THE PRINCIPALSHIP

FOURTH EDITION

THE PRINCIPALSHIP

A REFLECTIVE PRACTICE PERSPECTIVE

Thomas J. Sergiovanni

Trinity University
San Antonio, Texas

Allyn and Bacon
Boston • London • Toronto • Sydney • Tokyo • Singapore

Series editor: Arnis E. Burvikovs
Series editorial assistant: Patrice Mailloux
Marketing manager: Brad Parkins

Library of Congress Cataloging-in-Publication Data

Sergiovanni, Thomas J.
    The principalship : a reflective practice perspective / Thomas J. Sergiovanni.--4th ed.
      p. cm.
    Includes bibliographical references and index.
    ISBN 0-205-32185-2
    1. School principals--United States. 2. Educational leadership--United States. 3. School management and organization--United States. 4. School supervision--United States. 5. School improvement programs--United States. I. Title.

LB2831.92 .S47 2001
371.2'012'0973--dc21   00-025101

Printed in the United States of America

10 9 8 7 6 5 4 3 2 1   04 03 02 01 00

Credit: Pages 138–139: Excerpt from *Value-Added Leadership: How to Get Extraordinary Performance in Schools* by Thomas J. Sergiovanni, copyright © 1990 by Harcourt, Inc., reprinted by permission of the publisher.

CONTENTS

PREFACE

Everywhere one looks there is someone with an easy solution for improving schools. "Research says" if you put these correlates in place—if you teach, manage, or supervise using this list of behaviors—all will be well. Careers are built, journals are filled, and, for some with entrepreneurial bents, fortunes are amassed as the "solutions" are proposed.

The engine that drives this grand solutions machine is our search for simple answers. This searching, I fear, drives us to think in the rationalistic tradition about our work, to make unwarranted assumptions about the linearity and predictability that exist in the world, and to overestimate the tightness of links between research and practice. The result is the adoption of management theories and leadership practices that look great on paper, sound compelling when heard, and maybe even make us feel good, but that don't fit the actual world of schooling very well.

The term *rationalistic* is chosen over *rational* or *irrational* deliberately, for what is often thought to be irrational is actually rational, and vice versa. Winograd and Flores (1986) sort the differences as follows:

> *In calling it [traditional theory] "rationalistic" we are not equating it with "rational." We are not interested in a defense of irrationality or a mystic appeal to nonrational intuition. The rationalistic tradition is distinguished by its narrow focus on certain aspects of rationality which often lead to attitudes and activities that are not rational when viewed in a broader perspective. Our commitment is to develop a new ground for rationality—one that is as rigorous as the rationalistic tradition in its aspirations but that does not share the presuppositions behind it. (8)*

In a similar vein, Kozlov (1988) uses the categories "Neats" and "Scruffies" to sort researchers in the field of artificial intelligence as follows: "For a Neat, if an idea about thinking can't be represented in terms of mathematical logic, it isn't worth thinking about. For a Scruffy, on the other hand, ideas that can't be proved are the most interesting ones" (77–78).

It isn't easy for anyone to be a Scruffy. After all, it's very comfortable to be a Neat. You have all the answers and you fit nicely into our bureaucratic, technical, and rational culture. Fitting nicely reaps many career rewards. But still, many of us feel uncomfortable with the position of the Neats. A frequent first response to this uncomfortableness is to try to change the world to fit our theories and to damn those aspects of the world that will not cooperate. A better alternative, I propose, is for us to change our theories to fit the world. A scruffy world needs scruffy theories. Reflective practice, as I will argue in Chapter 2, is key to making scruffy theories work. John Stuart Mill wrote, "No great improvements in the lot of mankind are possible, until a great change takes place in the fundamental constitution of their modes of thought." His prophetic statement describes the situations we face today. If we want better schools, we are going to have to learn how to manage and lead differently. This book doesn't provide the answers, but it can help you find them.

The key to accepting the challenges of leadership in a scruffy world is for principals to understand leadership differently. When writing articles and books for principals, it is common to point out how important a principal is to the successful functioning of the school. Part of this ritual is to portray the principal as some sort of superhero who combines the best qualities of strong "instructional leadership" with a messianic ability to inspire people to great heights. It turns out that principals are indeed important, and their leadership is indeed indispensable, but in different ways than commonly thought.

From the perspective of the Neats, principals practice leadership directly by calculating what levers to pull to get the school structured differently and what buttons to push to get people motivated to do what is needed. Mystic principals rely less on rational calculation and more on their charismatic qualities to transform people. Both types of principals are highly visible players in the drama of leadership. Everything revolves around them. Should either of these types of principals fail to provide the needed leadership, things go awry.

Scruffy principals view the problem of leadership differently. Their leadership is much more subtle and aimed at building into the school substitutes for leadership. Substitutes, they argue, are the keys needed to encourage teachers and students to become self-managing. The sources of authority for leadership, as scruffy principals see it, need to be idea-based and anchored to moral commitments. Their job is to create new connections among people and to connect them to an idea structure. They do this by practicing leadership by bonding and binding. Their aim is to build a followership in the school. For the secret to leadership, they argue, is to have something worth following—something to which followers become morally committed.

A key theme in this book is that what we believe to be true about management and leadership depends on the metaphor we use to understand the school. Schools, for example, have traditionally been understood as *organizations* of one kind or another, and this metaphor encourages us to think about school organization structure, teacher motivation, power and authority, curriculum development, and supervision and evaluation in certain ways. If the metaphor were changed to *community*, these ways of viewing the world of school management and leadership would no longer make sense. Instead, a new management and leadership would need to be invented that would be more congruent with what communities are and how they function.

The concept of *lifeworld* is introduced in Chapter 10. We might think of the lifeworld as a school's local values, traditions, meanings, and purposes as embodied in traditions, rituals, and norms that define a school's culture. The lifeworld is important because it is at the core of a school's organizational character. Character is what gives a school a special focus, an idea structure, and an orientation toward purpose that has consistently been linked to more effective schooling as measured by levels of civility and student achievement. Chapter 10, new to this edition, also examines how standards can either help or hinder the development of a school's character depending on whether they are driven by that school's lifeworld or imported from afar. A layered system of standards is proposed as a solution to satisfying the need for rigor and direction without compromising either the lifeworld of schools or the need for external accountability.

Throughout the book, readers will find a number of inventories and questionnaires. Their purpose is to help raise and clarify issues, stimulate thought, encourage reflection, and provide a basis for discussion of concepts and ideas. They are not presented as fine-tuned measurement devices suitable for "research purposes," although faculties and groups may benefit from collecting school data and using results as a basis for discussion and reflection.

Readers are encouraged to read the last chapter (Chapter 15, "Administering as a Moral Craft") before examining the book's contents more systematically. Enhancing the principalship is the road on which this book journeys, and Chapter 15 lets readers know how the journey ends. Knowing the book's ending first may be helpful in providing an integrating perspective for the concepts, ideas, values, principles, and practices discussed in other chapters.

Thomas J. Sergiovanni

References

Kozlov, Alex. 1988. "Aristotle in the Fast Lane," *Discovery* 9(7), 77–78.
Winograd, Terry, and Flores, Fernando. 1986. *Understanding Computers and Cognition.* Norwood, NJ: Ablex.

ABOUT THE AUTHOR

Thomas J. Sergiovanni is Lillian Radford Professor of Education at Trinity University, San Antonio, Texas, where he teaches in the school leadership program and in the 5-year teacher education program. He is senior fellow at the Center for Educational Leadership and the founding Director of the Trinity Principals' Center. Prior to joining the faculty at Trinity, he was on the faculty of education administration at The University of Illinois, Urbana-Champaign, for 19 years, where he chaired the department for 7 years. A former associate editor of *Educational Administration Quarterly*, he serves on the editorial boards of *Teaching Education, Journal for a Just and Caring Education, Journal of Personnel Evaluation in Education, Teachers College Record,* and *Catholic Education: A Journal of Inquiry and Practice.* Among his recent books are *Moral Leadership* (1992), *Building Community in Schools* (1994), *Leadership for the Schoolhouse* (1996), *Supervision: A Redefinition* (1998), *Rethinking Leadership* (1999), and *The Lifeworld of Leadership: Creating Culture, Community, and Personal Meaning in Our Schools* (2000).

PART I

TOWARD A NEW THEORY

1

VIEWS OF THE PRINCIPAL'S JOB

Let's begin our examination of the principal's job with your perceptions of the tasks and functions that should make up this role and of their relative importance.

Imagine yourself as a candidate for the principalship of an 800-student junior high school in a community close to Philadelphia. You have taught for several years in a school and community much like this one; however, beyond temporary administrative assignments (e.g., chairing committees and project teams), you have had no full-time administrative experience. Your overall credentials and your background as a teacher are, nonetheless, sufficiently impressive that the search committee considers you one of its top three candidates. You have been invited to visit the school and to be interviewed by the committee and the superintendent for this job. To help you prepare for your visit, the committee informs you of a number of areas that they wish to explore and a number of issues that they wish to discuss. Among these are:

What do you consider to be the major tasks of a principal?

Which of these tasks do you believe to be most important?

As you plan your daily and weekly schedule, what proportion of time would you allocate to each of these tasks?

You want to be as prepared as possible for your visit and interview. Therefore, consider these questions and write down some of your ideas. Start by writing a brief general description of your perception of the role of the principal and her or his prime reasons for existing as part of the structure of schooling. Follow this general description with a listing of roles and task areas that you believe should define the principal's responsibilities. Curriculum and program development, supervision and evaluation, and student discipline are examples of task areas that might come to mind. As you examine your list, rank the tasks in order of their importance to you. Then, using 100 percent of the time available to you in an average work week, allocate percentages of time that you would try to spend in each area if you were to obtain this principalship.

In your deliberations about principalship responsibilities, roles, and tasks, you have probably been thinking in terms of the school in the ideal. You have been describing your perceptions of what is important and what you think the principal *ought* to do.

Ideal Conceptions of the Principalship

Definitions of the principal's roles and responsibilities have changed over time. Traditional definitions focused on the administrative processes and functions that must be emphasized for schools to work well. Effective principals, for example, are responsible for planning, organizing, leading, and controlling. *Planning* means setting goals and objectives for the school and developing blueprints and strategies for implementing them. *Organizing* means bringing together the necessary human, financial, and physical resources to accomplish goals efficiently. *Leading* has to do with guiding and supervising subordinates. *Controlling* refers to the principal's evaluation responsibilities and includes reviewing and regulating performance, providing feedback, and otherwise tending to standards of goal attainment.

The acronym POSDCoRB is another example of how administrative processes have been defined. Proposed in 1937 by Luther Gulick, POSDCoRB stands for planning, organizing, staffing, directing, coordinating, reporting, and budgeting. Lists such as these are continuously being revised. In 1955, for example, the American Association of School Administrators added such processes as stimulating staff and evaluating staff to the POSDCoRB list.

Gradually, lists of tasks and roles have given way to lists of competencies and proficiencies as the favored way to map out the territory of educational administration. For example, in 1997, the National Association of Elementary School Principals (NAESP) issued the document "Elementary and Middle School Proficiencies for Principals," which contained a list of 96 proficiencies grouped into 8 categories that define *expertness* in the principalship. It should be noted that in its 1986 study, 74 proficiencies were identified. Does this mean that more proficiencies are actually needed 11 years later? Or is it perhaps that the competency and proficiency movement has become more popular? The categories and the first three proficiencies listed for each category follow:

- Leadership Behavior. *The schools of proficient principals are marked by collegiality and a sense of common purpose. In the exercise of leadership, the proficient principal:*

    —*Demonstrates vision and provides leadership that appropriately involves the school community in the creation of shared beliefs and values.*
    —*Demonstrates moral and ethical judgment.*
    —*Demonstrates creativity and innovative thinking.*

- Communication Skills. *The image the principal projects affects how students, staff, parents, and the community perceive the school. In using communication skills, the proficient principal:*

—Articulates beliefs persuasively, effectively explains decisions, checks for understanding, and behaves in ways that reflect these beliefs and decisions.
—Writes and speaks clearly and concisely so the message is understood by the intended audience.
—Conveys opinions succinctly and distinguishes between facts and opinions when communicating priorities.

- Group Processes. *The proficient principal mobilizes others to collaborate in solving problems and accomplishing school goals. In facilitating group processes, the proficient principal:*

  —Understands group dynamics and applies effective group process skills.
  —Establishes a framework for collaborative action and involves the school community in developing and supporting shared beliefs, values, mission, and goals for the school.
  —Uses appropriate team-building skills.

- Curriculum and Instruction. *The proficient principal facilitates the establishment of a curriculum framework that provides direction for teaching and learning. In supervising the development and implementation of curriculum and instruction, the proficient principal:*

  —Maintains a visible presence in the classroom.
  —Works with staff and community representatives to identify a curriculum framework and common core of learning that support the mission and goals of the school.
  —Demonstrates to all stakeholders knowledge of the school's curriculum framework and common core of learning.

- To enlist the expertise of staff for improving instruction, the proficient principal:

  —Engages staff in the study of effective teaching practices.
  —Provides varied support strategies such as mentors, research, and support teams.
  —Seeks information and advice from a variety of sources.

- Assessment. *The proficient principal uses assessment to improve the school's programs and services. In assessing programs and services, student achievement, or staff performance, the proficient principal:*

  —Ensures that all parties understand the assessment criteria and procedures.
  —Seeks and encourages input from a variety of sources.
  —Seeks constructive suggestions from all parties.

- Organizational Management. *The origins of a school's organization lie in its shared beliefs, mission, and goals. In managing and organizing the school's day-to-day functions, the proficient principal:*

  —Possesses a clear view of the past, present, and future of the school.

—*Uses collaborative planning to help identify objectives that accomplish the school's mission and goals.*
—*Selects, assigns, and organizes staff in a way that assures the greatest potential for clarifying and accomplishing the school's mission.*

- Fiscal Management. *For proficient principals, sound fiscal management begins with the establishment of program goals and objectives. In fiscal management, the proficient principal:*

—*Understands the school district budget and its implications for the school.*
—*Involves members of the school community in developing budget priorities based on the mission and goals of the school.*
—*Prepares the school budget in accordance with school district budgeting procedures.*

- Political Management. *The proficient principal understands the dynamics of local, state, and national political decision making. In political management, the proficient principal:*

—*Develops strategies to attract appropriate financial support for public education.*
—*Involves community leaders in the development and support of the school's program.*
—*Uses effective strategies to deal with the political issues and forces that affect the school's operation. (National Association of Elementary School Principals, 1997:6–18)*

For parochial school principals, the religious dimension must be added to any array of roles and responsibilities that define the principalship. For example, in his analysis of the socialization of Catholic school principals, Augenstein (Augenstein, 1989; Augenstein and Konnert, 1991) defines the role requirements of the religious dimension as knowing about and making available church documents and other religious resources, providing for spiritual development, being a leader of prayer, creating an environment for religious education, integrating gospel values and other religious principles into the curriculum, and providing services to the parish and civic community. Other types of Christian, Jewish, and Muslim schools would have similar lists of added roles, responsibilities, and proficiencies that reflect their uniqueness. Modern lists of proficiencies provide a rendering of tasks and roles that are considerably more descriptive than the generic lists of the past and that emphasize much more the specific context of schooling, teaching, and learning.

In recent years, more emphasis is being given to what principals in schools are supposed to accomplish as a way of defining the job. The idea behind this trend is to determine the outcomes that schools should pursue and students should achieve. Much less attention is given to pointing out the processes that must be used. Presumably, principals in schools are expected to do whatever is necessary to achieve the outcomes. Defining the job this way has the advantage of freeing principals and others with whom they work from bureaucratic restrictions and constraints. Few scripts for the principal to follow are provided. Lists of things principals must do are kept to a minimum.

Defining the role of the principal in terms of outcomes, however, increases the likelihood that means will be separated from ends. Separating the two is risky business and can be troublesome in schools. For example, it is hard to specify all the important outcomes in advance. A tendency exists to specify outcomes that are easy to understand and easy to evaluate. As a result, many other outcomes that may be more important are overlooked. Furthermore, a difference exists between effective practices and good practices. What principals and teachers may do, for example, may work but may not be right. The outcomes approach tends to define effectiveness more in terms of what works than what is right, and this tendency raises important moral questions.

A Values Approach

One way to capitalize on the advantages of an outcomes-based approach to defining the role of the principal, while avoiding some of the disadvantages, is to adopt a values-based approach. When using this approach, assumptions and beliefs presumed to be important are specified and used as a basis for deciding what it is that principals and others should do. The specification of assumptions and beliefs provides a standard for determining what is good and bad, effective and ineffective, and acceptable and unacceptable. Sometimes the standards are backed up by hard research; other times they are backed up by informed and respected craft knowledge; and still other times they are reasoned expressions of philosophical positions, assumptions, and judgments. Using a values-based approach for defining the role of the principal not only ensures that what principals decide to do meets acceptable standards but it also provides the school with a set of indicators that defines its educational and moral health.

In 1996, the National Association of Secondary School Principals (NASSP), working cooperatively with the Carnegie Foundation for the Advancement of Teaching, published a report titled *Breaking Ranks: Changing an American Institution.* This report provides an example of using a values-based approach to define educational standards. *Breaking Ranks* provides a list of over 80 implementing recommendations for changing the American high school. The report is based on the belief that

> *if one theme could be extracted that is overarching and paramount, it is a message that the high school of the 21st century must be much more student-centered and above all much more personalized in programs, support services, and intellectual rigor. These seven recommendations are illustrative of what we envision: Every student will have a personal adult advocate; the Carnegie unit must be replaced or redefined; student anonymity must be banished; teachers should meet no more than 90 students per day; every student should have a Personal Plan of Progress; imaginative flexible scheduling must be the order of the day; every principal and teacher will have a Personal Learning Plan. (NASSP, 1996:vi)*

The recommendations from the report are grouped into 13 broad categories. The categories, along with examples of recommendations, are provided in Exhibit 1.1.

EXHIBIT 1.1   Breaking Ranks: Changing an American Institution Selected Recommendations

Curriculum

1. Each high school community will identify a set of essential learnings—above all, in literature and language, mathematics, social studies, science, and the arts—in which students must demonstrate achievement in order to graduate.
2. Teachers will design work for students that is of high enough quality to engage them, cause them to persist, and, when successfully completed, result in their satisfaction and their acquisition of learnings, skills, and abilities valued by society.
3. The content of the curriculum, where practical, will connect itself to real-life applications of knowledge and skills to help students link their education to the future.
4. Assessment of student learning will align itself with the curriculum so that students' progress is measured by what is taught.
5. Each student will have a Personal Plan for Progress to ensure that the high school takes individual needs into consideration and to allow students, within reasonable parameters, to design their own methods for learning in an effort to meet high standards.

Instructional Strategies

1. Each high school teacher will have a broad base of academic knowledge with depth in at least one subject area.
2. Teachers will be adept at acting as coaches and as facilitators of learning to promote more active involvement of students in their own learning.
3. Teachers will teach in ways that help students to develop into competent problem solvers and critical thinkers.

4. Teachers will convey a sense of caring to their students so that their students feel that their teachers share a stake in their learning.
5. Teachers will integrate assessment into instruction so that assessment does not merely measure students, but becomes part of the learning process itself.

School Environment

1. The high school community, which cannot be value-neutral, will advocate and model a set of core values essential in a democratic and civil society.
2. Experiences in high school will acknowledge multiple talents and ways of learning to help students achieve the meaningful success that leads to further achievement.
3. Every high school student will have a Personal Adult Advocate to help him or her personalize the educational experience.
4. The school will accord meaningful roles in the decision-making process to students, parents, and members of the staff to promote an atmosphere of participation, responsibility, and ownership.
5. Agreements that school systems negotiate with teachers, principals, and other personnel will be accompanied by a Student Impact Statement to help warrant that contracts and other agreements consider the best interests of students.

Technology

1. Schools will make technology integral to curriculum, instruction, and assessment, accommodating different learning styles and helping teachers to individualize the learning process.

EXHIBIT 1.1 *Continued*

2. High schools will equip individual classrooms with the technology necessary to prepare students for life in the 21st century.
3. Technology will be a key part of both initial and continuing teacher education to provide teachers with the knowledge and skills they need to integrate technology into the curriculum and to adapt it to instructional strategies. To achieve these ends, school districts will hire teachers who can use technology to obtain information and who can incorporate technology into teaching and learning.

Organization and Time

1. High schools will create small units in which anonymity is banished.
2. Each high school teacher involved in the instructional program on a full-time basis will be responsible for contact time with no more than 90 students during a given term so that the teacher can give greater attention to the needs of every student.
3. The Carnegie unit will be redefined or replaced so that high schools no longer equate seat time with learning.
4. Each high school will present alternatives to tracking and to ability grouping without restricting the range of courses and learning experiences it offers.
5. The academic program will extend beyond the high school campus to take advantage of learning opportunities outside the four walls of the building.

Assessment and Accountability

1. The school will review each student's Personal Progress Plan continually and indicate the extent of progress toward graduation and postsecondary transition options.

2. High schools will guarantee that students can meet performance standards in entry-level jobs. Recent graduates who fail to meet these basic standards will have the opportunity to return to school for additional studies.
3. Each high school will report annually to the community, disclosing school-wide assessment results and other pertinent information.
4. At least once every five years, each high school will convene a broadly-based external panel to offer a Public Description of the school, a requirement that could be met in conjunction with the evaluations of state, regional, and other accrediting groups.
5. Students will evaluate teachers and instruction on an ongoing basis in a variety of ways, providing regular feedback with regard to how effectively student learning goals are met.

Professional Development

1. Every high school will be a learning community for teachers and for the other professionals it employs.
2. Each educator will create a Personal Learning Plan that addresses his or her need to grow, stressing knowledge and skills related to improved student learning.
3. The principal of a high school, as a model for the staff, will pursue his or her own ongoing professional growth while helping to lead the professional development for the entire school.

Diversity

1. The principal, the school community, and the school board will promote policies, practices, and decisions that recognize diversity in accord with the core values of a democratic and civil society and within the mission of teaching and learning.

Continued

EXHIBIT 1.1   *Continued*

2. The curriculum will expose students to a rich array of viewpoints, perspectives, and experiences.
3. The teachers, adjunct teachers, paraprofessionals, support staff, volunteers, and members of the community who staff the high school will represent a wide array of talents, perspectives, and backgrounds.

Governance

1. Each high school will establish a site council to work with the principal in reaching decisions to make the school an effective organization for student learning.

Resources

1. New programs mandated for high schools will be restricted to those that support learning objectives identified in national goals or endorsed by district and state policies. Furthermore, programs mandated by government should be fully funded from the level at which the mandate originates.
2. Decisions regarding budget and staff allocations will be made at the site level, in accord with policy parameters set at the central level so as to ensure the input of those who know the situation best.

Ties to Higher Education

1. Secondary and higher education will collaboratively develop new and consistent standards concerning college admissions requirements.
2. High schools will hire educators who have prepared for teaching by studying in high schools that model best practice.

Relationships

1. A high school will regard itself as a community in which members of the staff collaborate to develop and implement the school's learning goals.
2. The high school will engage students' families as partners in the students' education.
3. The high school will require each student to participate in a service program in the community or in the school itself that has educational value.

Leadership

1. The principal will provide leadership in the high school community by building and maintaining a vision, direction, and focus for student learning.
2. Selection of high school principals will be based on qualities of leadership rooted in established knowledge and skills that result in dedication to good instructional practice and learning.
3. Teachers will provide the leadership essential to the success of reform, collaborating with others in the educational community to redefine the role of the teacher and to identify sources of support for that redefined role.
4. The leadership of students, parents, and others in the school community will enhance the work of the principal, who should recognize this potential for leadership by nurturing and supporting it.

Source: Breaking Ranks: Changing an American Institution. A Report of the Secondary School Principals Association on the High School for the 21st Century (pp. 11–99) by National Association of Secondary School Principals, 1996, Reston, VA: NASSP. Reprinted by permission. For more information concerning NASSP services and/or programs, please call (703) 860-0200.

A Standards-Based Approach

The use of standards is the latest attempt to define and describe what school principals and other administrators should do. Standards can be intimidating. They project a "gold standard" kind of image imbued with objectivity and scientific validity. But, as is the case with most prescriptions of what ought to be, standards are not objective. They represent the judgments of committees of experts, policy makers, and others. Different committees often come up with different standards. Still, the standards movement in educational administration seems grounded in what some research traditions (but not all) say are the principalship behaviors that contribute to effective schools. For this reason, they should not be taken lightly.

In 1996, the Council of Chief State School Officers adopted the list of standards for school leaders provided by the Interstate School Leaders Licensure Consortium (ISLLC). Neil Shipman, an assessment expert and director of ISLLC, and Joseph Murphy, a highly respected professor of educational administration and chair of ISLLC, describe the two-year effort as follows:

> *Forged from research on productive educational leadership and the wisdom of colleagues, the standards were drafted by personnel from 24 state education agencies and representatives from various professional associations. The standards present a common core of knowledge, dispositions, and performances that will help link leadership more forcefully to productive schools and enhanced educational outcomes. Although developed to serve a different purpose, the standards were designed to be compatible with the new National Council for the Accreditation of Teacher Education (NCATE)* Curriculum Guidelines *for school administration—as well as with the major national reports on reinventing leadership for tomorrow's schools. As such, they represent another part of a concerted effort to enhance the skills of school leaders and to couple leadership with effective educational processes and valued outcomes. (Council of Chief State School Officers, 1996:3)*

Unique to the consortium's work is that each standard is buttressed not only by the knowledge and performance thought to be needed for implementation but also by dispositions. *Dispositions* refer to the values, beliefs, and commonalities that seem most necessary for a principal to convert knowledge into performance that meets the standards. The ISLLC standards for school administrators appear as Appendix 1.1 at the end of this chapter. In a general way, this list of standards applies to parochial school principals, too. But there are important differences. In addition to being educational and managerial leaders, principals of religious-affiliated schools are expected to be spiritual leaders responsible for building a community of faith within the school that is embedded with pastoral qualities. Appendix 1.2, "Profile of an ICEL Graduate," provides an example of standards used by the Institute for Catholic Educational Leadership (ICEL) at the University of San Francisco to define the characteristics they expect of their graduates.

The Complex Nature of Managerial Work

Of interest is the extent to which statements of standards, recommendations, and needed proficiencies agree with reports from the "real world" that tell us what principals actually do and how they actually spend their time. We might think of such reports as descriptive studies of the principal's job. The 1973 publication of Henry Mintzberg's book, *The Nature of Managerial Work*, sparked a great deal of interest in descriptive studies of administration in education. Descriptive studies attempt to map out the actual roles and tasks of principals by focusing on what administrators actually do.

Mintzberg studied five executives, including a school superintendent. He relied on continued, detailed, and systematic observations of what these administrators actually did, almost moment by moment, over an extended period of time. His research has become a model for others who have studied the specific context of educational administration. In one such study, Sproul (1976) found that such words as *local, verbal, choppy,* and *varied* were most often used to describe the typical administrative workday. Choppiness, for example, was evidenced by the presence of many activities of brief duration. A composite administrator in Sproul's study engaged in 56 activities daily, each averaging about nine minutes, and participated in 65 events, each averaging six minutes. Events were described as periods of time one minute or longer during which administrators used one medium of communication such as the phone, a conversation, or a memo.

Similarly, Mintzberg found that the work of administrators was characterized by brevity, variety, and fragmentation, and that the majority of administrative activities were of brief duration, often taking only minutes. Activities were not only varied but also patternless, disconnected, and interspersed with trivia; as a result, the administrator often shifted moods and intellectual frames. These findings suggest a high level of *superficiality* in the work of administration. Mintzberg noted further that, because of the open-ended nature of administrative work, the administrator is compelled to perform a great number of tasks at an unrelenting pace. This contributes further to superficiality. Free time is only rarely available, and job responsibilities seem inescapable.

The administrators in Mintzberg's study demonstrated a preference for live action and for oral means of handling this action. They favored the job's current and active elements over abstract, technical, and routine elements. They preferred to visit with others personally, to talk on the telephone, and to conduct formal and informal conferences, rather than to rely on written means of communication. Because of this propensity for oral action, most of the business of the organization remained unrecorded and was stored in the administrator's memory. This, in turn, made delegation and shared decision making difficult. Mintzberg found that administrators are overloaded with *exclusive* knowledge about the organization and overburdened, as well, with incursions on their time as others seek this information. He observed further that administrators had difficulty in keeping on top of events and that no mechanisms existed to relieve them of minor responsibilities. Faced with the apparent requirement that one be involved in almost everything, the recourse was to treat work activities in a distinctly superficial manner.

School principals, too, often must deal with aspects of work superficially. The reasons for this can be understood as one examines the full range of responsibilities that principals have. Barth (1980) describes the extent of such responsibilities as follows:

> The principal is ultimately responsible for almost everything that happens in school and out. We are responsible for personnel—making sure that employees are physically present and working to the best of their ability. We are in charge of program—making sure that teachers are teaching what they are supposed to and that children are learning it. We are accountable to parents—making sure that each is given an opportunity to express problems and that those problems are addressed and resolved. We are expected to protect the physical safety of children—making sure that the several hundred lively organisms who leave each morning return, equally lively, in the afternoon.
>
> Over the years principals have assumed one small additional responsibility after another—responsibility for the safe passage of children from school to home, responsibility for the safe passage of children from home to school, responsibility for making sure the sidewalks are plowed of snow in winter, responsibility for health education, sex education, moral education, responsibility for teaching children to evacuate school buses and to ride their bikes safely. We have taken on lunch programs, then breakfast programs; responsibility for the physical condition of the furnace, the wiring, the playground equipment. We are now accountable for children's achievement of minimum standards at each grade level, for the growth of children with special needs, of the gifted, and of those who are neither. The principal has become a provider of social services, food services, health care, recreation programs and transportation—with a solid skills education worked in somehow. (4–6)

How is the challenge of superficiality in administrative work met by those who prescribe how administrators should behave? The well-known management consultant and theorist Peter Drucker recommended that principals set and stick to priorities. This is good advice, when it can be followed. Another well-known theorist, Chester Barnard (1938), suggested that administrators be more selective in the questions they address. In his words: "The fine art of executive decision-making consists of not deciding questions that are not pertinent, in not deciding prematurely, in not making decisions that cannot be made effectively, and in not making decisions that others should make" (194). How realistic are these prescriptions? When is it not possible to follow them? What gets in the way of following them? How might practicing principals react to them?

Following the Mintzberg research approach, Morris and colleagues (1984) studied elementary and secondary school principals in Chicago. They concluded:

> The principalship is a moving, dynamic occupation in almost a literal sense; the rhythm of the job, from arrival at the parking lot to the close of the business day, is typified by pace and movement, by frequent and abrupt shifts from one concern to another, and by the excitement pervading any institution dealing with young

people ..., the principal's job is different from other managerial positions because it is essentially an oral occupation, a job of talking. The principal governs the school mostly by talking with other people, usually one at a time, throughout the day. (209)

They noted that principals spend about 50 percent of their time outside the main office and in face-to-face contact with teachers and students. In their words:

A busy principal covers a great deal of ground. In making these rounds, from office to corridor to classroom to gymnasium to boilerroom to playground and back, the principal is managing the school. But it is management in a form unusual for most organizations because it is, in large part, administration at the work stations of other persons. This means that the principal carries the office around with him or her through at least 50% of the work day.... It is the principal who gets around, who visits teachers in their offices, who investigates areas of potential trouble, who smooths the flow of messages from one area of the building to another, who is on call and easily summoned by those needing assistance. (211)

Morris and colleagues (1984) noted that the job of building principal is open-ended; that is, the job becomes largely what each principal wishes to make of it. Despite a tightly structured paper hierarchy, principals have a great deal of auton-omy that allows their own values and preferences to influence the job (220). This open-endedness is not to suggest that principals are free to do whatever they wish, for they still must cope with constraints they face. It does suggest, however, that options do exist, that principals are not necessarily hopeless victims, and that principals do have some control over their priorities and the extent to which they pursue priorities.

Studies of principals at work indicate that the real world of school administration is often quite different from the world described in the theoretical literature and in principals' preferences. Appendix 1.3 is a portrait of one day in the life of an urban elementary school principal. How does this description of actual administrative work contrast with the views you had of the principal's job at the beginning of this chapter? Based on what this principal actually does and how she actually spends her time, write a brief job description for the principalship. How does this job description compare with that found and used in your school district? Does this description meet the proficiencies identified by the National Association of Elementary School Principals and with the standards set by the Interstate School Leaders Licensure Consortium?

Demands, Constraints, and Choices

Stewart (1982) describes managerial jobs "as consisting of an inner core of *demands*, an outer boundary of *constraints*, an in-between area of *choices*" (14). Demands are the things that principals must do. If they fail to do these things, sanctions are invoked, and often these sanctions are serious enough to endanger one's job. Demands are determined by school outcome specifications, legal requirements, bureaucratic rules and regulations, and the array of role expectations of important others such as superintendents, school board members, teachers, and parents. Constraints are determined by norms and values that exist in the community or school, availability of human and material resources, union contracts, space limitations, and the capability limitations of teachers and others with whom the principal must work. As with demands, principals who ignore constraints face the likelihood of threatened job security.

Although two principals may be subjected to the same demands and constraints, their leadership practices nonetheless typically vary. Within any demand-and-constraint set there are always choices in the form of opportunities to do the same things differently and to do other things that are not required or prohibited. It is in this area of choices that the opportunities for excellence exist. Whether these opportunities flourish depends on the latitude that principals are able to make for themselves. One hallmark of a successful principal is her or his ability to expand the area of choices and thus reduce demands and constraints. This extra margin of latitude makes an important difference in enhancing the overall effectiveness of the school.

In a 1988 National Association of Secondary School Principals study (Pellicer et al., 1988), respondents were asked to select from each of three pairs of statements the one that best characterized the role of the principal. Seventy-five percent chose "take initiative in developing and implementing school policy according to his or her professional judgment." This is compared to 25 percent who chose "primarily represent the interests of parents, leaders, and patrons of the school." Sixty-five percent chose "lead the school in new educational directions according to his or her best professional judgment." This is compared to 35 percent who chose "effectively and efficiently manage the day-to-day affairs of the school." Eighty-two percent chose "share decision making with the faculty on important issues." This is compared to 18 percent who chose "play the major role in establishing the agenda and deciding the important issues in the school" (p. 15). This study suggests that principals have clear and quite progressive views as to what they should be doing. Are highly successful principals more likely to come closer to the ideal than ordinary ones? How close do they come to this ideal in their everyday practice? A 1978 NASSP study, for example, found that successful school principals use time differently than do their more ordinary counterparts. Two of the NASSP researchers, Gorton and McIntyre (1978), studied time use by successful high school principals and found that real and ideal allocations of time corresponded fairly well. In a parallel study conducted by McCleary and Thomson (1979), the actual and ideal time allocations of a random sample of principals were surveyed. Table 1.1 summarizes the data from these studies, showing that although "successful" and "random" principals agree on how time should be spent, successful principals came closer to this ideal. The sum of differences between actual and ideal rankings for successful principals was 8, while that for randomly selected principals was 18.

The randomly selected principals, according to McCleary and Thomson (1979:16), appear to fall short of devoting the time they would like in two areas of responsibility: (1) program development and (2) professional development. They

TABLE 1.1   Comparing Rankings of Ideal and Actual Allocation of Time for Successful and Randomly Selected High School Principals

Task Areas	Successful Principals*			Random Principals**		
	Ideal Time Planned (Ranked biweekly)	Actual Time Spent (Ranked biweekly)	Difference	Ideal Time Planned (Ranked biweekly)	Actual Time Spent (Ranked biweekly)	Difference
Program development (curriculum, instructional leadership	1	3	2	1	5	4
Personnel (evaluation, advising, conferencing, recruiting)	2	1	1	2	2	0
School management (weekly calendar, office, budget, correspondence, memos, etc.)	3	2	1	3	1	2
Student activities (meetings, supervision, planning)	4	4	0	4	3	1
District office (meetings, task forces, reports, etc.)	5	5	0	9	6	3
Community (PTA, advisory groups, parent conferences)	6	6	0	8	8	0
Planning (annual, long range)	7	9	2	5	7	2
Professional development (readings, conferences, etc.)	8	8	0	6	9	3
Student behavior (discipline, attendance, meetings)	9	7	2	7	4	3
			Sum = 8			Sum = 18

*Data are used with permission from *The Senior High School Principalship, Vol. II: The Effective Principal* by Richard A. Gorton and Kenneth E. McIntyre, 1978, Reston, VA: National Association of Secondary School Principals.

**Data are used with permission from *The Senior High School Principalship, Vol. III: The Summary Report* by Lloyd E. McCleary and Scott D. Thomson, 1979, Reston, VA: National Association of Secondary School Principals.

report spending considerably more time than they would like dealing with problems of student behavior. According to these researchers, principals who are able to spend time as they intend credit this fact to their ability to delegate, to having capable assistant principals, to having faith in the competence of others, and to concentrating on priority goals. It appears that successful principals are able to devote more time and effort to a few critical areas; perhaps, as a result, they neglect other areas of comparatively less importance. Furthermore, they bring to their practice a high regard for those with whom they work and a commitment to the concept of empowerment.

The 1988 study noted little change in the way principals spend time and would like to spend time. "In general, the ways principals spend time and believe they should . . . have changed very little during the past decade" (Pellicer et al., 1988:17). Principals report spending less time on program development and planning than they would like and more time on student problems and working with the central office than they think they should. Unfortunately, the NASSP was not able to survey its members in 1998. If the survey had been conducted, would the ways principals spend their time differ? If your answer is yes, in what ways? Why do you think so?

The Changing Role

There is evidence that the role of the principal is changing. In the National Association of Elementary School Principals 1998 study of the principalship (Doud and Keller, 1998:2), for example, principals reported significant increases in responsibility (increases over 55 percent) in the following areas:

Areas of Responsibility	*Percent of Increase*
1. *Marketing/politics, etc., to generate supports for school and education*	70%
2. *Working with social agencies*	66%
3. *Planning/implementing of site-based staff development*	65.5%
4. *Development of instructional practice*	63.5%
5. *Curriculum development*	62.4%
6. *Working with site-based councils/ other constituencies*	61.6%
7. *Attention to issues related to potential legal liabilities*	58.1%

Keep in mind that large increases in percentages may not reveal corresponding large increases in emphasis if the amount of emphasis perceived earlier was very low. Still, the percentages do indicate emerging responsibility areas and new job pressures. The three leading responsibility indicators represent a cluster that is directly related to themes of increased autonomy at the local school site, increased emphasis on school choice, the need to market one's school effectively, and dealing with the politics involved. Curriculum development and instructional practice areas suggest the increased emphasis that is now being placed on individual schools to perform and to be held accountable to state standards.

Figure 1.1 shows the percentage of principals in the 1998 NAESP study who list the areas provided as one of the three in which they spend the most time. Despite dramatic increases in responsibility in dealing with marketing, choice, school-based management, curriculum, and teaching, it is the daily and continuous interaction with teachers, other staff, and students that consumes the lion's share of a

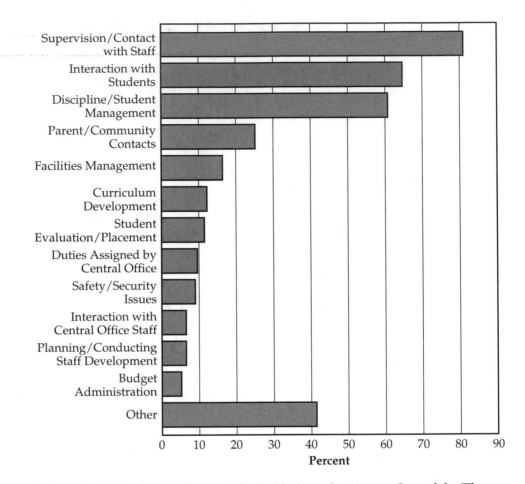

FIGURE 1.1   Percent of Respondents Listings the Area as One of the Three on Which They Spent the Most Time

Source: A Ten-Year Study: The K–8 Principal in 1998 (p. 10) by James L. Doud and Edward P. Keller, 1998, Alexandria, VA: National Association of Elementary School Principals. Reprinted with permission. National Association of Elementary School Principals. All rights reserved.

principal's time. Much of this interaction, of course, is consistent with the reported areas of increased responsibility. But much of it is not. As Doud and Keller point out, "Perhaps the biggest surprise among these rankings was the relatively low priority given to planning/conducting staff development. Despite the call of most site-based school management proponents and the priority given to staff development within many site-based school improvement planning processes, this finding clearly suggests that—within the prioritization of responsibility areas—staff development receives relatively little of the principal's time" (1998:12).

A 1998 EdSource study of California elementary, middle, and high school principals (EdSource, 1998:4) found that principals *prefer* to spend more time than is now the case on teaching and learning issues and tasks and less time than is now the case on issues and tasks that have to do with budget, parents, and students. Overall, the California principals surveyed reported spending about 16.8 percent *less* time than they would like in the areas of teaching and learning and about 15.4 percent *more* time than they would like in the areas of budget, parents, and students. They would make few changes in the amount of time now being spent in the areas of supervision and community relationships. The figures, summarized from the EdSource report, are provided in Table 1.2. The data suggest that increasingly the job of the principal is being defined by matters of teaching and learning, and this involves selecting teachers, helping and evaluating them, and, once selected, working with them in improving instruction. But how much authority do principals say they have to function effectively in these responsibility areas? Does the amount of authority match the amount of responsibility?

Figure 1.2 examines this question by comparing principals' perceptions of their primary authority with the authority they share with teachers and others. The good news is that significant sharing of responsibility with teachers was found in the areas of instructional improvement. There was some sharing of responsibility with teachers in the area of selection of teachers. But very few respondents reported

TABLE 1.2   How California Principals Spend Time: Real and Ideal

	Time Now Spent	Time Would Prefer to Spend	Difference
Teaching and Learning			
Instructional issues/ curriculum	14.5%	25.9%	−11.4%
School-wide planning, evaluation and reform	11.3%	16.7%	− 5.4%
Totals	25.8%	42.6%	−16.8%
Budgets, Parents and Students			
Budget, administration, maintenance	15.4%	7.5%	+ 7.9%
Parent engagement/ relations	13.3%	10.3%	+ 3.0%
Student contact and discipline	18.5%	14.0%	+ 4.5%
Totals	47.2%	31.8%	+15.4%
Supervision and Community			
Includes staff supervision, evaluation and external community relations	27.0%	25.6%	+1.4%

Source: California Principals: At the Center of School Improvement Efforts by EdSource Report, March 1998, Palo Alto, CA: EdSource. Reprinted by permission.

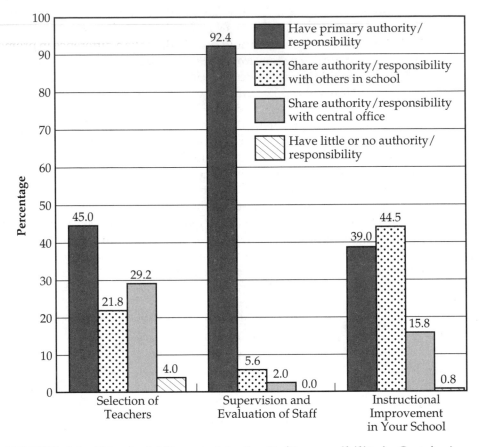

FIGURE 1.2   Principals' Reported Authority/Responsibility in Certain Areas

Source: A Ten-Year Study: The K–8 Principal in 1998 (p. 15) By James L. Doud and Edward P. Keller, 1998, Alexandria, VA: National Association of Elementary School Principals. Reprinted by permission. National Association of Elementary School Principals. All rights reserved.

sharing responsibility with teachers in the areas of supervision and evaluation of staff. These findings suggest that although some progress has been made in viewing the principal as a leader of leaders and the school as a community of leaders, the burdens of leadership continue to remain squarely on the shoulders of the principal. An important question is: Can new role definitions and responsibilities be effectively assumed by principals and schools without thinking through the question of redistributing the burdens of responsibility that now exist? If teachers were to accept more responsibility in the areas of supervision and evaluation by developing communities of practice and engaging in peer review, then principals would have more time for the emerging demands that they face in today's schools. Not only would such a redistribution of responsibilities be efficient, but it would represent a giant step toward increasing professionalism and enhancing capacity building among teachers.

A Look Ahead

In their monumental study of how principals make a difference in promoting quality schooling, Smith and Andrews (1989:8) concluded that strong principals functioned as forceful and dynamic leaders who brought to their practice high energy, initiative, tolerance for ambiguity, a sense of humor, analytical ability, and a practical stance toward life. They identified four broad areas of strategic role interaction between principal and teachers: (1) resource provider, (2) instructional resource, (3) communicator, and (4) visible presence. Their research reveals important differences in the ways teachers viewed strong, average, and weak principals across these four role dimensions. In every case, strong principals received more positive ratings than average and weak, and average principals more positive ratings than weak. Their findings are summarized in Exhibit 1.2. The Smith and Andrews research demonstrates the importance of principals giving prime attention to the schools' core technology, teaching and learning—a finding now well established in the literature (Teddlie, Kirby, and Stringfield, 1989).

Other studies of successful principals are examined in later chapters. These studies suggest that the ability to rely on symbolic and cultural leadership as enhancements of the more traditional technical, human, and educational leadership may provide an additional margin of latitude that expands choices in a world of demands and constraints. Furthermore, successful principals are able to expand their practice beyond the limits of traditional management theory, and this too may help account for their success in expanding choices.

Certain personal qualities of principals seem also to make a difference. For example, a pioneering study of the characteristics of principals of successful elementary schools, conducted by Goldhammer and colleagues in 1971, found that successful principals frequently tested the limits of bureaucracy and were driven by a commitment to schooling that resembled missionary zeal.

Less successful schools in the Goldhammer study were characterized by weak leadership, poor teacher and student morale, control by fear, traditional and ritualistic instructional programs, a general lack of enthusiasm, and principals who were "serving out their time." More successful schools, by contrast, were characterized by high morale, enthusiasm, and adaptability. They were uplifting places to visit and inhabit. The principals of those schools were able not only to recognize problems but also to face up to them with inspiring leadership and hard work. They displayed leadership supported by a belief system that included an overriding commitment to children, teaching, and teachers. They seemed to follow Drucker's (1967) advice to concentrate "efforts and energies in a few major areas where superior performance produces outstanding results" (24). They established priorities and stayed with priority decisions. They seemed to feel that they had no alternative but to do first things first. The characteristics shared by these principals of successful schools are described in Exhibit 1.3.

The studies of principals of successful schools reviewed in this chapter reveal a hopeful portrait. The work of successful principals corresponds more closely to what principals themselves say they should emphasize. Furthermore, in the face of

EXHIBIT 1.2   How Teachers Rate Their Principals:
A Comparison of Strong, Average, and Weak Leaders

	Percentage of Positive Ratings		
	Strong Leader (n=800)	*Average Leader (n=2,146)*	*Weak Leader (n=300)*
Principal as Resource Provider			
1. My principal promotes staff development activities for teachers.	95	68	41
2. My principal is knowledgeable about instructional resources.	90	54	33
3. My principal mobilizes resources and district support to help achieve academic achievement goals.	90	52	33
4. My principal is considered an important instructional resource person in this school.	79	35	8
Principal as Instructional Resource			
1. My principal encourages the use of different instructional strategies.	89	78	75
2. My principal is sought out by teachers who have instructional concerns or problems.	72	47	25
3. My principal's evaluation of my performance helps improve my teaching.	78	46	17
4. My principal helps faculty interpret test results.	54	35	9
Principal as Communicator			
1. Improved instructional practice results from interactions with my principal.	80	49	25
2. My principal leads formal discussions concerning instruction and student achievement.	85	41	17
3. My principal uses clearly communicated criteria for judging staff performance.	90	63	17
4. My principal provides a clear vision of what our school is all about.	90	49	17
5. My principal communicates clearly to the staff regarding instructional matters.	92	50	17
6. My principal provides frequent feedback to teachers regarding classroom performance.	68	29	18
Principal as Visible Presence			
1. My principal makes frequent classroom observations.	72	31	17
2. My principal is accessible to discuss matters dealing with instruction.	94	68	66
3. My principal is a "visible presence" in the building to both staff and students.	93	75	46
4. My principal is an active participant in staff development activities.	97	64	50

Source: From *Instructional Leadership: How Principals Make a Difference* (pp. 32–37) by Wilma F. Smith and Richard L. Andrews, 1989, Alexandria, VA: Association for Supervision and Curriculum Development. Copyright © 1989 by ASCD. Reprinted by permission. All rights reserved. This exhibit combines data from figures 2.4, 2.5, 2.6, and 2.7 in the original.

EXHIBIT 1.3   Characteristics of Successful Principals

1. Most did not intend to become principals. Most indicated that they had intended to teach, but were encouraged to become principals by their superiors.
2. Most expressed a sincere faith in children. Children were not criticized for failing to learn or for having behavioral difficulties. The principals felt that these were problems that the school was established to correct; thus the administrators emphasized their responsibilities toward the solution of children's problems.
3. They had an ability to work effectively with people and to secure their cooperation. They were proud of their teachers and accepted them as professionally dedicated and competent people. They inspired confidence and developed enthusiasm. The principals used group processes effectively; listened well to parents, teachers, and pupils; and appeared to have intuitive skill and empathy for their associates.
4. They were aggressive in securing recognition of the needs of their schools. They frequently were critical of the restraints imposed by the central office and of the inadequate resources. They found it difficult to live within the constraints of the bureaucracy; they frequently violated the chain of command, seeking relief for their problems from whatever sources that were potentially useful.
5. They were enthusiastic as principals and accepted their responsibilities as a mission rather than as a job. They recognized their role in current social problems. The ambiguities that surrounded them and their work were of less significance than the goals they felt were important to achieve. As a result, they found it possible to live with the ambiguities of their position.
6. They were committed to education and could distinguish between long-term and short-term educational goals. Consequently, they had established fairly well philosophies of the role of education and their relationship within it.
7. They were adaptable. If they discovered something was not working, they could make the necessary shifts and embark with some security on new paths.
8. They were able strategists. They could identify their objectives and plan means to achieve them. They expressed concern for the identification of the most appropriate procedures through which change could be secured.

Source: Keith Goldhammer et al. (1971). *Elementary School Principals and Their Schools.* Eugene, OR: Center for the Advanced Study of Educational Administration, pp. 2–3. Reprinted by permission.

the same demands and constraints, successful principals are able to find the necessary latitude that provides them with expanded choices and, thus, the extra margin needed for better performance. They do this, in part, because their view of how schools work and their conceptions of management theory and leadership practice are able to expand the concepts and practices of traditional management theory, and this is the theme of the next chapter.

References

Augenstein, John J. 1989. "Socialization Differences among Principals in Catholic Schools," *The Living Light* 25(3), 226–231.

Augenstein, John J., and W. William Konnert. 1991. "Implications of Informal Socialization Process of Beginning Elementary School Principals for Role Preparation and Initiation," *Journal of Educational Administration* 29(1), 39–50.

Barnard, Chester. 1938. *The Functions of an Executive.* Cambridge, MA: Harvard University Press.

Barth, Roland S. 1980. "Reflections on the Principalship," *Thrust for Educational Leadership* 9(5).

Council of Chief State School Officers. 1996. *Interstate School Leaders Licensure Consortium: Standards for School Leaders.* Washington, DC: Author.

Doud, James L., and Edward P. Keller. 1998. *A Ten-Year Study: The K–8 Principal in 1998.* Alexandria, VA: National Association of Elementary School Principals.

Drucker, Peter. 1967. *The Effective Executive.* New York: Harper & Row.

EdSource Report. 1998, March. *California's School Principals: At the Center of School Improvement Efforts.* Palo Alto, CA: Author.

Goldhammer, Keith, Gerald Becker, Richard Withycombe, Frank Doyel, Edgar Miller, Claude Morgan, Louis DeLoretto, and Bill Aldridge. 1971. *Elementary School Principals and Their Schools.* Eugene: University of Oregon, Center for the Advanced Study of Educational Administration.

Gorton, Richard A., and Kenneth E. McIntyre. 1978. *The Senior High School Principalship. Vol. II: The Effective Principal.* Reston, VA: National Association of Secondary School Principals.

Gulick, Luther, and L. Urwick (Eds.). 1937. *Papers on the Science of Administration.* New York: Institute for Public Administration.

McCleary, Lloyd E., and Scott D. Thomson. 1979. *The Senior High School Principalship. Vol. Ill: The Summary Report.* Reston, VA: National Association of Secondary School Principals.

Mintzberg, Henry. 1973. *The Nature of Managerial Work.* New York: Harper & Row.

Morris, Van Cleve, Robert L. Crowson, Cynthia Porter-Gehrie, and Emmanuel Hurwitz, Jr. 1984. *Principals in Action: The Reality of Managing Schools.* Columbus, OH: Merrill.

National Association of Elementary School Principals. 1997. *Elementary and Middle Schools: Proficiencies for Principals* (3rd ed.). Alexandria, VA: Author.

National Association of Secondary School Principals. 1996. *Breaking Ranks: Changing an American Institution.* A Report of the Secondary School Principals Association on the High School for the 21st Century. Reston, VA: Author.

Pellicer, Leonard O., Lorin W. Anderson, James W. Keefe, Edgar A. Kelley, and Lloyd E. McCleary. 1988. *High School Leaders and Their Schools. Vol. I: A National Profile.* Reston, VA: National Association of Secondary School Principals.

Smith, Wilma A., and Richard L. Andrews. 1989. *Instructional Leadership: How Principals Make a Difference.* Alexandria, VA: Association for Supervision and Curriculum Development.

Sproul, Lee S. 1976, November 13–14. "Managerial Attention in New Educational Systems." Seminar on Organizations as Loosely Couple Systems, University of Illinois, Urbana.

Stewart, Rosemary. 1982. "The Relevance of Some Studies of Managerial Work and Behavior to Leadership Research," in James G. Hunt, Uma Sekaran, and Chester A. Schriesheim (Eds.), *Leadership Beyond Establishment Views.* Carbondale: Southern Illinois University.

Teddlie, Charles, Peggy D. Kirby, and Sam Stringfield. 1989. "Effective versus Ineffective Schools: Observable Differences in the Classroom," *American Journal of Education* 97(3).

Appendix 1.1   Interstate School Leadership Consortium: Standards for School Leaders

Standard 1

A school administrator is an educational leader who promotes the success of all students by **facilitating the development, articulation, implementation, and stewardship of a vision of learning that is shared and supported by the school community.**

Knowledge
The administrator has knowledge and understanding of:

- learning goals in a pluralistic society
- the principles of developing and implementing strategic plans
- systems theory
- information sources, data collection, and data analysis strategies
- effective communication
- effective consensus-building and negotiation skills

Dispositions
The administrator believes in, values, and is committed to:

- The educability of all
- a school vision of high standards of learning
- continuous school improvement
- the inclusion of all members of the school community
- ensuring that students have the knowledge, skills, and values needed to become successful adults
- a willingness to continuously examine one's own assumptions, beliefs, and practices
- doing the work required for high levels of personal and organization performance

Performances
The administrator facilitates processes and engages in activities ensuring that:

- the vision and mission of the school are effectively communicated to staff, parents, students, and community members
- an implementation plan is developed in which objectives and strategies to achieve the vision and goals are clearly articulated

Source: Council of Chief State School Officers, 1996. *Interstate School Leaders Licensure Consortium: Standards for School Leaders* by The Council of Chief State School Officers, 1996, Washington, DC: The Council of Chief State School Officers. Reprinted by permission.

Appendix 1.1   *Continued*

- the vision and mission are communicated through the use of symbols, ceremonies, stories, and similar activities
- the core beliefs of the school vision are modeled for all stakeholders
- the vision is developed with and among stakeholders
- the contributions of school community members to the realization of the vision are recognized and celebrated
- progress toward the vision and mission is communicated to all stakeholders
- the school community is involved in school improvement efforts
- the vision shapes the educational programs, plans, and actions

- assessment data related to student learning are used to develop the school vision and goals
- relevant demographic data pertaining to students and their families are used in developing the school mission and goals
- barriers to achieving the vision are identified, clarified, and addressed
- needed resources are sought and obtained to support the implementation of the school mission and goals
- existing resources are used in support of the school vision and goals
- the vision, mission, and implementation plans are regularly monitored, evaluated, and revised

Standard 2

A school administrator is an educational leader who promotes the success of all students by **advocating, nurturing, and sustaining a school culture and instructional program conducive to student learning and staff professional growth.**

Knowledge
The administrator has knowledge and understanding of:

- student growth and development
- applied learning theories
- applied motivational theories
- curriculum design, implementation, evaluation, and refinement
- principles of effective instruction
- measurement, evaluation, and assessment strategies

- diversity and its meaning for educational programs
- adult learning and professional development models
- the change process for systems, organizations, and individuals
- the role of technology in promoting student learning and professional growth
- school cultures

Appendix 1.1   *Continued*

Dispositions
The administrator believes in, values, and is committed to:

- student learning as the fundamental purpose of schooling
- the proposition that all students can learn
- the variety of ways in which students can learn
- life long learning for self and others
- professional development as an integral part of school improvement

- the benefits that diversity brings to the school community
- a safe and supportive learning environment
- preparing students to be contributing members of society

Performances
The administrator facilitates processes and engages in activities ensuring that:

- all individuals are treated with fairness, dignity, and respect
- professional development promotes a focus on student learning consistent with the school vision and goals
- students and staff feel valued and important
- the responsibilities and contributions of each individual are acknowledged
- barriers to student learning are identified, clarified, and addressed
- diversity is considered in developing learning experiences
- life long learning is encouraged and modeled
- there is a culture of high expectations for self, student, and staff performance
- technologies are used in teaching and learning
- student and staff accomplishments are recognized and celebrated
- multiple opportunities to learn are available to all students

- the school is organized and aligned for success
- curricular, co-curricular, and extra-curricular programs are designed, implemented, evaluated, and refined
- curriculum decisions are based on research, expertise of teachers, and the recommendations of learned societies
- the school culture and climate are assessed on a regular basis
- a variety of sources of information is used to make decisions
- student learning is assessed using a variety of techniques
- multiple sources of information regarding performance are used by staff and students
- a variety of supervisory and evaluation models is employed
- pupil personnel programs are developed to meet the needs of students and their families

Appendix 1.1   *Continued*

Standard 3

A school administrator is an educational leader who promotes the success of all students by **ensuring management of the organization, operations, and resources for a safe, efficient, and effective learning environment.**

Knowledge
The administrator has knowledge and understanding of:

- theories and models of organizations and the principles of organizational development
- operational procedures at the school and district level
- principles and issues relating to school safety and security
- human resources management and development

- principles and issues relating to fiscal operations of school management
- principles and issues relating to school facilities and use of space
- legal issues impacting school operations
- current technologies that support management functions

Dispositions
The administrator believes in, values, and is committed to:

- making management decisions to enhance learning and teaching
- taking risks to improve schools
- trusting people and their judgments
- accepting responsibility

- high-quality standards, expectations, and performances
- involving stakeholders in management processes
- a safe environment

Performances
The administrator facilitates processes and engages in activities ensuring that:

- knowledge of learning, teaching, and student development is used to inform management decisions
- operational procedures are designed and managed to maximize opportunities for successful learning
- emerging trends are recognized, studied, and applied as appropriate
- operational plans and procedures to achieve the vision and goals of the school are in place

- organizational systems are regularly monitored and modified as needed
- stakeholders are involved in decisions affecting schools
- responsibility is shared to maximize ownership and accountability
- effective problem-framing and problem-solving skills are used
- effective conflict resolution skills are used

Appendix 1.1   *Continued*

- collective bargaining and other contractual agreements related to the school are effectively managed
- the school plant, equipment, and support systems operate safely, efficiently, and effectively
- time is managed to maximize attainment of organizational goals
- potential problems and opportunities are identified
- problems are confronted and resolved in a timely manner
- financial, human, and material resources are aligned to the goals of schools
- the school acts entrepreneurially to support continuous improvement

- effective group-process and consensus-building skills are used
- effective communication skills are used
- there is effective use of technology to manage school operations
- fiscal resources of the school are managed responsibly, efficiently, and effectively
- a safe, clean, and aesthetically pleasing school environment is created and maintained
- human resource functions support the attainment of school goals
- confidentiality and privacy of school records are maintained

Standard 4

A school administrator is an educational leader who promotes the success of all students by **collaborating with families and community members, responding to diverse community interests and needs, and mobilizing community resources.**

Knowledge
The administrator has knowledge and understanding of:

- emerging issues and trends that potentially impact the school community
- the conditions and dynamics of the diverse school community
- community resources

- community relations and marketing strategies and processes
- successful models of school, family, business, community, government and higher education partnerships

Dispositions
The administrator believes in, values, and is committed to:

- schools operating as an integral part of the larger community
- collaboration and communication with families
- involvement of families and other stakeholders in school decision-making processes
- the proposition that diversity enriches the school

- families as partners in the education of their children
- the proposition that families have the best interests of their children in mind
- resources of the family and community needing to be brought to bear on the education of students
- an informed public

Appendix 1.1   *Continued*

Performances
The administrator facilitates processes and engages in activities ensuring that:

- high visibility, active involvement, and communication with the larger community is a priority
- relationships with community leaders are identified and nurtured
- information about family and community concerns, expectations, and needs is used regularly
- there is outreach to different business, religious, political, and service agencies and organizations
- credence is given to individuals and groups whose values and opinions may conflict
- the school and community serve one another as resources
- available community resources are secured to help the school solve problems and achieve goals
- partnerships are established with area businesses, institutions of higher education, and community groups to strengthen programs and support school goals

- community groups to strengthen programs and support schools goals
- community youth family services are integrated with school programs
- community stakeholders are treated equitably
- diversity is recognized and valued
- effective media relations are developed and maintained
- a comprehensive program of community relations is established
- public resources and funds are used appropriately and wisely
- community collaboration is modeled for staff
- opportunities for staff to develop collaborative skills are provided

Standard 5

A school administrator is an educational leader who promotes the success of all students by **acting with integrity, fairness, and in an ethical manner.**

Knowledge
The administrator has knowledge and understanding of:

- the purpose of education and the role of leadership in modern society
- various ethical frameworks and perspectives on ethics

- the values of the diverse school community
- professional codes of ethics
- the philosophy and history of education

Appendix 1.1   *Continued*

Dispositions
The administrator believes in, values, and is committed to:

- the ideal of the common good
- the principles in the Bill of Rights
- the right of every student to a free, quality education
- bringing ethical principles to the decision-making process
- subordinating one's own interest to the good of the school community

- accepting the consequences for upholding one's principles and actions
- using the influence of one's office constructively and productively in the service of all students and their families
- development of a caring school community

Performances
The administrator:

- examines personal and professional values
- demonstrates a personal and professional code of ethics
- demonstrates values, beliefs, and attitudes that inspire others to higher levels of performance
- serves as a role model
- accepts responsibility for school operations
- considers the impact of one's administrative practices on others
- uses the influence of the office to enhance the educational program rather than for personal gain
- treats people fairly, equitably, and with dignity and respect

- protects the rights and confidentiality of students and staff
- demonstrates appreciation for and sensitivity to the diversity in the school community
- recognizes and respects the legitimate authority of others
- examines and considers the prevailing values of the diverse school community
- expects that others in the school community will demonstrate integrity and exercise ethical behavior
- opens the school to public scrutiny
- fulfills legal and contractual obligations
- applies laws and procedures fairly, wisely, and considerately

Standard 6

A school administrator is an educational leader who promotes the success of all students by **understanding, responding to, and influencing the larger political, social, economic, legal, and cultural context.**

Appendix 1.1   *Continued*

Knowledge
The administrator has knowledge and understanding of:

- principles of representative governance that undergird the system of American schools
- the role of public education in developing and renewing a democratic society and an economically productive nation
- the law as related to education and schooling
- the political, social, cultural and economic systems and processes that impact schools

- models and strategies of change and conflict resolution as applied to the larger political, social, cultural and economic contexts of schooling
- global issues and forces affecting teaching and learning
- the dynamics of policy development and advocacy under our democratic political system
- the importance of diversity and equity in a democratic society

Dispositions
The administrator believes in, values, and is committed to:

- education as a key to opportunity and social mobility
- recognizing a variety of ideas, values, and cultures
- importance of a continuing dialogue with other decision makers affecting education

- actively participating in the political and policy-making context in the service of education
- using legal systems to protect student rights and improve student opportunities

Performances
The administrator facilitates processes and engages in activities ensuring that:

- the environment in which schools operate is influenced on behalf of students and their families
- communication occurs among the school community concerning trends, issues, and potential changes in the environment in which schools operate
- there is ongoing dialogue with representatives of diverse community groups

- the school community works within the framework of policies, laws, and regulations enacted by local, state, and federal authorities
- public policy is shaped to provide quality education for students
- lines of communication are developed with decision makers outside the school community

Appendix 1.2   Profile of an ICEL Graduate

A graduate of the Institute for Catholic Educational Leadership is:

- OPEN TO GROWTH and, therefore, should be:

    —A visionary leader who articulates clearly the school's philosophy and mission to the various publics;
    —An educational leader who is cognizant of the lifelong process of learning and communicates this to colleagues and students.

- ACADEMICALLY AND PROFESSIONALLY COMPETENT and, therefore, should be:

    —A scholar who has demonstrated academic competence in all coursework;
    —A researcher who is knowledgeable of the latest findings in Catholic education and the field of education in general;
    —An educator who is aware of current methodologies and is able to apply them effectively when assessing the local school site;
    —A leader who is economically astute and possesses financial skills.

- A RELIGIOUS LEADER and, therefore, should be:

    —A person who has an understanding of Catholic education as an integral part of the Church's teaching mission;
    —A person of faith who is able to communicate this faith with others;
    —A person whose lifestyle is founded upon Gospel values and who is a role model for students, parents, and faculty;
    —A moral educator and leader.

- A COMMUNITY BUILDER and, therefore, should be:

    —An astute and sensitive leader who is able to assess the school climate and to foster a sense of community among all facets of the school;
    —A leader who builds a school's Catholic identity based upon its history, tradition, and rituals;
    —A collaborator who works well with other professionals in the Catholic, private, and public sectors;
    —A leader who stimulates the involvement of students, parents, and faculty in community service as a natural outgrowth of the school's mission;
    —A person of compassion and justice whose decisions respond to the needs of the individual as well as to the good of the entire community.

- COMMITTED TO DOING JUSTICE and, therefore, should be:

Source: "Ensuring the Catholicity of the Church's Schools: The University of San Francisco Responds to the Challenge" by Mary Peter Traviss and Gini Shimabukuro, March 1999, *Catholic Education: A Journal of Inquiry and Practice,* 2(3), pp. 338–339. Reprinted by permission.

Appendix 1.2   *Continued*

—An educator who integrates faith into culture and life in order to promote justice and service to others;

—An educator who encourages those within the school community to focus attention on local, national, and global needs;

—A leader who works to insure the integrity of each individual within the school community.

Appendix 1.3   A Day in the Life of an Urban Elementary Principal

When Mary Stewart arrived at Blaire Elementary School at 8:15 A.M., the teachers were stopping by the office to sign in on their way to their classrooms. Stewart removed her coat and boots, hanging them in the closet outside her office. She put on a pair of medium-heeled shoes, explaining to the researcher, " . . . the children like to see the principal a little dressed up." Joining her clerk in the outer office, the two of them reviewed the list of teachers who would be absent and the steps to be taken to secure substitutes. One substitute, sent by the central office "Sub Center," had already arrived, and Stewart asked the clerk to give her the regular teacher's file containing a class seating chart and lesson plans.

Returning to her desk, Stewart's eyes drifted to the Continuous Progress Program packet and accompanying memorandum from district offices which had arrived the previous afternoon. It was a reminder that the next reporting period was imminent and that all forms must be filed this coming Friday before the close of business. This meant that Stewart would be spending part of each of the next three days buttonholing the teachers to get their reports to her on each child, and then summarizing these figures in an all-school report. Stewart anticipated that she would have to divert some time from other managerial duties to get this paperwork finished on time.

As she reviewed her calendar, Stewart mentally prepared for a meeting with faculty representatives of the Professional Problems Committee. The Union contract provided that this group, elected by the teachers, must meet regularly with the principal. At 8:30, Stewart left her office for the short walk to the school library, where the committee members were gathering. Stewart called the meeting to order about 8:35. High on her list of items was the matter of selecting textbooks for next year. But before this discussion got underway, the teachers wanted to relay questions to Stewart that individual teachers had raised with them: a problem in supervising the third floor washrooms, a question about how next year's faculty advisor to the eighth grade graduating class was to be selected, and a problem in getting supplies during a particular free period when the office clerk was often not available. After promising to work on these problems, Stewart spent most of the remaining time discussing plans with the teachers to host upcoming meetings with publisher representatives. Together they also reviewed plans to form faculty textbook review committees, and procedures for selecting a common textbook for each grade level.

After the meeting, Stewart was approached by two teachers with individual questions. Miss La Pointe wanted to know whether Stewart would be available during eighth period. Stewart nodded and invited her to stop by the office at that time. Mr. Fields, the gym teacher, informed her that the basketball team did well at yesterday's game. They came close to beating Doyle, which is one of the best teams

Source: The Urban Principal: Discretionary Decision-Making in a Large Educational Organization (pp. 40–47) by Van Cleve Morris, Robert L. Crowson, Emanuel Hurwitz, Jr., and Cynthia Porter-Gehrie, 1981, Washington, DC: National Institute for Education, NIE-G-79-0019.

Appendix 1.3   *Continued*

in the district. Stewart congratulated him, and took the opportunity to ask how Marvin Goth was behaving in class lately. Fields said that Marvin still got "edgy," but in general was "doing a lot better."

As Stewart walked through the hallway back to her office, Mrs. Noyes motioned to her from inside the classroom. The students were already in their classrooms or moving quickly through the halls in the last moments before the class bell rang. Noyes told Stewart that she was scheduled to take the students on a field trip this morning, but that one of the parents had called at the last moment to say that she would not be able to come. This left Noyes one parent volunteer short. Should she cancel the trip? Stewart remembered that Mrs. Case would be volunteering in the reading center this morning. She offered to ask her if she would fill in.

On the way to the reading center, Stewart peeked into several classrooms. As she passed the student washrooms she quickly looked into each, checking to see that no students were present and that the rooms were in order. As one student hurried past her, she asked him why he was not in class. He said that he had arrived late. She checked to see that he had a late admittance slip, and then urged him to get to school on time in the future.

When she entered the reading center, she nodded in the direction of the reading teacher and motioned that she wanted to speak with Mrs. Case. Mrs. Case quickly joined her and agreed to help with the field trip. On her way out the door, Stewart complimented the reading teacher on a bulletin board entitled "Read for Experience."

Instead of returning to her office, Stewart continued to walk the halls on the second and third floors. On the third floor, she spent a few minutes studying the washroom situation. Then, stopping briefly at each classroom, she asked the teachers to be sure that only one student at a time was excused to use them. On her way back down the stairs, she detoured for a moment on the second floor to swing by a classroom with a substitute teacher, "just to see how he's doing." Finding the students somewhat unruly, she stepped into the classroom, fixing the well-known principal's stare on the children. As expected, her presence quieted the room. She greeted the substitute and inquired whether the regular teacher's substitute file was in order. He said that everything seemed fine, "they're just testing a little bit."

When Stewart returned to the office, she spoke briefly with the clerk, reviewing the arrival and assignment of substitute teachers. Stewart asked the clerk to inform the librarian that she would have to cover one of the classes during second period, if the substitute teacher did not arrive by then. Then Stewart picked up the mail that had arrived via the school system's delivery service. She asked the clerk to inform Mrs. Noyes that Mrs. Case would come on the field trip. She also asked the clerk to be sure that a teacher aide was available during seventh period to give out teaching supplies. As they talked, the clerk handed her two telephone messages.

Stewart entered her office, leaving the door to the outer office open. (A second door connecting directly to the hallway was kept closed. In this way, anyone who wanted to see Stewart had to go through the clerk. Stewart, herself, usually passed

Appendix 1.3 *Continued*

through the outer office in order to exchange information with the clerk on the way in or out of her own private office.) She quickly wrote a note to Mrs. Reynolds, on the second floor, informing her that the teacher aide would be available during seventh period to give out supplies. She also wrote a bulletin to all teachers in longhand: "Teachers: It appears that students from different classes are meeting at prearranged times in the third floor washrooms again. When excusing students to the washrooms, please be sure they use the nearest washroom, only. Thank you." She got up, walked to the outer office and taped the bulletin on the counter by the sign-in book. She also placed the note to Mrs. Reynolds in her mailbox.

Stewart returned to her office and placed a call to another principal who had left a message. The principal told her that he was calling a meeting of the district's science fair committee and would appreciate knowing when a convenient time would be for Stewart. They agreed to meet at 10:00 A.M. the following day at Blaire School. After the phone conversation, Stewart wrote a note to the cafeteria director, asking that coffee and some rolls be available the next morning in the conference room adjoining her office. She consulted the teachers' schedule and then also wrote a note to Mrs. St. Antoine, asking her to come to her office during seventh period. She got up, walked to the outer office and placed the notes in St. Antoine's and the cafeteria director's mailboxes.

Returning to her office, Stewart once again picked up the telephone and dialed the number of a representative from a photography company that took students' yearly pictures. No answer, so Stewart left a message that she called. She set the phone message at the corner of her desk, so that she "would remember his name when he calls again."

She then began to look at the morning mail and some items the clerk had placed in her "in" box:

- A personnel bulletin listing several openings in the system for teachers and administrators
- An announcement of a conference for reading teachers
- A set of rating cards to be completed for each teacher; these teacher rating cards were filled out each year by the principal and placed in the teachers' personal files.

Stewart placed the rating cards to one side on her desk, then got up, taking the other items to the outer office with her. She placed the conference announcement in the reading teacher's mailbox and tacked the personnel bulletin to the teacher's bulletin board. As she did so, the clerk informed her of an incoming telephone call.

Returning to her desk, she picked up the phone and heard the voice of the photographer's representative, glancing in recognition at the name on the earlier phone message. After some preliminary pleasantries, this: "Mr. Haskins, every year we make a selection from among several school photographers to take school pictures. You say you'd like to be considered this year? Fine, I'll be glad to include you in the

Appendix 1.3   *Continued*

group. Could you send me some materials—a list of the size and kind of photo to be included in each student's packet . . . maybe a sample packet, O.K.? Also the cost to the student, and the amount the school keeps for each packet sold. Also any other items that you make available, such as class pictures and teacher photographs."

Stewart went on to explain to the photographer that the eighth grade faculty sponsor participated in the selection. However, the sponsor for the following year had not yet been picked out. "I'll make sure that you get the information on the selection process and the date and time of the meeting when we ask all photographers to come to the school to demonstrate their work. However, I'd appreciate it if you would not meet directly with the faculty sponsor, except of course at the demonstration session. I look forward to seeing your materials, and thanks for your interest in the school."

Stewart put down the phone and turned to the researcher: "You know, its a pleasure dealing with these photographers. They really enjoy coming to the school, and I must say, the kids get a kick out of these sessions too." Then, turning to another subject, Stewart explained to the researcher that she had gotten a hurry-up phone call from downtown headquarters a day or so ago calling her to a special meeting on the Access to Excellence program. "It's scheduled for Friday at eleven, and that's just when I'll be putting the finishing touches on the Continuous Progress materials. I hope I can get them done in time. But, you know, these meetings . . . they're having more and more of them. They want to turn this school into an "academy," whatever that is. And we've got to go downtown and sit around for a couple hours to be told what it is. Then, no doubt, there'll be more meetings at district (headquarters) setting it up. Seems as if I spend more and more of my time away from here, going to meetings, meetings. Hard to keep on top of things here when I'm not around."

The researcher listened intently, and the two of them discussed the possibility of "academy" status and what that would mean for the school and for the community.

After a discussion of 15 minutes, Stewart looked at her watch and saw that it was nearly time for the primary grades recess. Breaking off the conversation with the researcher, she got up, walked through the outer office, and went to stand by the exit doors to the primary play area. When the bell sounded, the children were escorted through the building toward the exit. In the ensuing commotion, Stewart spoke sharply to a few boisterous children, telling them to "walk, don't run," and to "move slowly down the stairs."

She explained in an aside to the researcher that her customary practice was to accompany the youngsters out onto the playground where she and the teachers could supervise their play. However, today, she had to get back to the office to prepare a schedule for teacher rating conferences with each teacher. Returning to her desk, she assembled the teacher evaluation materials and got from her drawer the teachers' daily schedules. Allowing 20 minutes for each teacher, she began making up a conference schedule. In the middle of this activity, she was interrupted by

Appendix 1.3 *Continued*

three boys entering the outer office, with a teacher aide following close behind. One of the boys was crying and holding the back of his head. The aide explained that the injured boy had fallen and hit his head on a patch of ice near the rim of the play area. The other two boys, she reported, had been chasing the injured boy.

Stewart moved to the outer office and told the two chasers to sit down on a bench inside the hallway door. She inspected the head injury and found that it was beginning to swell at the point of impact. Sending a student helper to the cafeteria to fetch some ice, she asked the injured boy for his name, his home telephone number, and his mother's name. She then dialed the number and spoke with the mother. After hearing what had happened, the mother said that she would come pick him up as soon as she could get a neighbor to drive her to the school. The helper soon arrived back with the ice, and Stewart wrapped it in a paper towel and gave it to the boy to place on the bump. She told him to sit down on the bench and wait for his mother, whereupon she invited the two chasers into the inner office and closed the door. "Now look, you know you're not supposed to run where there is ice . . . it's too dangerous. Now that someone's hurt, the matter is serious. I want your parents to know about this." She filled out a form that requested a parent to come to school with the boys the following morning. With the boys still at her desk, she telephoned their homes and orally requested that a parent come to see her the next morning. She explained to the boys' mothers, "There's been an injury and your son was involved. Something must be done about their wild behavior during recess." She then sent the boys back to their classrooms, explaining that she would see them again in the morning.

As she gave them their hall passes, the injured boy's mother arrived. Stewart explained to her that two other boys had been involved and that she would be meeting with their parents in the morning. The mother asked her son, "Who did it?" and he replied it was "Jeff and Michael." "Those boys," the mother said, "why do they pick on him so much? Last week they pushed him in the bushes on the way home from school. Now they've gone too far." Stewart asked the mother to "Let me see if I can't work something out." She promised to call her back in the morning, after she met with the other parents.

As the boy and his mother left, Stewart looked up and saw that it was beginning to snow heavily. She went to the public address system and announced that students eating lunch at school would remain inside the building during the lunchtime recess.

Stewart returned to her desk and worked on the conference schedule, but was shortly interrupted by two phone calls. One concerned the placement of a student teacher in the school. The other was from her husband, asking if she would like to meet him downtown for dinner. As Stewart was finishing the schedule, the clerk brought in a master copy of the parents' bulletin for her to approve before it was duplicated. She set aside the schedule and read through the bulletin as the clerk waited to one side. She pointed out two typos and then placed her signature on the copy master. The clerk took it and left. A moment later she returned with the U.S.

Appendix 1.3   *Continued*

mail. Stewart took a quick glance at the envelopes before setting them to one side and continuing to finish the schedule. Stewart neatly copied the final schedule by hand and then asked the clerk to place a copy of the schedule in each teacher's mailbox.

Stewart then headed toward the cafeteria, speaking with students in the hall on the way, telling them to "slow down" and "go to your recess areas." She took a tray and moved through the lunch line. Instead of going to the faculty room, she returned to her office to eat. There, she was available for teachers who might want to stop by. As she ate, she looked through the U.S. mail: promotional material for textbooks, school administration booklets, and instructional supplies. Also an announcement of a tea at a local Catholic High School for the eighth graders. Stewart set this aside and threw out the rest.

A student asked to see Stewart. As student council president, she wanted to know when the next student council meeting would be (the last meeting had been cancelled because of snow). They picked a date and the student said that she would inform the council members. Stewart chatted for a few minutes with the girl about her plans for high school.

Getting up from her desk, Stewart carried her tray and the tea announcement to the outer office. She left the announcement in the eighth grade class sponsor's mailbox and returned her tray to the cafeteria. Then she began her tour of the hallways, inspecting the building as the students returned to their classes to settle down for the afternoon's course work.

When she returned to her office, the clerk handed her a phone message. Stewart dialed the phone for an in-house call and reached the building engineer. He told her that a small window at the back of the building had been broken during the lunch hour by some loitering high school students. He said he had covered it with some heavy cardboard, "but I thought you should know about it. Also, you know the art room . . . the shades in there have been damaged. The (art) teacher just lets the kids go wild in there during seventh and eighth periods. I think you should talk to him." Stewart agreed to check on it.

Miss La Pointe arrived. She had agreed to start a dramatic program in the school and wanted to report to Stewart the plans she was making for a Spring production. They discussed use of the auditorium, rehearsal schedules, the play La Pointe had selected, and the tryout announcement La Pointe had prepared. Toward the end of the seventh period, the conference was concluded and La Pointe left to return to her classroom. Stewart got up and, checking to make sure that the teacher's aide was on station in the outer office to give out supplies, headed for the art room to see the damaged shades and to make sure the students were under control.

When she returned to the office, Stewart found Mrs. St. Antoine waiting for her in the outer office. Stewart invited her into her own office and asked for an update about the plans for the eighth grade tea, dinner, and other graduation festivities. St. Antoine discussed with her the results of faculty and student committee meetings

Appendix 1.3 *Continued*

to that point. Then Stewart asked St. Antoine whether she was thinking about remaining eighth grade sponsor next year. St. Antoine seemed a bit embarrassed. She said that she enjoyed working with the students very much, but that there was some jealousy from some of the other eighth grade teachers who felt excluded. They discussed how some of the other eighth grade teachers might be brought more closely into the planning, and St. Antoine left agreeing that she would try to mend some of the fences that had been neglected.

Seeing that it was near the end of the day, Stewart checked her desk to see what remained to be done. Noting the stack of material in the "in" box, she looked through it. It contained several forms that required signing; they pertained to the ordering of supplies, teacher absences, and a field trip permission. Stewart signed all of the forms but one. It was a request to order a film. Stewart was unfamiliar with the film and wanted to discuss its nature and use with the teacher before signing.

Stewart put on her hat and coat and walked to the main exit doors just as the students were beginning to leave. Stationed just outside the exit, she called to the students inside the hallway and out on the playground to "slow down," and "watch out, its slippery." When the students were gone she returned to her office to find a tiny kindergartner sitting with tear-filled eyes next to the teacher aide. The aide explained that the girl's father was supposed to pick her up from school, but had not arrived. They tried to make some phone calls to find out who was coming for the girl, but could not get an answer. The girl suggested that they call her aunt, which they did. The aunt agreed to take the girl, but said no one could come and get her right now. Stewart agreed to bring the girl by the aunt's house. "There now," the aide told the girl, "the principal will take you to your aunt's house." Stewart placed a few items in a small brief case and was ready to leave. She waited as the aide and clerk prepared to leave also. As they put on their coats, she checked the teachers' sign-in sheets to be sure that they were all out of the building. Then she locked the office as they left together. Stewart reached for the small girl's hand and helped her down the slippery steps. Before going to her car, she muttered to the researcher, "I suppose I shouldn't be doing this . . . liability and all. But someone has to."

2

THE LIMITS OF TRADITIONAL MANAGEMENT THEORY

It is not by chance that some principals are more effective than others, even when all are faced with the same demands and constraints. Effective principals have a better understanding of how the world of schooling and school leadership works. They base their practice on a different theory, and this enables them to create a more effective practice.

Principals are faced with an important choice. On the one hand, they can base their practice on the assumption that predetermined solutions exist for most of the problems they face that are directly linked to research-based theories and techniques. On the other hand, they can base their practice on the assumption that few of the problems they face lend themselves to predetermined solutions. They can resign themselves to the difficult task of having to create knowledge in use as they practice. Principals who make the second choice realize that despite the attractiveness of the first, predetermined solutions can only be trusted to work for the few problems that are fixed and located in stable environments. They realize that the majority of problems and situations faced are characterized by ambiguity and confusion. These are problems located in a turbulent environment where practice is largely indeterminate. They would argue, as does Donald Schön, that the most important problems principals face are beyond the reach of technical, rational solutions. In Schön's words: "The practitioner must choose. Shall he remain on the high ground where he can solve relatively unimportant problems according to prevailing standards of rigor, or shall he descend to the swamp of important problems and nonrigorous inquiry?" (1987:3).

Mindscapes of Practice

The choice that a principal makes is largely dependent on her or his theory or "mindscape" of practice. Mindscapes influence what we see, believe, and do.

Although many scholars might take exception to the way I categorize mindscapes, three distinct views of schooling and administering can be identified, are worth describing and understanding, and can be evaluated for good fit with the real landscape of practice. The three are the mindscapes of the "Mystics," the "Neats," and the "Scruffies." Principals and researchers who are Mystics, Neats, or Scruffies have widely different conceptions of the nature of practice and of the relationships between this practice and knowledge from theory and research. For Mystics, no relationship whatsoever exists; for Neats, theoretical knowledge is superordinate to practice; and for Scruffies, theoretical knowledge is subordinate to practice. Their respective views can be summarized as follows.

- *Mystics* hold the view that educational administration resembles a nonscience; thus, scientific principles gleaned from theory and research have little relevance to practice. Scientific principles and practice are disconnected. Instead, practice is driven by the principal's tacit knowledge, intuitive feel for situations, sixth sense, and other more transcendental factors.
- *Neats* hold the view that educational administration resembles an applied science within which theory and research are directly and linearly linked to practice. The former always determine the latter, and thus knowledge is superordinate to the principal and designed to prescribe practice.
- *Scruffies* hold the view that educational administration resembles a craftlike science within which practice is characterized by interacting reflection and action episodes. Theory and research are only one source of knowledge. This knowledge is subordinate to the principal and is designed to inform but not to prescribe practice. Tacit knowledge and intuition develop and strengthen as they are informed by theory, research, experience, and the craft knowledge of others.

The mystical end of the continuum is characterized by the belief that no formal knowledge is of use, that the world is hopelessly phenomenological, that everything is relative, that only personal knowledge counts, that all knowing is tacit, that teaching and administrative skills are gifts, and that in the end it is one's intuition or other manifestation of some mysterious sixth sense that counts. Although many principals are card-carrying mystics, this view is not at the center of the debate regarding knowledge development and use in the principalship. Therefore, the emphasis in this discussion is on the position of the Neats and the Scruffies.

What about the Neats? They believe it is both possible and desirable to identify the one best way to practice. They search for the one best list of standards that specifies what everyone everywhere must learn. They adopt the one best list of school characteristics or the one best model of schooling in order to make schools effective. The Neats, for example, accept the research on effective teaching without question. They believe that a generic set of teaching effectiveness behaviors exists that can be applied by all teachers in all situations to all students. The research on effective schools, leadership styles, and conflict-management strategies are viewed similarly as truths to be accepted and applied. Principalship practice is considered to be a research-based technology that can be directly learned and routinely applied. To the Neats, the principal is presumed to function as a highly trained technician.

How does the view of the Neats fit the real world of practice? Not very well. Patterns of school practice are actually characterized by a great deal of uncertainty, instability, complexity, and variety. Value conflicts and uniquenesses are accepted aspects of educational settings. According to Schön (1983), these characteristics are perceived as central to the world of professional practice in all the major professions, including medicine, engineering, management, and education. He concludes: "Professional knowledge is mismatched to the changing characteristics of the situation of practice" (14). Although one may be comfortable in viewing the principalship as a logical process of problem solving with the application of standard techniques to predictable problems, a more accurate view may be a process of "managing messes" (16).

In the actual world of schooling, the task of the principal is to make sense of messy situations by increasing understanding and discovering and communicating meanings. Situations of practice are typically characterized by unique events; therefore, uniform answers to problems are not likely to be helpful. Teachers, supervisors, and students bring to their classrooms beliefs, assumptions, values, opinions, preferences, and predispositions. Thus, objective and value-free administrative strategies are not likely to address issues of importance. Uncertainty and complexity are normal aspects in the process of schooling. Intuition becomes necessary to fill in the gaps of what can be specified as known and what cannot. Yet, ordinary intuition will not do. Intuition must be *informed* by theoretical knowledge on one hand and adept understandings of the situation on the other.

Reflective Practice: The Paradigm of the Scruffies

The Scruffies' view of the principalship is that of a science of the practical—a science that stems from theories of practice and that provides principals with practical as well as theoretical mindscapes from which to work. The concept of *reflective practice* is critical to this new science.

Reflective practice is based on the reality that professional knowledge is different from scientific knowledge. Professional knowledge is created in use as professionals who face ill-defined, unique, and changing problems decide on courses of action. Ralph Tyler maintains that researchers don't have a full understanding of the nature of professional knowledge in education. He states:

> Researchers and many academics also misunderstand educational practices. The practice of every profession evolves informally, and professional procedures are not generally derived from systematic design based on research findings. Professional practice has largely developed through trial and error and intuitive efforts. Practitioners, over the years, discover procedures that appear to work and others that fail. The professional practice of teaching, as well as that of law, medicine, and theology,

is largely a product of the experience of practitioners, particularly those who are more creative, inventive, and observant than the average. (cited in Hosford, 1984:9)

Scientific studies in the various professions are important. But science, according to Tyler, "explains phenomenon, it does not produce practices" (cited in Hosford, 1984:10). Professionals rely heavily on informed intuition as they create knowledge in use. Intuition is informed by theoretical knowledge on the one hand and by interacting with the context of practice on the other. When teachers use informed intuition, they are engaging in reflective practice. When principals use informed intuition, they too are engaging in reflective practice. Knowing is in the action itself, and reflective professionals become students of their practice. They research the context and experiment with different courses of action. Schön (1983) suggests:

They may ask themselves, for example, "what features do I notice when I recognize this thing? What are the criteria by which I make this judgment? What procedures am I enacting when I perform this skill? How am I framing the problem that I'm trying to solve?" Usually, reflection on knowing-in-action goes together with reflection on the stuff at hand. There is some puzzling, or troubling or interesting phenomenon with which the individual is trying to deal. As he tries to make sense of it, he also reflects on the understandings which have been implicit in his action, understandings which he surfaces, criticizes, re-structures and embodies in further action.

It is this entire process of reflection-in-action which is central to the "art" by which practitioners sometimes deal with situations of uncertainty, instability, uniqueness, and value conflicts. (50)

To Schön (1984), reflection-in-action involves "on-the-spot surfacing, criticizing, re-structuring and testing of intuitive understandings of experienced phenomenon; often, it takes the form of a reflective conversation with the situation" (42). Reflection-in-action captures the principal at work as she or he makes judgments in trying to manage a very messy work context.

Life would be simpler if accepting the paradigm of the Scruffies meant the position of the Neats was false. The reality is that both are true. For simple problems that exist in stable environments under determinate conditions, thinking like a Neat will serve principals well. However, for complex problems that exist in turbulent environments under indeterminate conditions, thinking like a Scruffie makes more sense.

Take leadership, for example. For Scruffies, managing and leading resemble a game of golf in which the distance to the hole is always changing. You know the hole is straight ahead, but you can never be sure just how far away it is. You have a pretty good understanding of the distances that you can get from each club (club payoff), but you cannot choose a club based on where the hole is at the moment.

You must guess where the hole will be after you swing. Knowledge of club payoff remains important in this context, but it cannot be used directly. Instead, this knowledge becomes part of one's conceptual framework for making an educated guess in choosing the right club for an assumed distance. In this game, laws exist that determine where the hole will be next, but they cannot be fully understood.

The better golfers are those who develop an intuitive feel for past, current, and likely patterns of appearance of the hole as the game is played. Their play is neither whimsical nor random. Instead, they make mature, educated guesses (in the case of principals, informed professional judgments). These guesses combined with knowledge of club payoff helps them to win. Being familiar with the topographical features of each of the holes to be played, the play of the greens, the texture of the grass and rough, and the idiosyncrasies of each of the sand traps yields other pieces of information that might or might not come in handy should a hole pop up here rather than there. Having a firm fix on topography and club payoff is not enough if one cannot develop a feel for the patterns that are likely to emerge. However, and equally as important, being pretty good at predicting the patterns but having little understanding of course topography or club payoff will not be of much help.

The key to reflective practice can be found in William James's 1892 message to the teachers of Cambridge, Massachusetts. He pointed out the importance of "an intermediary inventive mind" in making practical application of scientific knowledge. In his words:

> The science of logic never made a man reason rightly, and the science of ethics . . . never made a man behave rightly. The most such sciences can do is to help us catch ourselves up and check ourselves, if we start to reason or behave wrongly; and to criticize ourselves more articulately after we have made mistakes. A science only lays down lines within which the rules of the art must fall, laws which the follower of the art must not transgress; but what particular thing he shall positively do within those lines is left exclusively to his own genius. (8)

The idea of reflective practice is still relatively new, and much more thinking needs to be given to its development and use in educational administration. It seems clear, nonetheless, that reflective principals are in charge of their professional practice. They do not passively accept solutions and mechanically apply them. They do not assume that the norm is the one best way to practice, and they are suspicious of easy answers to complex questions. They are painfully aware of how context and situations vary, how teachers and students differ in many ways, and how complex school goals and objectives actually are; they recognize that, despite difficulties, tailored treatments to problems must be the norm. At the same time, reflective professional practice requires that principals have a healthy respect for, be well informed about, and use the best available theory and research and accumulated practice wisdom. All these sources of information help increase understanding and inform practice. The rub is that no matter how reflective a principal tries to be, effectiveness will remain elusive if still based on traditional management theory. Management theory itself needs to be reinvented.

Changing Mindscapes

Traditional management enjoys official sanction in many state capitols and in many university preparation programs for school administrators. It is also the mindscape that dominates much of the literature on school improvement. It's no surprise, therefore, that this mindscape is entrenched in the thinking of many school principals and is difficult to change.

Consider, for example, the case of elementary school principal Jane. Jane now spends from one-third to one-half of her time trying to be an "instructional leader" as prescribed by a recent state law. This law requires that she evaluate every teacher in her building two times a year, using a state assessment instrument composed of a generic list of 50 teaching behaviors gleaned from dozens of independent research reports on "effective teaching." She is required as well to take into account the scores of students on the state's mandated standardized skills test as part of this evaluation. The instrument is several pages long and involves a good deal of paperwork in addition to one hour of classroom observation for each evaluation. Jane takes her responsibilities seriously and estimates that a conscientious job takes about three hours for each evaluation.

Teachers are required to develop "growth plans," which Jane must monitor as well. The growth plans indicate how each teacher intends to improve her or his teaching and thus earn higher evaluation scores. Jane estimates that she spends 180 hours or 22 days a year just conducting the required evaluations. She dreads the many hours it takes to collect, study, and comment on the growth plans and then figure out sensible, albeit efficient, ways to follow up what teachers claim they will do. She notices that the growth plans are often perfunctory in tone, and this bothers her.

Kim's comment

OR's

Among Jane's other instructional leadership responsibilities are daily monitoring of teachers to ensure that they follow the state-mandated standards for each of the subjects or courses taught and that they adhere to the proper time allocations as provided by the mandated schedule. Jane can keep tabs on this process by practicing "management by walking around," but is not able by relying on this process alone to demonstrate concretely to her superiors that her school is in compliance. Seeking to avoid a poor evaluation from her supervisors, Jane requires that teachers indicate the standards they are teaching to on their daily lesson plans, as well as the amount of time they spend teaching each of these objectives. She dutifully collects these lesson plans each Friday and examines them to be sure that teachers are in compliance. As time permits, Jane tries to write comments on the plans that might result in teachers thinking about their lessons more effectively and teaching better.

In Jane's school district, heavy emphasis is given to the state tests that are closely linked to the required standards. The results of these tests must be submitted to the school district's central office and by that office to the state department of education. The results are then published in the newspaper, with statewide comparisons made district by district and district comparisons made school by school. There is enormous pressure for schools to do well on the test comparisons. If the test scores in her school are not high enough, she hears about it from the superintendent's office. As part of her evaluation, for example, she must report to her supervisor the current year's test results and note progress (or lack of progress) made by comparing these results with test scores for the two previous years.

Sometimes Jane gets the impression that the superintendent wants the scores up at any cost and that all that counts is the bottom line. In turn, she puts enormous pressure on her teachers to be sure that the students do well on the tests. All teachers, for example, have been "inserviced" so that their day-by-day teaching should now be based on a popular teaching model made up of a series of specific steps thought to result in better student achievement. In addition to the evaluation system that is now in place and the monitoring of lesson plans and test scores, Jane spends much of her time coaching and monitoring the teachers to be sure that they are using the required teaching techniques.

In her school, Jane supervises a tightly connected "instructional management system" that seeks to link together measurable objectives, a highly specific curriculum, and required, detailed time schedules with a monitoring system of controls to ensure that teachers are doing what they are supposed to be doing and at the right time. Despite this management system, the results have been frustrating. Although there have been modest gains in test scores, particularly with respect to lower-level skills, a number of problems have emerged. The curriculum is becoming increasingly narrow, absentee rates are up, and Jane worries that teachers are using fewer and fewer of their talents and skills. She shudders at the harshness of the term *deskilled* that some people use to describe what is happening to teachers in her school, but is haunted by its imagery nonetheless.

A number of other "unanticipated consequences" from using this particular instructional management system are emerging. Teachers seem to be teaching more and more to the test. Furthermore, Jane is convinced that they are "showboating" the indicators that appear on the required teacher evaluation instrument when she is present and observing, but not using them at other times. She suspects that she is often observing staged lessons that allow for easy display of the indicators in the teachers' efforts to get higher evaluation scores. Higher scores increase their eligibility for merit-pay-ladder advancement, and, thus, Jane does not begrudge them.

Jane wonders what is wrong. Could Murphy's Law be true? Although from a traditional management perspective Jane can provide evidence that she is doing what she is supposed to, that the required instructional management system is in place, and that (at least overtly) teachers are doing what they are supposed to, Jane feels that appearances do not match reality and that things are just not working well. After much painful soul searching, she reaches the conclusion that something different must be done.

This conclusion is very disconcerting for Jane. She feels that she is on the verge of experiencing a professional career crisis that resembles the proverbial "midlife crisis." After all, Jane was an outstanding student during her years of graduate study in educational administration. She took the required workshops offered by the state-sponsored Leadership Development Academy and did so well that last summer she was asked to be an academy trainer. She knows how important such management ideas as POSDCoRB are to providing the kind of rational and efficient management needed for schools to work well. She knows how to demonstrate the leadership behaviors learned in a recent workshop, and last summer she developed workshops of her own on conflict management and on how to conduct a successful conference. She has earned a reputation for knowing how to handle people.

On the walls of Jane's office are displayed several plaques containing sayings of widely accepted management principles. Each of the plaques was given to her as an award for completing one of the Leadership Development Academy's workshops. One says, "If you can't measure it, you can't manage it." Another says, "What gets rewarded gets done." And a third says, "What gets measured gets taught"—a saying often repeated by her State Commissioner of Education as he shares his vision for schools in speeches throughout the state. Still other plaques remind Jane of the importance of having clear objectives, letting people know exactly what is expected of them, and being a rational and objective manager.

Jane is surrounded by the dimensions, principles, and expressions of traditional management theory—the theory of the Neats. Furthermore, this theory matches well her own mindscape of what management is, how schools are to operate if they are to function well, and the kind of leadership she should provide as a school principal. Finally, this mindscape is nurtured by the system of rewards in place in her school district. The more her practice reflects traditional management theory, the more successful she is assumed to be. It is no wonder Jane experiences dissonance and anxiety from the realization that it doesn't work very well. Changing one's mindscape is a little like changing one's religion.

In recent months, Jane has come to realize that for traditional management to work, schools need to be more tightly structured and predictable than is typically the case and people need to be more passive and uniform than is typical. At first, she responded to this awareness by continuing to do the same things, only doing them better. But gradually she accepted the reality that *when the world cannot be changed to fit your theory, you had better change your theory to fit the world.* This thought made more sense when she read somewhere about the differences between management and leadership. Management is concerned with doing things right, she remembered. Leadership is concerned with doing right things.

Jane realizes that successful principals are both effective managers and effective leaders. But if one has to choose between the two, the only sensible choice is to do right things, even if it means that you are not doing them in the way specified by the system. Arriving at this decision was an important and courageous milestone for Jane. Although anxious at first, she now feels comfortable with the idea that when bureaucratic and moral authority are in conflict, moral authority must always take precedence.

Jane was not known as a reckless person. Indeed, if anything, she was considered to be quite conventional and conservative in the way she did things. Thus, she began to respond to the looseness she found in the structure of schooling by bending rules and interpreting issues in a fashion that always reflected the spirit of the rule but not the letter. When Jane encountered the system tightening up because her supervisors practiced close supervision, or when she was forced by the system to ignore individual differences in people and situations, she would follow the opposite tack by emphasizing the letter of the rule but not the spirit. Perfunctory execution became part of her management repertoire—a skill she realized that teachers often used to advantage when locked into the same predicament.

During the evaluation of teachers using the standardized system, for example, Jane took liberties with the required procedures by not insisting that all the listed teaching behaviors be displayed by teachers, but only the ones that made sense, given the lessons or units they were teaching, the objectives they set, and the learning needs of their students. She would talk to teachers about what they wanted to accomplish in their lessons and how. She was sensitive to and respectful of the differences in personality that determined their teaching styles. She realized, for example, that reticent teachers had a harder time providing the kind of bubbling reinforcement and feedback that "win points" than did their more outgoing counterparts. Together, Jane and the teachers would look over the four-page list of required teaching behaviors, deciding on the 8 or 10 behaviors that seemed to make the most sense for the particular teaching episode to be evaluated and in light of particular teaching problems identified. The evaluation was then based on this shorter but more meaningful version.

Whenever Jane's supervisors got wind of what was going on and cracked down on her to comply more specifically with the system, Jane shifted her stratagem by routinely evaluating people with dispatch to save as much time as possible for other things. Once the evaluations were complete and the paperwork filed, Jane and her teachers were able to work more meaningfully and in better ways on the improvement of teaching. Jane is learning fast how to provide leadership in the complex, messy, and nonlinear scruffy world. Her mindscapes of management and leadership theory are changing to match the actual landscapes she encounters in practice.

The Limits of Traditional Management Theory

It would be a mistake for Jane to believe that traditional management theory is useless. She should not abandon it but should, rather, learn how to use it to her best advantage. Traditional management theory has its merits and limitations, and it is important for principals to know the difference.

- Traditional management theory is suited to situations of practice that are characterized by linear conditions. However, the usefulness of this theory ends where *nonlinear conditions* begin.
- Traditional management theory is suited to situations of practice that can be tightly structured and connected without causing unanticipated harmful effects. However, the usefulness of this theory ends where *loosely structured* conditions begin.
- Traditional management theory is suited to situations in which the need exists to bring about a routine level of competence and performance. However, the

usefulness of this theory ends when the goal is to bring about *extraordinary commitment and performance.*

Linear and Nonlinear Conditions

When deciding on management and leadership strategies, it is important to take into account the extent to which conditions are or are not *linear*. Linear conditions are characterized by:

Stable, predictable environments
Tight management connections
Loose cultural connections
Discrete goals
Structured tasks
Single solutions
Easily measured outcomes
Sure operating procedures
Determinate consequences of action
Clear lines of authority

Under linear conditions, simplicity, clarity, order, and predictability are present. Examples of administrative tasks that typically fit linear conditions include the routing of bus schedules, purchasing books, planning conference times, and other events and activities in which human interactions are simple, incidental, or nonexistent. Yet, even these tasks can quickly become nonlinear—for instance, an eight-inch snowstorm can create havoc with a bus schedule.

By contrast, nonlinear conditions are characterized by:

- Dynamic environments
- Loose management connections
- Tight cultural connections
- Multiple and competing goals
- Unstructured tasks
- Competing solutions
- Difficult-to-measure outcomes
- Unsure operating procedures
- Indeterminate consequences of action
- Unclear and competing lines of authority

The vast majority of human interactions that take place in schools can be described as nonlinear. Gleick writes in *Chaos Making a New Science:* "Nonlinearity means that the act of playing the game has a way of changing the rules" (1987:24). In nonlinear situations, every decision that is made in response to conditions at the base time (time 1) changes these conditions in such a way that successive decisions also made at time 1 no longer fit. It is difficult, therefore, for a principal to plan a series of steps, commit to a set of stepwise procedures, or otherwise make progressive management and leadership decisions based on the initial assumptions. When the context changes, the original sequence no longer makes sense. One cannot predict the conditions of time 2 until the conditions are experienced.

Under nonlinear conditions, management resembles following a compass when the position of north changes with each step you take. As Cziko (1989) phrases it: "A process demonstrating chaos is one in which strict deterministic causality holds at each *individual* step in an unfolding process, and yet it is impossible to predict the outcome over any *sequence* of steps in the process." In summary, nonlinear relationships between two events lead to consequences that are unpredictable. Furthermore, if the context for action changes, as is often the case in managing, leading, and teaching, the original sequence no longer makes sense.

Take, for example, application of motivation theories in an effort to increase teacher performance. Providing rewards to a teacher might result in a certain amount of motivation at time 1. This relationship may actually be linear, with the amount of motivation increasing proportionally as rewards are provided at times 2 and 3. However, more rewards can result in less motivation if they are no longer valued, if they are viewed as manipulative, or if they are taken for granted. Moreover, individual differences come to play, so that what person A values differs from what person B values. Person B may tire more quickly of the same rewards than does person A. While person A might feel manipulated as a result of receiving rewards and respond negatively, person B feels attended to and responds positively.

Although the typical textbook version of traditional management theory would have us believe otherwise, the consequences of using the same motivational strategies for different people and under different conditions typically are indeterminate and unpredictable. Their link to people and consequences is nonlinear. This is the case as well for leadership, conflict resolution, and other categories of management behavior. They are all linked to people and events in nonlinear ways. *The fact is that in management and leadership, identical situations and strategies give rise to different outcomes and consequences.*

Vaill (1989) aptly describes the nonlinear context for management as "permanent white water." White water is the frothy, turbulent water found in waterfalls, breakers, and rapids. This metaphor was suggested to Vaill by a manager who observed:

> *Most managers are taught to think of themselves as paddling their canoes on calm, still lakes. They are led to believe that they should be pretty much able to go where they want, when they want, using means that are under their control. . . . But it has been my experience that you never get out of the rapids! . . . There are lots of changes going on at once. The feeling is one of continuous upset and chaos. (2)*

Vaill points out that in management "things are only partially under control, yet the effective navigator of the rapids is not behaving randomly or aimlessly" (2). In summary, it is the dynamic nature of unfolding events resembling "permanent white water" that differentiates linear from nonlinear situations. Successful practice in the latter requires the kind of reflection that enables principals and teachers to constantly test what they know against what is happening.

Tight and Loose Structure

Weick (1976) has argued compellingly for viewing schools as loosely coupled organizations. His point is that whereas aspects of schools are connected to each other in such a way that one influences the other, these connections are often confounded by other connections and are rarely characterized by strong and direct influence. As March and Simon (1958:176) point out, loose coupling does not mean that decisions, actions, and programs in effect are unrelated, but that they are only loosely related to each other.

The issue of school goals and purposes provides a good example. It is generally assumed that there is a tight connection between stated goals and the policies, decisions, and actions that take place in an organization. Yet, the problem is that schools have multiple goals and are expected to achieve them. Sometimes the goals conflict with each other such that making progress toward one means losing progress toward another. Always thinking in terms of discrete goals or even discrete multiple goals with each attended to sequentially, therefore, does not fit the special character of schools' unique value systems. Under nonlinear and loosely structured conditions, schools don't achieve goals as much as they respond to certain values and tend to certain imperatives that ensure their survival over time (Parsons, 1951).

Hills (1982) points out that, rather than discrete goal attainment, school administrators bring to their practice what he calls "pattern rationality." Principals, by his way of thinking, respond to "a conception of a pattern development on a number of mutually limiting dimensions with respective gains in a given area having implications for other areas" (1982:7). Successful principals become surfers, skilled at riding the wave of the pattern as it unfolds. They respond to value patterns when discrete goals are in conflict with each other. Important to this concept of pattern rationality is the principal's concern with the costs and benefits of her or his actions.

Teachers respond similarly. Although the literature overwhelmingly portrays teaching as a rational and linear act whereby teaching behaviors and decisions about instructional materials and time are made in response to objectives and intended outcomes, a glimpse into the real world reveals that these connections are much looser and confounding. Goals and outcomes, for example, are selected as often as a result of available materials as are materials selected as a result of goals. Teaching styles and preferences determine objectives as often as objectives determine teaching styles and preferences. Outcomes become goals as often as goals determine outcomes. Teaching, similar to management, is largely nonlinear and indeterminate. Stated goals and objectives are constantly shifting and changing and are often displaced by others once the teaching begins and as it continues. Indeed, teachers are just as likely to discover their goals during and after their teaching than they are to state them beforehand.

Perhaps the most noticeable example of looseness in schools is the connection of teachers to rules. Principal Jane became aware of this reality the hard way as she tried to implement the required teaching evaluation system. When she was in class observing lessons using the instrument, she saw what she was supposed to because the teachers did what they were supposed to. Yet, when she left the classroom, teachers taught in ways that made sense to them and to their colleagues. They were more tightly connected to values, beliefs, and norms than they were to the imposed management system.

Ordinary and Extraordinary Commitment and Performance

The management and leadership needed to bring about "a fair day's work for a fair day's pay" and for transcending this minimum contract to achieve inspired and extraordinary commitment and performance in schools are different (see, for example, Bass, 1985; Burns, 1978; Herzberg, 1966; Kelly, 1988; Sergiovanni, 1990). Traditional management theory and practice can provide the former but not the latter. Principal Jane noted, for example, that by practicing traditional management she was able to get teachers to do what they were supposed to but could not get *sustained* and *extraordinary* results.

There are two reasons why traditional management theory and practice are limited to achieving minimums, not maximums. First, the theory is based on bureaucratic and personal authority. Relying on rules, mandates, procedures, regulations, and formal expectations to get someone to do something are examples of bureaucratic authority. When this form of authority is used teachers are expected to comply or else face negative consequences. When principals rely on their human relations skills to get people to comply, they are using personal authority. These skills enable principals to successfully trade meeting needs of teachers for compliance with their wishes. Both bureaucratic and personal authority are external. Teachers are motivated to respond for outside reasons rather than be motivated from within.

External authority works and most teachers and students respond to it. But external authority has the tendency to cause people to respond as *subordinates.* Good subordinates always do what they are supposed to but little else. Transcending ordinary competence for extraordinary commitment and performance requires that people be transformed from subordinates to *followers,* which requires a different kind of theory and practice. Subordinates respond to external authority, but followers respond to ideas, values, beliefs, and purposes. Traditional theory encompasses the former but not the latter.

Second, traditional management theory, with its bureaucratic roots, is heavily biased toward standardization and routinization. Though many aspects of schooling should be routinized, traditional theory seeks to routinize that which should be varied as well. For schools to excel, teachers and administrators need to be concerned with uniqueness and specialness in their interactions with each other and with students. The test of their effectiveness is their ability to ensure that every student is successful in achieving high academic, social, and personal goals—a task that cannot be accomplished by applying a standard recipe for organizing, presenting the curriculum, and engaging in teaching and learning. Standardization and routinization may be the formula for simple work that takes place in a stable environment where modest results are acceptable, but it is not the formula for extraordinary commitment and performance.

References

Bass, Bernard M. 1985. *Leadership and Performance Beyond Expectations*. New York: The Free Press.

Burns, James MacGregor. 1978. *Leadership*. New York: Harper & Row.

Cziko, Gary A. 1989. "Unpredictability and Indeterminism in Human Behavior: Arguments and Implications for Educational Research," *Educational Researcher* 18(3), 17–25.

Gleick, James. 1987. *Chaos Making a New Science*. New York: Viking Penguin.

Herzberg, Frederick. 1966. *Work and the Nature of Man*. New York: World.

Hills, Jean. 1982. *The Preparation of Educational Leaders: What's Needed and What's Next*. UCEA Occasional Paper No. 8303. Columbus, OH: University Council for Educational Administration.

Hosford, Philip L. 1984. "The Problem, Its Difficulties and Our Approaches," in Philip L. Hosford (Ed.), *Using What We Know about Teaching*. Alexandria, VA: Association for Supervision and Curriculum Development.

James, William. 1892. *Talks to Teachers on Psychology: And to Students on Some of Life's Ideals*. New York: Holt.

Kelly, Robert E. 1988, November–December. "In Praise of Followers," *Harvard Business Review*.

March, James G., and Herbert A. Simon. 1958. *Organizations*. New York: Wiley.

Parsons, Talcott. 1951. *Toward a General Theory of Social Action*. Cambridge, MA: Harvard University Press.

Schön, Donald A. 1983. *The Reflective Practitioner: How Professionals Think in Action*. New York: Basic Books.

Schön, Donald A. 1984. "Leadership as Reflection in Action," in Thomas J. Sergiovanni and John E. Corbally (Eds.), *Leadership and Organizational Culture* (pp. 64–72). Urbana-Champaign: University of Illinois Press.

Schön, Donald A. 1987. *Educating the Reflective Practitioner*. San Francisco: Jossey-Bass.

Sergiovanni, Thomas J. 1990. *Value-Added Leadership: How to Get Extraordinary Performance in Schools*. New York: Harcourt Brace Jovanovich.

Vaill, Peter B. 1989. *Managing as a Performing Art*. San Francisco: Jossey-Bass.

Weick, Karl E. 1976. "Educational Organizations as Loosely Coupled Systems," *Administrative Science Quarterly* 2, 1–19.

3

A NEW THEORY FOR THE PRINCIPALSHIP

To overcome the limits of traditional management and leadership, a new theory for the principalship must be developed—a theory more responsive to nonlinear conditions and loose structuring and that can inspire extraordinary commitment and performance. This theory should not replace but subsume the old. The role of traditional management must change, for example, from being the *strategic model* for developing school policies and practices to being a valued, albeit limited, *tactical option* within a new, more broadly based and powerful management theory. In constructing this new theory, many time-honored principles of traditional management will need to be rethought, expanded, and sometimes even inverted *whenever nonlinear and loosely structured conditions or extraordinary performance requirements are present.*

Toward a New Theory

The following subsections discuss examples of such principles. This discussion is brief because the purpose is to outline a set of basic ideas that contrast the two theories. Elaborations and further examples illustrating the principles are provided in subsequent chapters.

The Issue of How Schools Are Structured

The Traditional Rule
Schools are managerially tight but culturally loose.

The Problem
This traditional rule assumes that schools are structured and function much like the mechanical workings of a clock made of cogs and gears, wheels, drives, and pins all

tightly connected in an orderly and predictable manner. The task of management is to gain control of and regulate the master wheel and pin. The principal, for example, might put into place a well-oiled instructional delivery system composed of the "right" teacher evaluation system or the "right" alignment system or some other "right" control mechanism that defines in detail what teachers teach, and when and how. Once the master wheel and pin are under control, all the other wheels and pins will move responsively and the principal's intents will be accomplished.

Although many aspects of the school are indeed tightly connected in this clockworks fashion, other aspects are not. Furthermore, teachers and students are more tightly connected to values and beliefs than they are to management systems and rules (see, for example, Deal and Kennedy, 1982; March, 1984; Shils, 1961; Weick, 1982). The more typical view of how schools operate is that of clockworks gone awry—cogs, gears, and pins all spinning independently of each other. Although practices based on managerial tightness and cultural looseness can often get people to do what they are supposed to, the rule casts them in roles as subordinates and thus cannot inspire sustained and extraordinary commitment and performance. Furthermore, it is unable to provide the connections needed among loosely connected parts to get the job done well.

The Alternative
Schools are managerially loose but culturally tight.

Weick (1986) pointed out "that indeterminacy can be organized not just by rules, job descriptions, and a priori specifications, but also by such things as shared premises, culture, persistence, clan control, improvisation, memory and imitation." Weick continues:

> In a loosely coupled system you don't influence less, you influence differently. The administrator . . . has the difficult tasks of affecting perceptions, and monitoring and reinforcing the language people use to create and coordinate what they are doing. . . . Administrators model the kind of behavior they desire . . . identify key issues so they can centralize control over a few (not all) issues and help people see them similarly. Leaders in loosely coupled systems have to move around, meet people face-to-face, and to do their influencing by interaction rather than by rules and regulations. . . . Personnel selection is more crucial than in other systems, because the common premises that are selected into that system will guide how the dispersed activities are executed. (10)

The Issue of Strategic Planning

The Traditional Rule
Clarity, control, and consensus are important to effective management and are achieved by detailed planning. Therefore:

1. *State measurable outcomes* (indicate specifically what is to be accomplished).
2. *Provide behavioral expectations* (decide and communicate who will do what and how it will be done).

3. *Practice monitoring* (compare expected behavior with observed and correct when necessary).
4. *Measure outcomes* (compare observed outcomes with stated and correct when necessary).

The Problem

There are many paradoxes in management, and planning is one of them. By planning in a linear-stepwise way, one assumes that it is possible to control the future, but often one actually loses control. Detailed plans and surefire objectives take over from people, becoming scripts on the one hand that program future actions and self-fulfilling prophecies on the other that determine our destiny *even when we are no longer interested in either the journey or the destiny.* For linear conditions with tight structures, planning as traditionally conceived is a useful management *tactic* that can achieve the anticipated results, but as a *strategy,* traditional planning locks us into a course of action that often does not make sense once events are underway.

Further planning has the tendency to result in the "escalation of commitment" to a course of action that sustains itself irrationally long after the original course of action should have been abandoned (Staw, 1984). Sinking huge sums of money into facilities for the high school's interscholastic sports program makes it difficult to deemphasize sports even when doing so may be a good idea. Commitment to the teacher evaluation system that took so many hours of planning time to develop is likely to remain firm even in light of evidence that the teaching effectiveness research on which it is based is faulty and teacher morale is suffering as a result.

And, finally, the measurement aspects of traditional planning place severe limits on developing powerful strategies that encourage innovation and excellence. By establishing worth as the consistency that exists between stated and observed outcomes, too many worthwhile outcomes not stated or unanticipated don't count. New priorities and new courses of action are missed and innovation is discouraged—hardly conditions for excellence. Citing a study of planning in 75 corporations that appeared in the *Economist,* Peters (1989a) notes that firms without central planners tended to produce better results. A better strategy, Peters suggests, is that of General Bill Creech of the Tactical Air Command: "Organize as we fight . . . organize in accordance with the human spirit" as a way to best use talents of people, to respond to the idiosyncratic nature of situations, and to build esprit and small-group cohesiveness deep into the enterprise. It appears that planning, the sacred cow of traditional management, needs to be understood differently.

The Alternative

Clarity, control, and consensus are important to effective management and are achieved by planning strategically. Therefore:

1. *Be clear about basic directions* (set the tone and charter the mission).
2. *Provide purpose and build a shared covenant.* (What are our shared goals, values, and operating principles?)

3. *Practice tight and loose management* (hold people accountable to shared values but provide them with empowerment and enablement to decide what to do when and how).
4. *Evaluate processes and outcomes* (be sure that decisions and events embody shared values).

The principles that support this alternative rule are examined in some detail in subsequent chapters. Suffice to say here that in a nonlinear and loosely structured world, it makes managerial sense to allow people to make decisions in ways that make sense to them providing that the decisions they make embody shared values and commitments.

The Issue of Where to Fit People into the Improvement Planning Process

The Traditional Rule
When it comes to fitting people in:

1. *First emphasize ends* (determine objectives first).
2. *Then emphasize ways* (figure out how you will reach your objectives).
3. *Then emphasize means* (identify, train, place, and supervise people).

The Problem
Deciding where to fit people into the planning process influences the outcome in important ways (Hayes, 1985). Should one start with people first or fit them in after work requirements are identified? The traditional ends, ways, and means rule is compatible with a "cannonball" theory of management suitable for stable environments where targets don't move. Unfortunately, as Harry Quadracci (Peters, 1989b) points out, we live in a "cruise missile" world. Cannons are excellent weapons for hitting fixed targets under stable conditions; one need only identify the target (ends), take careful aim calculating distance and wind (ways), and give the order to fire to a well-trained crew (means). A hit is virtually guaranteed. However, hitting moving targets is another matter. Moreover, changing one's mind to enable hitting a better target than the initial one after the cannon has been fired is impossible. Yet, in the world of schooling most of our targets are moving, and different and more desirable targets are frequently discovered during the course of our actions. Cannons won't do here. Cruise missiles, to continue Quadracci's admittedly surly metaphor, have built into them the capacity to chase shifting targets and indeed to change targets after they are launched.

The Alternative
When it comes to school improvement:

1. *First emphasize means* (concentrate on people first, build them up, increase their commitment, link them to purposes, help them to be self-managing).

2. *Then emphasize ways* (let them figure out what to do and how).
3. *Then emphasize ends* (they will decide on and achieve objectives that are consistent with shared purposes).

Hayes (1985), who proposed this alternative rule, believes that it provides the basis for developing strategies that are more responsive to today's complex world. The key to concentrating on means first is to build up the capacity for people to be self-managing and to connect them to shared values and commonly held purposes. Kelly (1988:144) believes that self-management is an essential ingredient in being a good follower. Followers, he maintains, share a number of essential qualities:

- They manage themselves well.
- They are committed to the organization and to a purpose, principle, or person outside themselves.
- They build up their competence and focus their efforts for maximum impact.
- They are courageous, honest, and credible.

Once followership is built up, the other steps in the alternative rule's chain unfold in a manner that inspires performance and brings about extraordinary results. The traditional rule, by contrast, is based on authority and determinism. The likely result is the establishment of subordination rather than followership in the school, with mediocre rather than extraordinary results.

The Issue of Getting and Maintaining Compliance

The Traditional Rule
To manage compliance:

1. *Identify and announce your goals.* (What are your major objectives?)
2. *Use goals to develop work requirements* (decide how the work will be done).
3. *Use work requirements to develop your compliance strategy* (given the above, determine how you will get people to do what they are supposed to do).
4. *Observe involvement and commitment consequences and correct as necessary.* (Are people properly motivated? If not, determine ways to motivate them.)

The Problem
The organizational theorist Etzioni (1961) noted that one universal requirement of management is the need to obtain and maintain compliance. By compliance he means how schools get teachers and students involved in their work in the first place and how this involvement is maintained over time. A key point in his theory is that the strategy the manager uses to obtain and maintain involvement has a powerful influence on forming the kind of identification and attachment people have for their work and for the school itself, on shaping the goals of the school, and on the kind and character of work that takes place within the school as goals are pursued. *This is so, even when goals and work requirements are set first.* Goals and work

requirements are ultimately shaped to fit the means that schools use to get and keep teachers involved in their teaching and to get and keep students involved in their learning. These means then influence the kind and degree of involvement with work and school.

Given this influence, it is too chancy to let the involvement strategy evolve naturally as a result of stated goals and work requirements. Some involvement strategies can actually result in the emergence of dysfunctional school goals and work processes with negative effects. Consider, for example, a prison that has as its goal order among the inmates. To achieve this goal, it relies on the establishment of closely monitored daily routines and a system of compliance based on punishment for infractions. As a result, prisoners became alienated and would not choose freely to stay in prison. Alienated involvement reinforces the use of rules and punishment to maintain compliance. Changing the goal for this prison from order to rehabilitation will not likely be accomplished without changing what prisoners do and the means for ensuring compliance with the new system. Prisoners will have to come to see the value of rehabilitation, and the activities they engage in will have to be more meaningful to them.

Etzioni (1961) suggests that the strategies an organization or manager uses to get and keep people involved can be grouped into three broad categories:

1. *Coercive* (People, students, and teachers, for example, are forced by the threat of penalties.)
2. *Remunerative* (People are attracted by the promise of rewards such as money, career advancement, good grades, better working conditions, political advantage, enhanced social standing, and having psychological needs met.)
3. *Normative* (People are compelled because they believe what they are doing is right and good and/or because they find involvement intrinsically satisfying.)

Each of the three compliance strategies results in a particular kind of involvement, which in turn shapes the nature and character of school work and school goals. These relationships are illustrated in Table 3.1. Because the choice of compliance strategy is so important in determining what happens, the traditional rule needs to be inverted so that the principal and school begin first by deciding on the compliance strategy they will use.

The Alternative
To manage compliance:

1. *First establish your compliance strategy.* (How do we want to involve people in work and keep them involved? Use the strategy that reflects desired involvement.)
2. *Develop complementary work requirements.* (What kind of connections will people need to make for them to be properly involved?)
3. *Decide on work strategy.* (Given the connections desired, what kind of work designs and settings do we need?)

TABLE 3.1   How Compliance Is Achieved

	School A	School B	School C
The School's Dominant Compliance Strategy	*Coercion:* Force people by using bureaucratic controls and penalties for infractions	*Remunerative:* Provide people with rewards in exchange for involvement	*Normative:* Bond people to shared values, beliefs, and norms
Resulting Involvement of Teachers and Students	*Indifferent,* often alienated (they won't be involved unless they have to)	*Calculated* (they will be involved as long as they get something of value back in exchange)	*Moral* (they will be involved because they believe it is the right thing to do)
How the Work of Teaching and Learning Gets Done	*Routinely* (the hand works only)	*Instrumentally* (the mind drives the hand)	*Intrinsically* (mind, hand, and heart work together)
The Resultant Dominant Goal of Management	*Maintain order* by getting and keeping control	*Barter by making the best deal* and monitoring the deal, patching cracks that appear	*Develop and maintain a strong culture*

4. *Evaluate.* (What kind of commitment and involvement is observed? Make adjustments in compliance strategy if necessary.)

Moral involvement has the best chance of ensuring and maintaining inspired commitment and performance from students, teachers, and parents. Commitment to moral involvement does not preclude the occasional use of coercive and remunerative compliance, but it does suggest that the overarching framework for compliance must be normative.

The Issue of Developing a Motivational Strategy

The Traditional Rule
What gets rewarded gets done.

The Problem
This rule works—what gets rewarded does get done. But what happens when rewards are not available to principals, teachers, students, or parents? Unfortunately, the rule's flip side is true, too. What does not get rewarded does not get done.

Relying on rewards to obtain compliance leads to calculated involvement (Etzioni, 1961). Furthermore, this rule has a tendency to change other kinds of work involvement to calculated involvement. A student, for example, might be engaged in a learning activity because of its intrinsic interest. No gold stars, grades, or other external rewards are provided for her or his involvement. Once such rewards are introduced, the student's connection to the learning activity has a tendency to change from intrinsic to extrinsic. Take the rewards away and the student is not likely to engage further in the activity (Deci and Ryan, 1985; Greene and Lepper, 1974). By the same token, teachers who are engaged in certain kinds of activities for moral reasons—that is, because they feel a sense of obligation or believe that something is right or important to do—forsake moral involvement for calculated once rewards (or punishments) are introduced.

The Alternative

What is rewarding gets done, gets done well, and gets done without close supervision or other controls. What we believe in and feel obligated to do because of moral commitments gets done, gets done well, and gets done without close supervision or other controls.

Calculated involvement may be able to get people to do what they are supposed to as long as rewards are forthcoming, but it is not a potent enough strategy to inspire motivation and inspire people to become self-managing, to work without direction or supervision, and to remain engaged in their work even when extrinsic rewards are not available. A new theory of management for the principalship needs to subsume such ideas as what-gets-rewarded-gets-done into a broader motivational strategy that recognizes the importance of morality, emotions, and social bonds (Etzioni, 1988:xii). Although often underplayed and sometimes overlooked in traditional motivation theories, what counts most to people are what they believe, how they feel, and the shared norms and cultural messages that emerge from the small groups and communities with which they identify. Some principals, for example, have refused promotion or transfer because they felt a sense of obligation to see projects they initiated through to conclusion. They gave up extrinsic gains such as higher salaries, career advancement, and more prestige because of the obligation and commitment they had to what they were doing. Parents and teachers routinely sacrifice their own self-interests, wants, and needs to advance those of the children they have responsibility for raising.

Following Etzioni (1988), a new theory of management must provide for the development of motivation strategies that are based on all three motivation rules: what is rewarded gets done, what is rewarding gets done, and what is good gets done. In a new management theory, major emphasis would be given to the latter two. The three rules are depicted here:

The Rules	*Why People Behave*	*Motivational Type*	*Involvement*
What gets rewarded gets done	Extrinsic gain	Instrumental	Calculated
What is rewarding gets done	Intrinsic gain	Expressive	Intrinsic
What is good gets done	Duty/obligation	Moral	Moral

Controlling Events or Probabilities?

Both traditional and new management and leadership theories are about control. Control is intended to reduce ambiguity and indeterminancy, thus increasing reliability and predictability. For example, both clockworks and clockworks-gone-awry theories want the same thing—to get the cogs and gears moving in reliable and predictable ways. But how this control is sought differs depending on the theory one has in mind. The traditional theory seeks to increase control over events and people, which is a *power over* approach to leadership and management. The new theory, by contrast, seeks to control probabilities—the probability that shared goals and purposes are embodied and reached. This is a *power to* approach to management and leadership. Increasing the probability that shared goals and purposes will be realized means giving up control over events and people.

One important key to seeking and maintaining control is to solve the *coordination paradox*. As Mintzberg (1979) points out:

> *Every organized human activity ... gives rise to two fundamental and opposing requirements: the* division of labor *into various tasks to be performed and the* coordination *of these tasks to accomplish the activity. The structure of an organization can be captured simply as the sum total of ways in which it divides its labor into distinct tasks and then achieves coordination among them. (2)*

Every school faces the same control problem: How should the work of teaching and learning be divided, and, once divided, how should it be coordinated so that things make sense as a whole? Each person has something important to do, but it must be done in coordination with what others are doing if schools are to work well. As is the case with most problems of control, tackling the coordination paradox would be much easier if schooling was largely the linear and tightly structured world of the Neats and if the goal was to achieve a routine level of competence. All one would need to do would be to practice traditional management leadership. However, in a largely nonlinear, loosely structured Scruffy world with the goal of inspired levels of commitment and extraordinary performance, solving the paradox is more complex. Choosing the wrong control strategy can negatively shape the way teaching and learning takes place.

It is useful to think of six basic control strategies that can be used to help solve the coordination paradox: direct supervision, standardizing the work processes, standardizing outcomes, emphasizing professional socialization, emphasizing purposes, and structuring for collegiality and natural interdependence.* Although all six of the strategies might appropriately be used at one time or another, it makes a difference which of the six or which combination is the school's basic strategy for achieving control.

---

*This discussion of control strategies is based largely on the typology proposed by Mintzberg (1979). His typology reflects the conclusions of March and Simon (1958) and Simon (1957). Important to the discussion as presented here is the work of Peters and Waterman (1982) and Weick (1982). See also Sergiovanni (1987, 1990).

The key in deciding on an appropriate control strategy is whether it fits the kind and amount of complexity found in the work to be done and in the work environment. *This matching of strategy to complexity of work is critical, for if the strategy used does not fit, the level of complexity will change to match the strategy.* This is a variation of the ominous organizational rule: "Form should follow function or function will be shaped to fit the form." Accordingly, a simple control strategy applied to the normally complex work of teaching will simplify this work, with negative effects on what is learned and how it is learned. The six control strategies are summarized in the following paragraphs.

Direct Supervision

The simplest way to control the work of people who have different responsibilities is by having one of those persons take responsibility for the work of others by providing directions, close supervision, inspection, and otherwise executing the well-known planning, organizing, controlling, directing, motivating, and evaluating linear chain of management functions. In effect, as Mintzberg (1979) points out, one brain coordinates several hands. This simple approach to control works best for simple work that is done in a routine fashion. Direct supervision may be an appropriate control strategy for a fast-food restaurant, but not for schools where the work of teaching and learning is more complex.

Standardizing Work Processes

Mintzberg (1979) refers to standardizing work processes as coordination achieved on the drawing board before the work is actually undertaken. This strategy works best in jobs that are highly determinant and predictable. Work processes are standardized when what needs to be done is specified in great detail and how one does it is scripted. A "one best way" to get the job done is spelled out. A system of monitoring then is put into place to be sure that the best way is followed. Creating very detailed and tightly connected curriculum and teaching as well as evaluating alignment strategies that make up "instructional delivery systems" are examples of standardizing work processes. This strategy might be appropriate for Federal Express or for a fast-food restaurant, but not for schools where the work of teaching and learning is more complex.

Standardizing Outcomes

Standardizing outcomes is accomplished by requiring everyone to produce similar products or to reach the same level of performance. In schools we do this by relying heavily on standardized test scores, measurable objectives, and other detailed specifications of outcomes as a way to get people to do what they are supposed to do. The emphasis on standards, in the form of standards-based teaching, accreditation, and accountability are examples of recent attempts to standardize outcomes. Standardizing outcomes is different from standardizing work processes in that once the outcome requirements are set, people are thought to be essentially free to decide how they are going to accomplish them.

Providing discretion over means is a strength of this strategy. The question, however, is whether outcome requirements can be standardized and specified in sufficient detail and at the same time not result in undue narrowing of the curriculum and undue neglect of individual differences. Standardizing the outcomes ultimately compromises the degrees of freedom people have with respect to work processes. For example, defining quality schooling as levels of gains on standards-based tests may dictate how principals and students will spend time, what they will learn, and how they will learn it to the exclusion of other more suitable or better choices. Many of the problems associated with this strategy would be lessened if goals were viewed as values rather than objectives. Instead of designing down from the outcomes that are specified, the strategy would be to design out from shared values, goals, and commitments, leaving the specifics of "outcomes" and processes up to teachers and others. The only requirement would be that the decisions that they make embody the agreed upon values.

Professional Socialization

By relying on professional socialization, one need not standardize either work processes or outputs and still solve the coordination paradox (Mintzberg, 1979). *Professional socialization* refers to the upgrading and standardizing of the knowledge base for teaching and emphasizing one's professional obligations as a teacher. Once a professional level of training and socialization has been accomplished, teachers and other educational workers will presumably know what to do, when they ought to do it, and how to do it. Professional socialization is the way in which more advanced professions such as medicine solve the coordination paradox. As Mintzberg points out, "When an anesthesiologist and a surgeon meet in the operating room to remove an appendix, they need hardly communicate; by virtue of their respective training, they know exactly what to expect of each other" (7). Though professional socialization has much merit, it is less a strategy available to principals for solving the coordination paradox and more a long-term strategy to upgrade the teaching profession itself. As this upgrading occurs, issues of control will become less difficult to resolve.

Purposing and Shared Values

Weick (1982) noted that in schools

> *administrators must be attentive to the "glue" that holds loosely coupled systems together because such forms are just barely systems. In fact, this borderline condition is their strength, in the sense that it allows local adjustment and storage of novel remedies. It is also their point of vulnerability, because such systems can quickly dissolve into anarchy. . . . The effective administrator . . . makes full use of*

symbol management to tie the system together. People need to be part of sensible projects. Their action becomes richer, more confident, and more satisfying when it is linked with important underlying themes, values, and movements. (675)

Purposing and shared values provide the "glue" that bonds people together in a loosely connected world. Once common purposes and shared values are in place, they become compass points and mileposts for guiding what is to be done and how. As Selznick (1957) observed, "The need for centralization declines as the homogeneity of personnel increases.... [W]hen the premises of official policy are understood and widely accepted, centralization is more readily dispensable" (113).

The strategy is to identify shared values and then design what to do throughout the school from these values. Specific goals and purposes remain the responsibility of teachers and others to decide as long as they embody the values. (Purposing and shared values are key themes in the discussion of community that appears in the next chapter and of leadership in Part II.)

Collegiality and Natural Interdependence

Collegiality refers to the extent that common work values are shared and teachers work together and help each other as a result of these values. *Natural interdependence* has to do with the extent to which teachers must work together and cooperate to get the job done properly. In both cases the coordination paradox is solved by the process of informal communications and the need for people to cooperate with each other in order for each person to be successful.

Professional socialization, purposing and shared values, and collegiality and natural interdependence are unique in that they are able to solve the coordination paradox even under nonlinear circumstances and under loosely structured conditions. They do this by providing the kind of normative power needed to get people to meet their commitments. Once people are connected to norms, they are internally motivated to do the right thing—they become self-managing. Beyond the benefit of enhancing self-management, the quality of teaching and learning in a school is at stake. A new theory of management for the principalship must give primary attention to professional socialization, shared values, and collegiality and interdependence as control strategies because they match the complexity of teaching and learning at its best. Relying on the other control strategies, by contrast, does not match the complexity of good teaching and learning. The result is that teaching and learning become simplified as they are shaped by the control strategy. As Mintzberg (1979) notes, direct supervision is effective for simple work, but as work becomes more complex, the emphasis needs to shift from direct supervision to standardizing the work, to standardizing the outputs, and finally to emphasizing professional socialization, purposing, colleagueship, and natural interdependence. Relationships between choice of control strategy and the kind of teaching one is likely to receive is shown in Table 3.2.

TABLE 3.2   Control Strategies and Consequences

	Direct Supervision	Standardized Work	Standardized Outputs	Professional Socialization	Purposing and Shared Values	Collegiality and Inter-dependence
Strategy Concept	Simple	Simple	Simple	Complex	Complex	Complex
Management System	Complex	Complex	Moderate	Simple	Simple	Simple
Teachers' Behavior	Simple	Simple	Moderate	Complex	Complex	Complex
Authority for Leadership	Bureaucratic rules; the leader's personality	Bureaucratic rules; the leader's personality; management systems	The leader's personality; management systems	Professional values and norms	Moral values and norms	Professional values and norms; moral values and norms

Source: Adapted from Thomas J. Sergiovanni, *Moral Leadership: Getting to the Heart of School Improvement* (San Francisco: Jossey-Bass, 1992), p. 97.

When professional socialization, purposing and shared values, and collegiality are emphasized, they function as substitutes for leadership. This means that the principal does not have to provide as much direct leadership as would be the case if other control strategy choices were made. Leadership is much less intense and much more informal as issues of control and coordination take care of themselves naturally.

Direct supervision, standardizing work, and standardizing outputs are simple ideas that require complex management systems. For these ideas to work, structures must be in place and roles must be identified and delineated. Furthermore, expectations must be explicit and systems of monitoring must be in place to ensure that everything is functioning properly. As this management system becomes more complex, the discretion of teachers is narrowed. As a result, teaching becomes more simplified, routine, and standardized.

Exactly the opposite is the case with socialization, shared values, and collegiality. These are complex ideas that require very simple management systems to implement. Because of this simplicity, they allow teachers to function in complex ways, which enables them to make more responsive decisions that fit the unique circumstances that they face. In short, complex structures result in simple behaviors, and simple structures result in complex behaviors. Moreover, simple ideas require complex systems for implementation and complex ideas require simple systems. In the first case, teaching becomes simplified; in the second place, teaching is more complex. Understanding these seemingly paradoxical relationships is key to building a new and more effective practice of management for the principalship.

The New Theory and School Organization

Good organization provides the administrative structures, arrangements, and coordinating mechanisms needed to facilitate teaching and learning. What are the implications of the new management theory for how we organize schools?

Some Basic Principles of Organizing

Whatever decisions are made about organizing, the new theory suggests that they should reflect the following basic principles:

1. The principle of *cooperation:* Cooperative teaching arrangements facilitate teaching and enhance learning. Furthermore, they help overcome the debilitating effects of the isolation that currently characterizes teaching. In successful schools, organizational structures enhance cooperation among teachers.
2. The principle of *empowerment:* Feelings of empowerment among teachers contribute to ownership and increase commitment and motivation to work. When teachers feel like pawns rather than originators of their own behavior, they respond with reduced commitment, mechanical behavior, indifference, and, in extreme cases, dissatisfaction and alienation. In successful schools, organizational structures enhance empowerment among teachers.
3. The principle of *responsibility:* Most teachers and other school professionals want responsibility. Responsibility upgrades the importance and significance of their work and provides a basis for recognition of their success. In successful schools, organizational structures encourage teacher responsibility.
4. The principle of *accountability:* Accountability is related to empowerment and responsibility. It provides the healthy measure of excitement, challenge, and importance that raises the stakes just enough so that achievement means something. In successful schools, organizational structures allow teachers to participate in setting local standards and norms and then to be accountable for their decisions and achievements.
5. The principle of *meaningfulness:* When teachers find their jobs to be meaningful, jobs not only take on a special significance but also provide teachers with feelings of intrinsic satisfaction. In successful schools, organizational structures provide for meaningful work.
6. The principle of *ability-authority:* The noted organizational theorist Victor Thompson (1965) stated that the major problem facing modern organizations is the growing gap that exists between those who have authority to act but not the ability needed for their activism to be most effective, and those who have the ability to act effectively but not the authority to do so. This principle seeks to place those who have the ability to act in the forefront of decision making. In successful schools, organizational structures promote authority based on ability. In schools and school districts where it is necessary for authority to be formally linked to one's position in the organizational hierarchy, day-by-day practice is characterized by formal and informal delegation of this authority to those with ability.

As these principles are manifested in the ways in which schools are organized, schools increase their capacity to respond to their problems, principals are able to lead more effectively, teaching is enhanced, and learning increases.

The Language of Theory

The heart of any theory is the language used to describe and implement it. The words we use shape the way we think about management and leadership. Certain aspects of reality are highlighted and other aspects are covered up. For example, when schooling is described as an "instructional delivery system," one automatically thinks about such management issues as delivery, targets, and goals; steps, procedures, and schedules that promise the best delivery routes and timetables; the need to provide clear instructions to the deliverers of instruction; monitoring the delivery process; and evaluating to be sure that what is supposed to be delivered is delivered, and on time.

Getting the Words Right

What seems sensible and true can change when the language we use changes. Try thinking about schooling as a "learning community." What issues now come to mind, and how are they different?

Communities, for example, can be thought of as having "centers" that are repositories of shared values that give direction, order, and meaning to community life. The center is the cultural heart of any community. Edward Shils (1961) explains:

> *The center ... is a phenomenon of the realm of values and beliefs ... which govern the society. ... In a sense, society has an official "religion." ... The center is also a phenomenon of the realm of action. It is a structure of activities, of roles and persons, within the network of institutions. It is in these that the values and beliefs which are central are embodied and propounded. (119)*

Different management issues emerge from the metaphor of school as a learning community. How will this learning community be defined? What relationships among parents, students, teachers, and administrators are needed for us to be a community? What are our shared values, purposes, and commitments? How shall we work together to embody these? What kinds of obligations to the community should members have? How will obligations be enforced? What "wild cultures" exist (e.g., perhaps a student subculture excessively themed to football, beer, music, and sex; or one devoted to mediocre academic performance or to stealing hubcaps; or a faculty subculture more concerned with its own welfare than that of the school) that provide competing and work-restricting norms? How can these wild cultures be "domesticated" and thus subsumed under the overall culture that defines our learning community?

The fact that different management issues emerge from different metaphors for schooling suggests that validity in management and leadership is both subjective and objective. The management concepts, rules, and practices that are valid for schools as learning communities are not valid for schools as instructional delivery systems, and vice versa. Validity is subjective between conceptual systems and objective within (Lakoff and Johnson, 1980). The presence of both subjective and objective validity in management is one reason why it's so hard to have a successful argument with someone who uses a language system different from one's own. Furthermore, it is hard to think differently about leadership, management, and schooling unless you are willing to change your own language system—the metaphors and ultimately the mindscapes that create your reality.

The Power of Language

Another important aspect of the language we use is that it can become a source of power that forces others to think in our terms. This is particularly true in instances in which one person has more hierarchical authority than another. As Greenfield (1982) explains: "Language is power. It literally makes reality appear and disappear. Those who control language control thought—and thereby themselves and others" (8). He maintains that language can be used to dominate others by building categories of thinking and logic that they must use whether they want to or not. Getting others to think in your terms is a powerful form of domination. For example, superintendents who use the language of instructional delivery systems linked to state minimum competency standards and basic skills testing in their protocols for evaluating principals force principals to have to defend themselves in those terms no matter how effective they might be otherwise. A similar fate awaits teachers who are evaluated by principals who control the language of evaluation.

Domination is virtually total when one person not only controls the categories that another has to use but also controls the criteria for defining effectiveness. Imagine, for example, two children about to open their lunchboxes at school. One says to the other, "I bet you a soda that the fruit in my box is better than yours." The youngster then sets the criteria for *better* as follows: The redder the fruit and the rounder the fruit, the better. Unfortunately, the other child's lunchpail contains a banana. Had the second child been the one in control of the language criteria, there would be a different winner.

Winning and losing are functions of the language used (Sergiovanni, 1989). Lakoff and Johnson (1980) summarize the subjective nature of validity as follows:

Truth is relative to understanding, which means that there is no absolute standpoint from which to obtain absolute objective truths about the world. This does not mean that there are no truths; it means that truth is relative to our conceptual system, which is grounded in, and constantly tested by, our experiences and those of other members of our culture in our daily interactions with other people and with our physical and cultural environments. (193)

Perception is reality

Although the power of language is very real, it has not received much attention in the management literature.

One test of the adequacy of the language we use in discussing school theory and practice is whether it is beautiful or not. The language of traditional management theory lacks "aesthetic qualities." Such qualities are one important criterion that Kaplan proposes in his monumental book *Conduct of Inquiry* (1961) for validating theories. More pointedly, Mintzberg (1982) describes the language of traditional management theory as being *ugly*. In his words: "If a theory is not beautiful then the odds are good that it is not very useful" (250). Apply this rule, for example, to determine the "usefulness" of such concepts and ideas as instructional delivery system and learning community, instruction and teaching, training and education, POSDCoRB and purposing, objectives and goals, measuring and valuing, monitoring and coaching, bureaucratic and moral, quality control and obligation, and motivate and inspire.

Changing Our Metaphors

Because traditional management theory does not work well in nonlinear and loosely structured situations or under conditions that require extraordinary commitment and performance, a great deal is at stake in developing a new and better-fitting theory. For this to happen, our metaphors for management, leadership, and schooling must change. Subsuming "instructional delivery system" as a tactical option under the more encompassing and strategic "learning community" is an important beginning. What would schools be like if community was indeed the metaphor of choice? That is the topic of the next chapter.

References

Deal, Terrence E., and Allan A. Kennedy. 1982. *Corporate Cultures.* Reading, MA: Addison-Wesley.

Deci, Edward L., and Richard M. Ryan. 1985. *Intrinsic Motivation and Self Determinism in Human Behavior.* New York: Plenum Press.

Etzioni, Amitai. 1961. *A Comparative Analysis of Complex Organizations.* New York: The Free Press.

Etzioni, Amitai. 1988. *The Moral Dimension toward a New Economics.* New York: The Free Press.

Greene, David, and Mark R. Lepper. 1974. "How to Turn Play into Work," *Psychology Today* 8(4).

Greenfield, Thomas B. 1982, Winter. "Against Group Mind: An Anarchistic Theory of Education," *McGill Journal of Education* 17.

Hayes, Robert H. 1985, November–December. "Strategic Planning—Forward in Reverse?" *Harvard Business Review.*

Kaplan, Abraham. 1961. *Conduct of Inquiry: Methodology for Behavioral Sciences.* San Francisco: Chandler.

Kelly, Robert E. 1988, November–December. "In Praise of Followers," *Harvard Business Review.*

Lakoff, George, and Mark Johnson. 1980. *The Metaphors We Live By.* Chicago: University of Chicago Press.

March, James G. 1984. "How We Talk and How We Act: Administrative Theory and Administrative Life," in T. J. Sergiovanni and J. E. Corbally (Eds.), *Leadership and Organizational Culture* (pp. 18–36). Urbana: University of Illinois Press.

March, James G., and Herbert A. Simon. 1958. *Organizations.* New York: Wiley.

Mintzberg, Henry. 1979. *The Structuring of Organizations.* Englewood Cliffs, NJ: Prentice-Hall.

Mintzberg, Henry. 1982. "If You're Not Serving Bill and Barbara, Then You're Not Serving Leadership," in James G. Hunt, Una Sekaran, and Chester Schrlesheim (Eds.), *Leadership Beyond Establishment Views* (pp. 239–259). Carbondale: Southern Illinois University.

Peters, Tom. 1989a. "Structure vs. Spirit Battle Lines are Drawn," *San Antonio Light,* July 25.

Peters, Tom. 1989b. "Business Can Learn From Military Strategy," *San Antonio Light,* January 24.

Peters, Thomas J., and Robert H. Waterman. 1982. *In Search of Excellence.* New York: Harper & Row.

Selznick, Phillip. 1957. *Leadership in Administration.* New York: Harper & Row.

Sergiovanni, Thomas J. 1987. *The Principalship: A Reflective Practice Perspective.* Boston: Allyn and Bacon.

Sergiovanni, Thomas J. 1989. "Science and Scientism in Teaching and Supervision," *Journal of Curriculum and Supervision* 4(2), 93–106.

Sergiovanni, Thomas J. 1990. *Value-Added Leadership: How to Get Extraordinary Performance in Schools.* New York: Harcourt Brace Jovanovich.

Sergiovanni, Thomas J. 1992. *Moral Leadership.* San Francisco: Jossey-Bass.

Shils, Edward A. 1961. "Centre and Periphery," in *The Logic of Personal Knowledge: Essays Presented to Michael Polanyi.* London: Routledge and Kegan Paul.

Simon, Herbert A. 1957. *Administrative Behavior* (2nd ed.). New York: The Free Press.

Staw, Barry. 1984. "Leadership and Persistence," in T. J. Sergiovanni and J. E. Corbally (Eds.), *Leadership and Organizational Culture.* Urbana: University of Illinois Press.

Thompson, Victor A. 1965. *Modern Organizations.* New York: Knopf.

Weick, Karl E. 1982. "Administering Education in Loosely Coupled Schools," *Phi Delta Kappan* 27(2), 673–676.

Weick, Karl E. 1986, December. "The Concept of Loose Coupling: An Assessment," *Organizational Theory Dialogue.*

4

THE SCHOOL AS A MORAL COMMUNITY

Leadership is about many things. At the top of the list for a principal is protecting the character of his or her school. What most citizens want is for schools to reflect the values and beliefs that are meaningful in their lives. At the center of a school's institutional character are ideas and commitments that function as a source of authority for what people do. This authority establishes the form and content of values and purposes that determines initiatives aimed at achieving the school's own destiny.

Community strikes at the heart of a school's institutional character. It provides the substance for finding and making meaning and the framework for culture building. Think of community as a powerful antioxidant that can protect the school and help it achieve its goals. Communities are collections of people who come together because they share common commitments, ideas, and values. Schools can be understood as:

- Learning communities where students and other members of the school community are committed to thinking, growing, and inquiring, and where learning is an attitude as well as an activity, a way of life as well as a process
- Collegial communities where members are connected to each other for mutual benefit and to pursue common goals by establishing a sense of felt interdependence and mutual obligation
- Caring communities where members make a total commitment to each other and where the characteristics that define their relationships are moral in character
- Inclusive communities where economic, religious, cultural, and other differences are brought together into a mutually respective whole
- Inquiring communities where principals and teachers commit themselves to a spirit of collective inquiry as they reflect on their practice and search for solutions to the problems that they face

To understand community, one has to understand its story. What is the story of community? How does this story differ from other stories about schools? What narratives does the story of community encompass? What stories compete with community for our attention? The story of community includes unique ways of thinking about connections. In most schools, connections are understood using the narrative of social contracts.* In schools that are striving to become communities, connections are understood using the narrative of social covenants.

The major storyline in the narrative of social contracts involves a deal. Each of the parties to the contract gives up something to the other party in order to get something else back that is valued. In this narrative, teachers, parents, and others invest their talents and energy in the school and its children in exchange for certain benefits. Similarly, children endure the rituals of schooling in order to get the gold stars and praise they covet from teachers, the attention they want from their parents, and the grades they need to be admitted to college. This social contract with the school is maintained as long as each of the parties gets what it wants. When teachers no longer receive the contracted benefits, they are less willing to invest in the school. And when students no longer get the benefits they seek, they are less willing to endure the rituals of schooling. This narrative is about calculations involving trades that offer incentives in exchange for compliance. Self-interest is presumed to be paramount and "let's make a deal" is the order of the day.

The narrative of social contracts guides the practice of the principal of the Locke Elementary School. He promised the student body that if 2,000 books were read during the month of October, on Halloween night he would dress up like a witch and kiss a pig on the roof of the school building. This goal was achieved, and to the apparent delight of the students, the deed was done. The Locke principal believes that contracts are important motivational devices. He reasons that unless teachers, parents, and students get something tangible for their efforts, they will not be motivated. You can't expect managers to manage well, workers to be diligent, or football players to play hard unless there is something in it for them. So, the principal asks, how can we expect teachers to teach well, parents to parent well, students to learn well, and schools to improve themselves without incentives? How can we expect, for example, teachers and students to display proper behaviors without providing exhaustive lists of rules and regulations or outcome requirements that are linked to clear consequences for noncompliance?

Social Covenants

The major storyline in the narrative of social covenants is much less conditional. In this narrative, connections are more moral than calculated. Marriages, extended families, civic associations, faith communities, caring groups, and friendship networks are examples of affiliations characterized by covenantal relationships. In the

---

*This discussion of social contracts and social covenants is drawn from T. J. Sergiovanni, "Building Community in a Diverse Society," Department of Education, Trinity University, San Antonio, TX, 1998. © T. J. Sergiovanni. See also Sergiovanni (2000).

narrative of social covenants, connections among people are created when they are connected to shared ideas and values. Once achieved, this bonding of people and this binding to ideas forms a fabric of reciprocal roles, duties, and obligations that are internalized by members of the group. This is a fabric that cannot easily be torn apart when a person no longer likes the deal. This is a fabric that perseveres even when the fun is gone, when needs are not being met, and when self-interest must be sacrificed.

The narrative of social covenants guides the practice of the principal of the Rousseau Elementary School. She encourages teachers and students to develop together a framework of values and norms that informs how everyone in the school should lead their lives together. Connected to a larger vision of school purposes, critical values, and pedagogical beliefs, this covenant provides the basis for an ongoing discussion about how teachers, administrators, parents, and students can meet their commitments to each other and to the school. Students at Rousseau, for example, expect teachers to work hard, to be caring, and to teach well. Since relationships are reciprocal, teachers expect students to respond similarly. Students are given considerable latitude in deciding important things at Rousseau. They help decide how learning goals will be achieved and help make decisions about how they will spend their time. But decisions must be responsible ones that embody and enhance the school's covenant. Both teachers and students work hard to make reading fun and useful while also increasing mastery.

The Rousseau principal believes that when given the opportunity to make important decisions about school goals, purposes, values, and other important school matters, teachers and students will respond by being morally obliged to embody these decisions in their actions. Further, the bonding of school members together and their binding to shared ideas and ideals provides a normative environment that encourages moral responsiveness. Social contracts, she reasons, have important roles to play in the real world—but so do social covenants. The school is the place, she argues, to learn about social covenants, to practice developing them, and to use them in a practical way to govern affairs.

In comparing the two narratives, Sacks (1997) argues that a social contract is maintained by the promise of gain or the threat of external force. A social covenant is maintained by loyalty, fidelity, kinship, sense of identity, obligation, duty, responsibility, and reciprocity. A social contract, he points out, is instrumental, serving important political and corporate ends that ideally are in the national interest. A social covenant, by contrast, is concerned with quite different institutions—families, communities, friendship groups, and voluntary associations are examples. Social covenants provide the basis for our civil society. A healthy civil society also serves the national interest by being the moral foundation, bedrock, and wellspring that provides cultural purposes, unity, and strength. Social contracts are at the core of what connects people in the world of formal organizations, and social covenants are at the core of what connects people in the world of social organizations. The former are rules based; the latter are norms based.

A Theory of Community

Communities are organized around relationships and the felt interdependencies that nurture them (Blau and Scott, 1962). They create social structures that unify people and that bind them to a set of shared values and ideas. They are defined by their centers of values, sentiments, and beliefs that provide the needed conditions for creating a sense of "we" from "I."

In communities, members live their lives with others who have similar intentions. In ordinary organizations, relationships are constructed by others and become codified into a system of hierarchies, roles, and role expectations. Both ordinary organizations and communities must deal with issues of control, but instead of relying on external control measures, communities rely more on norms, purposes, values, professional socialization, collegiality, and natural interdependence. As the ties of community become established in schools, they become substitutes for formal systems of supervision, evaluation, and staff development. They become substitutes as well for the management and organizational schemes that seek to "coordinate" what teachers do and how they work together. Finally, they become substitutes for leadership itself.

The ties of community also redefine how empowerment and collegiality are understood. In ordinary organizations, empowerment is understood as having something to do with shared decision making, site-based management, and similar schemes. Within communities, empowerment focuses less on rights, discretion, and freedom, and more on commitments, obligations, and duties that people feel toward each other and toward the school. Collegiality in ordinary organizations results from administrative arrangements, such as variations of team teaching that force people to work together and team-building skills of principals. In communities, collegiality is something that comes from within. Community members are connected to each other because of felt interdependencies, mutual obligations, and other emotional and normative ties.

Community often means different things in different disciplines. Sociologists speak of the African American community, political scientists of the rural community, theologians of the spiritual community, and psychologists of the emotional community. To capture the spirit of these various uses, I define *community* as follows: Communities are collections of individuals who are bonded together by natural will and who are together bound to a set of shared ideas and ideals. This bonding and binding is tight enough to transform the individuals from a collection of "I"s into a collective "we." As a "we," members are part of a tightly knit web of meaningful relationships. This "we" usually shares a common place and over time comes to share common sentiments and traditions that are sustaining.

The theory of *gemeinschaft* and *gesellschaft* can help us to understand this definition and the forms it might take as schools become communities. *Gemeinschaft* translates to community and *gesellschaft* to society. Writing in 1887, Ferdinand Tonnies (1957) used the terms to describe the shifting values and orientations that were taking place in society as we moved first from a hunting and gathering society, to an agricultural society, and then on to an industrial society. Each of the societal transformations he described resulted in a shift away from *gemeinschaft* toward *gesellschaft*—that is, away from a vision of life as a sacred community toward a more secular society. Although *gemeinschaft* and *gesellschaft* do not exist in pure form in the real world, both are metaphors that bring to mind two "ideal types," two different ways of thinking and living, two different types of cultures, and two alternative visions of life.

Tonnies's basic argument was that as society moves toward the *gesellschaft* end of the continuum, community values are replaced by contractual ones. Among any collection of people, for example, social relationships do not just happen, they are willed. Individuals decide to associate with each other for reasons, and the reasons why they decide to associate are important. In *gemeinschaft*, natural will is the motivating force. Individuals decide to relate to each other because doing so has its own intrinsic meaning and significance. There is no selfish goal or benefit in mind for any of the parties to the relationship. In *gesellschaft*, rational will is the motivating force. Individuals decide to relate to each other to reach some goal, to gain some benefit. Without this benefit, the relationship ends. In the first instance, the ties among people are thick and laden with symbolic meaning; they are moral ties. In the second instance, the ties among people are thin and instrumental; they are calculated ties.

Since *gemeinschaft* and *gesellschaft* are ideal types, no organization or enterprise, including schools, will be exclusively one or the other. But it makes a difference which of the two world views, *gemeinschaft* or *gesellschaft*, is at the center, which worldview dominates the norms and values and the way of life in a particular organization or enterprise.

The modern formal organization is an example of *gesellschaft*. Within the organization, relationships are formal and distant, having been prescribed by roles and expectations. Circumstances are evaluated by universal criteria as embodied in policies, rules, and protocols. Acceptance is conditional. The more a person cooperates with the organization and achieves for the organization, the more likely she or he will be accepted. Relationships are competitive. Those who achieve more are valued more by the organization. Not all concerns of members are legitimate; legitimate concerns are bound by roles rather than needs. Subjectivity is frowned upon and rationality is prized. Self-interest prevails.

These same characteristics often undergird our present policies with respect to how schools are organized, how teaching and learning take place, how students are evaluated, how supervision is practiced, how principals and students are motivated and rewarded, and what leadership is and how it works. Most will agree that *gesellschaft* values make sense in getting such formal organizations as a corporation, army, research university, and hospital to work effectively. But applying the same values to the family, rural church, neighborhood, social club, and school, however, raises important epistemological questions. Are *gesellschaft* values appropriate? If they are not and we use them anyway, do we run the risk of creating standards of practice and norms of behavior that do not fit schools?

Gemeinschaft

Gemeinschaft, according to Tonnies (1957), exists in three forms: community by kinship, of place, and of mind. Community by *kinship* characterizes the special kinds of relationships among people that create a unity that is similar to that found in families and other closely knit collections of people. Community of *place* characterizes sharing a common habitat or locale. This type of sharing with others for sustained periods of time creates a special identity and a shared sense of belonging that connects people together in special ways. Community of *mind* emerges from the binding of people to common goals, shared values, and shared conceptions of being and doing. Together, the three forms represent webs of meaning that tie people together by creating a special sense of belonging and a strong common identity.

As schools struggle to become communities, they need to address questions such as the following: What can be done to increase the sense of kinship, neighborliness, and collegiality among the faculty of a school? How can the faculty become more of a professional community where everyone cares about each other and helps each other to grow, to learn together, and to lead together? What kinds of relationships need to be cultivated with parents that will enable them to be included in this emerging community? How can the web of relationships that exist among teachers and between teachers and students be defined so that they embody community? How can teaching and learning settings be arranged so that they are more like a family? How can the school, as a collection of families, be more like a neighborhood? What are the shared values and commitments that enable the school to become a community of mind? How will these values and commitments become practical standards that can guide the lives community members want to lead, what community members learn and how, and how community members treat each other? What are the patterns of mutual obligations and duties that emerge in the school as community is achieved?

Although not cast in stone, community understandings have enduring qualities. These understandings are taught to new members, celebrated in customs and rituals, and embodied as standards that govern life in the community. Furthermore, they are resilient enough to survive the passage of members through the community over time. As suggested by Bellah and his colleagues (1985), enduring understandings create a fourth form of community—community of *memory*. In time, communities by kinship, of place, and of mind become communities of memory by providing members with memories of common images and common learnings. Being a part of a community of memory sustains us when times are tough, connects us when we are not physically present, and provides us with a history for creating sense and meaning.

The Importance of Relationships

The web of relationships that stand out in communities are different in kind than those found in more *gesellschaft* organizations. They are more special, meaningful, and personalized. They result in a quality of connectedness that has moral over-tones. In addition, because of these overtones, members feel a special sense of obli-gation to look out for each other.

It is generally acknowledged that quality of relationships is an important ingre-dient in the make-up of a good school. A report issued by the Institute for Education and Transformation (1992) at the Claremont Graduate School, for example, points to quality of relationships and other relationship themes as the critical leverage point for school improvement. The quality of relationships determines the quality of the school. Or, in the words of Claremont president John Maguire, "If the rela-tionships are wrong between teachers and students, for whatever reason, you can restructure until the cows come home, but transformation won't take place" (Roth-man, 1992:1).

The Claremont researchers spent 18 months studying four culturally diverse schools—two elementary, one middle, and one high school. They interviewed stu-dents, teachers, custodians, secretaries, cafeteria workers, parents, and others inside the schools. More than 24,000 pages of data were collected and analyzed. "Our data strongly suggest that the heretofore identified *problems* of schooling (lowered achievement, higher dropout rates, and problems in the teaching profes-sion) are rather *consequences* of much deeper and more fundamental problems" (Institute, 1992:11). These deeper, more fundamental problems pointed to seven major issues that surfaced repeatedly throughout the study. Relationship themes are embedded in each of these issues with relationships themselves being consid-ered most important. The seven issues, as summarized from the institute's report, are presented here:

1. Relationships. *Participants feel the crisis inside schools is directly linked to human relationships. Most often mentioned were relationships between teachers and students. Where positive things about the schools are noted, they usually involve reports of individuals who care, listen, understand, respect others and are honest, open and sensitive. Teachers report their best experiences in school are those where they connect with students and are able to help them in some way. They also report, however, there is precious little time during the day to seek out individual students. . . . Students of color, especially older students, often report that their teachers, school staff and other students neither like nor understand them. Many teachers also report they do not always understand students ethni-cally different than themselves. When relationships in schools are poor, fear, name calling, threats of or incidents of violence, as well as a sense of depression and hope-lessness exist. This theme was prominently stated by participants and so deeply connected to all other themes in the data that it is believed this may be one of the two most central issues in solving the crisis inside schools.*

2. Race, Culture, and Class. *A theme which ran through every other issue, like that of relationships, was that of race, culture and class. This is a theme with much debate and very little consensus. Many students of color and some Euro-American students perceive schools to be racist and prejudiced, from the staff to the curricu-lum. Some students doubt the very substance of what is being taught. . . . Teachers*

are tremendously divided on such issues. Some are convinced that students are right about racism, others are not. . . . Students have an intense interest in knowing about one another's culture but receive very little of that knowledge from home or school.

3. Values. *There are frequently related conversations in the U.S. that suggest people of color and/or people living in economically depressed areas hold different basic values than others, and that it is these differences which create conflicts in schools and society. While cultural differences clearly do exist in the expression or prioritization of values, our data hold no evidence that people inside schools have significantly different fundamental values. Our data suggest that parents, teachers, students, staff and administrators of all ethnicities and classes, value and desire education, honesty, integrity, beauty, care, justice, truth, courage and meaningful hard work. Participants' writings and transcripts of discussions are filled with references to basic values. However, very little time is spent in classrooms discussing these issues and a number of restrictions exist against doing so. In the beginning of our research many participants initially assumed other participants held different values. The more we talked, the more this assumption was challenged. Students desire a network of adults (parents and teachers) with whom they can "really talk about important things," and want to have these conversations about values with one another.*

4. Teaching and Learning. *Students, especially those past fifth grade, frequently report that they are bored in school and see little relevance of what is taught to their lives and their futures. Teachers feel pressure to teach what is mandated and sometimes doubt its appropriateness for their students. Teachers also are often bored by the curriculum they feel they must teach. . . . Students from all groups, remedial and advanced, high school to elementary, desire both rigor and fun in their schoolwork. They express enthusiasm about learning experiences that are complex but understandable, full of rich meanings and discussions of values, require their own action, and those about which they feel they have some choice.*

5. Safety. *Related to disconnected relationships and not knowing about one another's differences is the issue of safety. Very few participants on campus or parents feel schools are safe places. This is particularly true in our middle school and high school. Teachers, students and staff fear physical violence. The influence of drugs, gangs and random violence is felt by students. Students feel physically safest inside classrooms and least safe in large gatherings between classes or traveling to or from school.*

6. Physical Environment. *Students want schools that reflect order, beauty, space and contain rich materials and media. The desire for clean, aesthetically pleasing and physically comfortable spaces is expressed by all. The food served to students is a persistent complaint. Many would like foods more typical of their homes and home cultures. The lack of any significant personal space such as lockers is problematic to students and also leads to feelings of being devalued. The depressed physical environment of many schools, especially those in lower socioeconomic areas, is believed by participants to reflect society's lack of priority for these children and their education.*

> 7. Despair, Hope, and the Process of Change. *Many participants feel a hopelessness about schools that is reflected in the larger society and in the music and art of our youth. Paradoxically, hope seemed to emerge following honest dialogues about our collective despair. Participants are anxious for change and willing to participate in change they perceive as relevant. We have strong indications that change inside schools might best be stimulated through participatory processes. In these self-driven research processes, participants came to openly discuss their hopes and dreams. Through this process, we understood there were shared common values around which we could begin to imagine a more ideal school. (12–16)*

The problematic relationships described in the report are the kinds of relationships that seem inevitably to evolve whenever schools are viewed as formal organizations. Furthermore, it is not likely that relationships will improve in schools unless this view is abandoned in favor of community.

The Pattern Variables

Sociologist Talcott Parsons (1951) used Tonnies's (1957) concepts of *gemeinschaft* and *gesellschaft* to describe different types of social relationships. He argued that any relationship can be described as a pattern that comprises five pairs of variables that represent choices between alternative value orientations. The parties to this relationship, for example, have to make decisions as to how they will orient themselves to each other. When taken together, these decisions represent a pattern giving rise to Parsons's now famous "pattern variables." The pairs of variables that comprise this pattern are now familiar to us:

> affective–affective-neutrality
> particularism–universalism
> diffuseness–specificity
> ascription–achievement
> collective orientation–self-orientation

In schools, for example, principals, teachers, and students have to make decisions about how they will perform their respective roles in relationship to others. Teachers have to decide: Will relationships with students be similar to a professional expert who treats students as if they were clients (affective-neutrality)? Or, will relationships be similar to a parent, with students treated as if they were family members (affective)? Will students be given equal treatment in accordance with uniform standards, rules, and regulations (universalism)? Or, will students be treated more preferentially and individually (particularism)? Will role relationships and job descriptions narrowly define specific topics for attention and discussion (specificity)? Or, will relationships be considered unbounded by roles and thus more inclusive and holistic (diffuseness)? Will students have to earn the right to be regarded as "good" and to maintain their standing in the school (achievement)? Or, will students be accepted completely, simply because they have enrolled in the school (ascription)? Do we decide that a certain distance needs to be maintained for professional interests and concerns to remain uncompromised (self-orientation)? Or, do we view ourselves as part of a teacher-student "we" that compels us to work intimately with students in identifying common interests, concerns, and standards for decision making (collective orientation)?

Parsons believed that the five pairs of pattern variables, when viewed as polar opposites on a continuum, can be used to evaluate the extent to which social relationships in an enterprise resemble communities or resemble more *gesellschaft*-like organizations. For example, although no school can be described as emphasizing one or another of the variables all the time or as never emphasizing any of the variables, schools can be fixed on this continuum based on the relative emphasis given to each of the polar opposites. This fixing across several pairs of variables can provide us with a kind of cultural "DNA" (a pattern of variables in Parsons's language) that can be used to place the school on a *gemeinschaft-gesellschaft* continuum. (See Appendix 4.1 for an assessment that can be used to evaluate your school on this continuum.)

In addition to Parsons's five variables, two other "polar opposites" are worth considering: substantive and instrumental, and altruistic love and egocentric love. Substantive and instrumental speak to the issue of means and ends. In organizations a clear distinction is made between means and ends communicating an instrumental view of human nature and society. In communities these distinctions are blurred; ends remain ends, but means are also considered ends.

Altruistic love and egocentric love address the issue of motivation. Like Tonnies, Rousseau (1991) believes that it is the motives that bring people together that are key in determining whether community will be authentically achieved. To Rousseau, it is altruistic love that is the deciding factor. Altruistic love is an expression of selfless concern for others that stems from devotion or obligation. It is more cultural than psychological. Egocentric love, more characteristic of organizations, is self-gratifying. Relationships are implicit contracts for the mutual exchange of psychological satisfactions.

Taken together, the seven pairs of variables portray different ties for connecting people to each other and for connecting them to their work. In school as community:

- Relationships are both close and informal.
- Individual circumstances count.
- Acceptance is unconditional.
- Relationships are cooperative.
- Concerns of members are unbounded and therefore considered legitimate as long as they reflect needs.
- Subjectivity is okay.
- Emotions are legitimate.
- Sacrificing one's self-interest for the sake of other community members is common.
- Members associate with each other because doing so is valuable as an end in itself.

- Knowledge is valued and learned for its own sake, not just as a means to get something or go somewhere.
- Children are accepted and loved because that's the way one treats community members.
- The bonding of relationship ties helps the school become a community by kinship and a community of place.
- The binding of idea ties helps the school become a community of mind.

In time, these collective sentiments bring people together as a community of memory and sustain them even when they become separated from each other.

Finding the Right Balance

It would be a mistake to take an either-or stance when selecting a framework for understanding schools. Doing so would create a false dichotomy between *gemeinschaft* and *gesellschaft*. Still, the use of ideal types is useful. The use of polar opposites along a common continuum is a strategy with a long tradition in sociology. *Gemeinschaft* and *gesellschaft* represent ideal types that do not exist in the real world in pure forms. They are, as Weber (1949) pointed out, polar mental representations that can help us categorize and explain on the one hand and track movement along a common continuum on the other. Thus, schools are never *gemeinschaft* or *gesellschaft*; they possess characteristics of both.

Although most schools are currently too *gesellschaft* and we need a realignment in favor *of gemeinschaft*, it is important to recognize that the *gesellschaft* perspective is both valuable and inescapable. We live, after all, in a *gesellschaft* world—a society characterized by technical-rationality, which has brought us many gains. Without *gesellschaft*, we would not have a successful space program or heart transplant technology. Nor would we have great universities, profitable corporations, and workable governmental systems. There would be no hope of cleaning up the environment, and as a nation we would not be able to defend ourselves.

Yet, we need to decide which theory should dominate which spheres of our lives. Most everyone will agree that the family, the extended family, and the neighborhood should be dominated by *gemeinschaft* values. The corporation, the research laboratory, and the court system, however, might well lean more toward *gesellschaft* values. In modern times, the school has been solidly ensconced in the *gesellschaft* camp with unhappy results. It's time that the school was moved from the *gesellschaft* side of the ledger to the *gemeinschaft*.

Problems with Community

Community theory is not without its problems. Although community is designed to bring people together in a common cause for altruistic reasons, its dimensions may comprise the same ingredients that create systems of "blood" that divide people (see, for example, Sergiovanni, 1992). The hard reality is that community, like fire, can be helpful or harmful. By its very nature, community is both inclusive and exclusive. It can bring some people together with good results while at the same time leaving others out. Further, community can exaggerate differences with others, causing fragmentation, disengagement, and conflict.

These are serious issues because the world is a diverse place.* Diversity raises important questions for how community should be understood, particularly as a construct for schooling. How, for example, do we reconcile the seemingly paradoxical problem of creating distinct school communities that are held together by common meanings and a shared sense of the common good within a society that is increasingly multicultural and that has a strong history of individualism? In schools, how do we identify a common purpose, develop a coherent practice, rally parents, teachers, students, and administrators to common themes, and construct a framework of shared norms when people are different, when parents have different expectations, when teachers bring different pedagogical philosophies and work styles to their practice, and when the potential for conflict over school purposes, organizational structures, curriculum designs, and assessment strategies is high?

Many voices suggest that in a postmodern world the very definition of *community* must be changed. Furman (1998), for example, claims that definitions of community based on shared conceptions and ideals that function as a unifying center are at odds with the purposes and practicalities of multiculturalism, and by implication denies the possibility that a productive moral leadership can emerge from this center. Furman proposes a postmodernist conception of community: "Postmodern community is community of difference. It is based on the ethics of acceptance of others with respect, justice, and appreciation and on peaceful cooperation within difference. It is inspired by the metaphor of an interconnected, interdependent web of persons engaged in global community" (p. 312). But even this definition has a unifying center. Acceptance of others and cooperation within differences are the universal values postmodernists claim are needed to guarantee feelings of belonging, trust, and safety that are essential to building community. These postmodernist "core values" place a high priority on building a community of relationships as a central part of the school's community of heart and mind.

Bringing Community and Diversity Together

One problem that contributes to worries about creating stifling communities with rigid centers that divide and exclude people is the perception that *centers* and *sameness* are the same. Communities of relationships, heart, and mind need not and should not be built on all-encompassing, narrowly defined, carbon-copy norms but on norms of caring and collaboration. Collaborative cultures share common beliefs in the value of both the individual and the group (Nias, Southworth, and Yeomans,

---

*This section is drawn from T. J. Sergiovanni, "Building Community in a Diverse Society," Department of Education, Trinity University, San Antonio, TX, 1998. © T. J. Sergiovanni. See also Sergiovanni (2000).

1989). Such norms as praise, appreciation, help, support, encouragement, and viewing differences as learning opportunities are common in collaborative cultures.

As Nias (1995) points out, collaborative cultures "should not be mistakenly viewed as conflict-free or cozy. Collaborative cultures are also built upon a belief in the value of openness, tempered by a respect for individual and collective security" (9). Nothing in the social sciences or in moral philosophy prohibits a community from holding in common the view that differences can be assets and should be respected.

Relying on his analysis of Taylor's work (1995), Etzioni (1995) offers "principled decentralization" as an antidote to possible divisions among different communities. Within a framework of principled decentralization, localized communities are developed in such a way that they embody a responsibility to encourage a variety of different voices and interests, not as isolated entities, but within a larger sphere of a pragmatic coalition built around common goals and ideas where an overlapping consensus has been established and bounded by a framework of mutual respect. Etzioni (1996/97) offers the *mosaic* as an image of community with bounded autonomy. A mosaic is comprised of a variety of elements of different shapes and colors that are held together by frame and glue. It symbolizes a society in which various communities maintain their cultural particulars while at the same time recognizing that they are integral parts of a more encompassing whole. Within this image, communities have firm commitments to both their uniqueness and their shared framework. And according to Etzioni (1996/97), community members have layered loyalties in the form of allegiance to two different dimensions of the whole. Principled decentralization, when accompanied by layered loyalties, embodies the metaphor mosaic in practice.

To these metaphors I would add the metaphor *neighborhoods within a city* to help us think about how nesting of communities within a broader community would work in schools. Imagine, for example, a 750-student, grades 1–6 elementary school in San Antonio or Toronto. There are five sections of each grade in this school. The school is organized into five "families," each comprising one set of grades located in its own corridor or area and designed to keep the same 150 youngsters and six teachers together as the youngsters travel through all six of their school years. The five families share the cafeteria, library, and other school facilities, abide by a few general schoolwide rules, and participate in some schoolwide traditions. At the same time, each of the families operates like an independent learning community or school within this larger school.

Though they share common elements, the families are unique in important ways. In the Toronto school, for example, one of the families is a French immersion school. The second has adopted the Basic School Principles as an organizing framework for planning and organizing the curriculum. A third family emphasizes Caribbean-Canadian themes in its humanities curriculum and uses the Constitution, the Charter of Rights and Freedoms, and other important civic documents as a framework for developing a constitutional society that guides how they will live their lives together. Still another family relies heavily on learning exhibitions, project learning, and other progressive ideas. In this family, the same teachers stay with the same youngsters for the first three years of their schooling, a pattern also repeated in grades 4–6. A fifth family spends Tuesdays and Thursdays out in the community visiting museums, conducting surveys, studying neighborhoods, engaging in scientific investigations in local streams, and in other ways using the community as a classroom. This family believes that schooling without walls is both motivating to students and pedagogically sound. The five families differ in how they handle the details of discipline, in what subjects get emphasized, in how the work of students is assessed, and in other important matters. While some learning outcomes are the same across all five families, other learning outcomes differ family by family.

Each of the five families functions much as does a neighborhood in a city by celebrating its unique purposes, habits, traditions, work patterns and culture. As parts of a mosaic, they bring different colors and hues to a larger portrait of learning in the school. But as neighborhoods in a city, they are also integral and interdependent parts of a whole that share values and commitments common across the school. All of the neighborhoods in this school as city are bound by certain beliefs: All students can learn if they try and if teachers work hard; caring and other virtues must be institutionalized into the culture of the school; teachers are members of communities of practice; parents should promise to accept their share of responsibility for making the school work; students are entitled to unconditional acceptance and have important contributions to make to the school; respect is not a rule but a standard that applies equally to everyone; form should follow function while making decisions about teaching and learning; character education is important; and so on. Though each of the families adopts a different curriculum and a different pedagogy, all five families are expected to engage students in authentic learning. The curriculum itself must be constructivist by nature without compromising attention to basic skills of literacy and numeracy thought to be important.

This list of common standards might be prefaced by two or three schoolwide rules such as no fighting, no drugs, and no weapons. These commonalities seem sufficient to ensure that despite similarities that might exist within school families (communities) and differences that might exist between them, ample guarantees are provided that ensure levels of civility, decency, and respect for everyone. Though layered, shared ideas and moral authority remain the reason for what goes on within the five families in the larger school. At the center of this moral authority are shared conceptions about individual rights of community members and their responsibilities to the larger good.

Eight conditions seem necessary for community theory to evolve in this direction:

1. Schools need to be redefined as collections of people and ideas rather than remain defined by brick and mortar. Thus within any school building, many independent and semi-independent schools might exist side by side.
2. Shared values that lead to the development of tightly knit communities of mind and heart need to be encouraged within schools, while, at the same time, respect for the defining differences that make a school unique need to be encouraged between schools. The goal should be to create communities nested

within communities, neighborhoods within cities, and schools within schools across the educational landscape.

3. Though some schools might function as schools within schools and others as freestanding schools connected to a larger complex of schools, all schools need to be tied together by common foundational values, by frame and glue to hold everything together.

4. Layered loyalties to one's own school community and to the larger community of schools needs to be cultivated.

5. Nothing in the concepts of nested communities, neighborhoods within a city or schools within a school should compromise the individual rights that students, parents, teachers, and other community members enjoy as part of a commitment to democratic values.

6. This emphasis on individual rights needs to be tempered by deliberately linking rights to responsibilities within a framework of commitment to civic virtue, defined as the willingness of each member of the community, individually and collectively, to sacrifice his or her self-interest on behalf of the common good.

7. Within practical limits, students and their families, as well as teachers, should be able to choose the particular school, school family, or school within school they wish to join. This "school" of choice should be part of a larger legal framework of school or schools and resourced at an equitable level.

8. Commitment to both individual rights and shared responsibilities that are connected to the common good should provide the basis for moral leadership.

What are the indicators of a good school? Cuban (1998) has proposed three simple ones:

1. Parents, students, and teachers are satisfied with their school, want to be there, and think it is important to invest in the school's success.

2. The school achieves its own *explicit* goals and purposes.

3. The school produces graduates who are committed to civic virtue and who demonstrate democratic behaviors, values, and attitudes.

I believe we are more likely to measure up to these simple yet powerful measures of goodness if we were to embrace a brand of community that is responsive to diversity.

Implications for School Management and Leadership

What are the implications of a theory of community for how we understand schools and how we arrange teaching and learning? With community as the theory, we would have to rethink the ways in which schools are organized and operated. As indicated in this chapter and in the recommendations of the National Association of Secondary School Principals outlined in Chapter 1, creating communities by kinship and of place, for example, might well mean the dissolution of the high school as we now know it into several small schools rarely exceeding 300 or so students. The importance of creating sustained relationships would require that students and teachers stay together for longer periods of time. Teaching in 50-minute sessions would have to be replaced with longer blocks of time. The curriculum would have to be rethought to accommodate a new schedule. Elementary schools, as outlined earlier, would have to give serious consideration to organizing themselves into smaller and probably multiage families. Discipline problems would no longer be based on psychological principles but moral ones, which would require abandoning such taken-for-granted notions as having explicit rules linked to clearly stated consequences that are uniformly applied in favor of the development of social contracts, constitutions, and normative codes. Inservice and staff development would move from the administrative side of the ledger to the teacher side as part of teachers' ongoing commitment to practice at the edge of their craft. Extrinsic reward systems would have to be deemphasized. The number of specialists would likely be reduced and pull-outs would be less common as families of teachers and students, similar to families of parents and children, take fuller responsibility for solving their own problems. Finally, all these changes would necessitate the invention of new standards of quality, new strategies for accountability, and new ways of working with people—that is, the invention of a new educational administration.

These and other issues associated with changing the metaphor for the school from formal organization to community are explored in subsequent chapters. Important to those discussions is the changing nature of the principal's role and the need to develop a new definition of what leadership is and how it works. It is argued that as community takes hold in schools, the principal emerges as a much more powerful leader than is now the case—a leader whose source of authority becomes increasingly moral.

References

Bellah, Robert N., Richard Madsen, William M. Sullivan, Ann Swidler, and Steven M. Tipton. (1985). *Habits of the Heart: Individualism and Commitment in American Life.* New York: Harper & Row.

Blau, Peter M., and W. Richard Scott. 1962. *Formal Organizations: A Comparative Approach.* San Francisco: Chandler.

Cuban, Larry. January 28, 1998. "A Tale of Two Schools," *Education Week* 33.

Etzioni, Amitai. (Ed.). 1995. *New Communitarian Thinking: Persons, Virtues, Institutions and Communities.* Charlottesville: University of Virginia Press.

Etzioni, Amitai. Winter 1996/97. "The Community of Communities," *The Responsive Community Rights and Responsibilities* 7(1), 21–32.

Furman, Gail C. 1998. "Postmodernism and Community in Schools: Unravelling the Paradox," *Educational Administration Quarterly* 34(3), 298–328.

Institute for Education and Transformation. 1992. "Voices from the Inside. A Report on Schooling from Inside the Classroom, Part I: Naming the Problem," Claremont, CA: The Claremont Graduate School.

Nias, Jennifer. 1995, November. *Teachers' Moral Purposes: Sources of Vulnerability and Strength.* the Johann Jacobs Foundation Conference on Teacher Burnout, Marbach Castle, Germany.

Nias, Jennifer, G. Southworth, and R. Yeomans. 1989. *Staff Relationships in the Primary School: A Study of Organizational Cultures.* London: Cassell.

Parsons, Talcott. 1951. *The Social System.* Glencoe, IL: Free Press.

Rothman, R. Dec. 2, 1992. "Study 'From Inside' Finds a Deeper Set of Problems," *Education Week* 12(13).

Rousseau, Mary F. 1991. *Community: The Tie That Binds.* New York: University Press of America.

Sacks, Jonathan. 1997. "Rebuilding Civil Society: A Biblical Perspective," *Responsive Community* 7(1), 11–20.

Sergiovanni, Thomas J. 1992. *Moral Leadership: Getting to the Heart of School Improvement.* San Francisco: Jossey-Bass.

Sergiovanni, Thomas J. 2000. *The Lifeworld of Leadership: Creating Culture, Community, and Personal Meaning in Our Schools.* San Francisco: Jossey-Bass.

Taylor, Charles. 1995. "Liberal Politics and the Public Sphere," in Amitai Etzioni (Ed.), *New Communitarian Thinking: Persons, Virtue, Institutions and Communities.* Charlottesville: University of Virginia Press.

Tonnies, Ferdinand. 1957. *Community and Society (Gemeinschaft und Gesellschaft).* (C. P. Loomis, trans. and ed.) New York: Harper & Row. (Originally published 1887.)

Weber, Max. 1949. *The Methodology of the Social Sciences.* (Edward A. Shils and Henry A. Finch, trans.) Glencoe, IL: Free Press.

Appendix 4.1　Profiles of Community:
Assessing Organizational and Community Values

The quality and kind of relationships that exist in a school provide an indication of the extent to which a school is oriented toward community values. Though no school can be described as emphasizing community values all of the time or never emphasizing community values, schools can be fixed on a *gemeinschaft-gesellschaft* continuum based on the relative emphasis given to each of the polar opposites.*

Below, the five pairs of pattern variables posed by Parsons (1951) and two other pairs that are closely related to the original five are discussed by asking you to participate in a thought exercise. The variables are represented in the form of a schedule arranged as polar opposites. Think of a school you know well. As the variables are discussed, use each of the pairs to describe three kinds of relationships in that school: the way teachers relate to students, the way teachers relate to each other, and the way administrators relate to teachers. In each case [circle a number] on the line scale in the schedule somewhere between the polar opposites that best places the relationship.

　　1. *Affective vs. Affective-Neutrality.* The parties that comprise the relationship are always interested in each other or are always disinterested. Actions toward each other are always determined by emotions (i.e., feelings of kinship, duty, or love) or are always devoid of feelings. In the first instance, teachers always relate to students as if they were teaching their own children. In the second instance, teachers always relate to students as skilled technicians who apply objective treatments to students who are clients. Principals are emotionally involved as they work with and relate to teachers. Or, principals adopt an emotionally detached, neutral attitude.

	Affective										Affective-Neutrality
Teacher-student	5	4	3	2	1	0	1	2	3	4	5
Among teachers	5	4	3	2	1	0	1	2	3	4	5
Administrator-teachers	5	4	3	2	1	0	1	2	3	4	5

　　2. *Collective Orientation vs. Self-Orientation.* The parties that comprise the relationship are always motivated by common interests or are always motivated by self-interest. In the first instance, any particular action or situation is always evaluated in terms of its collective significance as defined by agreed upon values that comprise a public moral code. In the second instance, any particular action or situation is always evaluated in terms of personal significance by a private standard. Teachers, for example, always choose to help each other get ready for "teacher evaluations" or to plan for the new year as a reflection of their commitment to a shared

*From Thomas J. Sergiovanni, *Building Community in Schools* (San Francisco: Jossey-Bass, 1994).

Appendix 4.1   *Continued*

sense of success. Or, teachers always choose to face "teacher evaluations" or to plan for the new year individually and privately as they compete with each other in pursuit of more personal gains. Principals are concerned with being sure that the best decisions are made even if lines of authority have to be compromised. Or, principals are concerned with maintaining proper lines of authority and thus insist on making decisions.

	Collective Orientation									Self-Orientation	
Teacher-student	5	4	3	2	1	0	1	2	3	4	5
Among teachers	5	4	3	2	1	0	1	2	3	4	5
Administrator-teachers	5	4	3	2	1	0	1	2	3	4	5

3. *Particularism vs. Universalism.* The parties that comprise the relationship always size up situations and make decisions on the basis of the specifics that define that situation or always on the basis of general protocols and rules. Actions are governed entirely by the particulars of the relationship itself or actions are governed entirely by the universal norms of the system itself. In the first instance, teachers always take into consideration the unique circumstances that define a discipline problem and then always create a unique resolution based on this consideration. (Thus, the same discipline problem may be handled differently on different occasions.) In the second instance, discipline problems are always categorized by predetermined protocols and then always dealt with according to universal rules. (Thus, the same discipline problem is always handled the same way whenever it appears.) Teachers judge students in accordance with particular and specific standards. The standards vary with students. Teachers judge the abilities of students by universal standards. The standards do not vary with the students.

	Particularism									Universalism	
Teacher-student	5	4	3	2	1	0	1	2	3	4	5
Among teachers	5	4	3	2	1	0	1	2	3	4	5
Administrator-teachers	5	4	3	2	1	0	1	2	3	4	5

4. *Ascription vs. Achievement.* The parties that comprise the relationship always value each other for who and what they are regardless of their achievements or always value each other for what they accomplish. Each always accepts the other as an absolute or acceptance is always contingent on one's achievements. In the first instance, students are always accepted, considered "good" and loved regardless of how well they do in school and how much they achieve. In the second instance, acceptance, attributions of being a good person, and love are always contingent upon and distributed based on the extent to which students are cooperative and achieve. Teachers accept each other, help each other, and respect each other

Appendix 4.1   *Continued*

because they are members of the same school faculty. Or, teachers accept, help, and respect each other differentially, in accordance with perceptions of relative worth and relative achievement.

	Ascription										Achievement
Teacher-student	5	4	3	2	1	0	1	2	3	4	5
Among teachers	5	4	3	2	1	0	1	2	3	4	5
Administrator-teachers	5	4	3	2	1	0	1	2	3	4	5

5. *Diffuseness vs. Specificity.* The parties that comprise the relationship always view each other in less defined ways that allow for broad interaction and for concern that is widely defined or always view each other in ways defined more narrowly by roles, role expectations, and preset work requirements. In the first instance, everything about the person is always relevant on any given occasion. In the second instance, relevance is always determined by role requirements and the requirements of the task at hand. Principals always view teachers as whole persons to be engaged fully. Or, principals always view teachers as cases to be treated in accordance with proper role definitions and expectations. Teachers are bonded to each other as total personalities who comprise a "family." Teachers relate to each other in more limited ways as defined by their jobs.

	Diffuseness										Specificity
Teacher-student	5	4	3	2	1	0	1	2	3	4	5
Among teachers	5	4	3	2	1	0	1	2	3	4	5
Administrator-teachers	5	4	3	2	1	0	1	2	3	4	5

One important characteristic that differentiates one school from another is the relationship that exists between means and ends. In some schools, a fairly clear distinction is made between means and ends. This distinction communicates an instrumental view of human nature and society. In other schools, by contrast, the distinctions are blurred. Ends remain ends but means too are considered as ends.

6. *Substantive vs. Instrumental.* The partners that comprise the relationship always view means as ends equal to ends or always make a clear distinction between means and ends. In the first instance, discipline policies and rules are always considered to be moral standards to be celebrated in their own right. [In the second instance, discipline policies and rules] are always considered as means to manage the behavior of students. The subjects taught are viewed entirely as knowledge to be valued and enjoyed, or are always viewed as content to be mastered in order to get good grades and high test scores. In the first instance principals emphasize improving the quality of the teacher's workplace because that is a good thing to do. In the second instance principals work to improve the quality of the teachers'

Appendix 4.1   *Continued*

workplace as a way to motivate them to perform. In the first instance, students are fed because loving, compassionate people feed hungry children. In the second instance, the purpose of the school breakfast program is to relieve the hunger that keeps children from learning. Students study only because they value knowledge as an end in itself or only to win approval, get promoted, or perhaps to qualify for the driver's education program.

	Substantive									Instrumental
Teacher-student	5	4	3	2	1	0	1	2	3	4	5
Among teachers	5	4	3	2	1	0	1	2	3	4	5
Administrator-teachers	5	4	3	2	1	0	1	2	3	4	5

7. *Altruistic Love vs. Egocentric Love.* Sometimes relationships between and among people are governed by altruistic love and at other times by egocentric love. Egocentric love is emotionally and physically self-gratifying. When egocentric love is the motive, each of the parties to the relationship enters into an implicit contract with the other for the exchange of needs and satisfactions that benefit both. Teachers, for example, develop special relationships with students, expecting in return cooperation and greater effort. Teachers help each other so that each will be more effective. Principals "love" their teachers for similar reasons.

Altruism is the benevolent concern for the welfare of others, as selflessness. Love, in this case, is defined as deep devotion and good will that comes from and contributes to feelings of brotherhood and sisterhood. Altruistic love is an expression of selfless concern for others that stems from devotion or obligation. The emphasis is on giving without concern for what one gets in return.

Strictly speaking, altruistic love and egocentric love are not opposite poles of the same continuum. But arranging them in this way is still useful for our purposes. Place your school on the continuum between the two to show the relative emphasis given to each.

	Altruistic Love								Egocentric Love		
Teacher-student	5	4	3	2	1	0	1	2	3	4	5
Among teachers	5	4	3	2	1	0	1	2	3	4	5
Administrator-teachers	5	4	3	2	1	0	1	2	3	4	5

Now use the score sheet that follows to summarize your ratings. By drawing in the profile lines, you will have an idea of where your school is on the *gemeinschaft-gesellschaft* continuum.

Appendix 4.1   *Continued*

Score Sheet: Profiles of Community

Teachers' relationships with students

5   4   3   2   1   0   1   2   3   4   5

Gemeinschaft   *Gesellschaft*

1. affective .... affective-neutrality
2. collective orientation .... self-orientation
3. particularism .... universalism
4. ascription .... achievement
5. diffuseness .... specificity
6. substantive .... instrumental
7. altruistic love .... egocentric love

Relationships among teachers

5   4   3   2   1   0   1   2   3   4   5

1. affective .... affective-neutrality
2. collective orientation .... self-orientation
3. particularism .... universalism
4. ascription .... achievement
5. diffuseness .... specificity
6. substantive .... instrumental
7. altruistic love .... egocentric love

Administrators' relationships with teachers

5   4   3   2   1   0   1   2   3   4   5

1. affective .... affective-neutrality
2. collective orientation .... self-orientation
3. particularism .... universalism
4. ascription .... achievement
5. diffuseness .... specificity
6. substantive .... instrumental
7. altruistic love .... egocentric love

P A R T **II**

PROVIDING LEADERSHIP

5

THE FORCES OF LEADERSHIP
AND THE CULTURE OF SCHOOLS

Principals are important! Indeed, no other school position has greater potential for maintaining and improving quality schools. These assertions are bolstered by findings that emerge from research and from more informal observation of successful schools. It is clear that when schools are functioning especially well and school achievement is high, much of the credit typically belongs to the principal. A recent governmental study, for example, reached the following conclusions (U.S. Senate, 1972):

> *In many ways the school principal is the most important and influential individual in any school. . . . It is his leadership that sets the tone of the school, the climate for learning, the level of professionalism and morale of teachers and the degree of concern for what students may or may not become. . . . If a school is a vibrant, innovative, child-centered place; if it has a reputation for excellence in teaching; if students are performing to the best of their ability one can almost always point to the principal's leadership as the key to success. (305)*

Although principals are important, their mere presence does not automatically result in the required leadership being provided. Often, circumstances prevent principals from becoming the leaders they want to be. Consider, for example, what one principal has to say about constraining circumstances:

> *I go almost every year to conventions for principals, and there's always a speech telling us we need to be educational leaders, not managers. It's a great idea. And yet the system doesn't allow you to be an educational leader. Everyone wants the power to run schools in one way or another—the central office, the union, the board, the parents, the special-interest groups. What's left for the principal to decide isn't always very much. There's so little we have to control or to change. The power, the authority, is somewhere else, though not necessarily the responsibility. (Boyer, 1983:219)*

Still, as we discussed in Chapter 1, many principals are able to rise above these and other difficulties. Key to realizing the potential for leadership in the principalship is to recognize that schools provide opportunities for expressing a *unique* form of leadership. These opportunities spring from special characteristics that schools possess.

As a result of their research, Blumberg and Greenfield (1980) conclude that "principals who lead seem to be highly *goal oriented* and to have a keen sense of *goal clarity*" (246). They point out that successful principals are alert to opportunities or create opportunities favoring their ability to affect what is going on in the school. Although they rely heavily on operational goals of a long-term nature, they emphasize day-by-day actions as well. They have a good sense of themselves, feel secure as individuals and as principals at work, and are able to accept failure as failure of an idea rather than of them as persons. These principals have a high tolerance for ambiguity and are able to work in loosely structured environments. With respect to authority, they test the limits of the boundaries they face and do not make premature assumptions about what they can or cannot do. They are sensitive to the dynamics of power existing in the school district and school community, and they are accomplished in establishing alliances and in building coalitions that enable them to harness this power on behalf of the school. Approaching problems from an analytical perspective, they are able to remove themselves from the situation; that is, they do not become consumed by the problems and situations they face.

When it comes to the "bottom line," most successful principals will tell you that getting the culture right and paying attention to how parents, teachers, and students define and experience meaning are two widely accepted rules for creating effective schools. We still have to worry about standards, the curriculum, teacher development, tests, resources, and the creation of appropriate management designs that help get things done. But these concerns will not matter much unless the right culture is in place and unless parents, teachers, and students interact with the school in meaningful ways.

In this chapter, the intent is to focus beneath these descriptions and to examine principal leadership as a set of forces available for improving and maintaining quality schooling. Suggestions are provided as to how principals can use these forces.

The Forces of Leadership

Leadership can be viewed metaphorically as comprising a set of forces. Each of the "forces" can be used by the principal to push the school forward toward effectiveness or to prevent it from being pushed back. Different forces have different consequences for school effectiveness.

Five "forces of leadership"—technical, human, educational, symbolic, and cultural—are discussed in the following subsections. All five are important. Technical, human, and educational are foundational forces that must be provided to ensure that schools will work. Symbolic and cultural are stretcher forces that help schools rise to levels of extraordinary commitment and performance.

The Technical Force

The first force available to principals is the power of leadership derived from using sound management techniques. This force is concerned with the technical aspects of leadership. When expressing the technical force, principals can be thought of as assuming the role of "management engineers," who emphasize such concepts as planning and time management, contingency leadership theories, and organizational structures. As management engineers, principals provide planning, organizing, coordinating, and scheduling to the school and are skilled at manipulating strategies and situations to ensure optimum effectiveness. The technical leadership force is very important because its presence, competently articulated, ensures that the school will be managed properly.

Proper management is a basic requirement of all organizations if they are expected to function properly day by day and to maintain support from external constituents. School boards and other segments of the public will not tolerate inefficient and poorly managed schools. Furthermore, it is clear from the research that poorly managed enterprises can have debilitating effects on workers. Hackman (1969:158), for example, found that "poor organization of work" resulted in such negative feelings among workers as frustration and aggression, anxiety, personal inadequacy, and even social rejection. It is apparent that workplaces need to be characterized by a degree of order and reliability that provides security for people *and* that frees them to focus wholeheartedly on major purposes and central work activities. The technical force of leadership serves this important need.

The Human Force

The second force available to principals is the power of leadership derived from harnessing the school's social and interpersonal potential—its human resources. This force is concerned with human aspects of leadership. Principals expressing this force can be thought of as assuming the role of "human engineer," emphasizing human relations, interpersonal competence, and instrumental motivational techniques. As human engineers, principals provide support, encouragement, and growth opportunities for teachers and others.

It is hard to imagine a school functioning properly without the strong presence of this human force of leadership. Schools are, after all, human intensive, and *the interpersonal needs of students and teachers are of sufficient importance that, should they be neglected, schooling problems are likely to follow.* High student motivation to learn and high teacher motivation to teach are prerequisite for quality schooling and must be effectively addressed by principals. This force is so fundamental that the development of human resources appears as either the dominant or underlying theme of each of this book's chapters.

The Educational Force

The third force available to principals is the power of leadership derived from expert knowledge about matters of education and schooling. This force is concerned with educational aspects of leadership. At one time, educational aspects were dominant in the literature of educational administration and supervision. Principals were considered to be instructional leaders, and emphasis on schooling characterized university training programs. In the latter part of the 1950s and during the 1960s, advances of management and social science theory in educational administration and supervision brought to center stage technical and human aspects of leadership; indeed, educational aspects were often neglected. As a result, the principalship was often viewed as a school management position separate from teaching. During this period, the original meaning of principal as "principal teacher" became lost. Goodlad (1978) has been a persistent critic of the displacement of educational aspects of leadership in favor of the technical and human. He states:

> But to put these matters (technical and human) at the center, often for understandable reasons of survival and expediency, is to commit a fundamental error which, ultimately, will have a negative impact on both education and one's own career. Our work, for which we will be held accountable, is to maintain, justify, and articulate sound, comprehensive programs of instruction of children and youth. *(326)*

Goodlad states further: "It is now time to put the right things at the center again. And the right things have to do with assuring comprehensive, quality educational programs in each and every school in our jurisdiction" (331).

Matters of education and schooling are again in the forefront. This new emphasis on the educational force of leadership is a happy result of recent school effectiveness and teaching effectiveness research and of other reports of research, such as Goodlad's *A Study of Schooling* (1983). Many national policy studies on the present status and future of education, such as the Carnegie Foundation for the Advancement of Teaching's report *High School: A Report on Secondary Education in America* (Boyer, 1983), have also contributed to enhancing this renewed emphasis on educational aspects of leadership. The following statement from Boyer's book (1983) regarding the preparation of principals is representative of current thought:

> New preparation and selection programs are required. Principals cannot exercise leadership without classroom experience. Specifically, we recommend that the preparation pattern for principals follow that of teachers. Without a thorough grounding in the realities of the classroom, principals will continue to feel uncomfortable and inadequate in educational leadership roles. Moreover, they will continue to lack credibility in instructional matters with their teachers. *(223)*

More recently, the Interstate School Leaders Licensure Consortium (Council of Chief State Officers, 1996) stated that "effective school leaders are strong educators, anchoring their work on central issues of learning and teaching and school improvement" (5). The first of seven principles used to guide the development of its licensure standards reads, "Standards should reflect the centrality of student learning" (7). Clearly, the educational force is receiving increased attention today.

When expressing the educational force, the principal assumes the role of "principal teacher" who brings expert professional knowledge and bearing to teaching, educational program development, and supervision. As principal teacher, the principal is adept at diagnosing educational problems; counseling teachers; providing for supervision, evaluation, and staff development; and developing curriculum.

Sometimes the educational force takes the form of principal as strong instructional leader, and at other times as knowledgeable colleague or leader of leaders who engages with teachers on an equal basis on matters of teaching and learning. The first expression of this educational force might be appropriate for new teachers, teachers with less than fully developed competencies, or teachers with doubtful commitment. The second expression is appropriate for more mature, competent, and committed teachers. Although instructional leadership might be appropriate for a particular circumstance or for a limited period of time, the overall goal is for principals to become leaders of leaders. As leadership builds, the principal strives to help the school become a community of leaders.

Technical, human, and educational forces of leadership—brought together in an effort to promote and maintain quality schooling—provide the critical mass needed for basic school competence. A shortage in any of the three forces upsets this critical mass, and less effective schooling is likely to occur. Studies of excellence in organizations suggest that despite the link between technical, human, and educational aspects of leadership and basic competence, the presence of the three does not guarantee excellence. Excellent organizations, schools among them, are characterized by other leadership qualities represented by symbolic and cultural forces of leadership.

The Symbolic Force

The fourth force available to principals is the power of leadership derived from focusing attention of others on matters of importance to the school. This force is concerned with the symbolic aspects of leadership. When expressing this force, the principal assumes the role of "chief," emphasizing selective attention or the modeling of important goals and behaviors, and signaling to others what is important and valuable in the school. Touring the school; visiting classrooms; seeking out and visibly spending time with students; downplaying management concerns in favor of educational concerns; presiding over ceremonies, rituals, and other important occasions; and providing a unified vision of the school through proper use of words and actions are examples of principal activities associated with this force.

The providing of *purposing* to the school is a major aspect of symbolic leadership. Vaill (1984) defines purposing as "that continuous stream of actions by an organization's formal leadership which has the effect of inducing clarity, consensus, and commitment regarding the organization's basic purposes." Leaders of the high-performing organizations he studied had in common the ability to provide purposing.

The symbolic force of leadership derives much of its power from the needs of persons at work to have a sense of what is important and to have some signal of what is of value. Students and teachers alike want to know what is of value to the school and its leadership; they desire a sense of order and direction, and they enjoy sharing this sense with others. They respond to these conditions with increased work motivation and commitment.

To understand the symbolic force, we need to look beneath the surface of what the principal does to what this behavior means. In symbolic leadership, what the principal stands for and communicates to others by his or her actions and words is important. In addition, providing meaning to teachers, students, and parents and rallying them to a common cause are the earmarks of effectiveness. Pondy (1978) suggests:

> *What kind of insights can we get if we say that the effectiveness of a leader lies in his ability to make activity meaningful for those in his role set—not to change behavior but to give others a sense of understanding what they are doing, and especially to articulate it so they can communicate about the meaning of their behaviors? (94)*

The noted administrative theorist James G. March (1984) echoes Pondy's thoughts as follows:

> *Administrators manage the way the sentiments, expectations, commitments and faiths of individuals concerned with the organization fit into a structure of social beliefs about organizational life. Administrative theory probably underestimates the significance of this belief structure for effective organizations. As a result, it probably underestimates the extent to which the management of symbols is a part of effective administration. If we want to identify one single way in which administrators can affect organizations, it is through their effect on the world views that surround organizational life; and those effects are managed through attention of the ritual and symbolic characteristics of organizations and their administration. Whether we wish to sustain the system or change it, management is a way of making a symbolic statement. (32)*

Technical aspects of leadership are managing structures and events; human aspects are managing psychological factors such as needs; and educational aspects are managing the substance of our work. By contrast, symbolic aspects are managing sentiments, expectations, commitments, and faith itself. Because symbolic leadership affects the faith that people have in the school, it provides the principal with a powerful force for influencing school events.

The Cultural Force

The fifth force available to principals is the power of leadership derived from building a unique school culture and refers to cultural aspects of leadership. It is clear from reviews of the successful schools literature that the building of a *culture* that promotes and sustains a given school's conception of success is key. When expressing this cultural force, the principal assumes the role of "high priest," seeking to define, strengthen, and articulate those enduring values, beliefs, and cultural strands that give the school its unique identity over time. As high priest, the principal is engaged in legacy building, and in creating, nurturing, and teaching an organizational saga (Clark, 1972) that defines the school as a distinct entity with an identifiable culture that builds institutional character.

Leadership activities associated with the cultural view include articulating school purposes and mission; socializing new members to the school; telling stories and maintaining or reinforcing myths, traditions, and beliefs; explaining "the way things operate around here"; developing and displaying a system of symbols (as exemplified in the fourth force) *over time;* and rewarding those who reflect this culture. The net effect of the cultural force of leadership is to bond students, teachers, and others together and to bind them to the work of the school as believers. The school and its purposes become revered, and in some respects they resemble an ideological system dedicated to a sacred mission. As persons become members of this strong and binding culture, they are provided with opportunities for enjoying a special sense of personal importance and significance. Their work and their lives take on a new importance, one characterized by richer meanings, an expanded sense of identity, and a feeling of belonging to something special—all of which are highly motivating conditions (Peters and Waterman, 1982).

Culture can be described as the collective programming of the mind that distinguishes the members of one school from another (Hofstede, 1980:13). Cultural life in schools is constructed reality, and school principals can play a key role in building this reality. School culture includes values, symbols, beliefs, and shared meanings of parents, students, teachers, and others conceived as a group or community. Culture governs what is of worth for this group and how members should think, feel, and behave. The "stuff" of culture includes a school's customs and traditions; historical accounts; stated and unstated understandings, habits, norms, and expectations; common meanings; and shared assumptions. The more understood, accepted, and cohesive the culture of a school, the better able it is to move in concert toward ideals it holds and objectives it wishes to pursue. Ultimately, the intent of cultural leadership is to transform the school from an organization inhabited by a collection of "I"s to a moral community—themes described in Chapter 4.

Practicing Symbolic and Cultural Leadership

Culture building and practicing the art of purposing in schools are the essentials of symbolic and cultural leadership forces. The expression of these forces requires vision and an understanding of the semantics of daily activities.

Expressing Symbolic Leadership

When principals are expressing symbolic aspects of leadership, they are typically working beneath the surface of events and activities; they are seeking to tap deeper meanings, deeper values. As Starratt (1973) suggests, leaders seek to identify the roots of meaning and the flow and ebb of daily life in schools so that they can provide students, teachers, and members of the community with a sense of importance, vision, and purpose above the seemingly ordinary and mundane. Indeed, they work to bring to the school a sense of drama in human life that permits persons to rise above the daily routine that often characterizes their day-by-day activities. Symbolic leaders are able to see the significance of what a group is doing and indeed could be doing. They have a feel for the dramatic possibilities inherent in most situations and are able to urge people to go beyond the routine, to break out of the mold into something more lively and vibrant. Finally, symbolic leaders are able to communicate their sense of vision by words and examples. They use language symbols that are easily understood but that also communicate a sense of excitement, originality, and freshness. These efforts provide opportunities for others in the school to experience this vision and to gain a sense of purpose, feeling that they share in the ownership of the school enterprise.

Lieberman and Miller (1984) find that principals often practice symbolic leadership as opportunists and under serendipitous circumstances. They note, for example,

> *when complementing a teacher for a well-constructed and well-taught lesson, an administrator is making a statement that excellence is recognized and rewarded. When meeting with a teacher whose classroom is in revolt, the principal is expressing concern about what happens behind the closed doors of the classroom and signals a change from previous administrators who gave high marks to a teacher needing improvement. When attending department meetings that focus on curricular issues, the principal is supporting dialogue and informed action. All of these events and actions may be defined as educational leadership—not rational, linear, and planned; but ad hoc, responsive and realistic. Educational leadership happens, when it happens at all, within the cracks and around the edges of the job as defined and presently constituted. (76)*

Bennis (1984) finds that compelling vision is the key ingredient of leadership among heads of the highly successful organizations he studied. *Vision* refers to the capacity to create and communicate a view of a desired state of affairs that induces commitment among those working in the organization. Vision becomes the substance of what is communicated as symbolic aspects of leadership are emphasized. Principal Tom Davis speaks of vision as follows:

> *I think the first thing I think I'd do real well is I have a vision about what the school should be and about what this school should be in particular. . . . And I think that's essential to a number of things. I think it's important to inspire staff, both emotionally and intellectually. I think it needs to serve that function. Explicitly, I function to bring back the broader vision, the broader view . . . to bear on all the little pieces. That's something I work at very hard . . . so, because I've got all these semi-autonomous, really capable human beings out there, one major function is to keep it all going in one direction.*

He continues:

So the vision . . . has to inform the board, the parents, and staff—all the relation-
ships. It's a whole community, so it all has to be part of it. The vision has to include
not only a vision of what you do with children, but what you do in the process of
doing it with children. It has to be all of one fabric. (Prunty and Hively, 1982:66)

Lieberman and Miller (1984) speak of the power of the principal as the school's
"moral authority," who by actions, statements, and deeds makes symbolic statements. In describing this power from case study notes involving student discrimination, they state:

Principals can maintain neutrality and let things progress as they always have;
even that is a moral statement. Or they may take an active stance, threatening the
assumptions of staff members and moving a school in more progressive or more
regressive directions. Principals condone or condemn certain behaviors and atti-
tudes; they model moral precepts as they go about the job. When the administrators
at Albion took the side of minority students in the lunchroom radio incident, they
gave a clear message to faculty that discrimination by race was not to be tolerated.
A powerful message was transmitted. Had there been administrative apathy, an
equally powerful point would have been made. (76)

Principals are cast into powerful symbolic roles whether they intend it or not
and whether they like it or not. Inaction, in certain circumstances, can be as powerful a symbolic statement as is action.

The Semantics of Cultural Leadership

To understand and practice symbolic and cultural leadership, the emphasis needs
to be on the semantics of leadership, not the phonetics. What the leader does represents the phonetics. What the leader's actions and behaviors mean to others represents the semantics. Focusing on semantics helps in the understanding that very
often it is the little things that count. One does not have to mount a white horse and
charge forward in a grand dramatic event in order to be a symbolic leader. Simple
routines and humble actions properly orchestrated can communicate very important messages and high ideas.

Saphier and King (1985), for example, point out that the content of symbolic
and cultural leadership need not be different from that of technical, human, and
educational leadership. In their words, "Cultures are built through the everyday
business of school life. It is the way business is handled that both forms and reflects
the culture. . . . Culture building occurs . . . through the way people use educational,
human and technical skills in handling daily events or establishing regular practices" (72). Dwyer reaches a similar conclusion. In describing his research (Dwyer
et al., 1983), Dwyer notes:

Another fundamental characteristic of these principals was the routine nature of
their actions. Instead of leaders of large-scale or dramatic innovation, we found
men and women who shared a meticulous attention to detail. We observed an

attention to the physical and emotional elements of the school environment, school-community relations, the teaching staff, schoolwide student achievement, and individual student progress. Their most essential activities included forms of monitoring, information control and exchange, planning, direct interaction with students, hiring and staff development, and overseeing building maintenance. (1984:37)

It is through such routines that the principal focuses attention, demonstrates commitments, and otherwise "embarks on a slow but steady campaign to create a consensus of values and beliefs in a setting" (Dwyer, 1989:22). Appendix 5.1 shows how Frances Hedges, one of the principals studied by Dwyer and his colleagues, managed to practice symbolic and cultural leadership by tending to both routine and varied aspects of her work.

Reitzug and Reeves (1992) have used the forces of leadership framework as the basis for describing how symbolic leadership is practiced by principals. They studied the principal of an 800-student elementary school. Both the school and the principal were considered to be exemplary by the district's teachers and administrators. As the researchers sorted the observed leadership behaviors into the forces category, they were able to develop a taxonomy of symbolic leadership forms. The taxonomy appears as Table 5.1. This taxonomy might be helpful in sorting the behaviors of Frances Hedges, Mary Stewart—described in Appendix 1.3—and other principals. The relationships between the five leadership forces and successful schooling are summarized in Table 5.2.

The Dynamic Aspects of School Culture

Appendix 5.2, "A Primer on School Culture," provides an overview of school culture and its dimensions. Included are discussions of why culture is an integral and unavoidable part of school life, the levels of school culture, how culture can be developed, and the dark side of school culture.

All schools have cultures, but successful schools seem to have strong and functional cultures aligned with a vision of quality schooling. Culture serves as a compass setting to steer people in a common direction; it provides a set of norms defining what people should accomplish and how, and it is a source of meaning and significance for teachers, students, administrators, and others as they work. Strong and functional cultures are *domesticated* in the sense that they emerge deliberately—they are nurtured and built by the school leadership and membership.

Once shaped and established in a school, strong culture acts as a powerful socializer of thought and programmer of behavior. Yet, the shaping and establishment of such a culture don't just happen; they are, instead, a negotiated product of the shared sentiments of school participants. When competing points of view and competing ideologies exist in the school, deciding which ones will count requires some struggling. Principals are in an advantageous position to strongly influence the outcome of this struggle. They are, for example, in control of the communica-

TABLE 5.1   Taxonomy of Symbolic Leadership Forms

Technical	Human	Educational
Planning	Consideration	Diagnosing educational
Coordinating	Support	problems
Scheduling	Concerns	Coaching/counseling
Budgeting	Individuality	teachers on instruc-
Accounting	Autonomy	tional matters
Initiating structure	Encouragement	Supervision of
Forms management	Reinforcement	instruction
	Growth opportunities	Evaluation of instruction
	Building morale	Program development
	Shared decision	Curriculum development
	making	Staff development
	Conflict management	Discussing instructional
	Discipline	program
	Team building	Providing growth
	Counseling	opportunities

Symbolic/Culture

Actions	Language	Artifacts
Way time is spent	Conversations	Documents
Where energy is committed	Questions asked	Agendas
Meetings attended	Topics discussed	Handbooks
Where meetings are located	Announcements	Letters
Which items result in follow-up	Feedback given	Memos
Presiding over ceremonies, rituals	Gestures	Mission/vision
Things rewarded	Nonverbal	statements
Downplaying one type of activity	communication	Newsletters
(e.g., management) in favor of	Stories	Policy books
another (e.g., educational)	Jokes	School philosophies
Modeling	Myths	Slogans
Touring school	Legends	Teacher bulletins
Visiting classrooms	Favorite sayings	Grant proposals
Spending time with students, staff	Slogans	Written correspon-
Rituals	Recurring phrases	dence
Rites of passage	Rumors	Other documents
Ceremonies	Content of documents	School products
Way that resources are acquired	Songs sung	Badges, pins, buttons
What resources are requested	Books read	Displayed objects
Way that resources are expanded		Bulletin boards
Decisions made		
Materials distributed		*Artifacts (intangible)*
Gifts given		
Procedures/policies developed		Heroes
		Cultural network

TABLE 5.2   The Forces of Leadership and Excellence in Schooling

Force	Leadership Role Metaphor	Theoretical Constructs	Examples	Reactions	Link to Excellence
Technical	"Management engineer"	Planning and time management strategies Contingency leadership theories Organizational structure	Plan, organize, coordinate, and schedule Manipulate strategies and situations to ensure optimum effectiveness	People are managed as objects of a mechanical system. They react to efficient management with indifference but have a low tolerance for inefficient management.	Presence is important to achieve and maintain routine school competence but not sufficient to achieve excellence. Absence results in school ineffectiveness and poor morale.
Human	"Human engineer"	Human relation supervision Psychological theories of motivation Interpersonal competence Conflict management Group-cohesiveness	Provide needed support Encourage growth and creativity Build and maintain morale Use participatory decision making	People achieve high satisfaction of their interpersonal needs. They like the leader and the school and respond with positive interpersonal behavior. A pleasant atmosphere exists that facilitates the work of the school.	
Educational	"Principal teacher"	Professional knowledge and bearing Teaching effectiveness Educational program design Clinical supervision	Diagnose educational problems Counsel teachers Provide supervision and evaluation Provide inservice Develop curriculum	People respond positively to the strong expert power of the leader and are motivated to work. They appreciate the assistance and concern provided.	Presence is essential to routine competence. Strongly linked to, but still not sufficient for, excellence in schooling. Absence results in ineffectiveness.

Table 5.2 *Continued*

Force	Leadership Role Metaphor	Theoretical Constructs	Examples	Reactions	Link to Excellence
Symbolic	"Chief"	Selective attention Purposing Modeling	Tour the school Visit classrooms Know students Preside over ceremonies and rituals Provide a unified vision	People learn what is of value to the leader and school, have a sense of order and direction, and enjoy sharing that sense with others. They respond with increased motivation and commitment.	
Cultural	"High priest"	Climate, clan, culture Tightly structured values—loosely structured system Ideology "Bonding" motivation theory	Articulate school purpose and mission Socialize new members Tell stories and maintain reinforcing myths Explain SOPs Define uniqueness Develop and display a reinforcing symbol system Reward those who reflect the culture	People become believers in the school as an ideological system. They are members of a strong culture that provides them with a sense of personal importance and significance and work meaningfulness, which is highly motivating.	Presence is essential to excellence in schooling though absence does not appear to negatively affect routine competence.

Source: Adapted from "Leadership and Excellence in Schooling," by Thomas J. Sergiovanni, 1984, *Educational Leadership, 41*(5), page 12. Used by permission.

tions system of the school and thus can decide what information to share and with whom. Furthermore, they control the allocation of resources and are able to reward desirable (and sanction undesirable) behavior. Bates (1981) elaborates on the principal's influence in shaping school culture:

> *The culture of the school is therefore the product of conflict and negotiation over definitions of situations. The administrative influence on school language, meta-phor, myths and rituals is a major factor in the determination of the culture which is reproduced in the consciousness of teacher and pupils. Whether that culture is based on metaphors of capital accumulation, hierarchy and domination is at least partly attributable to the exercise of administrative authority during the negotiation of what is to count as culture in the school. (43)*

Can a culture emerge in a school based on agreements to disagree, on the maintenance of ambiguity over certainty, and on norms of variety and playfulness rather than order? Key for the concept of culture is the importance of collective ideology, shared values and sentiments, and norms that define acceptable behavior. The actual substance of culture is, by contrast, less important. Thus, not all schools with strong cultures are characterized by "harmony." Indeed, agreeing to disagree may well be the core value of a given school culture. This is often the case with respect to colleges and universities and to school research and development enterprises.

School Culture Building

Culture building requires that school leaders give attention to the informal, subtle, and symbolic aspects of school life. Teachers, parents, and students need answers to questions such as these: What is this school about? What is important here? What do we believe in? Why do we function the way we do? How are we unique? How do I fit into the scheme of things? Answering these questions imposes an order on one's school life that is derived from a sense of purpose and enriched meanings. Purpose and meaning are essential in helping the school become a community of mind. As Greenfield (1973) states:

> *What many people seem to want from schools is that schools reflect the values that are central and meaningful in their lives. If this view is correct, schools are cultural artifacts that people struggle to shape in their own image. Only in such forms do they have faith in them; only in such forms can they participate comfortably in them. (570)*

What is the purpose of leadership conceived as a cultural force? "The task of leadership is to create the moral order that binds them [leaders] and the people around them," notes Greenfield (1984:159). Quinn (1981) states: "The role of the leader, then, is one of orchestrator and labeler: taking what can be gotten in the way of action and shaping it—generally after the fact—into lasting commitment to a new strategic direction. In short, he makes meanings" (59). Leadership as culture building is not a new idea but one that is solidly embedded in our history and well known to successful school and other leaders. In 1957, Selznick wrote:

> *The art of the creative leader is the art of institution building, the reworking of human and technological materials to fashion an organism that embodies new and enduring values. . . . To institutionalize is to* infuse with value *beyond the technical requirements of the task at hand. The prizing of social machinery beyond its technical role is largely a reflection of the unique way it fulfills personal or group needs. Whenever individuals become attached to an organization or a way of doing things as persons rather than as technicians, the result is a prizing of the device for its own sake. From the standpoint of the committed person, the organization is changed from an expendable tool into a valued source of personal satisfaction. . . . The institutional leader, then, is primarily an expert in the promotion and protection of values. (28)*

In 1938, noted theorist Chester Barnard stated the following about executive functions: "The essential functions are, first to provide the system of communications; second, to promote the securing of essential efforts; and third, to formulate and define purpose." He continued: "It has already been made clear that, strictly speaking, purpose is defined more nearly by the aggregate of action taken than by any formulation in words" (vii).

Successful Schools and Central Zones

One of the findings revealed in the successful schools literature and in the community-building literature is that these schools have central zones comprising values and beliefs that take on sacred characteristics. Indeed, it might be useful to think of them as having an official "religion" that gives meaning and guides appropriate actions. As repositories of values, these central zones are sources of identity for teachers and students from which their school lives become meaningful. The focus of cultural leadership, then, is on developing and nurturing these central zone patterns so that they provide a normative basis for action within the school.

In some respects, the concept of central zone suggests that successful schools are tightly structured. This means that they are closely organized in a highly disciplined fashion around a set of core ideas spelling out the way of life in the school and governing the way in which people should behave. This is in contrast to recent developments in organizational theory that describe schools as being loosely structured entities (these developments were discussed in Part I). Cohen, March, and Olsen (1972), for example, speak of educational organizations as being "organized anarchies." Similarly, Weick (1982) uses the phrase "loose coupling" to describe the ways in which schools are organized. Indeed, Weick believes that one reason for ineffectiveness in schools is that they are managed with the wrong theory in mind.

Contemporary thought, Weick (1982) argues, assumes that schools are characterized by four properties: the existence of a self-correcting rational system among people who work in highly interdependent ways; consensus on goals and the means to obtain these goals; coordination by the dissemination of information; and predictability of problems and responses to these problems. He notes that, in fact, *none* of these properties is a true characteristic of schools and how they function. Principals in loosely coupled schools, he argues, need to make full use of symbol management to tie the system together. In his words: "People need to be part of sensible projects. Their action becomes richer, more confident, and more satisfying when it is linked with important underlying themes, values and movements" (675). He further states: "Administrators must be attentive to the 'glue' that holds loosely coupled systems together because such forms are just barely systems" (675). Finally, Weick notes that

> *the administrator who manages symbols does not just sit in his or her office mouthing clever slogans. Eloquence must be disseminated. And since channels are unpredictable, administrators must get out of the office and spend lots of time one on one—both to remind people of central visions and to assist them in applying these visions to their own activities. The administrator teaches people to interpret what they are doing in a common language. (676)*

Some commentators on the successful schools literature point out that these schools are not loosely coupled or structured at all but instead are tightly coupled (Cohen, 1983). A more careful study of this literature leads one to believe that successful schools are *both* tightly coupled and loosely coupled, an observation noted as well by Peters and Waterman (1982) in their studies of America's best-run corporations. There exists in successful schools a strong culture and clear sense of purpose that defines the general thrust and nature of life for their inhabitants. At the same time, a great deal of freedom is given to teachers and others as to how these essential core values are to be honored and realized. This combination of tight structure—around clear and explicit themes representing the core of the school's culture—and of autonomy—so that people can pursue these themes in ways that make sense to them—may well be a key reason why these schools are so successful.

The combination of tight structure and loose structure matches very well three important human characteristics associated with motivation to work, commitment, enthusiasm, and loyalty to the school:

1. The need for teachers, students, and other school workers to find their work and personal lives meaningful, purposeful, sensible, and significant
2. The need for teachers, students, and other school workers to have some reasonable control over their work activities and affairs and to be able to exert reasonable influence over work events and circumstances
3. The need for teachers, students, and other school workers to experience success, to think of themselves as winners, and to receive recognition for their success

People are willing to make a significant investment of time, talent, and energy in exchange for enhancement and fulfillment of these three needs (Hackman and Oldham, 1980; Peters and Waterman, 1982). The concept of combined tight and loose coupling in schools is developed further in Part III of this book as the importance of school goals and purposes is discussed. In the language of community, focusing on central zones of values, shared conceptions, covenants, and other idea structures are key to building a community of mind.

References

Barnard, Chester I. 1938. *The Functions of the Executive.* Cambridge, MA: Harvard University Press.

Bates, Richard. 1981. "Management and the Culture of the School," in Richard Bates and Course Team (Eds.), *Management of Resources in Schools: Study Guide I* (pp. 37–45). Geelong, Australia: Deakin University.

Bennis, Warren. 1984. "Transformation Power and Leadership," in Thomas J. Sergiovanni and John E. Corbally (Eds.), *Leadership and Organizational Culture.* Urbana-Champaign: University of Illinois Press.

Blumberg, Arthur, and William Greenfield. 1980. *The Effective Principal: Perspectives on School Leadership.* Boston: Allyn and Bacon.

Boyer, Ernest. 1983. *High School: A Report on Secondary Education in America.* New York: Harper & Row.

Clark, Burton R. 1972. "The Organizational Saga in Higher Education," *Administrative Science Quarterly* 17(2), 178–184.

Cohen, Michael. 1983. "Instructional Management and Social Conditions in Effective Schools," in Allan Odden and L. Dean Webb (Eds.), *School Finance and School Improvement: Linkages in the 1980's.* Yearbook of the American Educational Finance Association.

Cohen, Michael D., James G. March, and Johan Olsen. 1972. "A Garbage Can Model of Organizational Choice," *Administrative Science Quarterly* 17(1), 1–25.

Council of Chief State School Officers. 1996. *Interstate School Leaders Licensure Consortium: Standards for School Leaders.* Washington, DC: Author.

Dwyer, David. 1984. "The Search for Instructional Leadership: Routines and Subtleties in the Principal's Role," *Educational Leadership* 41(5).

Dwyer, David. 1989. "School Climate Starts at the Curb," *School Climate—The Principal Difference* (pp. 1–26). Monograph Series #1. The Connecticut Principals' Academy. Hartford, CT.

Dwyer, David, Ginny Lee, Brian Rowan, and Steven Bossert. 1983. *Five Principles in Action: Perspectives on Instructional Management.* San Francisco: Far West Laboratory for Educational Research and Development.

Goodlad, John L. 1978. "Educational Leadership: Toward the Third Era," *Educational Leadership* 23(4), 322–331.

Goodlad, John L. 1983. A *Study of Schooling.* New York: McGraw-Hill.

Greenfield, Thomas B. 1973. "Organizations as Social Inventions: Rethinking Assumptions about Change," *Journal of Applied Behavioral Science* 9(5).

Greenfield, Thomas B. 1984. "Leaders and Schools: Willfulness and Non-Natural Order in Organization," in Thomas J. Sergiovanni and John E. Corbally (Eds.), *Leadership and Organizational Culture.* Urbana-Champaign: University of Illinois Press.

Hackman, J. Richard, and Greg R. Oldham. 1980. *Work Redesign.* Reading, MA: Addison-Wesley.

Hackman, Ray C. 1969. *The Motivated Working Adult.* New York: American Management Association.

Hofstede, G. 1980. *Cultures Consequences.* Beverly Hills, CA: Sage Publications.

Lieberman, A., and L. Miller. 1984. *Teachers, Their World, and Their Work.* Arlington, VA: Association for Supervision and Curriculum Development.

March, James G. 1984. "How We Talk and How We Act: Administrative Theory and Administrative Life," in Thomas J. Sergiovanni and John

E. Corbally (Eds.), *Leadership and Organizational Culture* (pp. 18–35). Urbana-Champaign: University of Illinois Press.

Peters, Thomas J., and Robert H. Waterman, Jr. 1982. *In Search of Excellence.* New York: Harper & Row.

Pondy, Louis. 1978. "Leadership Is a Language Game," in Morgan W. McCall, Jr. and Michael M. Lombardo (Eds.), *Leadership: Where Else Can We Go?* Durham, NC: Duke University Press.

Prunty, John J., and Wells Hively. 1982, November 30. "The Principal's Role in School Effectiveness: An Analysis of the Practices of Four Elementary School Leaders." National Institute of Education (G 8-01-10) and CEMRL, Inc.

Quinn, James B. 1981, Winter. "Formulating Strategy One Step at a Time," *Journal of Business Strategy.*

Reeves, Jennifer Esler, and Ulrich C. Reitzug. 1992. "'Miss Lincoln Doesn't Teach Here': A Descriptive Narrative and Conceptual Analysis of a Principal's Symbolic Leadership Behavior," *Educational Administration Quarterly* 28(2), 185–219.

Saphier, John, and Matthew King. 1985. "Good Seeds Grow in Strong Cultures," *Educational Leadership* 42(6), 67–74.

Selznick, Philip. 1957. *Leadership and Administration: A Sociological Interpretation.* New York: Harper & Row.

Starratt, Robert J. 1973. "Contemporary Talk on Leadership: Too Many Kings in the Parade?" *Notre Dame Journal of Education* 4(1), 5–14.

United States Senate, Select Committee on Equal Educational Opportunity. 1972. "Revitalizing the Role of the School Principal," in *Toward Equal Educational Opportunity* (pp. 305–307). Senate Report No. 92-0000.

Vaill, Peter B. 1984. "The Purposing of High Performing Systems," in Thomas J. Sergiovanni and John E. Corbally (Eds.), *Leadership and Organizational Culture* (pp. 85–104). Urbana-Champaign: University of Illinois Press.

Weick, Karl E. 1982. "Administering Education in Loosely Coupled Schools," *Phi Delta Kappan* 27(2), 673–676.

Appendix 5.1   Frances Hedges and Orchard Park Elementary School

The year 1982 marked Orchard Park Elementary School's 35th year in the city of Hillsdale. Surrounding the school were rows of white, grey, pale green and pastel yellow houses, whose neatly trimmed yards were, by late summer, straw-colored from lack of water. The neighborhood itself was quiet, but the noises from a nearby freeway attested to its urban setting. The community's only distinctive landmark was an old church which occupied a large corner lot adjacent to the school. Its three onion-shaped spires had for years cast a sense of permanence over the entire community.

"Permanent," however, would be a somewhat misleading description of the area. Prior to 1960, white, middle-class families of Italian descent predominated in the neighborhood. Over the next few years increasing numbers of ethnic minorities moved out of the city's poorer neighborhoods to areas like Orchard Park's community, seeking better schools and better living conditions. As a result, Orchard Park's neighborhood lost its homogeneity, and some of its quiet, as a number of racial conflicts marred the community's tranquility. The school also was affected, and staff had to find a way to adapt the program to the needs of the newer students.

The new student body at Orchard Park Elementary School was characterized by a diversity of racial groups from various ethnic backgrounds. District records showed that as many as 10 different language groups were represented in the school's student population. Fifty-nine percent of the students were black; 13 percent reflected Spanish heritage; 16 percent were Asian (Chinese, Filipino, Samoan, Laotian, and Vietnamese); and 11 percent were white. Other ethnic groups composed the remaining one percent. The majority of the students' families were of low- or lower-middle income status. These students were energetic and active, frequently exhibiting aggressive behavior that stemmed more from overexuberance than from any other motivation. Groups at play were observed to be multiethnic and solicitous of affection and approval from teachers and the principal. Warm hugs exchanged between staff members and students were common occurrences on the playground.

Orchard Park employed 25 teachers, the majority of whom were very experienced. There were few signs of negativism, criticism or conflict among these teachers despite the fact that their instructional approaches differed markedly. Generally, they were supportive of the school and particularly of the principal. One teacher told us that there was only one reason for staff turnover at Orchard Park—retirement. Further evidence of their satisfaction with the status quo came at the end of the year of our study. The staff, together with the community, rallied to prevent the transfer of their principal and came together to hold a "Principal Appreciation" gathering to honor Hedges' leadership.

Source: Excerpted from "School Climate Starts at the Curb," *School Climate—The Principal Difference* by David Dwyer, 1989. Hartford: The Connecticut Principals' Academy. Reprinted by permission.

Appendix 5.1   *Continued*

The center of attention at that ceremony, Frances Hedges, was a 60-year-old black woman who had served at Orchard Park for six and a half years. She conveyed to all who met her a sense of elegance through her well-matched clothes, golden earrings, oversized glasses and neatly fashioned white hair. Her appearance contrasted to the casual style adhered to by most of her staff; she was easily distinguished as the person in charge.

Long before coming to Orchard Park, Hedges had attended a teachers' college in her hometown, originally intending to become a child psychologist. But economic considerations prevented her from pursuing this goal. Instead, she spent 21 years as a classroom teacher, mostly in the district that includes Orchard Park. After receiving a Masters Degree in educational administration, she gradually climbed to her current position by working as a reading resource teacher, a district program coordinator, and a vice principal.

Hedges' manner with staff and students was personable. Whether discussing professional matters or just making small talk, she conveyed warmth and friendliness through smiles and laughter. She was generous with compliments to both students and teachers. She also communicated often and comfortably through touches, hugs and embraces. As a result, she frequently was referred to by both students and teachers as Orchard Park's "mother figure."

Hedges' way of acting was consistent with her philosophy. She strongly adhered to what she termed "humanistic" beliefs about education. She explained:

> *My philosophy is that if we are warm and humane and nurturing, we maximize the learning of children. There is just no way to separate out those basic needs.*

Believing that she was "acutely sensitive to...children's needs as well as adults' needs," Hedges strove to keep everyone in her learning community "reasonably happy" and worked to help everyone strengthen their self-concepts.

Attending to the basic needs of children logically led to Hedges' attention to safety and order in her school. She was a strict disciplinarian and never hesitated to reprimand children for misbehavior. Her harsh words, however, always would be followed by her efforts to help children understand their mistakes and become more responsible for their own behavior. She said:

> *I believe that if we are really going to change the behavior of children, we can't just say "stop that," without going a step further and really having some kind of dialogue about what took place, why, and what are the options.*

Her philosophy of education also included tenets about instruction. She strongly believed in the importance of academics, particularly reading. She pronounced:

Appendix 5.1   *Continued*

Reading is by far our number one priority. I believe that if children don't know how to read, they really cannot make it in this world.

Thus, Hedges' beliefs about education were related to her concerns for both the social and academic well-being of her students. It came as no surprise to find that her goals for the school reflected those convictions.

Hedges' primary goal at Orchard Park was to build a program conducive to the emotional and social growth of her students. She wanted her staff both to instill in each child a love for learning and to foster an awareness of social responsibility. She was adamant that her staff actively seek to strengthen students' self-concepts. These goals, she believed, were pre-eminent. They were a foundation upon which successful academic experiences could be built.

The principal's concern for the academic growth of her students was always stated from a "whole-child" perspective. Delineating her academic goals, she said:

We work very hard to try to make sure that in the six or seven years that boys and girls are in elementary school, that they leave this school operating at grade level or above. . . . I'd like to see them at grade level for at least their last two years so that they can go into junior high school as much stronger and more confident children.

Hedges actively promoted both her social and academic goals to her faculty. During the year of our study with her, she utilized a district mandate to develop and implement an integrated, three-year instructional plan as a major vehicle to communicate her goals and develop her staff's commitment to them. Evidence that she had been very successful in this aspect of her work accumulated as we interviewed teachers about their beliefs and goals. In virtually all instances, their statements echoed Hedges' own.

How did Frances Hedges bring about the warm and productive climate at Orchard Park? Hedges demonstrated a propensity for direct, face-to-face interaction with participants in her setting. In total, 51 percent of her activities were verbal exchanges of varying length. The other glaring fact in the Orchard Park story is that her routine actions directly affected the climate at Orchard Park, making it conducive to teaching and learning.

Both the value she placed on students' emotional well-being and her goal to improve students' self-esteem contributed to a vision of school climate as an important end in itself. In addition, her beliefs about schools and schooling linked climate to instruction in several ways: she considered students' emotional well-being as an important precursor to their learning; she regarded an orderly, disciplined environment as a necessary condition for teaching and learning to take place; and she believed that the improvement of teachers' instructional practices was best achieved in a setting that built on the positive aspects of their skills. Thus, she strove

Appendix 5.1   *Continued*

to maintain an environment that contributed to the happiness, safety, and productivity of all participants.

We see in many of Hedges' routine actions the keys to the development and maintenance of Orchard Park's social milieu. Her actions, as she supervised students in the building and on the playgrounds, attended simultaneously to the need to maintain safety and order at the school and to build students' self-esteem. She monitored their conduct and corrected them when necessary, exchanging her views about responsible behavior and reinforcing school rules. She constantly reminded students to pick up trash, bus their trays in the cafeteria, play in the correct areas of the playyard, walk instead of run in the hallways, refrain from pushing and shoving, and be quiet in the corridors and auditorium. She utilized these same actions to carry out her more social goals: she frequently stopped to talk to students, expressing delight at seeing them or remarking about the clothes they were wearing. Children often approached her to describe important events in their lives. Many of these brief interactions were concluded with a hug exchanged between the principal and the youngster.

An additional strategy Hedges used in her supervision of students was to model appropriate behavior. She might, for example, pick up a piece of trash and deposit it in a container or take a food tray to the cafeteria kitchen as she reminded students of the rules, often mentioning that they should keep the school as tidy as they would their homes.

Hedges' desire to counsel students played a large part in her interactions with children, especially those who had committed some infraction of school rules. We witnessed many instances of her counselor-like approach as she dealt with students whom she had seen misbehaving or who had been sent to her for fighting, stealing, acting inappropriately in class, or failing to complete their school work. In all instances, she carefully took the time to listen to what the students had to say about their behavior. Hedges explained this strategy in terms of her humanistic philosophy:

> *If you don't do something, [children] feel . . . that their problems are falling on deaf ears. I tell the staff all the time, "You really do have to take the time out, let a child explain what happened, and be willing to at least listen, whether it's what that particular child wants, or not . . . it's just that someone has listened."*

Students were aware that Hedges would act vigorously and appropriately if they misbehaved as well as listen to their problems. When infractions were serious, Hedges would tell students that she was going to phone their parents to report incidents . . . she always followed through. As a result Orchard Park's students understood that their principal was serious about discipline and true to her word.

We mentioned earlier the importance that Hedges placed on building on the positive aspects of people in the school. This approach was most apparent in her dealings with problem students as she implemented special plans to communicate

Appendix 5.1   *Continued*

to them that, despite misbehavior, they were still worthy human beings and could act responsibly. We observed one instance in which Hedges appointed the worst offenders in the school as "Chair Captains" and allowed them to pick their own squads who would help set up and take down chairs in the auditorium. The youngsters saw this as an important and enjoyable responsibility that gave them status among their peers. In another instance, Hedges urged that a child who had a particularly negative attitude toward school be assigned to the traffic detail. His teacher remarked that this made a dramatic improvement in the boy's classroom behavior and attitude.

When infractions were serious. Hedges often assigned offenders work projects around the school that would contribute to the school's overall welfare. She tenaciously pursued alternatives to suspension. One teacher reported of the principal's efforts to deal with problem students:

> [Hedges] has a relationship with almost all of the children that regularly act out, the ones that are really on your blacklist . . . if it's your child that's constantly acting out, you would almost want her to say, "Doggone! Let's give up on that kid." But she never really does.

Hedges not only worked creatively with problem students but encouraged growth in responsibility among all students at Orchard Park. For example, she taught leadership to all members of the school's student council.

Orchard Park's teachers also were encouraged to promote positive social values in the school through classroom activities. In an unusual departure from Hedges' policy of permitting a good deal of staff autonomy concerning the selection of classroom materials, for example, she established a schoolwide focus on her social goals through the introduction of a set of self-esteem materials. At the first faculty meeting of the year, Hedges presented the materials and asked staff members to use them as a regular part of their programs. Although the use of these materials was not systematically monitored, her message was clear to her staff. Subsequently, teachers were observed using an array of esteem-building activities in their classrooms, including magic circle activities, life box materials, and art projects to stimulate discussions about feelings and attitudes.

Thus Hedges aggressively pursued a positive school climate at Orchard Park. By demonstrating her values in her daily interactions and conversations. Hedges encouraged an environment in which staff members shared her child-centered approach. Participants in the setting directly and indirectly exhibited their satisfaction: there was very little vandalism by students in the school, teachers felt lucky to be at the school and left only because of retirement, and the district held a waiting list of teachers anxious to join this faculty.

Hedges also directly or indirectly manipulated such important elements of the organization as class size and composition, scheduling, staff assignments, the scope and sequence of curriculum, the distribution of instructional materials, and even

Appendix 5.1   *Continued*

teaching styles. On the surface, a principal actively and successfully engaged in shaping the conditions for and of instruction in a school seems perfectly natural—principals are supposed to be instructional leaders, right? But we also know that teachers enjoy and expect autonomy in matters related to classroom instruction. It is not uncommon for teachers to actively or passively resist principals' instructional improvement campaigns.

Hedges was able to transcend this problem for two reasons. First, her own 21 years of experience as a classroom teacher and reading specialist legitimated her expertise in the eyes of her faculty. The second ingredient to Hedges' success at influencing her staff's classroom practices was her ability to establish a culture of instruction at the school, facilitated by the emphasis she placed on building on people's strengths and emphasizing the positive. Thus, experience coupled with style enabled her to provide information to teachers without alienating them. Her staff regarded her as competent and nonthreatening. They not only accepted her suggestions, but actively sought her advice and counsel.

While there were many strategies that Hedges used to influence instruction both directly and indirectly at the school, the most potent and pervasive was the informal classroom visit. Hedges monitored instruction by regularly dropping into teachers' classrooms. These visits provided opportunities to make suggestions that did not carry the onus that might accompany recommendations made as the result of formal classroom evaluations. On many of Hedges' informal visits, we observed her assisting teachers by working with students and making brief constructive and supportive comments to her staff.

These often-repeated behaviors were key features in her strategy to reduce teachers' anxieties about her visits. She mentioned that she spent time building positive rapport with teachers before providing suggestions for changes in their instructional patterns:

> *I operate with the idea that we really are all a team. If I can just ... give [the staff] enough strokes on those positives, then I can get [at] those areas that are not so well done.*

When Hedges did feel a need to comment on teachers' deficiencies, she did so in a low-key, nonthreatening manner without embarrassing, confronting, or demeaning them.

Hedges also promoted a norm of teacher-to-teacher sharing because she did not see herself as the only source of instructional expertise in the school. She often advised teachers to talk with their colleagues for assistance or ideas. Frequently this required Hedges to organize opportunities for staff members to get together. For example, she commonly arranged for the school's reading specialist to help teachers create reading centers in a classroom or help classroom teachers evaluate those students who required remedial instruction. There were many instances of Hedges

Appendix 5.1   *Continued*

arranging meetings between teachers who were successful with new methods and teachers who were less successful. In this way, she served as a "linking agent" or "information broker." Because Hedges' classroom visits were regular, her recommendations were timely and the staff found them very helpful. Hedges also used classroom visits as opportunities to impress upon children the importance she attached to academic success. By publicly complementing students on their individual or group successes, she not only strengthened their self-esteem, but created an ethos about learning that children would want to share....

Her philosophy is marked by simple tenets: all people are fundamentally good; everyone can learn and grow in a warm and nurturing environment; any successful enterprise is the result of teamwork and everyone can and must contribute to the whole. From experience, Hedges adds to these beliefs a strongly held value regarding the importance of reading as an essential skill that children must master to realize their highest potential. These humane attributes are wrapped in her tough-minded awareness about the importance of setting limits and making children and staff responsible for their own behavior.

Hedges leads her school by continually communicating her beliefs to parents, students, and staff members through her routine actions. By constant word and deed she demonstrates how the vision she holds of the "good" school must work. Mostly she proceeds through patient, subtle suggestions and reminders. Occasionally, she mandates changes or additions to organizational structures, procedures, and curricula. But the key to her success is the relentless pursuit of her goals and her talent in getting others to adopt those goals.

Over years at Orchard Park, staff have experimented with procedures and techniques Hedges has recommended. They have been continually bombarded with her rationale. As they experience success, the procedures and rationales become embedded in their own experiences and slowly alter their own beliefs. Slowly, a working consensus about the "right" way to teach and run a school emerges. As those beliefs fade into assumptions and become habituated, an organizational culture is born. Its progenitor, its patient nurseryman, was Frances Hedges.

Appendix 5.2   A Primer on School Culture

In every school there are observable behavioral regularities defined by the rules of the game for getting along. These rules are norms that define for people what is right and correct to do, what is acceptable, and what is expected. Norms are expressions of certain values and beliefs held by members of the work group. When trying to understand how norms emerge and work, the metaphor of culture can be helpful. Some experts may debate whether schools really have cultures or not, but the issue is less the reality of culture and more what can be learned by thinking about schools as cultures. The metaphor school culture helps direct attention to the symbols, behavioral regularities, ceremonies, and even myths that communicate to people the underlying values and beliefs that are shared by members of the organization.

External Adoption and Internal Integration

Schein believes that the term *culture* "should be reserved for the deeper level of *basic assumptions* and *beliefs* that are shared by members of an organization, that operate unconsciously, and that define in a basic 'taken-for-granted' fashion an organization's view of itself and its environment" (Schein, 1985:6). The concept of culture is very important, for its dimensions are much more likely to govern what it is that people think and do than is the official management system. Teachers, as suggested earlier, are much more likely to teach in ways that reflect the shared assumptions and beliefs of the faculty as a whole than they are in ways that administrators want, supervisors say, or teacher evaluation instruments require.

Following Argyris (1964), Merton (1957), and Parsons (1951), Schein (1985) points out that schools and other organizations must solve two basic problems if they are to be effective: external adoption and survival and internal integration. The problems of *external adoption and survival* are themed to:

1. Mission and strategy (how to reach a shared understanding of the core mission of the school and its primary tasks)
2. Goals (developing a consensus on goals that are linked to the core mission)
3. Means (reaching consensus on the managerial and organizational means to be used to reach goals)
4. Standards (reaching consensus on the criteria to be used to determine how well the group is doing in fulfilling its goals and whether it is meeting its commitments to agreed-upon processes)
5. Correction (reaching consensus on what to do if goals are not being met)

The problems of *internal integration* are themed to:

1. Developing a common set of understandings that facilitates communication, organizes perceptions, and helps to categorize and make common meanings

Appendix 5.2   *Continued*

2. Developing criteria for determining who is in and out and how one determines membership in the group
3. Working out the criteria and rules for determining who gets, maintains, and loses power
4. Working out the rules for peer relationships and the manner in which openness and intimacy are to be handled as organizational tasks are pursued
5. "Every group must know what its heroic and sinful behaviors are; what gets rewarded with property, status and power; and what gets punished in the form of withdrawal of the rewards and, ultimately, excommunication" (Schein, 1985:66)
6. Dealing with issues of ideology and sacredness: "Every organization, like every society, faces unexplainable and inexplicable events, which must be given meaning so that members can respond to them and avoid the anxiety of dealing with the unexplainable and uncontrollable" (Schein, 1985:66).

As issues of external adoption and internal integration are solved, schools and other organizations are better able to give full attention to the attainment of their goals and have the means for allowing people to derive sense and meaning from their work lives—to see their work as being significant. In summarizing his stance, Schein (1985) notes that culture is *"a pattern of basic assumptions—invented, discovered or developed by a given group as it learns to cope with its problems of external adaptation and internal integration—that has worked well enough to be considered valid and, therefore, to be taught to new members as the correct way to perceive, think, and feel in relation to those problems"* (9). Because the assumptions have resulted in decisions and behaviors that have worked repeatedly, they are likely to be taken for granted. This point is important because the artifacts of culture, such as symbols, rites, traditions, and behaviors, are different from the actual content and substance of culture; the basic assumptions that govern what is thought to be true, what is right, and for all intents and purposes, what is reality for the school. As mentioned in earlier discussions of culture, the central zone that Shils (1961) speaks of is composed of assumptions, values, and beliefs. The values and beliefs are often manifest, but the assumptions are typically tacit.

Levels of Culture

Because assumptions and basic beliefs are typically tacit, they are inferred from manifestations of cultures such as the school's climate (Dwyer, 1989) and the rites and rituals of the school's organizational life (Deal, 1985). To account for both, it is useful to think about dimensions of school culture as existing at least four levels (Dyer, 1982; Schein, 1981; 1985). The most tangible and observable level is represented by the *artifacts* of culture as manifested in what people say, how people behave, and how things look. Verbal artifacts include the language systems that are

Appendix 5.2   *Continued*

used, stories that are told, and examples that are used to illustrate certain important points. Behavioral artifacts are manifested in the ceremonies and rituals and other symbolic practices of the school. The interpersonal life of the school as represented by the concept of school climate is an important artifact of culture.

Less discernible but still important is the level of *perspectives*. Perspectives refer to the shared rules and norms to which people respond, the commonness that exists among solutions to similar problems, how people define the situations they face, and the boundaries of acceptable and unacceptable behavior. Often, perspectives are included in statements of the school's purposes or its covenant when these include ways in which people are to work together as well as the values that they share.

The third level is that of *values*. Values provide the basis for people to judge or evaluate the situations they face, the worth of their actions and activities, their priorities, and the behaviors of people with whom they work. Values not only specify what is important but often the things that are not important. In schools the values are arranged in a fashion that represents the covenant that the principal, teachers, and others share. As discussed in Chapter 8, this covenant might be in the form of an educational or management platform, statements of school philosophy, mission statements, and so forth.

The fourth level is that of *assumptions*. Assumptions are "the tacit beliefs that members hold about themselves and others, their relationships to other persons, and the nature of the organization in which they live. Assumptions are the nonconscious underpinnings of the first three levels—that is, the implicit, abstract axioms that determine the more explicit system of meanings" (Lundberg, 1985:172).

Identifying the Culture of Your School

The four levels of culture provide a framework for analyzing the culture of a school. Because assumptions are difficult to identify firsthand, they often must be inferred from what is found at the artifacts, perspectives, and values levels. Much can be learned from examining the school's history. Deal (1985) points out, for example, that

> *each school has its story of origin, the people or circumstances that launched it, and those who presided over its course thereafter. Through evolutionary development—crises and resolutions, internal innovations and external pressures, plans and chance occurrences—the original concept was shaped and reshaped into an organic collection of traditions and distinctive ways. Throughout a school's history, a parade of students, teachers, principals, and parents cast sustaining memories. Great accomplishments meld with dramatic failures to form a potentially cherishable lore. (615)*

The following questions might be helpful in uncovering a school's history:

Appendix 5.2   *Continued*

How does the school's past live in the present?

What traditions are still carried on?

What stories are told and retold?

What events in the school's history are overlooked or forgotten?

Do heroes and heroines exist among teachers and students whose idiosyncrasies and exploits are still remembered?

In what ways are the school's traditions and historical incidents modified through reinterpretation over the years? Can you recall, for example, a historical event that has evolved from fact to myth?

Believing that an organization's basic assumptions about itself can be revealed through its history, Schein (1985) suggests that the organization's history be analyzed by identifying all major crises, crucial transitions, and other times of high emotion. For each event identified, reconstruct how management dealt with the issue, how it identified its role, and what it did and why. Patterns and themes across the various events identified should then be analyzed and checked against current practices. The next step is to identify the assumptions that were behind the actions taken in the past and check whether those assumptions are still relevant for present actions.

To uncover beliefs, ask what are the assumptions and understandings that are shared by teachers and others, though they may not be explicitly stated. These may relate to how the school is structured, how teaching takes place, the roles of teachers and students, what is believed about discipline, and the relationship of parents to the school. Sometimes assumptions and understandings are written down somewhere in the form of a philosophy or other value statements. Whether that is the case or not, beliefs can best be understood by being inferred from examples of current practices.

According to Schein, one important set of basic assumptions revolves around the theme of what is believed about human nature and how these beliefs then affect policies and decisions. To address this issue, he suggests that an attempt be made to identify organizational heroes and villains, successful people, and those who are less successful, and compare the stories that are told about them. He recommends as well that recruitment selection and promotion criteria be examined to see if indeed they are biased toward selecting a certain type of person into the organization and promoting that type. An analysis of who gets rewarded and who gets punished can also be revealing. Do patterns emerge from this sort of analysis? Are there common assumptions about people that begin to emerge?

Values can be identified by asking what things the school prizes. That is, when teachers and principals talk about the school, what are the major and recurring value themes underlying what they say? When problems emerge, what are the values that seem to surface as being relied on in developing solutions?

Appendix 5.2   *Continued*

Norms and standards can be identified by asking what are the oughts, shoulds, do's, and don'ts that govern the behavior of teachers and principals, and examining what behaviors get rewarded and what behaviors get punished in the school. What are the accepted and recurring ways of doing things, the patterns of behavior, the habits and rituals that prevail?

Hansen (1986) suggests that teachers discuss the following questions when seeking to identify the culture of their school: Describe your work day both in and outside of the school. On what do you spend your time and energy? Given that most students forget what they learn, what do you hope your students will retain over time from your teaching? Think of students whom you are attracted to—those whom you admire, respect, or enjoy. What common characteristics do these students share? What does it take for a teacher to be successful in your school? What advice would you give to new teachers who want to be successful? What do you remember about past faculty members and students in your school? If you were to draw a picture or take a photo or make a collage that represented some aspect of your school, what would it look like? How are students rewarded?

The Dark Side of School Culture

The benefits of a strong school culture are clear. Culture represents an effective means of coordination and control in a loosely connected and nonlinear world. Its covenant or center of purposes and shared values represents a source of inspiration, meaning, and significance for those who live and work in the school. These qualities can lead to enhanced commitment and performance that are beyond expectations. As a result, the school is better able to achieve its goals.

Yet, there is a dark side to the concept of school culture, as well. Weick (1985) points out, for example, that

> *a coherent statement of who we are makes it harder for us to become something else. Strong cultures are tenacious cultures. Because a tenacious culture can be a rigid culture that is slow to detect changes and opportunities and slow to change once opportunities are sensed, strong cultures can be backward, conservative instruments of adaptation. (385)*

Furthermore, the presence of a strong norm system in a school can collectively program the minds of people in such a way that issues of reality come into question. If this is carried to the extreme, the school might come to see reality in one way but its environment in another. Finally, there is the question of rationality. As commitment to a course of action increases, people become less rational in their actions. Strong cultures are committed cultures, and in excess, commitment takes its toll on rational action.

Appendix 5.2   *Continued*

Schein points out that as organizations mature, the prevailing culture becomes so entrenched that it becomes a constraint on innovation. Culture preserves the glories of the past and hence becomes valued as a source of self-esteem and as a means of defense rather than for what it represents and the extent to which it serves purposes (Schein, 1985).

The Importance of a Loyal Opposition

If the purposes and covenants that constitute cultural centers are highly dynamic and fluid, school cultures are likely to be weak and ineffectual. By the same token, if they are cast in granite, they can squelch individuality and innovation. The alternative is to build a resilient culture—one that can bend to change here and there, but not break; that can stretch in a new direction and shrink from an old, but still maintain its integrity; a culture that is able to bounce back and recover its strength and spirit, always maintaining its identity. Key to resiliency is the cultivation of a small but energetic loyal opposition made of

> *people with whom we enjoy an honest, high-trusting relationship but who have conflicting visions, goals or methods. . . . The task of the (loyal opposition) is to bring out the best in us. We need to be grateful for those who oppose us in a high-trust way, for they bring the picture of reality and practicality to our plans. (Block, 1987:135–136)*

Block believes that it is important when working with the loyal opposition that the leader communicate the extent to which they are valued. Leaders can do this, in his view, by reaffirming the quality of the relationship and the fact that it's based on trust. They should be clear in stating their positions and the reasons why they hold them. They should also state in a neutral way what they think positions of the loyal opposition are. The leader reasons as follows:

> *We disagree with respect to purpose, goals, and perhaps even visions. Our task is to understand their position. Our way of fulfilling that task is to be able to state to them their arguments in a positive way. They should feel understood and acknowledged by our statement of their disagreement with us. (Block, 1987:137)*

With this kind of relationship in place, the leadership and the loyal opposition are in a position to negotiate differences in good faith.

Appendix 5.2   *Continued*

References

Argyris, Chris. 1964. *Integrating the Individual and the Organization.* New York: Wiley.

Block, Peter. 1987. *The Empowered Manager.* San Francisco: Jossey-Bass.

Deal, Terrence E. 1985. "The Symbolism of Effective Schools," *The Elementary School Journal* 85(5).

Dwyer, David C. 1989. "School Climate Starts at the Curb," in *School Climate—The Principal Difference.* Hartford: The Connecticut Principals' Academy.

Dyer, W. G., Jr. 1982. *Patterns and Assumptions: The Keys to Understanding Organizational Culture.* Office of Naval Research, Technical Report TR-O NR-7.

Hall, John W. 1972. "A Comparison of the Halpin and Croft's 'Organizational Climates' and Likert and Likert's 'Organizational Systems,'" *Administrative Science Quarterly* (17), 586–590.

Hansen, Corwith. 1986. "Department Culture in a High-Performing Secondary School." Unpublished dissertation, Teachers College, Columbia University.

Likert, Rensis. 1961. *New Patterns of Management.* New York: McGraw-Hill.

Likert, Rensis. 1967. *The Human Organization: Its Management and Value.* New York: McGraw-Hill.

Lundberg, Craig C. 1985. "On the Feasibility of Cultural Intervention in Organizations," in Peter J. Frost, Larry F. Moore, Meryl Reis Louis, Craig C. Lundberg, and Joanne Martin (Eds.), *Organizational Culture.* Beverly Hills, CA: Sage Publications.

Merton, Robert K. 1957. *Social Theory and Social Structure.* New York: The Free Press.

Parsons, Talcott. 1951. *The Social System.* New York: The Free Press.

Schein, Edgar H. 1981. "Does Japanese Management Style Have a Message for American Managers?" *Sloan Management Review* 24(1), 55–68.

Schein, Edgar H. 1985. *Organizational Culture and Leadership.* San Francisco: Jossey-Bass.

Shils, Edward A. 1961. "Centre and Periphery," in *The Logic of Personal Knowledge: Essays Presented to Michael Polanyi.* London: Routledge and Kegan Paul.

Weick, Karl E. 1985. "The Significance of Culture," in Peter J. Frost, Larry F. Moore, Meryl Reis Louis, Craig C. Lundberg, and Joanne Martin (Eds.), *Organizational Culture.* Beverly Hills, CA: Sage Publications.

6

THE STAGES OF LEADERSHIP
A Developmental View

Not every situation a principal faces requires the same leadership strategy. The principal of a highly competent and well-motivated faculty will have to proceed one way and the principal of a developing and uncommitted faculty will have to proceed another way. As is the case with most craftlike fields where one must create her or his practice in use depending on circumstances, no one best approach to leadership will work. Instead, principals must practice leadership in light of the context they face. In this chapter we are concerned with four leadership strategies and tactics that are available to principals, each being appropriate at different times during the development of an effective school (Sergiovanni, 1990, 1994):

1. *Bartering.* Principals and teachers strike a bargain within which the leader gives to those led something they want in exchange for what the leader wants. The emphasis in bartering is on trading wants and needs for cooperation and compliance. This approach works best when the principal and teachers do not share common goals and interests—when their stakes in the school are different.
2. *Building.* Principals provide the climate and interpersonal support that enhances teachers' opportunities for fulfillment of individual needs for achievement, responsibility, competence, and esteem. The emphasis in building is less on trading and more on providing the conditions that enable teachers to experience psychological fulfillment. Once a minimum level of common effort has been achieved, this approach is recommended to shift the emphasis from extrinsic to intrinsic rewards.
3. *Bonding.* Principals and teachers develop together a set of shared values about the relationships they want to share and the ties they want to create so that together they can become a community of learners and leaders—a community of colleagues. The emphasis in bonding is on relationships characterized by mutual caring and the felt interdependence that comes from mutually held

obligations and commitments. This approach strives to shift the emphasis from what the principal provides to obligations and commitments teachers feel toward each other.

4. *Binding.* Principals and teachers together commit themselves to a set of shared values and ideas that ties them together as a "we." The emphasis in binding is on developing common commitments and conceptions about purposes, teaching and learning, and the relationships that bring people together as a community of mind, heart, and practice. Binding is recommended as a means to establish the moral authority that calls on teachers to be morally responsive.

Taken together the strategies can be thought of as developmental stages, each suited to different levels of school competence and excellence. The stages are elaborated in Table 6.2 later in this chapter. But first, let's turn our attention to the sources of authority for leadership—the assumptions and theories that principals use to legitimize their practice.

The Sources of Authority for Leadership

When leadership is viewed as developmental stages, the emphasis is not on which leadership strategy is best, but which of the strategies makes most sense given the stage of school improvement in question. Leadership by bartering, for example, makes most sense in schools that are not working very well. Leadership by bonding, by contrast, makes sense when basic competence is not the issue and when a healthy interpersonal climate has been established. Each of the stages and leadership strategies can be understood by examining the sources of authority for leadership and by being linked to the transactional and transformational leadership types provided by Burns (1978).

The challenge for principals is to provide the leadership needed to achieve a basic level of competence and then to transcend this competence to get extraordinary commitment and performance not only when rewards are available but when they are not. Sustained commitment and performance require an approach to leadership that connects people to work for moral reasons. Moral reasons emerge from the purposes, values, and norms that form the cultural center of the school. This center bonds people together in a common cause. For this reason, the leadership that is required is referred to as *bonding* leadership. Bonding leadership is key in cultivating self-management among teachers. This leadership is contrasted with the more common traditional and human resources approaches to leadership as follows:

1. *Traditional leadership* practices emphasize hierarchy, rules, and management protocols and rely on bureaucratic linkages to connect people to work by forcing them to respond as subordinates.
2. *Human resource leadership* practices emphasize leadership styles, supportive climates, and interpersonal skills and rely on psychological linkages to motivate people to work by getting them to respond ultimately as self-actualizers.

3. *Bonding leadership* practices emphasize ideas, values, and beliefs and rely on moral linkages to compel people to work by getting them to respond as followers.

Traditional leadership practices rely on bureaucratic values as their source of authority. Teachers (and students, too, since this discussion of sources of authority and their implicit assumptions applies to the leadership that both principals and teachers use in relating to students) are expected to comply with the rules and to follow the provided scripts or face the consequences. In a sense, they trade compliance to avoid problems with the system. Bureaucratic authority has a place even in the most progressive of schools. Yet, when this source of authority is central, the following assumptions seem to be implicit:

Teachers are subordinates in a hierarchically arranged system.

Principals are trustworthy, but you cannot trust teachers.

The goals and interests of teachers and principals are not the same; therefore, principals must be watchful.

Hierarchy equals expertise; thus, principals know more than do teachers about everything.

External accountability works best. (Sergiovanni and Starratt, 1993:25)

The consequences of relying on a leadership based primarily on bureaucratic authority have been carefully documented. Without proper monitoring, principals wind up being loosely connected to bureaucratic systems complying only when they have to (Sergiovanni, 1990–1991; Weick, 1976). When this monitoring is effective, teachers respond as technicians who execute predetermined scripts and whose performance becomes narrowed. They become, to use the jargon, "deskilled" (McNeil, 1986; Rosenholtz, 1989; Wise, 1979). When teachers are not able to use their full talents and when they are caught in the drudgery of routine, they become separated from their work, viewing teaching as a job rather than a vocation and treating students as cases rather than persons.

Very few people mean to advocate a leadership practice based primarily on bureaucratic authority or mean to accept the implicit assumptions that are behind this practice. Not many principals, for example, believe that teachers as a group are not trustworthy and do not share the same goals and interests about schooling as they do. Even fewer would accept the idea that hierarchy equals expertise, and, thus, they know more about everything than do teachers. Even so, most principals are likely to feel that teachers are subordinates in a hierarchically arranged system and that external monitoring works best. For this reason, supervision based on external monitoring persists. Principals still rely heavily on "expect and expect," predetermined standards, inservicing teachers, and direct supervision.

Human resources leadership practices rely heavily on personal expertise and skill in motivating and manipulating people as their source of authority. Essentially the idea is to figure out which psychological buttons to push when motivating teachers, and if the right ones are chosen, then teachers willingly trade compliance with the principal's wishes for getting needs met. When principals place personal authority at the center of their leadership practice, the following assumptions seem to be implicit:

> The goals and interests of teachers and principals are not the same. As a result, each must barter with the other so that both get what they want by giving something that the other party wants.

> Teachers have needs and if these needs are met at work, their work gets done as required in exchange.

> Congenial relationships in pleasant interpersonal climates make teachers easier to work with and more apt to cooperate with the principal.

> Principals must be experts at reading the needs of teachers and otherwise handling them in order to barter successfully for their cooperation and commitment. (Sergiovanni and Starratt, 1993:27)

The typical reaction of teachers to personal authority is to respond when rewards are available, but not otherwise. Teachers become involved in their work for calculated reasons, and as such, their performance is difficult to sustain over time without continually renegotiating the bartering arrangement.

Bonding leadership practices rely heavily on moral values as their source of authority. Moral authority is derived from obligations and duties that teachers feel toward each other and toward the school as a result of their connection to widely shared values, ideas, and ideals. When moral authority is in place, teachers respond to shared commitments and to the felt interdependence that comes from the sense of "we" that is created. As moral authority becomes the center of a principal's practice, the school is transformed into a moral community. Moral authority, for example, is the central tenant of the discussion on building community that appears in Chapter 4. The sources of authority and their relationship to leadership practice are summarized in Table 6.1.

The Stages of Leadership

In 1978, James MacGregor Burns proposed a theory of leadership that has shaped the way leadership practice is now understood. According to Burns, leadership is exercised when persons with certain motives and purposes mobilize resources so as to arouse and satisfy the motives of followers. He identified two broad kinds of leadership: transactional and transformative. *Transactional leadership* focuses on basic and largely extrinsic motives and needs; *transformative leadership* focuses on higher-order, more intrinsic, and ultimately moral motives and needs. This latter point is important to understanding Burns's theory. Burns (1978:20) described transformational leadership, for example, as a process within which "leaders and followers raise one another to higher levels of morality and motivation." Transfor-

TABLE 6.1   The Sources of Authority for Leadership and Practice

Source	Assumptions When Use of This Source Is Prime	Leadership/Supervisory Strategy	Anticipated Consequences
Bureaucratic Authority			
Hierarchy Rules and regulations Mandates Role expectation Teachers are expected to comply or face consequences.	Teachers are subordinates in a hierarchically arranged system. Supervisors are trustworthy, but you cannot trust subordinates very much. Goals and interests of teachers and supervisors are not the same; thus, supervisors must be watchful. Hierarchy equals expertise; thus, supervisors know more than do teachers. External accountability works best.	"Expect and inspect" is the overarching rule. Rely on predetermined standards to which teachers must measure up or face sanctions. Directly supervise and closely monitor the work of teachers to ensure compliance. Figure out how to motivate them and get them to change.	With proper monitoring, teachers respond as technicians executing predetermined scripts. Their performance is narrowed.
Personal Authority			
Motivation technology Interpersonal skills Human relations leadership Teachers will want to comply because of the congenial climate provided and to reap rewards offered in exchange.	The goals and interests of teachers and supervisors are not the same but can be bartered so that each gets what each wants. Teachers have needs, and if those needs are met at work, the work gets done as required in exchange. Congenial relationships and harmonious interpersonal climates make teachers content, easier to work with, and more apt to cooperate.	Develop a school climate characterized by congeniality among teachers and between teachers and supervisors. "Expect and reward." "What gets rewarded gets done."	Teachers respond as required when rewards are available but not otherwise. Their involvement is calculated and performance is narrowed.
Moral Authority			
Felt obligations and duties derived from widely shared community values, ideas, and ideals Teachers respond to shared commitments and felt interdependence.	Schools are professional learning communities. Communities are defined by their center of shared values, beliefs, and commitments. In communities: What is considered right and good is as important as what works and what is effective. People are motivated as much by emotion and beliefs as by self-interest. Collegiality is a professional virtue.	Identify and make explicit the values and beliefs that define the center of the school as community. Translate the above into informal norms that govern behavior. Promote collegiality as internally felt and morally driven interdependence. Rely on ability of community members to respond to duties and obligations. Rely on the community's informal norm system to enforce professional and community values.	Teachers respond to community values for moral reasons. Their practice becomes collective and their performance is expansive and sustained.

Source: Adapted from Thomas J. Sergiovanni, 1992, "Moral Authority and the Regeneration of Supervision," in Carl Glickman, Ed., *Supervision in Transition*, pp. 203–214, ASCD Yearbook. Association for Supervision and Curriculum Development, © Thomas J. Sergiovanni. All rights reserved. See also T. J. Sergiovanni, 1992, *Moral Leadership*, pp. 30–42. San Francisco: Jossey-Bass.

mative leadership is in two stages, one concerned with higher-order psychological needs for esteem, autonomy, and self-actualization, and the other with moral questions of goodness, righteousness, duty, and obligation.

In his ground-breaking examination of the moral dimension in management and motivation, Etzioni (1988) provides a compelling case for moral authority as a source of motivation and basis for management. Etzioni acknowledges the importance of extrinsic and intrinsic motivation, but points out that ultimately what counts most to people is what they believe, how they feel, and the shared norms and cultural messages that emerge from the groups and communities with which they identify. Morality, emotion, and social bonds, he maintains, are far more powerful motivators than are the extrinsic concerns of transactional leadership and the intrinsic psychological concerns of the early stages of transformative leadership.

In transactional leadership, leaders and followers exchange needs and services in order to accomplish *independent* objectives. It is assumed that leaders and followers do not share a common stake in the enterprise, and thus some kind of bargain must be struck. This bargaining process was described earlier as a form of *leadership by bartering*. The wants and needs of followers and the wants and needs of the leader are traded and a bargain is struck. Positive reinforcement is given for good work, merit pay for increased performance, promotion for increased persistence, a feeling of belonging for cooperation, and so forth.

In transformative leadership, by contrast, leaders and followers are united in pursuit of higher-level goals that are common to both. Both want to become the best. Both want to shape the school in a new direction. When transformative leadership is practiced successfully, purposes that might have started out being separate become fused.

Initially, transformative leadership takes the form of *leadership by building*. Here the focus is on arousing human potential, satisfying higher-order needs, and raising expectations of both leader and follower in a manner that motivates both to higher levels of commitment and performance. Burns points out that ultimately transformative leadership becomes moral because it raises the level of human conduct and ethical aspiration of both leader and led. When this occurs, transformative leadership takes the form of *leadership by bonding*. Here the leader focuses on arousing awareness and consciousness that elevate school goals and purposes to the level of a shared covenant that bonds together leader and follower in a moral commitment. Leadership by bonding responds to such intrinsic human needs as a desire for purpose, meaning, and significance in what one does. The key concepts associated with transformative leadership by bonding are cultural and moral leadership.

Leadership by bartering, building, and bonding, when viewed sequentially, make up the stages of leadership for school improvement referred to earlier. Bartering provides the push needed to get things started; building provides the push needed to create the psychological support system necessary for people to respond to higher levels of need fulfillment; and bonding provides the inspiration needed for performance and commitment that are beyond expectations.

School improvement initiatives become real only when they are institutionalized as part of the everyday life of the school. To this effort, *leadership by bonding* is the fourth stage of school improvement. *Binding* seeks to routinize school improvements by linking teachers morally to purposes and to the norms that emerge from their being members of communities of practice. The key is connecting people to a set of ideas and ideals about the work of the school. This binding of ideas provides guidelines as to what to do and helps people become self-managing.

When practicing leadership by binding, the principal *ministers* to the needs of the school and works to serve others so that they are better able to perform their responsibilities. In addition to manager, minister, and servant, the leader functions as a "high priest" by protecting the values of the school. The high priest function is an expression of the cultural force of leadership discussed in Chapter 5.

Each of the stages of leadership can be thought of as comprising distinct school improvement strategies. However, tactically speaking, bartering, building, bonding, and binding can be thought of as leadership styles to be used simultaneously for different purposes or people within any of the stages. A recalcitrant teacher, for example, may well require leadership by bartering regardless of one's overall strategy.

Leadership by bartering is an especially effective strategy when the issue is one of competence. However, once competence has been achieved, one needs to look to leadership by building and bonding for the strategies and tactics that will help transcend competence to inspire commitment and extraordinary performance. The stages of leadership and their relationship to school improvement are summarized in Table 6.2.

Operationalizing Charismatic Leadership

Transformational leadership sounds similar to the concept of *charisma*. This similarity can be troublesome because depending on how charisma is defined, one could conclude that leadership ability is based on endowed gifts of birth and personality. If this is the case, then some principals have it and others don't, and those who don't can't get it. This is the conclusion to be reached if one accepts the metaphysical definition that comes from the Greek language in which *charisma* means the ability to perform miracles, to predict the future, and to possess divinely inspired gifts.

In recent years, the social science literature has moved away from considering charisma as having something to do with "divine personality" to more ordinary definitions themed either to one's ability to influence and inspire others or to attributions of this ability. Instead of worrying about a mysterious charismatic personality, the emphasis is on identifying behaviors that encourage people to *attribute* charismatic qualities to the leader.

Leaders thought to be charismatic have the ability to touch people in meaningful ways. As a result, these people respond to their leaders and to the ideas and values that they stand for with unusual commitment and effort. The typical result is performance that is beyond expectations.

There is growing consensus that this charismatic leadership does not exist as something concrete or objective but is a perception—indeed an attribute that cannot be separated from followership. Followers attribute charisma to the leader. Furthermore, no leader is thought to be charismatic by everyone. There needs to be a

TABLE 6.2   The Stages of Leadership and School Improvement

Leadership Type	Leadership Styles	Stages of School Improvement
Transactional Leadership	Leadership as "bartering"	*Getting started* by: Exchanging human needs and interests that allow satisfaction of independent (leader and follower) but organizationally related objectives
Transformational Leadership	Leadership as "building"	*Muddling through* by: Arousing human potential, satisfying higher needs, raising expectations of both leader and followers that motivate to higher levels of commitment and performance
	Leadership as "bonding"	*Seeking a transformative breakthrough* by: Arousing awareness and consciousness that elevate organizational goals and purposes to the level of a shared covenant and that bond together leader and followers in a moral commitment
	Leadership as "binding"	*Promoting self-management* by: Turning improvements into routines so that they become second-nature
		Ministering to the needs of the school, being of service, guarding the values
		Connecting people to an idea structure that guides what to do

connection between what the leader does and the meanings, if any, that followers derive. Conger (1989:23–24) points out that in order for leadership behaviors to "induce the perception of charisma, their specific character has to be seen by followers as *relevant* to their situation. If followers do not think their leader's formulation of a strategic vision matches their own aspirations, they are less likely to perceive him or her as a charismatic leader."

According to attribution theory (i.e., Kelly, 1973), followers search for the meaning of the leader's behavior. We attribute a set of generalizations to the leader based on what we see and hear and what we think it means to us. We might conclude, for example, that Bill is a wishy-washy principal, Terry is a manager but little else, and Mary is the kind of principal who is a real leader. Our conclusions result from our own needs, our values, our conceptions of what good leadership is, and our own experiences. If there is a match between the behaviors we observe and what we think they mean, then the attribution is a positive one. If not, it is negative.

TABLE 6.2 *Continued*

Leadership Concepts	Involvement of Followers	Needs Satisfied	Effects
Management skills Leadership style Contingency theory Exchange theory Path-goal theory	Calculated	Physical Security Social Ego	Continual performance contingent on parties keeping the bargain struck. "A fair day's work for a fair day's pay."
Empowerment Symbolic leadership "Charisma"	Intrinsic	Esteem Competence Autonomy Self- actualization	Performance and commitment are sustained beyond external conditions. Both are beyond expectations in quantity and quality.
Cultural leadership Moral leadership Covenant Building followership	Moral	Belonging Purpose Meaning Significance	
Procedures Institutional leadership Servant leadership Leadership by outrage Kindling outrage in others	Moral	Belonging Purpose Meaning Significance	Performance remains sustained

Source: Adapted from Sergiovanni (1990).

These attributions result in different kinds of commitments to the leader and different levels of effort. After an exhaustive survey of the literature on charismatic leadership and attribution theory, Yukl (1989:205) concludes: "Charisma is believed to result from follower perceptions of leader qualities and behavior. These perceptions are influenced by the context of the leadership situation and the follower's individual and collective needs."

Behavioral Dimensions of Charisma

Conger and Kanungo (1987, 1988) propose a theory that identifies the leadership behaviors that influence followers to attribute charismatic qualities to a leader. The dimensions identified do not constitute a personality type but rather a set of leadership behaviors that can be duplicated by principals with varying personalities. Moreover, independent of the charismatic issue, the leadership behaviors result in extraordinary levels of commitment and performance (Conger, 1989). Conger and Kanungo (1987, 1988) propose that followers are more likely to attribute charisma to leaders

> who advocate a vision that challenges the status quo but still is close enough to be accepted by followers
>
> who demonstrate convincingly that they are willing to take personal risks, incur high costs, and even make self-sacrifices to achieve their vision
>
> who act in unconventional ways in implementing the vision
>
> whose vision and actions are timely in the sense that they are sensitive to the values, beliefs, and needs of followers on the one hand and to the opportunities inherent in the situation at hand on the other
>
> who respond to existing dissatisfaction or, if needed, who create dissatisfaction in the status quo
>
> who are able to communicate confidence in themselves and their proposals and who are enthusiastic about the future prospects for successful implementation of proposals
>
> who rely on expert power to influence others by demonstrating that they know what they are talking about and can propose solutions that help others to be successful (summarized from Yukl, 1989:208–209)

According to Conger (1989), the behavioral dimensions of charismatic leadership are manifested in four stages. Stage one involves sensing leadership opportunities and formulating a vision. The leader detects unexploited opportunities and deficiencies or problems in the current situation and formulates a vision that responds. Key to stage one is being sensitive to the needs of followers and other constituents. Success of the proposed vision depends on whether it helps followers and others satisfy their own needs.

Stage two involves communicating the vision in a fashion that makes it clear that the current situation is unacceptable and the proposed vision is an attractive alternative. If the proposed alternative is responsive to the needs of followers and other constituents, then it is likely to be accepted even though it represents a radical departure from the present. As Conger (1989) points out, "Since the vision is a perspective shared by the followers and promises to meet their aspirations, it tends to be very acceptable despite its radical departure from the present situation" (29).

Stage three involves building trust with followers and other constituencies by demonstrating sincerity and commitment to the proposed vision. As Conger (1989) explains, "Thus the leader must build exceptional trust among subordinates in himself and in the goals he articulates. The charismatic leader does this through personal risk taking, unconventional expertise, and self-sacrifice. These qualities set the charismatic leader apart from others" (33).

Stage four involves demonstrating the means to achieve the vision through modeling, empowering others, and the use of unconventional tactics.

One of the ways to test the efficacy of the ideas Conger and Kanungo propose is to examine leaders you know from personal experience whom you consider to possess charismatic qualities. To what extent do they exhibit the behavioral dimensions just described? As you review the dimensions, which one seems to function as the linchpin that holds the others together?

The "charismatic leaders," "bonding leaders," and "transformative leaders" discussed in this chapter share one common quality: *the ability to respond to the needs of followers.* They are able to help others reach higher levels of need fulfillment, to extract more meaning from their work lives, and to see that what they are doing is something special and significant. When these needs are addressed, followers invariably respond with higher levels of commitment, effort, and performance.

Why Leadership by Bonding and Binding Works

Bonding and binding leadership works because:

- They are aligned with a realistic view of how schools actually work; thus their practices are practical.
- They are based on a theory of human rationality that enhances both individual and organizational intelligence and performance.
- They respond to higher-order psychological and spiritual needs that lead to extraordinary commitment, performance, and satisfaction.

When a school leader chooses a theory from which to practice, a particular image of rationality is assumed whether or not it fits the real world. A better fit between theory and practice will occur by starting the other way around. *First* choose the image of rationality that fits the real world, and *then* find a theory that fits that image of rationality.

Shulman (1989) provides three images of human rationality. All three are true to a certain extent, but some are more true than others. It makes a difference which of the three or which combination of the three provides the strategic basis for one's leadership practice. The three are provided below. Using a total of 10 points, distribute points among the three to indicate the extent to which you believe each to be true.

1. Humans are rational; they think and act in a manner consistent with their goals, their self-interests, and what they have been rewarded for. If you wish them to behave in a given way, make the desired behavior clear to them and make it worth their while to engage in it.
2. Humans are limited in their rationality; they can make sense of only a small piece of the world at a time and they strive to act reasonably with respect to their limited grasp of facts and alternatives. They must therefore construct conceptions or definitions of situations rather than passively accept what is presented to them. If you wish them to change, engage them in active problem solving and judgment—don't just tell them what to do.

3. Humans are rational only when acting together; since individual reason is so limited, men and women find opportunities to work jointly on important problems, achieving through joint effort what individual reason and capacity could never accomplish. If you want them to change, develop ways in which they can engage in the change process jointly with peers. (Shulman, 1989:171)

The first image of rationality fits traditional management theories and leadership by bartering practices very well. The second and third images, by contrast, are better accommodated by the Scruffie view of management discussed in Chapter 2 and leadership by building and bonding. Within the second and third images, rationality is achieved by helping people make sense of their world. As sense builds, some of the limits on rationality are overcome. The ability to make sense builds when people are able to construct their own definitions of situations and are involved with the leader in active problem solving. The limits, however, are typically too great for anyone to do it alone. Thus, a key strategy for sense building is the pooling of human resources and the fostering of collegial values in an effort that expands individual reason and capacity to function successfully.

Leadership as bartering responds to physical, security, social, and ego needs of people at work. In his well-known motivation-hygiene theory, Herzberg (1966) pointed out that these needs and the job factors that accommodated them had less to do with commitment and performance beyond expectations than with meeting ordinary basic job requirements. He pointed out that should the needs not be met, worker performance and commitment are likely to fall below a satisfactory level. But when the needs are met, all that results is that workers meet basic job requirements. However, when such job factors as opportunities for achievement, challenge, responsibility, recognition for one's accomplishment, and opportunities to demonstrate competence were present, then such higher-order needs as esteem, competence, autonomy, and self-actualization were likely to be met. These factors and needs are related to leadership by building. They are the bridges that leader and followers must cross together as they move from ordinary performance to performance that is beyond expectations.

The strength of leadership by bonding and binding is the ability to focus on arousing awareness and consciousness to elevate school goals and purposes to the level of a shared covenant that bonds leader and followers together and binds them to a set of ideas that comprise moral commitments. Leadership by bonding and binding responds to such higher-order needs as the desire for purpose, meaning, and significance in what one does. Both can provide the necessary cultural cement that holds people and organizations together.

Idea-Based Leadership

When values and beliefs become institutionalized into the everyday management life of the school, then management know-how, hierarchical authority, interpersonal skill, and personality are ultimately transcended as the leader becomes one who administers to the needs of the school and its members. The principal doesn't become less important, only differently important. On the one hand, she or he becomes the guardian of the values of the school's covenant, and on the other hand, she or he becomes a capable administrator who works hard to help others meet their commitments to the school. Once at this stage, leadership and followership become very, very close. As pointed out earlier, followers manage themselves well by thinking for themselves, exercising self-control, accepting responsibility and obligation, and believing in and caring about what they are doing (Kelly, 1988:144). Both followers and leaders are attracted to and compelled by the same things: ideas, values, and commitments. Thus, over time, leaders seek to restructure the chain of command so that followers are not connected to leaders in a hierarchical sense, but so that both leaders and followers respond to the same ideas, values, and commitments.

Traditional chain of command   *New chain of command*
(hierarchical authority)   *(moral authority)*
Leaders   *Ideas, values, commitments*
↓   ↓
Followers   *Leaders as followers and*
followers as leaders

When this happens, hierarchical authority and authority derived from one's personality give way to purpose and management. The leader is neither boss nor messiah but administrator.

The authority vested in the leader as boss is organizational and hierarchical; the authority vested in the leader as messiah is charismatic and interpersonal; and the authority vested in the leader as administrator is obligatory, stemming from the obligations that come from serving shared values and purposes (Sergiovanni, 1990:150).

School principals are responsible for "ministering" to the needs of the schools they serve, as defined by the shared values and purposes of the school's covenant. They minister by furnishing help and by being of service to parents, teachers, and students. They minister by providing leadership in a way that encourages others to be leaders in their own right. They minister by highlighting and protecting the values of the school. The principal as minister is one who is devoted to a cause, mission, or set of ideas and accepts the duty and obligation to serve this cause. Ultimately, her or his success is known by the quality of the followership that emerges in the school. The quality of followership is a barometer that indicates the extent to which moral authority has replaced bureaucratic. When moral authority drives leadership practice, the principal is at the same time a leader of leaders, follower of ideas, minister of values, and servant to the followership.

References

Burns, James MacGregor. 1978. *Leadership*. New York: Harper & Row.

Conger, Jay A. 1989. *The Charismatic Leader*. San Francisco: Jossey-Bass.

Conger, Jay A., and Rabindra N. Kanungo. 1987. "Towards a Behavioral Theory of Charismatic Leadership in Organizational Settings," *Academy of Management Review* 12(4), 637–647.

Conger, Jay, and Rabindra N. Kanungo. 1988. "Behavioral Dimensions of Charismatic Leadership," in J. A. Conger and R. N. Kanungo (Eds.), *Charismatic Leadership*. San Francisco: Jossey-Bass.

Etzioni, Amitai. 1988. *The Moral Dimension toward a New Theory of Economics*. New York: The Free Press.

Herzberg, Frederick. 1966. *Work and the Nature of Man*. Cleveland: The World Publishing Company.

Kelly, H. H. 1973. "The Process of Causal Attribution," *American Psychologist* 28(2), 107–128.

Kelly, Robert E. 1988, November–December. "In Praise of Followers," *Harvard Business Review*.

McNeil, Linda. 1986. *Contradictions of Control: School Structure and School Knowledge*. New York: Routledge and Kegan Paul.

Rosenholtz, Susan. 1989. *Teachers' Workplace: The Social Organization of Schools*. New York: Longman.

Sergiovanni, Thomas J. 1990. *Value-Added Leadership: How to Get Extraordinary Performance in Schools*. San Diego, CA: Harcourt Brace Jovanovich.

Sergiovanni, Thomas J. 1990–1991. "Biting the Bullet: Rescinding the Texas Teacher Appraisal System," *Teacher Education in Practice* 6(2), 89–93.

Sergiovanni, Thomas J. 1994. *Building Community in Schools*. San Francisco: Jossey-Bass.

Sergiovanni, Thomas J., and Robert J. Starratt. 1993. *Supervision: A Redefinition* (5th ed.). New York: McGraw-Hill.

Shulman, Lee. 1989. "Teaching Alone, Learning Together: Needed Agenda for New Reforms," in T. J. Sergiovanni and J. H. Moore (Eds.), *Schooling for Tomorrow: Directing Reforms to Issues that Count*. Boston: Allyn and Bacon.

Weick, Karl E. 1976. "Educational Organization as Loosely Coupled Systems," *Administrative Science Quarterly* 21.

Wise, Arthur E. 1979. *Legislated Learning: The Bureaucratization of the American Classroom*. Berkeley: University of California Press.

Yukl, Gary A. 1989. *Leadership in Organizations* (2nd ed.). Englewood Cliffs, NJ: Prentice-Hall.

7

BECOMING A COMMUNITY OF LEADERS

The idea of community has appeal to most principals, and many schools are quick to label themselves as caring communities and learning communities. Yet, when the conversation shifts to a discussion of school as a community of leaders, many principals begin to feel uncomfortable. The literature, for example, frequently encourages principals to provide strong and direct leadership in making schools effective. As a result, leadership is part of an interaction influence system within which the leader, acting alone, interacts with others in an effort to influence what they think and do.

As discussed in Chapter 6, we have come to understand this approach as leadership by bartering. The leader and the led strike bargains within which the leader gives to the led something they want in exchange for something the leader wants. Within this view, leaders may have lofty visions and may want to do the right thing, but exercising leadership still means controlling events and people in a way that makes events occur the way leaders think they should. Progressive leaders, however, are not supposed to be dictatorial. Instead, they are encouraged to share some of *their* responsibility for leadership with others and delegate some of *their* authority to others. When they do this, so it is believed, the likelihood that others will respond better and thus be more likely to do what the leader thinks is good for the school is increased.

Struggling to make the school a community changes all of this. Leadership by bartering may be necessary in the beginning, but then the emphasis shifts to leadership by building, bonding, and binding. In creating community, what matters most is what the community shares together, what the community believes in together, and what the community wants to accomplish together. It is this shared idea structure, this community of mind, that becomes the primary source of authority for what people do. Together, principals and teachers become followers of the dream and are committed to making it real. Within this view, leadership is nothing more than a means to make things happen. Because not only the principal but all of the followers have an equal obligation to embody community values, principals and teachers must share equally together in the obligation to lead.

Practical Issues

Striving to make the school a community of leaders is a good idea that doesn't need much justification. After all, most will agree the more that leadership is cultivated in a school, the more likely it is that everyone will get a chance to use their talents fully and the more committed everyone is likely to be. Furthermore, in a democracy such as ours, the more that leadership is shared and expressed, the better it is presumed to be. Exercising leadership for the good of everyone is considered to be one of the responsibilities of citizenship. An additional consideration is that, given today's complex world, shared leadership is necessary for schools to work well.

In their review of the literature on school improvement, Lieberman and Miller (1986) reached a similar conclusion. They found that any effort to improve schools must be grounded in the social realities of the classroom as revealed in the lives of teachers and their work. This is the same conclusion they reached in their 1978 epic, "The Social Realities of Teaching." In their words*:

> *What we have rediscovered are some tried and true notions that have become enriched and expanded over time. Among them:*
>
> > *Working with people rather than working on people.*
> >
> > *Recognizing the complexity and craft nature of the teacher's work.*
> >
> > *Understanding that there are unique cultural differences in each school and how these affect development efforts.*
> >
> > *Providing time to learn.*
> >
> > *Building collaboration and cooperation, involving the provisions for people to do things together, talking together, sharing concerns.*
> >
> > *Starting where people are, not where you are.*
> >
> > *Making private knowledge public, by being sensitive to the effects of teacher isolation and the power of trial and error.*
> >
> > *Resisting simplistic solutions to complex problems; getting comfortable with reworking issues and finding enhanced understanding and enlightenment.*
> >
> > *Appreciating that there are many variations of development efforts; there is no one best way.*
> >
> > *Using knowledge as a way of helping people grow rather than pointing up their deficits.*

*Source: Reprinted by permission of the publisher from Lieberman, Ann, and Miller, Lynne, *Rethinking School Improvement: Research, Craft, and Concept* (New York: Teachers College Press, © 1986 by Teachers College, Columbia University. All rights reserved.), p. 108 (Lines 21–24); p. 109 (Lines 1–5).

Supporting development efforts by protecting ideas, announcing expectations, making provisions for necessary resources.

Sharing leadership functions as a team, so that people can provide complementary skills and get experience in role taking.

Organizing development efforts around a particular focus.

Understanding that content and process are both essential, that you cannot have one without the other.

Being aware of and sensitive to the differences in the worlds of teachers and other actors within or outside of the school setting. (Lieberman and Miller, 1986:108–109)

In a recent update of the social realities theme, Lieberman and Miller (1999) state:

Perhaps the greatest lesson we have learned from our study of teachers and schools in the midst of change is that a new view of teaching and community is being crafted, one that takes place not only inside classrooms and schools but outside as well, one that respects diversity and confronts differences, that represents a sensitivity to and engagement with the whole life of students as they live it. The creation of new learning communities that include rather than exclude, that create knowledge rather than merely apply it, and that offer both challenge and support provide the greatest hope for teachers who are in the process of transforming themselves, their world, and their work. (91)

This emphasis on creating new learning communities for teachers as a vehicle for change leads them to propose eight new understandings about the social realities of teaching and their link to teacher development and school improvement:

Creating a seamless web of values, practices and organizational structures.

Making professional development integral to school life.

Supporting teacher learning outside of school.

Leading and learning as a collective responsibility.

Maintaining balance [among competing demands].

Establishing conditions that support the new social realities of teaching.

Learning about and understanding the change process.

Protecting and nurturing hope, passion and commitment. (Lieberman and Miller, 1999:84–90)

Lieberman and Miller's lists suggest that successful school improvement efforts depend on reaching into the invisible aspects of school life and tapping the energy and commitment of teachers up close. Teachers have to take initiative, accept responsibility, and become active leaders. Together, principal and teachers must become a community of leaders.

New Leadership Values for the Principalship

Becoming a community of leaders requires adopting new leadership values such as purposing, followership, empowerment, accomplishment, collegiality, intrinsic motivation, quality control, simplicity, reflection, and outrage. Together the values provide the substance for practicing leadership by bonding and by binding. They are considered in the following subsections in the form of leadership principles.

Purposing and Shared Values

Harvard Business School professor Abraham Zaleznik (1989) believes that the failure of management is the substitution of process for substance. The importance of management processes to school effectiveness should not be underestimated, but such processes are not substitutes for substance. It is important, for example, to know how to get from A to B, and sound management can help; however, the substance of administrative leadership is concerned with whether B is better than A and why. Furthermore, having determined the direction, substance is the means by which one brings together divergent human resources, inspires commitment, and achieves extraordinary performance.

Management processes alone turn workers into *subordinates*. Substances, by contrast, build *followership*. Subordinates comply with management rules and procedures and with the leader's directives; the job gets done. Followers, however, respond to ideas, ideals, values, and purposes; as a result, the job gets done well.

In his classic book *The Functions of the Executive* (1938), Barnard stated: "The inculcation of belief in the real existence of a common purpose is an essential executive function"(87). The inculcation of belief comes from the embodiment of purposes as leaders act and behave, or, in the words of Vaill, from *purposing*. He defines purposing as "that continuous stream of actions by an organization's formal leadership which has the effect of inducing clarity, consensus and commitment regarding the organizations basic purposes"(1984:91). Vaill (1984) conducted extensive studies of high-performing systems (HPS) from a broad spectrum of U.S. society. He examined the characteristics held in common by these systems and the kind of leadership found within them. Key to success was the presence of purposing. "HPS's are clear on their broad purposes and on near-term objectives for fulfilling these purposes. They know why they exist and what they are trying to do. Members have pictures in their heads which are strikingly congruent" (86). He continues, "Commitment to these purposes is never perfunctory.... [M]otivation as usually conceived is always high" (86).

Purposing is a key characteristic found by others who have studied successful schools in the United States. This research establishes the importance of shared goals and expectations and approved modes of behavior that create a strong school culture. Important to this culture are the norms and values that provide a cohesion and identity and that create a unifying moral order from which teachers and students derive direction, meaning, and significance. One example is Joan Lipsitz's (1984) study of four successful middle schools. She found that the four schools achieved unusual clarity about the purposes of intermediate schooling and the students they teach, and made powerful statements, both in word and in practice, about their purposes. There was little disagreement about what they believed and little discrepancy between what they said they were doing and what they were actually doing.

It is through purposing and the building of shared values and agreements that a school culture emerges.

> *The concept of culture refers to the total way of life in a society, the heritage of accumulated social learnings that is shared and transmitted by the members of that society. To put it another way a culture is a set of shared plans for living, developed out of necessities of previous generations, existing in the minds of the present generation, taught directly or indirectly to new generations. (White, 1952:15)*

Purposing involves both the vision of the leader and a set of agreements that the group shares. Bennis (1984) describes vision as "the capacity to create and communicate a compelling vision of a desired state of affairs, a vision . . . that clarifies the current situation and induces commitment to the future" (66). Vision is an important dimension of purposing and without it the very point of leadership is missed, but the vision of the school must also reflect the hopes and dreams, the needs and interests, the values and beliefs of everyone who has a stake in the school—teachers, parents, and students. In the end, it is what the school stands for that counts. In successful schools, consensus runs deep. It is not enough to have worked out what people stand for and what is to be accomplished. A binding and solemn agreement needs to emerge that represents a value system for living together and that provides the basis for decisions and actions. This binding and solemn agreement represents the school's covenant.

When both vision and covenant are present, teachers and students respond with increased motivation and commitment and their performance is beyond expectations. The affirming of values that accompanies purposing is a motivational force far more powerful than the bureaucratic and psychological transactions that characterize leadership by bartering and building. They become the very basis upon which we construct our reality and from which we derive sense and meaning. As Gardner (1986) points out,

> *A great civilization is a drama lived in the minds of people. It is a shared vision; it is shared norms, expectations and purposes. . . . If we look at ordinary human communities, we see the same reality: A community lives in the minds of its members—in shared assumptions, beliefs, customs, ideas that give meaning, ideas that motivate. (7)*

Building Followership

In his book *Every Employee a Manager*, Meyers (1971) observes that the more management like jobs were, the more readily workers accepted responsibility and responded with increased motivation. By *managementlike,* he meant having the freedom to plan, organize, and control one's life, to make decisions, to accept responsibility, and to be held accountable for one's actions in light of this responsibility. Empowering every employee to be a manager is a goal of leadership by bonding because it contributes to leadership density. *Leadership density* refers to the extent to which leadership roles are shared and leadership itself is broadly based and exercised. To understand leadership density, one needs to understand how closely leadership and followership are linked and what the differences are between being a good follower and a good subordinate. Good followers manage themselves well. They think for themselves, exercise self-control, and are able to accept responsibility and obligation, believe in and care about what they are doing, and be self-motivated; therefore, they are able to do what is right for the school, do it well, do it with persistence, and, most importantly, do it without close supervision (Kelly, 1988). Followers are committed people—committed perhaps to a set of purposes, a cause, a vision of what the school is and can become, a set of beliefs about what teaching and learning should be, a set of values and standards to which they adhere, a conviction.

By contrast, good subordinates do what they are supposed to but little else. They want to know specifically what is expected of them, and with proper monitoring and supervision will perform accordingly. They are dependent on their leaders to provide them with goals and objectives and the proper ways and means to achieve them. They want to know what the rules of the game are and will play the game as required to avoid problems. For them and their leaders, life is comfortable and easy. For the school and the children they teach, excellence escapes and mediocrity becomes the norm.

Subordinates are not committed to causes, values, or ideas, but respond instead to authority in the form of rules, regulations, expectations of their supervisors, and other management requirements. This is a crucial distinction. Subordinates respond to authority; followers respond to ideas. The standard dictionary definition of a follower is one who is in the service of a cause or of another person who represents a cause; a follower is one who follows opinions and teachings—a disciple. Because followership is linked to ideas, it is difficult for principals to help others transcend subordinateness for followership in schools, without practicing leadership by purposing.

The concept of followership proposes a number of paradoxes. It turns out that effective following is really a form of leadership (Kelly, 1988). Commitment to a cause and the practice of self-management are hallmarks of good leadership and they are hallmarks of good followership as well. The successful leader, then, is one who builds up the leadership of others and who strives to become a leader of leaders. A successful leader is also a good follower—one who follows ideas, values, and beliefs. When followership is established, bureaucratic and psychological authority are transcended by moral authority. A new kind of hierarchy emerges in the school, one that places purposes, values, and commitments at the apex and teachers, principals, parents, and students below in service to these purposes.

Enabling Others to Function Autonomously on Behalf of Shared Purposes

There are three dimensions to enablement: (1) empowering principals, teachers, parents, and others by giving them the discretion they need to function autonomously on behalf of school goals and purposes; (2) providing them with the support and training they need to function autonomously; and (3) removing the bureaucratic obstacles that keep them from being autonomous.

Bonding leaders practice the principle of power investment. They distribute power among others in an effort to get more power in return. They know that it is not power over people and events that counts, but power over the likelihood that accomplishments and shared goals and purposes will be realized. To gain control over the latter, they recognize that they need to delegate or surrender control over the former. In a nonlinear and loosely connected world, they are resigned to the reality that delegation and empowerment are unavoidable.

Except for the most routine of jobs, the major problem facing management in the United States today is the gap existing between ability and authority (Thompson, 1961). Those who have the authority to act typically don't have the necessary technical ability, and those with the ability to act typically don't have the necessary authority. Leadership by empowerment can remedy this situation by lending to those with the ability the necessary authority to act.

Empowerment without purposing is not what is intended by this value. The two must go hand in hand. When directed and enriched by purposing and fueled by empowerment, teachers and others respond not only with increased motivation and commitment but with surprising ability as well. They become smarter, use their talents more fully and grow on the job. Thus, the first question that bonding leaders ask when thinking about empowerment is: Empowered to do what? The empowerment rule that they follow is *everyone is free to do the things that make sense to them, providing the decisions they make about what to do embody the values that are shared.* Furthermore, the best empowerment strategy is not to focus on teachers or to focus on any other particular role group, but to think about empowering the school site. It is principals, teachers, and parents, bonded together in a common cause, who are given the necessary discretion that they need to function effectively. Empowerment is the natural complement to accountability. One cannot hold teachers, parents, and schools accountable without giving them the necessary responsibility to make the decisions that they think are best. The mistake of equating empowerment with freedom must be avoided. Empowerment has to do with obligation and duty. One is not free to do what he or she pleases, but free to make sensible decisions in light of shared values.

Viewing Leadership as Power to Accomplish

Successful leaders know the difference between power *over* and power *to*. There is a link between leadership and power, and indeed leadership is a special form of power—power to influence. There are, however, two conceptions of power: power over and power to. Power over is controlling and is concerned with "How can I control people and events so that things turn out the way I want?" Power over is concerned with dominance, control, and hierarchy. One needs to be in a position of dominance, control, and hierarchy to exercise power over. One needs to have access to rewards and punishments, "carrots," and "bully" sticks. In reality, however, most principals don't have many carrots or bully sticks. Furthermore, people don't like carrots or bully sticks and resist power over leadership both formally and informally. Thus, this approach is rarely effective.

The concept of power over raises certain ethical questions relating to dominance and manipulation. Power to, however, is not instrumental but facilitative. It is power to do something, to accomplish something, and to help others accomplish something that they think is important. In power to, far less emphasis is given to what people are doing and far more emphasis is given to what they are accomplishing.

Putting Collegiality First

When combined with purposing, leadership density, and enablement, collegiality is an important strategy for bringing about the kinds of connections that make schools work and work well in a nonlinear and loosely structured world. Too often, however, collegiality is confused with congeniality (Barth, 1986). *Congeniality* refers to the friendly human relationships that exist among teachers and is characterized by the loyalty, trust, and easy conversation that result from the development of a closely knit social group. *Collegiality*, by contrast, refers to the existence of high levels of collaboration among teachers and between teachers and principal and is characterized by mutual respect, *shared work values*, cooperation, and specific conversations about teaching and learning. When congeniality is high, a strong, informal culture aligned with social norms emerges in the school; however, the norms may or may not be aligned with school purposes. Sometimes the norms contribute to and at other times interfere with increased commitment and extraordinary performance. By contrast, when collegiality is high, a strong, professional culture held together by shared work norms emerges in the school. The norms are aligned with school purposes, contributing consistently to increased commitment and extraordinary performance.

Research independently reported by Little (1981) and Rosenholtz (1989) provides compelling support for the importance of collegiality and building a professional culture of teaching on the one hand and in enhancing commitment and performance on the other. Both researchers found that the kind of leadership principals provided influences the collegial norm structure of the school. Rosenholtz found that teachers in high collegial schools described their principals as being supportive and as considering problems to be schoolwide concerns that provided opportunities for collective problem solving and learning. Teachers and principals in less collegial schools, by contrast, reported being isolated and alienated. In her research, Little found that norms of collegiality were developed when principals clearly communicated expectations for teacher cooperation; provided a model for collegiality by working firsthand with teachers in improving the school; rewarded expressions of collegiality among teachers by providing recognition, release time, money, and other support resources; and protected teachers who were willing to go against expected norms of privatism and isolation by engaging in collegial behaviors. Although norms of collegiality can be enhanced within traditionally organized school structures, these structures often provide obstacles that prevent collegiality from developing fully. One advantage of the community image of schooling that was outlined in Chapter 4, which gave emphasis to smallness, shared goals, and moral connections, is that these characteristics can provide the opportunities for collegiality to be expressed within communities of practice.

Emphasizing Intrinsic Motivation

Traditional management theory is based on the principle "what gets rewarded gets done." It makes sense to base motivational strategies and practices on this principle; however, when this principle becomes the overriding framework for making decisions about how to lead and how to encourage and reward good performance, typically the result is the opposite of that which is anticipated. In the long run, the job just doesn't get done. The problem with "what gets rewarded gets done" is that it results in calculated involvement of people with their work. When rewards can no longer be provided, the work no longer will be done. Work performance becomes contingent on a bartering arrangement rather than being self-sustaining because of moral principle or a deeper psychological connection. A better strategy on which to base our efforts is "what is rewarding gets done." When something is rewarding, it gets done even when "no one is looking"; it gets done even when extrinsic rewards and incentives are scarce or nonexistent; it gets done not because somebody is going to get something in return but because it's important. The power of intrinsic motivation is well documented in both research and practice and is a key element in bonding leadership.

Understanding Quality Control

Perhaps on no issue do ordinary and highly successful leaders differ more than in their beliefs about and concepts of quality control. To ordinary leaders, quality control is considered to be a management problem solvable by coming up with the right controls such as scheduling, prescribing, programming, testing, and checking. Although successful leaders recognize that such managerial conceptions of quality control have their place, they are likely to view the problem of quality control as being primarily cultural rather than managerial. Quality control, they have come to learn, is in the minds and hearts of people at work. It has to do with what teachers and other school employees believe, their commitment to quality, their sense of pride, the extent to which they identify with their work, the ownership they feel for what they are doing, and the intrinsic satisfaction they derive from the work itself. It is for this reason that quality control is not viewed so much as planning, organizing, scheduling, and controlling as it is viewed as purposive, enablement, leadership density, collegiality, and intrinsic motivation as a way to build identity and commitment.

Valuing Simplicity

Highly successful principals believe in lean, action-oriented, uncomplicated organizational structures. To them, "small is beautiful" and "simple is better." Smallness has the advantage of encouraging primary group relationships among teachers and students, providing more readily for empowerment, and increasing one's identity and feeling of belongingness. Simplicity is action-oriented and to the point. It places emphasis on what needs to be accomplished and how best to do it without undue emphasis on protocols and procedural matters.

Reflection in Action

Leaders of highly successful schools view with suspicion quick fixes, sure-fire remedies, and one-best-way prescriptions for teaching and learning, supervising, and evaluating. Instead, they bring to their work a more complex view of schooling (see, for example, Brandt, 1985; Glatthorn, 1984; Joyce and Weil, 1980). No single model of teaching is sufficient to address all the aims of schooling. The issue, for example, is not didactic and informal versus structured and direct, but costs and benefits of various approaches to teaching and learning. What is gained and what is lost by using a particular approach? Given one's present situation, are the gains worth the losses? Similarly, no single method of supervision and evaluation is sufficient for all teachers and all situations.

Successful principals resist accepting a direct link between research and practice. They recognize instead that the purpose of research is to increase one's understanding and not to prescribe practices (Tyler, 1984). Paying close attention to theory and research, they heed well the success stories emerging from practice, but they have a conceptual rather than an instrumental view of such knowledge (Kennedy, 1984). Knowledge viewed instrumentally is evidence for directly prescribing action. Knowledge viewed conceptually is information for informing thought and enhancing professional judgment—the prerequisites for action.

Leadership by Outrage

The standard prescription that emerges from traditional management is that leaders should be cool, calculated, and reserved in everything they say or do. Studies of successful leaders (e.g., Lipsitz, 1984; Peters and Waterman, 1982; Sergiovanni, 1990; Vaill, 1984) reveal quite a different image. Indeed, successful leaders typically bring to their practice a sense of passion and risk that communicates to others that if something is worth believing in then it's worth feeling strongly about. In his extensive studies of successful leaders, Vaill (1984) found that their leadership practice was characterized by *time, feeling,* and *focus.* Successful leaders put in extraordinary amounts of time, have strong feelings about the attainment of the system's purposes, and focus their attention and energies on key issues and variables. These characteristics are key contributors to building purposing in the enterprise. According to Vaill,

> *Purposing occurs through the investment of large amounts of micro- and macro-Time, through the experience and expression of very strong Feeling about the attainment of purposes and importance of the system, and through the attainment of understanding of the key variables in the system success (Focus). All leaders of high-performance systems have integrated these three factors at a very high level of intensity and clarity. (1984:103)*

Vaill noted that feeling was the important link between time and focus. His successful leaders cared deeply about the welfare of their particular enterprise, its purposes, structure, conduct, history, future security, and underlying values and commitments. They cared deeply enough to show passion; and when things were not going right, this passion often took the form of outrage.

Leadership by outrage is a symbolic act that communicates importance and meaning and that touches people in ways not possible when leadership is viewed only as something objective and calculated. Leaders use outrage to highlight issues of purpose defined by the school's shared covenant, and this outrage adds considerable value to their leadership practice.

The linking of outrage to purposes is very important. Bonding leaders, for example, know the difference between real toughness and merely looking tough or acting tough. Real toughness is always principle-value based. Bonding leaders expect adherence to common values but promote wide discretion in how these values are to be implemented (they practice enablement and emphasize followership). They are outraged when they see these values ignored or violated. The values of the common core represent nonnegotiables that comprise cultural strands that define a way of life in the school. No matter how free people may be to do and decide, they are expected to embody the values that are shared and make up the school's covenant. When this is not the case, outrage is expressed.

Kindling Outrage in Others

Outrage is not owned by the principal alone. When purposes are established, followership is understood, enabling is provided, collegiality is in place, and leadership by outrage is modeled by the designated leader; then, expressing outrage becomes an obligation of every person connected with the school. When the ideals and commitments that are shared are compromised, outrage is expressed. Bonding leaders work hard at *kindling outrage in others.*

The Worth of the Leadership Values

None of the leadership values considered alone is powerful enough to make the difference in bringing about quality schooling. Indeed, a critical connectedness exists among them, and leadership is best understood as comprising interdependent parts. Practicing enabling leadership in the form of individual empowerment—for example, without practicing leadership that emphasizes purposing and the building of a covenant of shared values is more likely to result in laissez-faire management than in quality schooling. Furthermore, emphasizing management at the expense of leadership by providing controls and regulations, by emphasizing authority, by attempting to regulate the flow and work of schooling will not allow the practice of convincing and meaningful empowerment. A school that builds a covenant of shared values composed of technical statements of objectives, targets, and outcomes that fail to inspire; that are lacking in symbolic representations; and that do not allow principals, parents, teachers, and students to derive sense and meaning from their school lives will not likely be characterized by extraordinary commitment and performance.

Constructivist Leadership

Lambert (Lambert et al., 1995:33) defines *leadership* as involving a reciprocal process that enables members of a school community to construct meaning that leads toward a common purpose. To Lambert, engaging in reciprocal relationships is the way we make sense of our worlds, continually define ourselves, and grow together. She refers to this kind of leadership as *constructivist* and views it as being less a role to be assumed by some and more a function to be assumed by all. Key to constructivist leadership is building capacity among people and in schools. Schools that are good at helping members construct meaning and craft common purposes are likely to be highly skilled at capacity building and in developing broad participation. This combination, Lambert (1998) points out, promotes learning and encourages acceptance of a collective responsibility for the success of the school. When the purpose of leadership becomes constructing meaning, facilitating learning, and developing collective responsibility, leadership is linked directly to the very heart of a school's culture.

A Community of Leaders

In a major breakthrough, Rost (1991) offers a definition of *leadership* that can help connect its practice to community building. "Leadership is an influence relationship among leaders and followers who intend real changes that reflect their mutual purposes" (102). This definition contains four key elements—all of which, Rost argues, must be present for relationships between and among people to be called leadership. If any one of the four is missing, then these relationships might better be thought of as management or some other expression—they may have merit, but they just aren't leadership. The four elements are as follows:

1. *The relationship is based on influence.*
2. *Leaders and followers are the people in this relationship.*
3. *Leaders and followers intend real change.*

4. Leaders and followers develop mutual purposes. (Rost, 1991:102–103)

Rost (1991) points out that conceiving of leadership as an influence relationship means that it is interactive and multidirectional. Leadership does not exist if influence is just top down. Furthermore, influence, in his definition, means the use of persuasion and not rewards and punishments or position and legal power. It is not leadership if a person orders, requires, seduces, or threatens another's compliance.

For something to be called leadership, according to Rost (1991), both followers and leaders must be doing the leadership. They need not be equal in the relationship nor must everyone be leading all the time, but in any given period of time or for any given episode, both share the burdens and obligations of leadership. Furthermore, for leader and followers to intend real changes, leadership acts must be purposeful; they must be motivated not by personal gain or by bureaucratic requirements, but by a desire to better serve purposes. Finally, the purposes themselves must be shared by both leaders and followers. In the ideal, they are developed together.

Rost's (1991) definition relies on the importance of compelling ideas and shared commitment to these ideas. Furthermore, the roles of followers and leaders are blurred. With shared ideas as the source of authority, everyone is a follower first, and when anyone takes the initiative to lead, followership becomes redefined as leadership. Leadership flourishes when leaders and followers view each other as being credible. The stronger this credibility, the more likely people will allow themselves to be influenced by leadership acts, no matter what their source.

To Rost and Smith (1992:199), credibility can be thought of as encompassing five Cs: *character,* defined as honesty, trust, and integrity; *courage,* defined as the willingness to change and to stand up for one's beliefs; *competence,* defined in both technical and interpersonal senses; *composure,* defined as being graceful under pressure and displaying emotion appropriately; and *caring,* defined as being concerned with the welfare of others.

The credibility of the Five Cs suggests that certain relationship requirements must be met before leadership can be fully and widely expressed in a school—before the school, in other words, can become a community of leaders. Not surprisingly, the relationship requirements are *gemeinschaft.* How open are we to each other? Do we have the courage to speak, to express our true feelings, to ask for help, and to stand up for what we believe? Can we speak knowledgeably about teaching and learning? Are we sensitive to the views of others? Do we care about each other, our work, and the students we serve? How do we embody this caring? Becoming a community of leaders means that not only does everyone share in the obligations and responsibility of leadership in an effort to facilitate the work of the school, but everyone shares in the obligations and responsibilities of caring. Not only does leadership involve doing, but it involves being. Are we willing to care enough to accept responsibility together for the burdens of leadership?

References

Barnard, Chester. 1938. *The Functions of the Executive.* Cambridge, MA: Harvard University Press.

Barth, Roland. 1986. "The Principal and the Profession of Teaching," *Elementary School Journal* 86(4).

Bennis, Warren. 1984. "Transformative Power and Leadership," in Thomas J. Sergiovanni and John E. Corbally (Eds.), *Leadership and Organization Culture* (pp. 64–71). Urbana: University of Illinois.

Brandt, Ron. 1985. "Toward a Better Definition of Teaching," *Educational Leadership* 42(8).

Gardner, John. 1986, March. "The Tasks of Leadership." Leadership Papers No. 2. Leadership Studies Program, Independent Sector, Washington, DC.

Glatthorn, Alan. 1984. *Differentiated Supervision.* Alexandria, VA: Association for Supervision and Curriculum Development.

Joyce, Bruce, and Marsha Weil. 1980. *Models of Teaching* (2nd ed.). Englewood Cliffs, NJ: Prentice-Hall.

Kelly, Robert E. 1988, November–December. "In Praise of Followers," *Harvard Business Review.*

Kennedy, Mary. 1984. "How Evidence Alters Understanding and Decisions," *Educational Evaluations and Policy Analysis* 6(3), 207–226.

Lambert, Linda. 1998. "How to Build Leadership Capacity," *Educational Leadership* 55(7), 17–19.

Lambert, Linda, Deborah Walker, Diane P. Zimmerman, Joanne E. Cooper, Morgan Dale Lambert, Mary E. Gardner, and P. J. Ford Slack. 1995. *The Constructivist Leader.* New York: Teachers College Press.

Lieberman, Ann, and Lynne Miller. 1978. "The Social Realities of Teaching," *Teachers College Record* 80(1), 54–68.

Lieberman, Ann, and Lynne Miller. 1986. "School Improvement: Themes and Variations" in Ann Lieberman (Ed.), *Rethinking School Improvement: Research, Craft, and Concept.* New York: Teachers College Press.

Lieberman, Ann, and Lynne Miller. 1999. *Teachers—Transforming Their World and Their Work.* New York: Teachers College Press.

Lipsitz, Joan. 1984. *Successful Schools for Young Adolescents.* New Brunswick, NJ: Transaction Books.

Little, Judith. 1981. *School Success and Staff Development in Urban Desegregated Schools.* Boulder, CO: Center for Action Research.

Meyers, Scott. 1971. *Every Employee a Manager.* New York: McGraw-Hill.

Peters, Thomas J., and Robert H. Waterman. 1982. *In Search of Excellence.* New York: Harper & Row.

Rosenholtz, Susan. 1989. *Teacher's Workplace: A Social-Organizational Analysis.* New York: Longman.

Rost, Joseph. 1991. *Leadership for the Twenty-first Century.* New York: Praeger.

Rost, Joseph, and A. Smith. 1992. "Leadership: A Post-Industrial Approach," *European Management Journal* 10(2).

Sergiovanni, Thomas J. 1990. *Value-Added Leadership: How to Get Extraordinary Performance in Schools.* San Diego, CA: Harcourt Brace Jovanovich.

Thompson, Victor. 1961. *Modern Organization: A General Theory.* New York: Knopf.

Tyler, Ralph. 1984. Quoted in Philip L. Hosford, "The Problem, Its Difficulties, and Our Approaches," in P. L. Hosford (Ed.), *Using What We Know about Teaching.* Alexandria, VA: Association for Supervision and Curriculum Development.

Vaill, Peter B. 1984. "The Purposing of High-Performance Systems," in T. J. Sergiovanni and J. E. Corbally (Eds.), *Leadership and Organizational Culture.* Urbana: University of Illinois Press.

White, Robert W. 1952. *Lives in Progress: A Study of the Natural Growth of Personality.* New York: Dryden Press.

Zaleznik, Abraham. 1989. *The Managerial Mystique: Restoring Leadership in Business.* New York: Harper & Row.

PART III

BUILDING COMMUNITY

8

CHARACTERISTICS OF
SUCCESSFUL SCHOOLS

Since the beginning of schooling in the United States, the relationship between quality of schools and quality of learning for students has been accepted as an article of faith. However, with the 1964 publication of Benjamin Bloom's *Stability and Change in Human Characteristics* and the 1966 publication of James Coleman and colleagues' *Equality of Educational Opportunity*, this faith was broken. Many teachers and principals joined the general public in a widespread acceptance of the belief that schools were not very important.

Coleman's study suggested that social inequality, poverty, and segregated schooling were key elements in determining inadequate levels of learning for many students and that improving learning would require the correction of these social factors. Regardless of one's race or region, it was the home environment (social class and income of parents, exposure to books, need for achievement, and modeling differentials) that was far more important in explaining differences in learning outcomes of students than were school facilities, teacher salaries, or even the curriculum itself.

Bloom's classic work on the development of educational capacity reinforced the primacy of nonschool over school factors in determining the amount and extent of student learning. He noted, for example:

> By about 4, 50% of the variation in intelligence at age 17 is accounted for . . . in terms of intelligence measured at age 17; from conception to age 4, the individual develops 50% of his mature intelligence; from ages 4 to 8 he develops another 30%; and from ages 8 to 17, the remaining 20%. . . . We would expect the variations in the environments to have relatively little effect on the I.Q. after age 8, but would expect such a variation to have marked effect on the I.Q. before that age, with the greatest effect likely to take place between the ages of about 1 to 5. (Bloom, 1964:68)

As these ideas became accepted, principals and teachers came to believe that the home or basic educational capacity, not the school, accounted for major differences in student achievement. Some principals and teachers welcomed this news, seeing within it a legitimate excuse for their own results. After all, they reasoned, the research shows clearly that poor student performance is linked to conditions beyond control of the school.

The 1980s provided quite a different picture as to the relationship between schooling and quality of learning for students. The belief that schooling does make a difference became once more the accepted stand. Quality schooling indeed leads to quality learning, and an important key to quality schooling is the amount and kind of leadership that school principals provide directly and promote among teachers and supporting staff.

These assertions are supported by hundreds of studies on school effectiveness and success. For example, a classic study conducted in 1978 by Gilbert Austin compared 18 high-achieving and 12 low-achieving schools carefully selected from among all schools in Maryland, using that state's accountability data. Schools selected were considered "outliers" for scoring outside the average statistical band of test scores for all Maryland schools. This research indicated that one difference between high- and low-achieving schools was the impact of the principal. In higher-achieving schools, principals exerted strong leadership, participated directly and frequently in instructional matters, had higher expectations for success, and were oriented toward academic goals. It seems clear from this study, and many others like it, that quality of schooling is greatly influenced by leadership from the principal.

Many experts point out that the influence principals have on fostering school effectiveness is indirect (see, for example, Hallinger and Murphy, 1985; Hallinger and Heck, 1996). The work of the Far West Lab, for example, concluded that principal behaviors have a direct effect on the school's overall climate and on its instructional organization (factors such as class size, school size, time available for learning, curriculum pacing and sequencing, staff development, and staff evaluation). These factors, in turn, seem related to student achievement and other effectiveness indicators (Bossert et al., 1982). Essentially, there is an interplay of *initiating variables,* defined as principal dispositions and behaviors, which influence *mediating variables,* defined as school climate and organizing for learning, which affects *school results variables* such as student achievement and other dimensions of goodness. These relationships are summarized in Appendix 13.1, "Studying the Climate of Your School."

Principal leadership is only part of the answer to establishing successful schools. Many experts and many supporting studies point out that equally significant—perhaps even most significant—is the amount and quality of leadership density that exists in schools. *Leadership density* refers to the total leadership available from teachers, support staff, parents, and others on behalf of the school's work. Of course, the principal plays a key role in building and maintaining leadership density. In this sense, principal leadership can be understood as an enabling process. Principals practice enabling leadership when they help teachers, students, and staff to function better on behalf of the school and its purposes, to engage more effectively in the work and play of the school, and to promote the achievement of the school's objectives. It is crucial to build up the leadership capacity of others, and in this sense the principal is a leader of leaders.

Effectiveness and School Success

Are *effective* and *good* schools the same? The terms are often used interchangeably to describe the same school or to communicate the same level of accomplishment, but this can cause confusion. *Effectiveness* has both common and technical meanings. It is commonly understood to mean the ability to produce a desired effect. Thus, in a sense, any school that produces effects desired by some group would be considered effective by that group. Yet, technically speaking, within educational circles, school effectiveness has taken on a specific and special meaning. An effective school is understood to be a school whose students achieve well in basic skills or basic competency standards as measured by achievement tests. The dimensions of management, teaching, and leadership that are included in the school effectiveness model have been convincingly linked to this limited view of effectiveness, but not to broader, higher order, and more qualitative intellectual and academic views of effectiveness.

The question remains: What is a good school? How does one know such a school when it is seen? Can "goodness" be defined? Just how does one determine if a school is doing a good job or not? Such questions usually receive quick answers. For example:

- Graduates of good high schools get jobs or are admitted to college in larger numbers.
- Test scores of students are at or above average for similar groups of students.
- High school teachers remark that incoming students from the junior high are well prepared.
- Students spend approximately two hours each evening on homework.
- A survey of the number of books checked out of the school library during the last year reveals that students in that school check out more books than students in other area schools.
- The average salary of former students 10 years after graduation is high.
- Attendance at school is up.
- Teachers agree as to what the purposes of schooling are.
- Discipline problems are on the decline.
- Students select tougher courses.
- Teachers report that students are working harder.
- Students report that teachers are working harder.
- Surveys indicate that students are satisfied with their school.
- Parents indicate that if they had to choose between sending their children to this or another school, they would choose this one.

- Faculty members carefully plan lessons.
- Tax referenda are passed.
- The accrediting team praises the school.
- Faculty members are available to students.
- The Christmas play, the Chanukkah program, and other seasonal pageantry are well attended year after year, and parents report being pleased with the results.
- The school has a winning football team.
- Faculty members work together, share ideas, and help one another.
- The number of Merit Scholars is increasing.
- Teacher turnover is low.
- The number of students referred to mental health services is low when compared with similar schools.
- More students study foreign languages.
- More students study art.
- More students study physics.
- Morale of faculty is high.

This list of responses could easily be extended. Clearly, the problem of defining a good school is more complex than it seems at first appearances. Indeed, educators and parents alike often have difficulty in coming to grips with an adequate description, definition, or list of criteria. When lists are developed, they typically differ depending on who is deciding.

In a study of 638 respondents affiliated with 10 high schools in England and Wales, MacBeath and his associates (1995) sought to identify indicators of school goodness. They asked pupils, teachers, parents, members of the school management team, support staff, and governors or school board members to provide their own indicators of a good school. Teachers listed:

- Good communications among members of the staff
- Good staff development
- Good working environment
- Happy and well-motivated pupils
- Help is given to all students to achieve what they are capable of

Parents listed:

- Welcoming and friendly atmosphere
- Caring staff who communicate well with pupils
- Good discipline
- Extra time spent with the children
- Good relationships between teachers and parents

Pupils listed:

- Pupils are nice to each other

- Everyone is treated fairly
- Friendly atmosphere
- Teachers control the class but are not too strict
- Teachers help you with things you're not good at

Senior management listed:

- Pupils are safe
- All members of the school community work together toward clear objectives
- High-quality information is provided to parents and visitors
- Rules are applied evenly and fairly
- Pupils are helped to achieve what they are capable of

Support staff listed:

- Good up-to-date resources
- Clean, warm, and comfortable classrooms
- Support staff is given credit when due
- Friendly and welcome environment
- Staff development involves all staff

Members of the board of governors listed:

- Excellent reputation with the local community
- Strong leadership from senior management
- Happy and welcoming environment
- Pupils are being helped to reach their individual potential
- A safe place for pupils and teachers

The problem of determining goodness and differentiating it from effectiveness is compounded by the fact that often schools look "effective" but may not be "good." Many schools rated in the top group according to state standards-based assessments are not rated as such because they provide superior teaching, have better faculties, or improved educational programs; instead, they are rated highly simply because the values of the home are more closely aligned with the values of the school. As Comer and his colleagues (N.A.K. Production Associates, 1993) pointed out, "In general, children whose parents are part of the social mainstream have the best opportunities for success in school, because the values and social skills they acquired from their parents and care-givers are consistent with those of the school, its teachers and administrators" (6). They compellingly argue that "mainstream children—those from social networks where the attitudes, values and behavior most closely resemble those of the school, and its teachers and administrators— have the best chance of meeting the expectations of the school" (9). Mainstream students, for example, are more likely to thrive in the competitive environment the school provides, respond to a pattern of schooling that prizes individuality over community and competition over cooperation, accept docile roles as recipients of an instructional delivery system, look and act the way teachers want them to, learn how to be test savvy, and show up for school even if it's boring. The reason is that these expectations of the school are mirrored in the culture of the family. These same expectations are less likely to be reinforced in the families of students in schools whose ratings are in the lower third.

As has been the case in previous years, the results of the 1995 National Assessment of Educational Progress revealed that test scores are related to parental income, with high-income families having children who score higher than the children in low-income families. Further, despite a rise in the test scores of poor, central city, and minority children, they still scored lower on average than did other children.

Good schools, as Comer and his associates so compellingly argue, do not expect families and students to bear all of the burdens of alignment with the values of the school. Instead, they work hard to align themselves with the values of the home. They are committed to respond with empathy and to respect those values. In short, many, but not all, of the schools that place in the upper third of a given state's rankings can be considered good; there are also many good schools in the lower third.

Nonetheless, intuitively, "goodness" is a known quality no matter how difficult it is to precisely articulate its essence. Lipsitz (1984), for example, found that the principals of the good schools she studied had difficulty in articulating what it was that made their schools special or what the dimensions of goodness were. "You will have to come and see my school" was the typical and predictable response.

Similarly, we know good schools when we experience them, although we cannot always specify their precise components. In good schools, things "hang together"; a sense of purpose exists, rallying people to a common cause; work has meaning and life is significant; teachers and students work together and with spirit; and accomplishments are readily recognized. To say that good schools have high morale or achieve higher test scores or send more students to college—and to leave it at that—is to miss the point. Goodness is all of this and more.

Should we expect more from our schools than the satisfaction of knowing that they are performing "up to the standard" and that students are competent performers as measured by such typical indicators as test scores? The situation is sufficiently poor in some schools that, if they were indeed to achieve such a modest standard, it would be cause for celebration. Most surveys indicate that basic skill learning and developing fundamental academic competence (the indicators of effectiveness common to the school effectiveness literature) are paramount school goals in the minds of parents and teachers. But the question of goodness does not end with this emphasis. Pushed a bit further, most parents and teachers provide a more expansive view of school success. Educational goals typically espoused by parents include developing a love of learning, critical-thinking and problem-solving skills, aesthetic appreciation, curiosity and creativity, and interpersonal competence. Parents want a complete education for their children (see, for example, Goodlad, 1983). Indeed, our society requires a complete education for its youth if it is to survive and flourish. What is needed is that our young become cultured and educated citizens, able to participate fully in our economic and social society, not just trained workers with limited potential for such participation. These aspirations include all of America's youth, including urban and rural poor and minority students, for whom the more limited definitions of school effectiveness are often applied.

Characteristics of Successful Schools

It is fashionable to talk about the correlates of effective schools. Many school districts and even states settle on a particular list of such correlates (e.g., strong instructional leadership from the principal, academic focus on the basic skills, safe and orderly environment, high expectations for students, close monitoring of instruction by supervision and testing) to apply uniformly to all schools. Recent research and reasoned thought, however, suggest that *correlates* may be too strong a designation, and uniform application of any particular list may be hazardous for the long-term health of the school. The research and thought, however, do provide us with a number of insights in the form of general characteristics that can help us decide what counts in our own unique situation.

Research Revelations

The seminal work of Brookover and Lezotte (1979), Brookover and colleagues (1979), and Edmonds (1979) consistently revealed that effective schools are characterized by high agreement among staff as to goals and purposes, a clear sense of mission, and the active presence of purposing. Studies by Bossert and his colleagues (1982) and by Greenfield (1982) revealed that goal orientation and the articulation and modeling of school purposes by principals are also common characteristics.

Blumberg and Greenfield's (1980) research revealed that successful principals are proactive and direct behaviors at building and articulating a vision of what the school is and can become. This notion of vision is supported, as well, by the case study research of Prunty and Hively (1982) and of Newberg and Glatthorn (undated). Nearly all these studies, as well as that of Rutter and his colleagues (1979), identify the concept of ethos (shared goals and expectations and associated approved modes of behavior) or strong school culture as being an important characteristic. Important to this culture are norms and values that provide for cohesion and identity and that create a unifying moral order or ideology from which teachers and students derive direction, meaning, and significance.

Duttweiler's (1988, 1990) review of the more recent literature (Purkey and Smith, 1982; Roueche and Baker, 1986; Stedman, 1987; Wayson, 1988; Wimpelberg, Teddlie, and Stringfield, 1989) reveals a more comprehensive picture of what constitutes an effective school than that provided by earlier studies. Although Duttweiler continues to use the word *effective* to describe these schools, she has redefined the term. The following characteristics emerge from her synthesis (Duttweiler, 1990:72–74).

Effective Schools Are Student Centered

Effective schools make an effort to serve all students, create support networks to assist students, involve students in school affairs, respect and celebrate the ethnic and linguistic differences among students, and have student welfare as a first priority. They use community volunteers, parents, teacher aides, and peer tutors to provide close, personal attention to students. They involve students in many of the activities of running a school. Student needs are given priority over other concerns. An atmosphere of cooperation and trust is created through a high level of interaction between students and teachers.

Effective Schools Offer Academically Rich Programs

Student development and the provision of a well-rounded academic program are the primary goals. Effective schools address higher- as well as lower-order cognitive objectives, provide an enriched environment through a variety of options, have an active cocurricular program, provide in-depth coverage of content, and appropriately monitor student progress and provide feedback.

Effective Schools Provide Instruction That Promotes Student Learning

Effective schools have a distinctive normative structure that supports instruction. They design their programs to ensure academic success and to head off academic problems. Teachers and administrators believe that all students can learn and feel responsible for seeing that they do. Teachers and administrators believe in their own ability to influence students' learning. Teachers communicate expectations to students, provide focused and organized instructional sessions, adapt instruction to student needs, anticipate and correct student misconceptions, and use a variety of teaching strategies. In general, effective schools set high standards, closely and regularly monitor performance, and recognize and reward effort and success.

Effective Schools Have a Positive School Climate

Effective schools have a clear organizational personality, characterized by stated missions, goals, values, and standards of performance. They have a sense of order, purpose, and direction fostered by consistency among teachers; an atmosphere of encouragement in which students are praised and rewarded; a work-centered environment; and high optimism and expectations for student learning. Teachers and principals commit themselves to breaking down institutional and community barriers to equality. They create a learning environment that is open, friendly, and culturally inviting. Using community resources, they acknowledge the ethnic and racial identity of their students. They provide encouragement and take a positive approach to discipline. Administrators model the behaviors that they say are important.

Effective Schools Foster Collegial Interaction

Effective schools strive to create professional environments for teachers that facilitate the accomplishment of their work. Teachers participate in decisions affecting their work, have reasonable control or autonomy to carry out work, share a sense of purpose and community, receive recognition for contributions to the organization, and are treated with respect and dignity by others in the workplace. Teachers work together as colleagues to carry out instruction, plan curriculum, and refine teaching practices.

Effective Schools Have Extensive Staff Development

The teacher evaluation system is used to help teachers improve their skills. Inservice is practical, on-the-job training tailored to meet the specific needs of staff members. The emphasis is on the exchange of practical teaching techniques and on making training an integral part of a collaborative educational environment. Teachers and administrators conduct inservice programs and are provided with ample staff-development opportunities to help them develop further. Administrators and teachers are encouraged to reflect on their practices.

Effective Schools Practice Shared Leadership

Instructional leadership does not depend solely on the principal. School administrators understand and use a leadership style appropriate for professionals; solve problems through collaboration, team, or group decision making; know their staff members and delegate authority; communicate and build cohesiveness; and use their positions to recognize and reward accomplishments of both staff and students. While no single leadership style dominates, common leadership features include setting and maintaining direction for the school and facilitating the work of teachers by adopting a wide range of supportive behaviors. Involvement in decision making is a critical element. Involvement begins with members of the school community developing the goals, mission, and values of the school. Decisions are made with input from those to be affected by the decision.

Effective Schools Foster Creative Problem Solving

Staff members in effective schools are unwilling to accept defeat or settle for mediocrity. They turn their problems into challenges, design solutions, and implement them. They go about their tasks with commitment, creativity, persistence, and professionalism. Resources such as time, facilities, staff expertise, and volunteers are used to maximum advantage to facilitate the process of teaching and learning.

Effective Schools Involve Parents and the Community

There is a partnership linkage between the school and the community. Effective schools establish a variety of methods for communicating as well as working with parents and the community. They involve parents and community members in the teaching and learning activities of the school, include them in the decision-making process, have them serve as resources to extend the efforts of the school, and depend on them to be advocates as well as to provide good public relations for the school. They make sure that parents are involved in all aspects of their children's learning. Effective schools are contributory partners to the community they serve. They teach young people that they have a responsible part to play in society and that their contributions are valued and needed.

To this list, Stedman (1987) adds ethnic and racial pluralism, student responsibility for school affairs, and shared governance with parents and teachers. Stedman's conclusions are interesting because they rely on studies of successful schools conducted in the 1960s and early 1970s, as well as more recent studies, and thus provide a more "longitudinal" view.

Academic Press and Community Together

Recent research points to academic press and community as important factors in promoting student achievement. The two contribute to the development and strengthening of a school's organizational character—its unique focus, purpose, and sense of well-being. As Sebring and Bryk (1996) explain, these schools where student achievement is high "are safe, orderly, and respectful; they demand that students do significant academic work; and the teachers and staff work hard to provide the students with moral and personal support" (5). The researchers relied on personalism as a measure of community. *Personalism* refers to the extent to which students feel personally known and cared for. *Academic press* refers to the extent to which expectations are strongly communicated that students will work on intellectually challenging tasks, come to class prepared, and complete all assignments. These themes are accomplished by widespread and intense concern on the one hand and by support on the part of teachers on the other. Extra help is provided when needed and students are praised when they try and do well.

Sebring and Bryk (1996) found that emphasizing *both* academic press and personalism had a significantly greater influence on students being academically engaged than did an emphasis on just one factor or the other factor alone. *Academic engagement,* considered a prerequisite for student achievement, is defined as the extent to which students are connected to their academic work, try hard, are persistent, and are committed to learning. The relationships between academic press, personalism, and academic engagement are shown in Figure 8.1.

In their study of urban Catholic high schools that were effective with low-income minority children, Bryk, Lee, and Holland (1993) were able to link academic press (high expectations combined with clear and strongly held norms) and a strong sense of community with increases in academic achievement. Neither high communality and low academic press nor high academic press and low communality schools were very effective—a finding supported by Shouse (1996) in his national sample of high schools serving large numbers of low-income students.

It appears that personalism and academic press together are important in helping schools become caring and focused communities that are able to generate the necessary social capital that helps youngsters not only perform well but behave well. But neither caring nor academic performance can be scripted. Both must emerge from a particular school's sense of what is important, a particular school's inventory of values and purposes, and a particular school's commitment to do well and to manifest other characteristics that provide it with uniqueness, focus, and ultimately character.

The Importance of Character

Hill, Foster, and Gendler (1990) provide evidence of the link between school character and school effectiveness. These researchers studied 13 high schools in New York and Washington, D.C. Some of these schools were Catholic, others were pub-

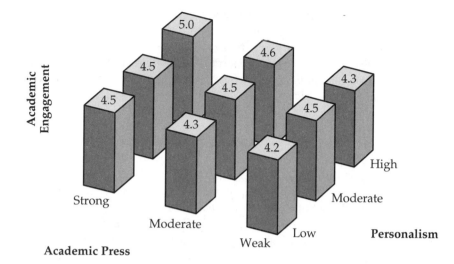

**FIGURE 8.1   Influence of Academic Press and Personalism on Academic
Engagement in Elementary Schools**

Source: "Student-Centered Learning Climate" by P. B. Sebring and A. S. Bryk in P. B. Sebring et al. (Eds.),
Charting Reform in Chicago: The Students Speak. Chicago: Consortium on Chicago School Research, 1996,
p. 13. Reprinted by permission.

Note: All the scales constructed for this graph were placed on a 0- to 10-point scale. The level of academic
engagement in schools were students report high personalism and strong press toward academic
achievement is significantly higher than in any other category of schools.

lic comprehensive schools, and still others were public magnet schools. The
researchers found that the more successful schools in this sample (the Catholic
schools and the public magnet schools) had unique, clear, and simple purposes centered on improving student academic performance and attitudes and on providing
the care, concern, and necessary arrangements to help the school achieve its unique
goals. The Catholic and public schools with unique and clear missions were labeled
as "focus schools," and their more undifferentiated and less effective public school
counterparts were labeled as "zoned schools." In the words of Hill, Foster, and
Gendler:

> *Focus schools [both Catholic and public] resemble one another and differ from
> zoned comprehensive public schools in two basic ways. First, focus schools have
> clear uncomplicated missions centered on the experiences the school intends to pro-
> vide its students and on the ways it intends to influence its students' performance,
> attitudes and behavior. Second, focus schools are strong organizations with the
> capacity to initiate action in pursuit of their missions, to sustain themselves over
> time, to solve their own problems, and to manage their external relationships. . . .
> Students and staff in each focus school consider their school special, a unique cre-
> ation that reflects their efforts and meets their needs. . . . (vii)*

Zoned public schools, in contrast, had diffuse missions defined by the demands of external funders and regulators. They are also profoundly compromised organizations, with little capacity to initiate their own solutions to problems, define their internal character, or manage their relationships with external audiences. Because zoned schools are essentially franchises reflecting a standard model established by central authorities, staff and students have less reason to consider the schools uniquely their own. (vii)

The researchers found that not only did focus schools concentrate on student outcomes but they also had established social covenants that communicated reciprocal role responsibilities for parents, students, teachers, and administrators. Further, they had developed a strong commitment to caring and were able to rally everyone around a set of values and ideas aimed at increasing levels of caring and civility as well as academic performance. Perhaps most important, these schools had a great deal of discretion. They were able to develop unique ways of doing things by being relatively unencumbered by bureaucratic mandates and structures from the outside. Their success, the researchers argued, is built around themes of uniqueness and specialness. They have specific educational and ethical principles or central zones that are used to guide behavior. These central zones function as a moral center that is able to deeply involve students and teachers in the life of the school. Zoned schools, by contrast, were much more differentiated with a one-size-fits-all mentality that provided few authentic alternatives and much less discretion—resulting in the erosion of institutional character.

In a recent analysis of the research, Hill and Celio (1998) identify characteristics of effective schools that are widely accepted—even by reformers who disagree on the means to make schools effective. The characteristics are accepted, for example, by those who oppose market approaches to reform and those who support market approaches. *Effectiveness* was defined as high rates of student learning. The characteristics include small school size; personalization; high expectations for students; collaboration among teachers; a simple, focused, and coherent curriculum; aggressive leadership; consistent standards for student behavior; family support; and peer support. Hill and Celio point out that though all the characteristics are important, none alone is sufficient to improve student learning. They describe the characteristics as follows:

- *Small schools allow faculty to know one another personally and to collaborate outside the big-school compartments of grade level and academic discipline. Small size also allows the principal to know every teacher and every student.*
- *Personalization, sometimes a consequence of small size, means that adults pay attention to the needs and development of every student and prevent emotional crises and learning plateaus from becoming serious problems.*
- *High expectations for all students lead faculty to regard a student's learning difficulties as a problem to be solved, not evidence of a permanent incapacity.*
- *Teacher collaboration implies that teachers coordinate their instruction so that students accumulate knowledge and understanding from course to course, and that teachers share responsibility for students' overall development.*

- *Aggressive school leadership focuses adult attention on the school's overall goals and fosters constant self-criticism, so that teachers do not assume that routines that worked for students in the past will also work today.*
- *Simple curricula focus the faculty's attention on a relatively small number of subjects, drawing all students toward learning a common core of challenging subjects.*
- *Consistent high standards for student behavior both inside and outside the school signal the school's commitment to learning and protects students from disruption by (and the temptation to disrupt) their peers. Such standards also eliminate corrosive doubts about the school's fairness toward students from different social classes and ethnic groups.*
- *Family support for the school ensures that parents will provide opportunities for homework and reinforce the school's demands on student time and attention.*
- *Supportive peer groups, which schools can foster at least in part by providing extracurricular opportunities and maintaining high standards for student behavior, weaken anti-school forces in the cool youth culture. (Hill and Celio, 1998, 30–31)*

Reflective Practice

Although lists of general characteristics are helpful, they should not be readily translated into specific prescriptions for management and leadership practice. What needs to be done to increase effectiveness and how one does it are situationally specific. What works for a failing school, for example, will not necessarily work for a competent school. What works for low socioeconomic status schools will not necessarily work for middle socioeconomic status schools. The early studies on school-effectiveness, for example, pointed out the importance of strong instructional leadership by the principal. The principal's job, according to this view, is to establish procedures and criteria for evaluating teachers, observe classrooms regularly and meet with teachers to discuss and improve classroom practices, and reward teachers for excellence in teaching. Furthermore, every effort must be made to ensure that what the teacher teaches is aligned with carefully delineated purposes, and both purposes and content are aligned with tests. Directing and monitoring the affairs of teaching and learning are essential to the principal's role.

Clearly, such principalship behaviors and expectations make sense in many situations but not in others. Being a strong instructional leader may be a good idea in schools where teachers are poorly trained or lacking in commitment, but it is not a good idea in schools where competence and commitment are not issues. In some schools, for example, teachers know more than the principal about matters of teaching and learning. To persist in providing strong instructional leadership in such a situation locks in teachers as instructional followers or subordinates and puts a cap on the total amount of leadership available in the school to promote better teaching and learning.

A number of researchers (e.g., Gersten, Carnine, and Green, 1982; Pajak and Glickman, 1989) have found that the leadership provided by lead teachers, assistant principals, grade-level heads, central office supervisors, department chairpersons, and teams of teachers are often the most critical factors in improving teaching and learning. What seems crucial to school improvement is not so much who provides the leadership but how much leadership there is. To that end, the principal as the leader of leaders may well be a more appropriate role where competence and commitment are not issues than would the role of instructional leader.

In summary, indiscriminate application of school-effectiveness research findings and, in particular, the development of generic lists of correlates or indicators that are subsequently applied uniformily to schools pose serious questions about the proper use of research and can result in negative, unanticipated consequences for teaching and learning. Wimpelberg, Teddlie, and Stringfield (1989) put it more bluntly: "It is patently foolish to attempt 'effective schools' changes in schools that are wholly different from the settings in which 'effective schools' correlates were isolated" (103). List of effectiveness characteristics as proposed by knowledgable researchers remain useful if viewed as general indicators. They are not so much truths to be applied uniformly, but rather as understanding that can help principals and others make more informed decisions about what to do and how in improving schools.

Perhaps Cuban (1998) is right. Searching for a single answer to the question "What is a good school?" may be misguided. Good schools might be traditional or progressive; have principals who use direct leadership and thus empower staff less or who use indirect leadership and thus empower staff more; rely on literature-based reading programs or phonics-based reading programs; use interest groups or rely on direct teaching; have gerbils and rabbits walking around the classroom or don't. What really matters in defining goodness, Cuban maintains, is:

1. "Are parents, staff, and students satisfied with what occurs in the school?"
2. "Is the school achieving the explicit goals it has set for itself?"
3. "Are democratic behaviors, values, and attitudes evident in the students" who graduate from this school? (p. 48)

References

Austin, Gilbert. 1978. "Process Evaluation: A Comprehensive Study of Outlines." Baltimore: Maryland State Department of Education. ERIC: ED 160 644.

Bloom, Benjamin S. 1964. *Stability and Change in Human Characteristics*. New York: Wiley.

Blumberg, Arthur, and William Greenfield. 1980. *The Effective Principal: Perspective on School Leadership*. Boston: Allyn and Bacon.

Bossert, Steven T., D. D. Dwyer, B. Rowan, and G. V. Lee. 1982. "The Instructional Management Role of the Principal," *Educational Administration Quarterly* 18(3), 34–64.

Brookover, Wilbur B., C. Brady, P. Flood, J. Schweigen, and J. Wisenbater. 1979. *School Systems and School Achievement: Schools Can Make a Difference*. New York: Praeger.

Brookover, Wilbur B., and Lawrence W. Lezotte. 1979. *Changes in School Characteristics Coincident with Changes in School Achievement*. East

Lansing: Institute for Research on Teaching, Michigan State University.

Bryk, Anthony S., Valerie E. Lee, and Peter B. Holland. 1993. *Catholic Schools and the Common Good*. Cambridge, MA: Harvard University Press.

Coleman, James, Ernest Q. Campbell, Carol J. Hobson, James McParland, Alexander M. Mood, Frederick D. Weinfeld, and Robert L. York. 1966. *Equality of Educational Opportunity*. Vol. 2. Washington, DC: U.S. Government Printing Office, OE-38001.

Cuban, Larry. 1998, January 28. "A Tale of Two Schools How Progressives and Traditionalists Undermine Our Understanding of What Is 'Good' in Schools," *Education Week* pp. 33, 48.

Duttweiler, Patricia Cloud. 1988. "New Insights from Research on Effective Schools," *Insights*, No. 4. Austin, TX: Southwest Educational Development Laboratory.

Duttweiler, Patricia Cloud. 1990. "A Broader Definition of Effective Schools: Implications from Research and Practice," in T. J. Sergiovanni and J. H. Moore (Eds.), *Target 2000: A Compact for Excellence in Texas's Schools*. Austin: Texas Association for Supervision and Curriculum Development.

Edmonds, Ronald. 1979. "Some Schools Work and More Can," *Social Policy* 9(2), 28–32.

Gersten, Russell, Douglas Carnine, and Susan Green. 1982, December. "The Principal as Instructional Leader: A Second Look," *Educational Leadership* 40, pp. 47–50.

Goodlad, John. 1983. A *Place Called School*. New York: McGraw-Hill.

Greenfield, William. 1982. A *Synopsis of Research on School Principals*. Washington, DC: National Institute for Education.

Hallinger, Philip, and Ronald H. Heck. 1996. "Reassessing the Principal's Role in School Effectiveness: A Review of the Empirical Research 1980–1995," *Educational Administration Quarterly* 32(1), 5–44.

Hallinger, Philip, and Joseph Murphy. 1985. "Assessing the Instructional Management Behavior of Principals," *The Elementary School Journal* 86(2), 217–247.

Hill, Paul T., and Mary Beth Celio. 1998. *Fixing*

Urban Schools. Washington, DC: The Brookings Institution Press.

Hill, Paul T., Gail E. Foster, and Tamar Gendler. 1990. *High Schools with Character*. Santa Monica, CA: RAND Corporation.

Lipsitz, Joan. 1984. *Successful Schools for Young Adolescents*. New Brunswick, NJ: Transaction.

MacBeath, John, Brian Boyd, Jim Rand, and Steve Bell. 1995. *Schools Speak for Themselves toward a Framework for Self-Evaluation*. London: The National Union of Teachers.

N.A.K. Production Associates and Association for Supervision and Curriculum Development. 1993, March 29. *Creating Learning Communities: The Comer Process*. Teleconference Coordinators Handbook.

Newberg, Norman A., and Allan A. Glatthorn. Undated. "Instructional Leadership: Four Ethnographic Studies of Junior High School Principals." Washington, DC: National Institute for Education (G-81–008).

Pajak, Edward F, and Carl D. Glickman. 1989. "Dimension of School District Improvement," *Educational Leadership* 46(8), 61–64.

Prunty, John J., and Wells Hively. 1982. "The Principal's Role in School Effectiveness: An Analysis of the Practices of Four Elementary School Leaders." Washington, DC: National Institute for Education (G-8-01-10) and CEMRL, Inc.

Purkey, S. C., and M. S. Smith. 1982. "Synthesis of Research on Effective Schools," *Educational Leadership* (40)3, 64–69.

Roueche, J. E., and G. A. Baker. 1986. *Profiling Excellence in America's Schools*. Arlington, VA: American Association of School Administrators.

Rutter, M., B. Maughan, P. Mortimore, J. Ouston, and A. Smith. 1979. *Fifteen Thousand Hours: Secondary Schools and Their Effects on Children*. Cambridge, MA: Harvard University Press.

Sebring, Penny Bender, and Anthony S. Bryk. 1996. "Student Centered Learning Climate," in Penny Bender Sebring et al. (Eds.), *Charting Reform in Chicago: The Students Speak*. A report sponsored by the Consortium on Chicago School Research. Chicago: University of Chicago.

Shouse, Roger C. 1996. "Academic Press and a Sense of Community: Conflict, Congruence, and Implications for Student Achievement," *Social Psychology of Education* 1, 47–68.

Stedman, Lawrence C. 1987. "It's Time We Changed the Effective Schools Formula," *Phi Delta Kappan* 69(3), 215–227.

Wayson, W. W. 1988. *Up from Excellence: The Impact of the Excellence Movement on Schools*. Bloomington, IN: Phi Delta Kappan Foundation.

Wimpelberg, Robert K., Charles Teddlie, and Samuel Stringfield. 1989. "Sensitivity to Context: The Past and Future of Effective Schools Research," *Educational Administration Quarterly* 25(1), 82–108.

9

BECOMING A COMMUNITY
OF MIND

No finding is more important to building a successful school than the link that exists between the school being able to develop social capital for all its students and their subsequent engagement with the school, behavior as school members, and academic performance. This is the message underlying the theme of Chapter 8 and a message reiterated in other chapters throughout this book.

Social capital consists of norms, obligations, and trusts that are generated by relationships among people in a school or school community (Coleman, 1988, 1990; Gamoran, 1996). Schools develop social capital by being caring communities (see, for example, Bryk and Driscoll, 1988; Battistich et al., 1994; Sergiovanni, 1994).

In schools we can think of social capital as having three dimensions—all linked to the development of human capital or the enhancement of the capacity of students, teachers, parents, and others to function more effectively. As social capital grows, so does human capital (Coleman, 1987).

> *Human capital is created by changes in persons that bring about skills and capabilities that make them able to act in new ways.*
>
> *Social capital, however, comes about through changes in the relations among persons that facilitate action.... Human capital facilitates productive activity, social capital does as well. For example, a group within which there is extensive trustworthiness and extensive trust is able to accomplish much more than a comparable group without that trustworthiness and trust (Coleman, 1988:S100–S101).*

This relationship is particularly important in schools, for society assigns to schools the official responsibility for the development of human capital.

The dimensions of social capital are academic, intellectual, and professional capital. *Academic capital* is linked to a school's increased capacity to develop a deep culture of teaching and learning and to focus attention of parents, teachers, and students on this endeavor. *Intellectual capital* refers to the ability of the school and its staff to learn, relearn, inquire, and grow in its ability to identify and solve problems, and in its ability to develop the ways and means to improve teaching and learning. *Professional capital* refers to the development of heightened levels of collegiality that link teachers morally to common goals and shared visions and to each other as members of a shared practice of teaching. Academic capital is created as schools become focused communities. Intellectual capital is created as schools become learning communities. Professional capital is created as schools become moral communities—places where teachers are committed to each other and to the parents and students they serve as parts of a web of reciprocal role responsibilities (Sergiovanni, 1998).

Social capital building in schools depends largely on the cultivation of a community of mind. In Chapter 4, *community* was defined as collections of individuals who are bonded together by natural will and who are together bound to a set of shared ideas and ideals. This bonding and binding is tight enough to transform them from a collection of "I"s into a collective "we." As a "we," members are part of a tightly knit web of meaningful relationships. This "we" usually shares a common place and over time comes to share sentiments and traditions that are sustaining.

When this definition of community is applied to schools, they become transformed from formal organizations to focused, caring, learning, and inquiring communities. Key to this transformation is building new kinds of relationships among people. This requires restructuring living and learning environments in ways that enhance the identity of teachers and students with each other, with the work of the school, and with the school itself. The aim is to build new connections among people and between them and their work that are idea- and norm-based, and to sanctify and ritualize these connections in ways that make them traditions rich in meaning and significance. As connections build, schools become communities by relationship, of place, of mind, and of memory.

Among the four dimensions of community, none is more important than the struggle to create a community of mind that bonds everyone together in special ways and binds them to a shared ideology. Schools, for example, cannot become caring communities unless caring is valued and unless a norm system develops that points the way toward caring, rewards caring behaviors, and frowns on non-caring behaviors. Nor can schools become focused, learning, or inquiring communities without valuing these respective images and without developing norm systems that guide their quest for embodying these images.

Community emerges from a network of shared ideologies. Ideologies are coherent sets of beliefs that tie people together and that explain their work to them in terms of cause and effect relationships (Trice and Beyer, 1984). Ideologies are the means by which we make sense of our lives, find a direction, and commit ourselves to courses of action. In communities, ideologies shape what principals and teachers believe and how they practice. They influence, as well, the norm structure and behavior of students.

The Importance of Goals

Goals are an important part of a school's community of mind. Nonetheless, disagreement exists among those who study schools as to how the term *goals* should be defined and understood, and even as to whether goals actually make a difference in the decisions that principals and teachers make about schooling. Many prominent organizational theorists doubt whether organizations actually have goals; for example, Perrow (1981) states: "The notion of goals may be a mystification, hiding an errant, vagrant, changeable world" (8). He continues:

> *Do organizations have goals, then, in the rational sense of organizational theory? I do not think so. In fact, when an executive says, "This is our goal" chances are that he is looking at what the organization happens to be doing and saying, "Since we are all very rational here, and we are doing this, this must be our goal." Organizations in this sense, run backward; the deed is father to the thought, not the other way around. (8)*

Other organizational theorists have commented that schools are loosely structured (Bidwell, 1965; Weick, 1976), suggesting that parts tend to operate independently of one another. Teachers, for example, work alone in classrooms; their work is not visible to others. Close supervision under these circumstances is difficult, and continuous evaluation of teaching is impossible. No mechanism exists to ensure that school mandates, such as stated goals, are reflected in actual teaching. Coordination of the work of several teachers is difficult to achieve.

Because direct supervision and tight coordination are difficult to implement successfully in loosely structured schools, principals need to rely on the management of symbols to rally teachers to a common cause. Although schools may be loosely structured in the way they are organized, effective schools combine this loosely structured characteristic with a tightly structured core of values and beliefs. This core represents the cultural cement that bonds people together, gives them a sense of identity, and provides them with guidelines for their work.

But are symbols the same as goals? At one level, symbols and goals share common characteristics and similar functions. Weick's view is that symbols are more like *charters* than goals. They tell people *what* they are doing and *why* they are doing it. They reveal to people the importance and significance of their work. Goals, however, provide direction and are devices for telling people when and how well they are doing things (Weick, 1982:676).

The more generally goals are stated, the closer they approximate symbols. As goals become more precise, they tend to lose symbolic value and to resemble instrumental objectives designed to program daily school activities. They serve less to provide a sense of purpose or to instill a feeling of significance and more to guide what teachers should be doing at a given moment. Goals as symbols sacrifice precision, detail, and instrumentality to gain significance and meaning. They seek to capture the spirit of teachers at work. Objectives, however, sacrifice significance and meaning in an attempt to gain instrumental power over what teachers are doing at a given moment and to provide ready measures of how well they are performing these tasks.

Experts who describe schools as being loosely structured maintain that instrumental control is difficult to achieve. Behind closed classroom doors, they argue, teachers follow the beat of a different drummer—selecting learning materials and deciding on what and how to teach not in response to objectives, but in response to available materials, their own intuitions and abilities, their perceptions of student needs, time constraints, and other situational characteristics. Tight school structures, they maintain, simply cannot reach into the classroom and challenge this de facto autonomy of the teacher no matter how detailed such structures might be or how eloquently they might be described. Because the influence of direct control is blunted by de facto teacher autonomy, the significance of goal-symbols as a means of influence in schools is increased.

Goals as Patterns

Hills (1982) points out that in the real world, principals rarely find themselves in a position where they can pursue goals one at a time. The problem they face is that schools have multiple goals. Furthermore, sometimes the goals conflict with each other. Making progress toward one goal may mean losing progress toward another. Always thinking in terms of discrete goals or even discrete multiple goals with each attended to sequentially by the principal, therefore, does not fit the special character of the school's unique value system. Under loosely structured conditions, schools don't achieve goals as much as they respond to certain values and tend to certain imperatives that ensure their survival over time.

Parsons (1951), for example, identified four imperatives that must be balanced against each other in such a way that each is maximized in order for the school or any other institution to survive. The neglect of any of these imperatives causes the other to decline, which means trouble for the school. The imperatives are *goal attainment; internally maintaining day-to-day stability and functions; adopting to external demands, concerns, and circumstances;* and, finally, *tending to the cultural patterns and norms* that hold the school together over time. External adoption, for example, often threatens internal stability and upsets cultural patterns. Maintaining cultural patterns often interferes with goal attainment, and so forth.

Rather than discrete goal attainment, Hills points out that principals bring to their practice what he calls "pattern rationality." They behave in response to "a conception of pattern development on a number of mutually limiting dimensions with respective gains in a given area having implications for others" (1982:7). Successful principals become surfers, skilled at riding the wave of the pattern as it unfolds. They respond to value patterns when discrete goals are in conflict with each other. Important to the concept of pattern rationality is that principals be concerned with the costs and benefits of their actions.

Goals as Symbols

School boards, state departments of education, and other groups and institutions expect schools to have goals. Goal statements are therefore necessary to symbolically portray the school as being rational and thus legitimate to outsiders. Rational schools are supposed to have goals and purposes and are supposed to pursue them deliberately. Schools, for example, are expected to behave rationally by accrediting agencies, state governments, the local press, the local school board, and other groups. Thus, stated goals and purposes are necessary to obtain legitimacy from these and other groups.

It is clear that some discrepancy exists between stated goals and what schools actually do. This gap is more evident as goals take the form of actual intents (specifying exactly what we will accomplish) than the form of beliefs (specifying what is important and valued). Statements of beliefs provide the language necessary to bond people together in a common cause, to provide them with a sense of direction, and to establish a standard by which they can evaluate their actions and from which meanings for their actions can be derived. The more successful the school, the stronger is this bonding and the stronger is the link between beliefs, decisions, and actions.

Findings from the successful schools research parallel those of Peters and Waterman (1982) in their studies of excellent business corporations. In their words: "Every excellent company we studied is clear on what it stands for, and takes the process of value shaping seriously. In fact, we wonder whether it is possible to be an excellent company without clarity of values and without having the right sorts of values" (280). They continue:

> *Virtually all of the better performing companies we looked at in the first study had a well-defined set of guiding beliefs. The less well-performing institutions, on the other hand, were marked by one of two characteristics. Many had no set of coherent beliefs. The others had distinctive and widely discussed objectives, but the only ones that they got animated about were the ones that could be quantified (the financial objectives, such as earnings per share and growth measures). (281)*

In describing his many years of experience at the helm of IBM, Thomas Watson, Jr. (1963) highlights the importance of goals and symbols as statements of beliefs as follows:

> *I firmly believe that any organization, in order to survive and achieve success, must have a sound set of beliefs on which it premises all its policies and actions. Next, I believe that the most important single factor in corporate success is faithful adherence to these beliefs. And, finally, I believe that if an organization is to meet the challenge of a changing world, it must be prepared to change everything about itself except those beliefs as it moves through corporate life. In other words, the basic philosophy, spirit, and drive of an organization have far more to do with its relative achievements than do technological or economic resources, organizational*

structure, innovation, and timing. All these things weigh heavily in success. But they are, I think, transcended by how strongly the people in the organization believe in its basic precepts and how faithfully they carry them out. (4–6)

Corporations, of course, are different from schools. They are generally considered to be more quantitative, impersonal, and instrumental. Schools, by contrast, are much more human-intensive. Although values are important to both, they are presumed to be more central to the inner workings of schools. Thus, providing examples from the corporate world illustrating the importance of goals, values, and beliefs should serve as notice to principals and other educators that such statements are even more important to schools.

Statements of belief provide the common cement, bonding people together as they work on behalf of the school. Operationally, such beliefs form an *education platform* for the school and principal. Educational platforms should be thought of as encompassing the defining principles and beliefs that guide the actions of individuals and that provide a basis for evaluating these actions. Leaders of successful schools have well-defined educational platforms from which they operate. Indeed, successful schools contain fairly well-developed educational platforms serving as guides to teachers and others as they live and work in the school. Platforms are not objectives or specifications of what exactly is to be accomplished; instead, they contain guiding principles from which individuals decide what to do and how to do it. The more loosely structured the school, the more important is the concept of educational platform in bringing about cohesion and concerted action. Platforms are the means by which mission statements and broad goals and purposes are articulated into practice.

When taken together, platforms, mission statements, and broad goals and purposes constitute a covenant of shared values that functions as the cultural center of the school—the repository of that which is held sacred by all. As pointed out in Chapter 3, at the heart of any culture is what the noted sociologist Edward A. Shils (1961) calls the "central zone." He believes that all societies and organizations within societies have central zones that provide a sense of order and stability and a source for the development of norms that gives meaning and significance to the lives of people. The school's central zone represents a repository for the emotions and values that become the basis for moral authority.

Centers evolve naturally in schools in response to human needs, but if left unattended they can take the form of "wild cultures." Wild cultures are driven by emotions and values that may or may not be compatible with school goals, may or may not be supportive of improved teaching and learning, may or may not be growth oriented, and may or may not be good for students. One of the jobs of the principal is to try to unravel and make manifest the wild culture so that it can be examined and understood. Doing so helps those involved come to grips with what is in relation to the values and beliefs that are desired. The idea is to "domesticate" this culture so that it emerges as a system of shared values and beliefs that define for all a way of life that is committed to quality teaching and learning. The goal of domestication is to create community.

When domesticated, the center that defines the school culture becomes the basis for collective decision making and the basis for moral action. The actions and behaviors of parents, teachers, students, and others are driven less by self-interest and more by what the school community considers to be right and good. In this chapter, *center* is referred to as the *covenant* of shared values that determines for the school what is right and good, points to the school's mission, defines obligations and duties, and spells out what must be done to meet commitments.

Purposing Is the Linchpin

Key to domesticating the culture of the school along the lines of community is the building of a covenant of shared values that replaces more implicit and informal norms. Zaleznik (1988) believes that "the failure of American management is the substitution of process for substance." He attributes this substitution to an exaggerated belief that schools can be improved by perfecting management systems, structures, and programs and by emphasizing human relationships in order to better control what people do. Too often, process and relationship means become ends in themselves, resulting in vacuous school improvement strategies (Sergiovanni and Duggan, 1990).

To Zaleznik, "leadership is based on a compact that binds those who lead and those who follow into the same moral, intellectual and emotional commitment" (1988:15). Purposing is what principals do to develop this compact. Purposing involves both the vision of the leader and the covenant that the group shares.

Vision in school leadership needs to be understood differently than the way it emerges from the corporate sector. Peters and Austin (1985), for example, point out that vision should start with a single person and suggest that one should be wary of "committee visions." There is some truth to this observation, but there are problems as well. Principals and superintendents have a responsibility and obligation to talk openly and frequently about their beliefs and commitments. They are responsible for encouraging a dialogue about what the school stands for and where it should be headed. Vision, however, should not be construed as a strategic plan that functions like a road map charting the turns needed to reach a specific reality that the leader has in mind. It should, instead, be viewed more as a compass that points the direction to be taken, that inspires enthusiasm, and that allows people to buy into and take part in the shaping of the way that will constitute the school's mission (Bricker, 1985). The fleshing out of this vision requires the building of a shared consensus about purposes and beliefs that creates a powerful force bonding people together around common themes. This bonding provides them with a sense of what is important and some signal of what is of value. *With bonding in place, the school is transformed from an organization to a community.*

Often overlooked is the importance of the personal visions of teachers. As Barth (1986) points out:

> *All of us who entered teaching brought with us a conception of a desirable school. Each of us had a personal vision and was prepared to work, even fight, for it. Over*

*time our personal visions became blurred by the visions, demands, and require-
ments of others. Many teachers' personal visions are now all but obliterated by
external prescriptions. (478)*

Vision is a noun that describes what principals and others bring to the school.
Purposing is a verb that points to what principals do to bring about a shared consensus tight enough and coherent enough to bond people together in a common cause
and to define them as a community, but loose enough to allow for individual self-
expression.

Purposes in Action

Purposes let people know where the school is going, why, and how. Sometimes
purpose statements contain bedrock beliefs that comprise value assumptions about
the nature of people. The following four beliefs, for example, are based on Purkey
and Novak's (1988) proposal for an approach to schooling they call *invitational education:*

1. Teachers, parents, students, and everyone else with whom the school works are
   able, valuable, and responsible and should be treated accordingly.
2. Education should be a collaborative, cooperative activity.
3. Teachers, parents, students, and everyone else with whom the school works
   possess untapped potential in all areas of human endeavor.
4. Human potential can best be realized by places, policies, and processes that are
   designed to invite development and by the actions and behaviors of people
   who are intentionally inviting.

When adopted, the four beliefs become a policy platform from which decisions
are made about how to organize the school and its curriculum, how people are to
work together, and the tone of teaching that is expected. The first belief, for example, frames policies about success and failure. If the principal and teachers believe
that every parent is worthy of respect and can learn, then they will find ways for
parents to improve their parenting skills, to learn about how to help their children
at home with their lessons, and so forth. Excuses such as "they are barely literate
themselves" and "they don't speak English" would not be acceptable. This formula
applies as well to student success.

Similarly, the second belief frames policies in the direction of cooperation
rather than competition. Good policies and practices in a school committed to those
beliefs are those that do things *with* people rather than *to* people. They give parents,
teachers, and students voices, and they listen to these voices. Similar guidelines for
action can be derived from beliefs three and four.

Sometimes purposes take the form of a set of common principles that combine
beliefs with understandings and expectations. "The Common Principles" of the
Coalition of Essential Schools, a national effort to restructure secondary schools
founded by Theodore Sizer, is an example of this approach. Sizer believes that no

two good schools are quite alike. Instead, each should be a creation of its unique school-community. Thus, advocating common principles rather than proposing a model to be emulated makes sense. The principles of the coalition are as follows:

1. An Essential school should focus on helping adolescents learn to use their minds well. Schools should not attempt to be "comprehensive" if such a claim is made at the expense of the school's central intellectual purpose.

2. The school's goals should be simple: that each student master a limited number of essential skills and areas of knowledge. While these skills and areas will, to varying degrees, reflect the traditional academic disciplines, the program's design should be shaped by the intellectual and imaginative powers and competencies that students need, rather than by "subjects" as conventionally defined. The aphorism "less is more" should dominate. Curricular decisions should be guided by the aim of thorough student mastery and achievement rather than by an effort merely to "cover content."

3. The school's goals should apply to all students, although the means to these goals will vary as those students themselves vary. School practice should be tailor-made to meet the needs of every group or class of adolescents.

4. Teaching and learning should be personalized to the maximum feasible extent. Efforts should be directed toward a goal that no teacher have direct responsibility for more than 80 students. To capitalize on personalization, decisions about the course of study, the use of students' and teachers' time, and the choice of teaching materials and specific pedagogics must be unreservedly placed in the hands of the principal and staff.

5. The governing practical metaphor of the school should be student-as-worker, rather than the more familiar metaphor of teacher-as-deliverer-of-instructional-services. A prominent pedagogy will be coaching, to provoke students to learn how to learn and thus to teach themselves.

6. Students entering secondary school studies should be those who can show competence in language and elementary mathematics. Students of traditional high school age but not yet at appropriate levels of competence to enter secondary school studies should be provided intensive remedial work to help them meet these standards. The diploma should be awarded upon a successful final demonstration of mastery for graduation—an "exhibition." This exhibition by the student of his or her grasp of the central skills and knowledge of the school's program may be jointly administered by the faculty and by higher authorities. The diploma is awarded when earned, so the school's program proceeds with no strict age grading and with no system of credits collected by time spent in class. The emphasis is on the students' demonstration that they can do important things.

The tone of the school should stress values of unanxious expectation ("I won't threaten you but I expect much of you"); of trust (until abused); and of decency (the values of fairness, generosity, and tolerance). Incentives appropriate to the school's particular students and teachers should be emphasized, and parents should be treated as essential collaborators.

7. The principal and teachers should perceive themselves as generalists first (teacher and scholars in general education), and specialists second (experts in one particular discipline). Staff should expect multiple obligations (teacher-counselor-manager), and demonstrate a sense of commitment to the entire school.

8. Ultimate administrative and budget targets should include, in addition to total student loads per teacher of 80 or fewer pupils, substantial time for collective planning by teachers, competitive salaries for staff, and an ultimate per pupil cost not to exceed that at traditional schools by more than 10 percent. To accomplish this, administrative plans might include the phased reduction or elimination of some services now provided for students in many traditional comprehensive secondary schools. (Sizer, 1989:2–4)

Sometimes the substance of a school's covenant comprises a commitment to a set of ideals and beliefs or "theory" about the nature of schooling. This is the case in the Key School in the Indianapolis, Indiana, School District. This school is organized around Howard Gardner's (1983) theory of multiple intelligences. Gardner proposes that people are possessed by seven relatively autonomous intellectual competencies: linguistic and mathematical (the two now emphasized almost exclusively in schools), musical, spatial, bodily-kinesthetic, and two personal intelligences (one focusing on self-understanding and the other on the understanding of others). The Key School gives all seven of these intelligences equal emphasis through the use of an interdisciplinary curriculum. Belief in a common approach to teaching and a common conception of human potential is the core element that bonds together the Key School faculty into a common cause.

"Expeditionary learning" (Outward Bound USA Convenor, 1992), one of several models of schools advocated by New American Schools, is another example of how school purposes can provide the kind of idea structure that gives direction and guides decisions that schools make. Those involved in this movement seek to transform schools into centers of expeditionary learning. They believe that learning is an expedition into the unknown that requires bringing together personal experience and intellectual growth to promote self-discovery and construct knowledge. Schools committed to the expeditionary learning approach are not provided with scripts to implement but with design principles and components. As is the case with the essential schools movement, the design principles and components serve to inform the decisions that schools make. The principles, along with a handful of key program components that provide a standard for how the principles should be implemented, appear in Table 9.1.

Characteristics of Purpose Statements

There is no recipe for developing a covenant of shared values. It is a "personal" statement that is developed and owned by a particular school-community. A good

TABLE 9.1   **Expeditionary Learning Outward Bound® Design Principles and Components**

Principles

1. **The Primacy of Self-Discovery:** Learning happens best with emotion, challenge, and the requisite support. People discover their abilities, values, "grand passions," and responsibilities in situations that offer adventure and the unexpected. They must have tasks that require perseverance, fitness, craftsmanship, imagination, self-discipline, and significant achievement. A primary job of the educator is to help students overcome their fear and discover they have more in them than they think.

2. **The Having of Wonderful Ideas:** Teach so as to build on children's curiosity about the world by creating learning situations that provide matter to think about, time to experiment, and time to make sense of what is observed. Foster a community where students' and adults' ideas are respected.

3. **The Responsibility for Learning:** Learning is both a personal, individually specific process of discovery and a social activity. Each of us learns within and for ourselves and as a part of a group. Every aspect of a school must encourage children, young people, and adults to become increasingly responsible for directing their own personal and collective learning.

4. **Intimacy and Caring:** Learning is fostered best in small groups where there is trust, sustained caring, and mutual respect among all members of the learning community. Keep schools and learning groups small. Be sure there is a caring adult looking after the progress of each child. Arrange for the older students to mentor the younger ones.

5. **Success and Failure:** All students must be assured a fair measure of success in learning in order to nurture the confidence and capacity to take risks and rise to increasingly difficult challenges. But it is also important to

experience failure, to overcome negative inclinations, to prevail against adversity, and to learn to turn disabilities into opportunities.

6. **Collaboration and Competition:** Teach so as to join individual and group development so that the value of friendship, trust, and group endeavor is made manifest. Encourage students to compete, not against each other, but with their own personal best and with rigorous standards of excellence.

7. **Diversity and Inclusivity:** Diversity and inclusivity in all groups dramatically increases richness of ideas, creative power, problem-solving ability, and acceptance of others. Encourage students to investigate, value, and draw on their own different histories, talents, and resources together with those of other communities and cultures. Keep the schools and learning groups heterogeneous.

8. **The Natural World:** A direct and respectful relationship with the natural world refreshes the human spirit and reveals the important lessons of recurring cycles and cause and effect. Students learn to become stewards of the earth and of the generations to come.

9. **Solitude and Reflection:** Solitude, reflection, and silence replenish our energies and open our minds. Be sure students have time alone to explore their own thoughts, make their own connections, and create their own ideas. Then give them opportunities to exchange their reflections with each other and with adults.

10. **Service and Compassion:** We are crew, not passengers, and are strengthened by acts of consequential service to others. One of a school's primary functions is to prepare its students with the attitudes and skills to learn from and be of service to others.

Continued

TABLE 9.1   *Continued*

Components

1. **Schedule, Structure, Teacher-Student Relationships:** Implementing Expeditionary Learning will require a complete reconsideration of the relationships among staff and students, as well as the schools' arrangements of time and space. Schools should be prepared to eliminate the 50-minute period as the basic scheduling unit and to replace it with a schedule organized to accommodate learning expeditions that may engage students full time for periods of days, weeks, or months.

   Interdisciplinary learning expeditions will replace subject-separated classes. Tracking will be eliminated; Teachers will work with the same group of students for periods of several years.

2. **Curriculum:** Expeditionary Learning engages the learner in situations that provide not only context but consequence. The curriculum makes intellectual learning and character development of equal importance and encourages self-discovery.

3. **Assessment:** Expeditionary Learning uses real-world performance as the primary way to assess effectiveness in teaching and learning. The International Baccalaureate is used as a framework for establishing world-class standards.

4. **Staff Development:** Expeditionary Learning depends on and invests in the ongoing development and renewal of staff. An apprenticeship model, flexibility in hiring or reassignment, and a substantial investment in year-round staff growth is required.

5. **Linkages to Community and Health Service Organizations:** To provide necessary support to students and their families, expeditionary centers will develop working relations with the appropriate service agencies.

6. **Budget:** Expeditionary Learning achieves its goals through reorganization of existing resources and should not require significant additional funding after an initial period of transition.

Sources: Expeditionary Learning Outward Bound.® (1993). *The Expeditionary Learning Reader* Expeditionary Learning: Cambridge, MA. Vol. 1. The above principles have been informed by Kurt Hahn's "Seven Laws of Salem," by Paul Ylvisaker's "The Missing Dimension," and by Eleanor Duckworth's *"The Having of Wonderful Ideas" and Other Essays on Teaching and Learning* (New York: Teachers College Press, Columbia University, 1987).

convenant, however, should communicate a school's key purposes. Here are some general characteristics of purposes that might be helpful to schools. Purposes should have the following criteria:

1. Clear enough so that you know you are achieving them
2. Accessible enough so that they can be achieved with existing resources
3. Important enough to reflect the core values and beliefs that are shared by those with a stake in the school
4. Powerful enough that they can inspire and touch people in a world that is managerially loose and culturally tight
5. Focused and few in number so that it is clear as to what is important and what isn't
6. Characterized by consonance (the purposes should "hang together" as a group); it should be clear that contradictory purposes can be managed
7. Difficult enough to evoke challenge and cause people to persevere, to persist
8. Resilient enough to stand the test of time and thus not be easily changed

9. Flexible enough to be changed after careful consideration

Taken together, a good set of purposes should encourage cooperation within the school, and not competition. Cooperative purposes encourage people to work together by allowing each member to share in what the group achieves or attains. Everyone benefits when anyone is successful. Competitive purposes, by contrast, pit one person against another. Each member receives rewards independent of the success of the group and contingent only on her or his own performance, regardless of how well the group does.

Both Discipline and Discretion Are Key

Shared purposes, covenants, design principles, and other agreements should provide enough discipline to ensure that focus, clarity, and harmony characterize what teachers do. This discipline, however, must be achieved without taking away the discretion teachers need to make decisions in light of the unique circumstances that they face. A good idea structure, in other words, doesn't tell people what to do but informs the decisions they make about what to do. This is a theme that will be explored in detail in Chapter 10, "Layered Standards, Holistic Assessment." One way to achieve both discipline and discretion is by striking a balance among instructional, problem solving, and expressive outcomes (Eisner, 1969, 1979) as curriculum experiences are planned. Instructional outcomes are set beforehand and in fairly specific ways. They are stated in terms of what the student is supposed to be able to do as a result of teaching. Curriculum and teaching decisions are made by designing down from the instructional outcomes. Problem-solving outcomes are shaped by the decisions made about problems that students must solve and exhibitions they must master and perform. Expressive outcomes are discovered during and after the teaching of trusted subject matter and the use of trusted teaching activities—trusted means that they are known for their ability to stimulate learning.

In a sense, instructional outcomes represent baseball strike zones. Teaching to them represents the pitching of learning into a particular strike zone. Balls and strikes must be called to keep track of how effective the teaching is in achieving the outcomes. For example, in teaching a lesson or unit on the jury system, we might state the following instructional outcomes: (1) the student will be able to differentiate between the roles and functions of various principles in a jury trial (e.g., prosecuting attorney, defense attorney, bailiff, types of witnesses) and (2) the student will be able to write two coherent paragraphs that describe the differences in rules of evidence for civil trials as opposed to criminal trials. If the student performs according to the specified behaviors, then we have a strike. If she or he does not, then it's a ball. When a ball is called, the teaching pitches do not count, even though what the student learns may be as important or more important than the instructional outcome that was stated. The student, for example, may not be able to differentiate the rules of evidence as required, but is able to detect flaws in arguments better than before. The student may not be able to differentiate the various roles very well, but she or he has a greater appreciation for the fairness and effectiveness of the judicial system. Sorry, it's still a ball. The learning doesn't count because it does not fit into the strike zone.

In the real world of teaching, good teachers often change their minds as they teach. Sometimes they chase a student's ideas and wind up at a place different than originally intended. The strike zone that counts for them moves to another position; however, the strike zone that counts officially stands still, converting perfectly sound and sensible strikes into balls.

When using only instructional outcomes, the curriculum intended, the curriculum taught, and the curriculum learned must always be aligned with each other. Thus, once outcomes are set (discipline), teachers have increasingly less say over the taught and learned curriculum (discretion). It often makes sense to insist that students be able to demonstrate exactly what they are supposed to demonstrate. Thus, instructional outcomes have an important role to play, but so do problem solving and expressive outcomes. Balance is needed among the three if both discipline and discretion are to be achieved.

Problem-solving outcomes are harder to nail down in a specific way beforehand, but they are hardly serendipitous. By carefully crafting a problem, we can increase the likelihood that certain kinds of outcomes will emerge. Eisner (1979) explains:

> *The problem-solving objective differs in a significant way from the behavioral [instructional] objective. In the problem-solving objective, the students formulate or are given a problem to solve—say to find out how deterrents to smoking might be made more effective, or how to design a paper structure that will hold two bricks sixteen inches above a table, or how the variety and quality of food served in the school cafeteria could be increased within the existing budget. (101)*

It's not enough just to state the problem; certain criteria need to be provided that set a standard for how the problem will be solved. The more specific the criteria, the more the range of outcomes becomes narrowed. The forms of the solution, however, remain infinite. With instructional outcomes, both questions and answers are set ahead of time. With problem-solving objectives, the question is set but the answer is not definite.

Problems-based learning provides a happy balance between discipline and discretion for both teachers and students. Teachers might agree, for example, on the problems that students will solve in a given unit, course, or grade level. However, because no single answer or no one solution exists for the typical problem, teachers have flexibility in making choices about what will be studied, what materials will be used, what teaching approaches to use, what learning settings to invent, and so forth. Furthermore, students have discretion; within the parameters of the problem, they decide how they will learn and what they will learn. As teachers monitor learning, they make decisions that shape what students are doing and that are shaped by what students are doing. Despite discretion, a certain coherence and focus is maintained by the parameters the problem provides.

Problem-solving outcomes play a major role in organizing the curriculum, arranging learning experiences, teaching, and evaluating in schools that are committed to the principles of both the Coalition of Essential Schools and expeditionary learning. These schools rely heavily on exhibitions of mastery as the construct for organizing the curriculum, for teaching and learning, and for evaluating.

Expressive outcomes, according to Eisner (1969), are what one ends up with, whether intended or not, after being engaged in a learning experience. "Expressive outcomes are the consequences of curriculum activities that are intentionally planned to provide a fertile opportunity for personal purposing and experiences" (26). The emphasis is on the activity itself, the learning experience that the student will be engaged in, and the content or the subject matter, not the specifics of what the student will learn as a result of this engagement.

Although expressive outcomes are not anticipated prior to the actual teaching, they represent valued learnings nonetheless. Good teachers, for example, know and trust the potential of certain ideas, activities, and experiences to promote learning. They know that when students engage in them, good things happen. Although the teacher cannot say exactly what students will get out of the experience, she or he has always found that they learned a great deal when engaging in the learning activity.

Instructional outcomes, problem-solving outcomes, and expressive outcomes all have important roles to play in curriculum planning. When brought together, they allow teachers to make decisions that reflect the discipline necessary for purposeful community building. Furthermore, this discipline is achieved without compromising the discretion needed to make informed decisions in light of the ambiguities found in the typical teaching and learning situation. Discretion increases the likelihood that effective teaching and learning decisions will be made and that effective caring decisions will be made. Discretion allows the building of an inquiring community as teachers puzzle together over what decisions make the most sense. In addition, discretion embodies professional community by allowing teachers to take control of their practice.

Providing the Necessary Leadership

Shared goals and purposes, agreed-upon covenants, and other statements of what is believed are the nerve center of a successful school. They provide the necessary signals, symbols, substance, and direction needed for coordinated action on behalf of quality in schooling. The clarity and coherence they provide cannot be duplicated by close supervision, management controls, and other regulatory measures, for these latter practices require a much tighter connection among school parts, roles, and activities than is typically found in schools. Loosely structured schools achieve coordinated action by creating a powerful normative system that serves to socialize newcomers and to provide reinforcement to those already socialized. Furthermore, this normative system provides a source of meaning and direction to those who live and work in the school.

Principal leadership in tight value and loose decision-making schools is more complicated than first seems apparent. It requires the balancing of both flexible and resilient leadership styles. Effective principals display a great deal of resiliency when concerned with the school's goal structure, educational platform, and overall philosophy. At the same time, they display a great deal of flexibility when concerned with the everyday articulation of these values into teaching and learning practices and designs. Before continuing with this discussion, let's examine the Style Flexibility Index (SFI) and the Style Resilience Index (SRI) shown in Exhibits 9.1 and 9.2. The items in these indexes were suggested by W. J. Reddin's (1970) discussion of style flexibility and style resilience. Respond to each of the indexes and obtain flexibility and resilience scores. Keep in mind that both indexes suggest only how you might be perceived on these dimensions by others with whom you work.

Now let's examine the concepts of flexibility and resilience. Flexibility is perhaps best understood by understanding its relationship to drifting. As leadership concepts, both flexibility and drifting comprise the same behaviors. Yet, expressions of these behaviors might result in effectiveness in one situation and ineffectiveness in another. When the behavior expressed matches the situation, the principal will be viewed as being highly flexible. When the exact same behavior is expressed in inappropriate situations, the principal is viewed as drifting.

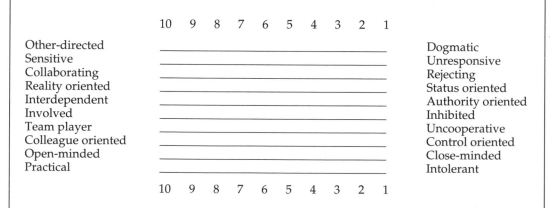

EXHIBIT 9.1   Style Flexibility Index

Think of occasions, situations, and incidents when you, as a school principal, were interacting directly with teachers about *day-to-day and week-to-week decisions involving instructional materials, subject-matter content, classroom organization, and the provision of teaching and learning*. As a result of this interaction, indicate how teachers would describe you, using the 10 paired statements provided below.

	10 9 8 7 6 5 4 3 2 1	
Other-directed		Dogmatic
Sensitive		Unresponsive
Collaborating		Rejecting
Reality oriented		Status oriented
Interdependent		Authority oriented
Involved		Inhibited
Team player		Uncooperative
Colleague oriented		Control oriented
Open-minded		Close-minded
Practical		Intolerant
	10 9 8 7 6 5 4 3 2 1	

Scoring: Sum the scores given to each of the 10 scales of the Style Flexibility Index. Scores will range from a low of 10 to a high of 100. The higher the score, the more flexible one is perceived to be. An improved indication of style flexibility would be obtained by having teachers actually describe their principal.

EXHIBIT 9.2   Style Resilience Index

Think of occasions, situations, and incidents when you, as a principal, were interacting directly with teachers about *general goals and purposes, educational platform, and overall philosophy of the school.* As a result of this interaction, indicate how teachers would describe you, using the 10 paired statements provided below.

	10 9 8 7 6 5 4 3 2 1	
Clear goals	_____	Inconsistent
Fulfills commitments	_____	Uncommitted
Willpower	_____	Avoids conflict
Individualistic	_____	Conforming
Decisive	_____	Indecisive
Reliable	_____	Disorganized
Self-confident	_____	Avoids rejection
Simplifies issues	_____	Ambiguous
Persistent	_____	Yielding
Tough-minded	_____	Wavering
	10 9 8 7 6 5 4 3 2 1	

Scoring: Sum the scores given to each of the 10 scales of the Style Resilience Index. Scores will range from a low of 10 to a high of 100. The higher the score, the more flexible one is perceived to be. An improved indication of style flexibility would be obtained by having teachers actually describe their principal.

Reddin (1970) points out that style flexibility in leadership is characterized by high ambiguity tolerance, power sensitivity, an open belief system, and other-directedness. Highly flexible principals are comfortable in unstructured situations, are not control oriented, bring to the work context very few fixed ideas, and display a great deal of interest in the ideas of others. These characteristics are very desirable when articulated within the loosely structured discretionary space of schools, but in matters of the school's goal structure and educational platform, flexibility by the principal is often viewed negatively by teachers and others. When this is the case, the principal's style can be described as drifting rather than flexible. Drifting suggests a lack of direction and an absence of commitment to a purpose or cause.

Rigidity is the concept that Reddin suggests to understand counterproductive expressions of resilience. The resilient leadership style is characterized by willpower, tough-mindedness, self-confidence, and self-discipline. Principals of effective schools display these qualities when dealing with aspects of the school's value core. Expressing these same qualities, when dealing with the day-to-day decisions that teachers make in classrooms as they work with students, would result in the principal's being perceived as rigid. The two dimensions of resilience and flexibility are illustrated in Figure 9.1 in the form of a leadership grid. Note that, at the base of the grid, resiliency ranges from a low score of 0 to a high of 100. Plot your score from the Style Resilience Index on this dimension of the grid. To the left is the flex-

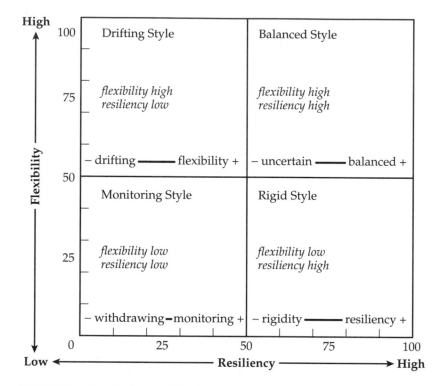

FIGURE 9.1   Styles for Flexible and Resilient Principal Leadership

ibility dimension, ranging from 0 to 100. Plot your score from the Style Flexibility Index on this dimension.

High resiliency scores combined with low flexibility scores would place one in the lower right corner of the grid and represent the Rigid style. A flexibility score of 80 combined with a resiliency score of 30, however, would place one in the upper left quadrant of the grid, representing the Drifting leadership style. High scores on both flexibility and resilience would place one in the upper right quadrant—the Balanced leadership style. Low scores on both dimensions would place one in the lower left quadrant—the Monitoring style. Let's examine each of the four styles with reference to principals as they manage issues of tight and loose coupling in schools.

The Drifting style can work when important values are not at stake and might be appropriate for issues common to the school's loosely structured, high discretionary area. However, when principals are flexible in dealing with the school's core of values, they appear to teachers to be drifting and are not viewed as able to provide necessary purposing and direction.

The Rigid style can work for issues relating to the school's core of values. Using this style with teachers on issues of providing for daily teaching and learning, however, is likely to be viewed negatively. Instead of appearing resilient, principals will be seen as autocratic and their style as rigid.

The Monitoring style can work in instances in which jobs can be programmed in such detail that the emphasis is less on persons and goals and more on monitoring the work flow, thus ensuring reliability. Teacher-proof designs for schooling support the Monitoring style. The enforcement of school rules and providing drill-practice work in teaching and learning might be examples appropriate for the Monitoring style. When principals use this style excessively or in the wrong instances, they are viewed as having withdrawn their concern for people as individuals and for goals and purposes.

The Balanced style provides flexible leadership in the articulation of the school's values, goals, and platform as teachers work day by day. At the same time, this style provides resilient leadership with respect to the promotion and maintenance of important values. This approach characterizes principal leadership found in successful schools. The concept of balanced leadership characteristic of successful schools should be the cornerstone of one's management platform and is an important dimension of reflective practice in the principalship.

Appendix 9.1 provides an inventory of assumptions that school faculties can use to begin a conversation about what they believe and what they don't believe about teaching and learning and about the nature of school knowledge. The assumptions they settle on can become values used to "design out" how they relate with students, how teaching and learning is planned and practiced, and how curriculum and evaluation decisions are made. Further, Appendix 9.1 can be used to assess the extent to which assumptions, values, and beliefs that are held are actually being implemented in your school. If, for example, you are lukewarm to most of the assumptions, then that reluctance should be embodied in the actual practices you observe in your school. To help in your assessment, "reality check" questions are provided for the first 13 items themed to assumptions about Motivation, Conditions for Learning, and Social Learning. These questions can serve as prompts for you to assess what your reality check response would be to the remaining assumptions.

References

Barth, Roland. 1986. "The Principal and the Profession of Teaching," *Elementary School Journal* 86(4).

Battistich, V., D. Solomon, M. Watson, and E. Schaps. 1994. *Students and Teachers in Caring Communities and School Communities.* Paper presented at the annual meeting of the American Educational Research Association, April 4–8, New Orleans.

Bidwell, Charles E. 1965. "The School as a Formal Organization," in James G. March (Ed.), *Handbook of Organization* (pp. 972–1022). Chicago: Rand McNally.

Bricker, H. 1985. As quoted in Robert H. Hayes, "Strategic Planning Forward in Reverse?" *Harvard Business Review*, Nov.-Dec.

Bryk, A. S., and M. E. Driscoll. 1988. *The School as Community: Theoretical Foundations, Contextual Influences and Consequences for Students and Teachers.* Madison: National Center on Effective Schools, University of Wisconsin.

Coleman, J. 1987. "Families in Schools," *Educational Research* 16(6), 32–38.

Coleman, J. 1988. "Social Capital in the Creation of Human Capital." *American Journal of Sociology* 94 (Supplement), S95–S120.

Coleman, J. 1990. *Foundations of Social Theory.* Cambridge, MA: Harvard University Press.

Eisner, Elliot. 1969. "Instructional and Expressive Educational Objectives: Their Formulation and Use In Curriculum," in W. James Popham (Ed.), *Curriculum Evaluation: Instructional Objectives.* AERA Monograph Series. Chicago: Rand-McNally.

Eisner, Elliot. 1979. *The Educational Imagination: On the Design and Evaluation of School Programs.* New York: Macmillan.

Gamoran, A. 1996. "Student Achievement in Public Magnet, Public Comprehensive and Private City High Schools," *Educational Evaluation and Policy Analysis* 18(1), 1–18.

Gardner, Howard. 1983. *Frames of Mind: The Theory of Multiple Intelligences.* New York: Basic Books.

Hills, Jean. 1982. "The Preparation of Educational Leaders: What's Needed and What's Next?" UCEA occasional paper No. 8303. Columbus, OH: University Council for Educational Administration.

Outward Bound USA Convenor. 1992. "Expeditionary Learning: A Design for New America's Schools." A proposal to the New American Schools Development Corporation. Greenwich, CT: Author.

Parsons, Talcott. 1951. *Toward a General Theory of Social Action.* Cambridge, MA: Harvard University Press.

Perrow, Charles. 1981. "Disintegrating Social Sciences," *New York University Education Quarterly* 10(2), 2–9.

Peters, Thomas J., and Robert H. Waterman, Jr. 1982. *In Search of Excellence: Lessons from America's Best-Run Companies.* New York: Harper & Row.

Peters, Tom, and Nancy Austin. 1985. *A Passion for Excellence.* New York: Random House.

Purkey, William W., and J. M. Novak. 1988. *Education: By Invitation Only.* Bloomington, IN: Phi Delta Kappan Foundation.

Reddin, W. J. 1970. *Managerial Effectiveness.* New York: McGraw-Hill.

Sergiovanni, T. J. 1994. *Building Community in Schools.* San Francisco: Jossey-Bass.

Sergiovanni, T. J. 1998. "Leadership as Pedagogy, Capital Development and School Effectiveness," *International Journal of Leadership in Education* 1(1), 37–46.

Sergiovanni, Thomas J., and Brad Duggan. 1990. "Moral Authority: A Blueprint for Managing Tomorrow's Schools," in T. J. Sergiovanni and J. H. Moore (Eds.), *Target 2000: A Compact for Excellence in Texas's Schools.* The 1990 Yearbook of the Texas Association for Supervision and Curriculum Development. San Antonio, TX: Watercress Press.

Shils, Edward A. 1961. "Centre and Periphery," in *The Logic of Personal Knowledge: Essays Presented to Michael Polanyi.* London: Routledge and Kegan Paul.

Sizer, Theodore R. 1989. "Diverse Practice, Shared Ideas: The Essential School," in H. J. Walberg and J. J. Lane (Eds.), *Organizing for Learning: Toward the 21st Century.* Reston, VA: National Association of Secondary School Principals.

Trice Harrison, M., and Ganice M. Beyer. 1984. "Studying Organizational Cultures through Rites and Ceremonials," *Academy of Management Review* 9(4), 653–669.

Watson, Thomas J., Jr. 1963. *A Business and Its Beliefs: The Ideas That Helped Build IBM.* New York: McGraw-Hill.

Weick, Karl. 1976. "Educational Organizations as Loosely Coupled Systems," *Administrative Science Quarterly* 21(2), 1–19.

Weick, Karl. 1982. "Administering Education in Loosely Coupled Systems," *Phi Delta Kappan* 27(2), 673–676.

Zaleznik, Abraham. 1988, September 3. Quoted in Doran P. Levin, "G.M. Bid to Rejuvenate Leadership." *The New York Times.*

Appendix 9.1   Assumptions about Learning and Knowledge

Instructions: Somewhere along each line, make a mark that best represents your own feelings about each statement.

Example: School serves the wishes and needs of adults better than it does the wishes and needs of children.

strongly agree	agree	no strong feeling	disagree	strongly disagree

Reality Check.   In my school, most decisions made by the teachers and administrators serve the wishes and needs of adults better than the wishes and needs of children.

strongly agree	agree	no strong feeling	disagree	strongly disagree

I. Assumptions about Children's Learning

Motivation
Assumption 1.   Children are innately curious and will explore their environment without adult intervention.

strongly agree	agree	no strong feeling	disagree	strongly disagree

Reality Check 1.   In my school, we provide many opportunities for students to explore their environment.

strongly agree	agree	no strong feeling	disagree	strongly disagree

Assumption 2.   Exploratory behavior is self-perpetuating.

strongly agree	agree	no strong feeling	disagree	strongly disagree

Source: Adapted from "So You Want to Change to an Open Classroom" by Roland S. Barth, 1971, *Phi Delta Kappan* 53(2), 98–99. The "reality checks" have been added.

Appendix 9.1   *Continued*

Reality Check 2.   In my school, we make decisions that assume students are capable of being self-managing learners.

strongly agree	agree	no strong feeling	disagree	strongly disagree

Conditions for Learning

Assumption 3.   Children will display natural exploratory behavior if they are not threatened.

strongly agree	agree	no strong feeling	disagree	strongly disagree

Reality Check 3.   We work hard to eliminate threats and fear.

strongly agree	agree	no strong feeling	disagree	strongly disagree

Assumption 4.   Confidence in self is highly related to capacity for learning and for making important choices affecting one's learning.

strongly agree	agree	no strong feeling	disagree	strongly disagree

Reality Check 4.   We make decisions that build self-confidence among learners.

strongly agree	agree	no strong feeling	disagree	strongly disagree

Assumption 5.   Active exploration in a rich environment, offering a wide array of manipulative materials, will facilitate children's learning.

strongly agree	agree	no strong feeling	disagree	strongly disagree

Appendix 9.1   *Continued*

Reality Check 5.   We encourage active exploration and offer a wide variety of manipulative materials for learning.

strongly agree	agree	no strong feeling	disagree	strongly disagree

Assumption 6.   Play is not distinguished from work as the predominant mode of learning in early childhood.

strongly agree	agree	no strong feeling	disagree	strongly disagree

Reality Check 6.   Opportunities for play are a natural part of the pedagogy in the early grades of my school.

strongly agree	agree	no strong feeling	disagree	strongly disagree

Assumption 7.   Children have both the competence and the right to make significant decisions concerning their own learning.

strongly agree	agree	no strong feeling	disagree	strongly disagree

Reality Check 7.   We involve students in significant decisions concerning their own learning.

strongly agree	agree	no strong feeling	disagree	strongly disagree

Assumption 8.   Children will be likely to learn if they are given considerable choice in the selection of the materials they wish to work with and in the choice of questions they wish to pursue with respect to those materials.

strongly agree	agree	no strong feeling	disagree	strongly disagree

Appendix 9.1 *Continued*

Reality Check 8. We give students considerable choice in the selection of learning materials and the choice of learning questions.

strongly agree	agree	no strong feeling	disagree	strongly disagree

Assumption 9. Given the opportunity, children will choose to engage in activities that will be of high interest to them.

strongly agree	agree	no strong feeling	disagree	strongly disagree

Reality Check 9. Our decisions reflect the belief that students will choose to engage in learning that interests them.

strongly agree	agree	no strong feeling	disagree	strongly disagree

Assumption 10. If a child is fully involved in and is having fun with an activity, learning is taking place.

strongly agree	agree	no strong feeling	disagree	strongly disagree

Reality Check 10. Our decisions reflect the belief that involvement and enjoyment are good indicators that learning is taking place.

strongly agree	agree	no strong feeling	disagree	strongly disagree

Social Learning
Assumption 11. When two or more children are interested in exploring the same problem or the same materials, they will often choose to collaborate in some way.

strongly agree	agree	no strong feeling	disagree	strongly disagree

Reality Check 11. We encourage students to collaborate with each other whenever possible.

strongly agree	agree	no strong feeling	disagree	strongly disagree

Appendix 9.1   *Continued*

Assumption 12.   When children learn something that is important to them, they will wish to share it with others.

| strongly agree | agree | no strong feeling | disagree | strongly disagree |

Reality Check 12.   We encourage students to share what they learn with others.

| strongly agree | agree | no strong feeling | disagree | strongly disagree |

Intellectual Development
Assumption 13.   Concept formation proceeds very slowly.

| strongly agree | agree | no strong feeling | disagree | strongly disagree |

Assumption 14.   Children learn and develop intellectually not only at their own rates but in their own styles.

| strongly agree | agree | no strong feeling | disagree | strongly disagree |

Assumption 15.   Children pass through similar stages of intellectual development, each in their own way and at their own rates and in their own time.

| strongly agree | agree | no strong feeling | disagree | strongly disagree |

Assumption 16.   Intellectual growth and development take place through a sequence of concrete experiences followed by abstractions.

| strongly agree | agree | no strong feeling | disagree | strongly disagree |

Assumption 17.   Verbal abstractions should follow direct experience with objects and ideas, not precede them or substitute for them.

| strongly agree | agree | no strong feeling | disagree | strongly disagree |

Appendix 9.1   *Continued*

Evaluation
Assumption 18.   The preferred source of verification for a child's solution to a problem comes through the materials with which he or she is working.

strongly agree	agree	no strong feeling	disagree	strongly disagree

Assumption 19.   Errors are necessarily a part of the learning process; they are to be expected and even desired, for they contain information essential for further learning.

strongly agree	agree	no strong feeling	disagree	strongly disagree

Assumption 20.   Those qualities of a person's learning that can be carefully measured are not necessarily the most important.

strongly agree	agree	no strong feeling	disagree	strongly disagree

Assumption 21.   Objective measures of performance may have a negative effect on learning.

strongly agree	agree	no strong feeling	disagree	strongly disagree

Assumption 22.   Learning is best assessed intuitively, by direct observation.

strongly agree	agree	no strong feeling	disagree	strongly disagree

Assumption 23.   The best way of evaluating the effect of the school experience on the child is to observe him or her over a long period of time.

strongly agree	agree	no strong feeling	disagree	strongly disagree

Appendix 9.1   *Continued*

Assumption 24.   The best measure of a child's work is his or her work.

strongly agree	agree	no strong feeling	disagree	strongly disagree

Knowledge
Assumption 25.   The quality of being is more important than the quality of knowing; knowledge is a means of education, not its end. The final test of an education is what a person *is*, not what he or she *knows*.

strongly agree	agree	no strong feeling	disagree	strongly disagree

Assumption 26.   Knowledge is a function of one's personal integration of experience and therefore does not fall into neatly separate categories or "disciplines."

strongly agree	agree	no strong feeling	disagree	strongly disagree

Assumption 27.   The structure of knowledge is personal and idiosyncratic; it is a function of the synthesis of each individual's experience with the world.

strongly agree	agree	no strong feeling	disagree	strongly disagree

Assumption 28.   Little or no knowledge exists that is essential for everyone to acquire.

strongly agree	agree	no strong feeling	disagree	strongly disagree

Assumption 29.   It is possible, even likely, that an individual may learn and possess knowledge of a phenomenon and yet be unable to display it publicly. Knowledge resides with the knower, not in its public expression.

strongly agree	agree	no strong feeling	disagree	strongly disagree

10

LAYERED STANDARDS, HOLISTIC ASSESSMENT

Everyone wants good schools—an aspiration shared by people in all walks of life. Few would disagree that we should be able to identify the good schools we have now, to learn from them, and to increase their number. Further, most people believe that providing schools and their publics with information as to where they are now, given their own goals and aspirations and the goals and aspirations of the state, is a reasonable idea. Schools need this information to plan the next steps, new directions, and other initiatives on the road to improvement. But it is not likely that any of these things will happen unless our schools are involved at the ground floor in standards and assessment. Ground-floor involvement of each school means having a good, practical, broad, realistic, and *lifeworld* serving definition of what is a good school in the first place.

The term *lifeworld* needs some explaining (see, for example, Sergiovanni, 2000). Borrowing from the philosopher and sociologist Jurgen Habermas (1987), we might think of the lifeworld as a school's local values, traditions, meanings, and purposes. In the best of circumstances the lifeworld determines and legitimizes local initiatives aimed at achieving a school's own destiny (Sergiovanni, 2000). The lifeworld includes the traditions, rituals, and norms that define a school's culture. Lifeworlds differ as we move from school to school, and these differences lay the groundwork for developing a school's unique character. As character builds, the capacity of a school to serve the intellectual, social, cultural, and civic needs of its students increases. School character helps schools be more effective. *Effectiveness* is broadly defined as achieving higher levels of pedagogical thoughtfulness, developing relationships characterized by caring and civility, and achieving increases in the quality of student performance on both conventional and alternative assessments.

The evidence from a wide variety of sources (i.e., Coleman and Hoffer, 1987; Bryk, Lee, and Holland, 1993; Hill, Foster, and Gendler, 1990) leads to the conclusion that schools that function as focused communities where unique values are important, schools where caring for each other is the norm, schools where academic matters count, and schools where social covenants are established that bring parents, teachers, students, and others together in a shared commitment to the common good are able to use the values of the lifeworld and to get surprisingly good results. This link between the lifeworld of a school and that school's effectiveness establishes local authority as a necessary ingredient in any school effectiveness equation.

More than Effective

It is much easier to identify what is an "effective" school than to struggle with a deeper definition of what is a "good" school. Sara Lawrence Lightfoot's research, reported in her book *The Good High School* (1983), is an example of searching for a more meaningful and expansive definition of effectiveness. She provided portraits of six very different but very good high schools. What emerges from her seminal study is that a single list of indicators for a good school is not so easily achieved. She found that good schools have invented ways to effectively serve different neighborhoods, contain a diverse mix of goals and purposes, and use unique ways to achieve these goals and purposes. Further, good schools have principals who provide a unique blend of leadership strategies and styles. Goodness is about the kind of wholeness and purpose and the kind of responsiveness to unique characteristics and needs that contribute to school character. Goodness builds from and grows from what a particular school and its community values. The lifeworld of a school, not externally imposed organizational structures or outside mandates, is the key to this broader view of effectiveness.

The Role of Standards

Building diverse schools that are characterized by a commitment to both caring and academic competence is a good idea. But it is difficult to create this kind of community within a standards movement that imposes on all schools the same expectations and the same outcomes for learning.[*] For these reasons, the present standards movement may have to be realigned. Standardized standards and assessments place community building at risk and compromise the discretion that parents, teachers, students, and local communities need to decide for themselves what their goals and purposes should be, what values they should pursue, and what they want their schools to accomplish. We can avoid this problem of diluting local discretion by switching to layered standards and a system of holistic assessments.

*This discussion of standards draws on Chapters 5 and 6, "Layered Standards and Shared Accountability" and "Whole Child, Whole School, Holistic Assessment" in Thomas J. Sergiovanni, *The Lifeworld of Leadership: Creating Culture, Community and Personal Meaning in Our Schools*. San Francisco: Jossey-Bass, 2000. Used with permission.

Switching our approach to standards is not the same as doing away with standards. Setting standards for what students need to know, for what levels of civility should characterize student behavior, for what schools need to do, and for how parents, teachers, and even governors and legislators should define their roles is, most would agree, a good thing for students, a good thing for schools, and a good thing for the state. Standards are most useful when they are accompanied by assessments that can be used to determine where we are with respect to our goals and that can help us to get better. The right standards and the right kinds of assessments can help us define the common good and come together in a common quest to pursue that good. When this happens, both standards and assessments play an important role in helping build the kind of focused and caring communities that research tells us are both good and effective for our students.

As now construed, however, standards too often erode local discretion, place the school's organizational character at risk, compromise its ability to be responsive to local needs and aspirations, and ultimately hamper its efforts to provide effective teaching and learning.

Standardized standards advocates are quick to point out that parents, teachers, testing experts, politicians, and corporate leaders are typically represented on state-appointed committees charged with writing standards or with jurying standards. But the vast majority of ordinary people do not have a direct role or say in this process. Though representative government may be the best way to handle most decisions that affect our lives, when the issues have to do with our children, their social and mental health, their civic and intellectual development, and their spiritual and moral growth, then we may well need democratic government in the form of direct participation of those affected by the issues at hand. The state, of course, has an important role to play in this process. And so do parents, teachers, students, and other citizens in local school communities. Granted, there are some things that everyone should learn, but there are also some things that might be learned by some people but not others, in one school but not another school, in one state but not another state.

The Ends Usually Determine the Means

Many politicians and other policy makers point out that we need not worry about the lifeworld of schools because local control is alive and well. They note that even though ends are specified by the state or by some other external agency, local schools are given autonomy over the means by which they will achieve the mandated ends. But as states move in the direction of specifying all of the standards across the curriculum and then testing to see if these standards have been met, it is more likely that this accountability system will determine for all teachers and all schools within a state the details of both the curriculum to be taught and the kind of teaching that will be needed for it to be learned. When this happens, the state has virtually complete control over the educational process.

Who controls what and how has direct consequences, as well, for the kind of profession teaching will become and for the lifeworlds of individual teachers. If a vital lifeworld is needed in every individual school to provide the character, discretion, sense of community, motivation, and commitment that teachers and students need to be responsive and effective, then we have to worry about the potential for erosion of these characteristics as, across the board, standardized standards and assessments are put into place. McMullin (1999) raises this concern as follows: "It occurred to me . . . the movement to statewide and even national standards for students (and teachers) is an attempt to make one large school for the whole country. Has anyone considered whether this is the best thing to do? How do we make space for regional, local and individual differences? Is it possible for a one-size-fits-all educational system to really fit everyone?" How one answers McMullin's question depends in part on that person's view of how objective standards really are.

How Objective Are Standards?

The word *standard* can be intimidating to many parents and teachers. The dictionary, for example, thinks of a standard as something set up by an authority as a rule to measure the quality and quantity of something. Thus, many ordinary citizens come to think of a learning standard or a school standard as something similar to the gold standard—a scientific and objective measure of something valuable with which ordinary people had better not tamper. Thus, parents rarely ask what a standards-based, state-assigned school rating, such as exemplary or needs improvement or proficient, means. They just assume that whatever is being measured should be measured and whatever the ratings are, they must be scientific ones. But standards are neither god-like nor scientific. They are, instead, subjective. Some standards are good and some are bad. Some standards are measured properly and some are not. In some cases, the rating scheme that evaluates the extent to which a standard is met is set too high. And in other cases, the rating scheme is set too low. There is no atomic clock that provides a precise and sure metastandard against which other standards of measurement can be compared.

Instead, standards are set by people who make human decisions about what they believe or think is appropriate or is not appropriate. Not surprisingly, these people often differ. One group, for example, might prefer some, accept others, and reject still other standards, whereas another group in the same room dealing with the same standards might prefer, accept, or reject different ones.

While conceding that there might be some controversy in agreeing on standards in the social studies and other soft areas, many people might assume that standard setting is noncontroversial, and thus an easy task in the hard sciences such as mathematics or science or in the basic skills areas such as reading. But the evidence indicates otherwise. In California, for example, the crafting of science standards by a state-appointed committee turned out to be a difficult task. The committee splintered into two major groups. One group favored an inquiry approach and pushed for standards that would help students think like scientists, experience science firsthand, learn general scientific principles, and be able to solve scientific problems. The other group favored a content acquisition approach and pushed for standards that were more graded, content oriented, and amiable to direct instruction. In the end, the committee members struck a compromise that neither side celebrated but one with which both sides could live. Once the committee's work was done, it was up to the California State Board of Education to decide whether to accept the compromise package or some other combination of standards. The board decided to approve a set of standards that reflected the views of the more traditional commissioners (Olson, 1998; Hoff, 1998). So much for viewing educational standards as being akin to the gold standard.

What about standards in skill areas such as reading? In 1993, the U.S. Department of Education commissioned the National Council of Teachers of English, the International Reading Association, and the Center for the Study of Reading at the University of Illinois at Urbana to develop and recommend a set of national standards in reading. When the standards were submitted, the Department of Education rejected the work and subsequently terminated funding of the project. One of the drafters of the standards explained the rejection as follows: "The standards were excessively concerned with 'process' and insufficiently concerned with 'products' or 'outcomes'" (Clinchy, 1995:11). Yes, even in the basic skills areas, such as reading, different ideologies lead to different conclusions. Standard setting in the real world resembles a game of winning and losing rather than a process of scientific inquiry into a discipline in search of some sort of truth. Simply put, standards are subjective reflections of the principles of those who set them. Different people set different standards. Thus, the process is as much political as it is anything else. If you want standards that you like, make sure the people who set the standards are people with whom you agree.

Local Authority

Despite the problems just discussed, standards have the potential to provide needed focus and to rally the resources of a school and school district in a common direction. Testing is a powerful tool that can help assess how well standards are being achieved. Both can provide clues as to how a school can get better. If standards and testing, per se, are not the issue, what is? The issue is the erosion of the lifeworld of schools and school districts. Instead of standards and accountability being derived from the needs, purposes, and interests of parents, teachers, and students in each school, the standards and accountability systems determine what the needs, purposes, and interests are and scripts the behavior of teachers and students accordingly. When the lifeworld of a school is the source of authority for what happens, then testing reflects local passions, needs, and values. Standards remain rigorous and true but are not presumed to be standardized. Although tests possess the proper psychometric properties and the integrity of their substance is maintained, the specifics of what is tested reflects local values and preferences. Further, the worth of individual students, of teachers, and of schools themselves is not determined by some narrow definition of effectiveness and achievement but by a range of assessments that respond to both local and state visions and needs.

Layered Standards as an Alternative

Both uniqueness and discretion at the school site are needed for school culture and character to flourish and for the school to then be able to function most effectively in improving student performance, levels of civility, and other dimensions of goodness. But both are compromised by the present standardized "one-best-way" system of accountability that most states now share. Is the answer to do away with standards and accountability? Most would agree that the answer is no. Schools work well when the lifeworld is at the center, functioning as a source of authority that leads to the crafting of systems of standards and accountability that serve local needs and interests rather than dominate them.

Can such a system be created? Yes, if we are willing to adopt a layered approach to establishing standards and a shared approach to accountability that includes a strong local component. Yes, if we are willing to abandon thinking in terms of a one-best-way to do things in schools. Yes, if we are able to bring together the state, the local school district, and individual schools as partners in search of a common good. Before moving on to what a system of layered standards and assessments might look like, let's summarize with some assumptions (Sergiovanni, 2000:89–91):

- It is reasonable for the state to participate in setting standards for schools. It is equally reasonable for school boards, parents, and teachers at the local school and even students to participate in setting standards, too. We just have to figure out who has responsibility for what.
- When standards and assessment are set by the state alone, standardization is likely to emerge with schools becoming more and more similar as a result. When school boards, parents, teachers, and students at the local school level participate in the setting of standards and determining assessments, schools become standardized in some few areas but diverse in most other areas.
- The advantage of a standards setting and assessment system that combines some common understandings with many diverse understandings is that it is consistent with the American democratic ideal, honors diversity, and provides the basis for real choice.
- Choice only has meaning when students, parents, and teachers are provided with different options from which to choose. Providing real choices requires creating new programs and new images of schools. This is hard to do unless schools have responsibility for setting most of the standards they will pursue, for participating in the assessments of these standards, and for making this information public.
- The state should assume major responsibility for developing standardized standards and assessments for all schools in the skill areas of reading, math, and writing.
- The school board, parents, teachers, and students at the local school level should share responsibility for developing standards and assessments in advanced math, science, literature, history, social science, art, music, English,

and other areas. Since school districts and schools within them differ, it should be expected that many of these standards will differ as one moves from district to district and from school to school within the same district.

- Since the abilities and dispositions of parents, teachers, and students at the local school level vary with respect to how to write standards and how to craft assessments, the state has a responsibility to provide both technical assistance and financial resources for professional development.
- The state has a responsibility to provide a centralized standards bank from which local authorities might draw as needed. Some local authorities may choose to withdraw and use standards from this bank "as is," and others might choose to withdraw and use standards from this bank as frameworks for creating their own standards. It should be expected that different standards will be withdrawn, reflecting unique local values, needs, and purposes.
- Students should participate by setting standards for themselves and by assessing their own performance. Student assessments should count along with state, school district, and local school assessments in evaluating a school.
- No single set of standards and no single assessment system should dominate the other. If it is decided that schools must be rated and compared with each other, then no single rating source should determine a school's score or a school's category designation.

Social and Emotional Learning

Before using these assumptions to propose an actual system of layered standards and holistic assessment, we have to deal with the issue of scope. What kinds of standards should be included? What range of assessments will be needed to authentically measure and evaluate these standards? We have, for example, established that good schools are identified by strong performance on such measurable indicators as test scores. But we have also suggested that good schools are known by other criteria. One of the limits of our present approach to assessment is that the goals and curriculum areas that are emphasized are likely to be those most easily stated as standards and most easily measured. This can result in the neglect of important learning and development areas that not only have intrinsic value but have instrumental value, too. Neglected areas may lead to more effective and efficient basic skills acquisition and to the mastery of academic and related disciplines. The whole area of social and emotional learning (SEL) provides many examples (see, for example, Goleman, 1995; Sternberg and Wagner, 1995; Gardner, 1983, 1993). Elias and his colleagues point out:

> *Social and emotional competence is the ability to understand, manage and express the social and emotional aspects of ones life in ways that enable the successful management of life tasks such as learning, forming relationships, solving everyday problems, and adopting to the complex demands of growth and development. It includes self-awareness, control of impulsivity, working cooperatively, and caring*

about oneself and others. Social and emotional learning is the process through which children and other adults develop the skills, attitudes and values necessary to acquire social and emotional competence. (Elias et al., 1997:2)

A short time ago, certain goals were considered as "frills," such as helping students to acquire knowledge, skills, work habits, and values for success at work; to be motivated; to function effectively as members of peer groups and families; to develop self-knowledge and worth; and to cultivate social skills. But in today's world, such goals are considered essential not only to be successful in school learning but to be successful in the world of work and to participate successfully in the civic life of our society (Elias et al., 1997).

A Holistic Approach

Gardner (1993) believes that many of our problems with standardized standards and assessments could be solved by viewing assessment as obtaining information about the skills and potentials of students for the purposes of providing useful feedback to them and to the local community. This definition of assessment obtains information naturally in a *situated context* and in the course of ordinary performance of teaching and learning. Tests, by contrast, are formal, artificial, and decontextualized. To Gardner, assessments have "ecological validity" in the sense that they are validated by the content of learning itself. Teachers and students work closely and continuously together, like master and apprentice, and this relationship builds confidence in the teacher's ability to make sound assessment decisions.

Furthermore, Gardner (1993) points out that most tests focus exclusively on linguistic and logical mathematical intelligences. If youngsters have strengths in these intelligences, they will test well. If they do not have strengths in these areas, they will not test well. Assessments can be engineered to address the other intelligences, making the assessments intelligence fair—for example: "Spatial intelligence can be assessed by having an individual navigate around an unfamiliar territory; bodily intelligence by seeing how a person learns and remembers a new dance or physical exercise; interpersonal intelligence by watching an individual handle a dispute with a salesclerk or navigate her way through a difficult committee meeting" (176). Gardner believes that assessments should be much more sensitive to individual differences, developmental needs, and many forms of expertise. Assessments should also allow for the use of more intrinsically interesting materials. Tests are sort of like box scores, providing information in the form of runs, hits, and errors inning by inning. An assessment approach provides more vivid ways to communicate the drama and excitement of the game itself. Each approach has a role to play. Right now we emphasize the write up of box scores and are only beginning to learn how to provide more vivid and meaningful portrayals of what has been learned and how to communicate this information to various audiences. If we want to be responsive to what parents, teachers, and students want and need, we will have to give more attention to this deeper form of assessment.

The Quality Review Process

One possibility worth exploring in putting into place a system of layered standards and holistic assessment is to borrow from the experiences of New York and Illinois with the school quality review process. This process was imported from the United Kingdom to the United States by Thomas Sobol in 1992 when he was New York State Commissioner of Education. With Sobol's departure as commissioner, the review process received less attention in New York but has been implemented in many schools in the state of Illinois.

The process requires putting together a team of state and local representatives, parents, teachers, students, and other local citizens who make three- to five-day-long visits to a school and engage in a holistic and in-depth assessment of what is going on. Team members visit classrooms and faculty meetings; examine student work; review documents; interview students, teachers, and parents; and engage in other sorts of activities. Of particular interest are the school improvement plans that the local school has developed and the extent to which these plans are being implemented. The quality review process requires a direct examination of practice, an analysis of self-review information, and the preparation of a report. Both the school's own goals and external standards are used in reviewing the school and in providing information.

Ancess (1996) identifies five principles as being key to the review process: "(1) responsiveness to the culture of the school, (2) reliance on the team's collective perspective to safeguard against subjectivity, (3) development of building-level capacity, (4) stimulation of inquiry, and (5) support for professionalism" (5). The review process, for example, is driven by the school's own goals, own sense of mission, and own values and beliefs rather than those of reviewers. No template from the outside is brought into the process to assess the extent to which a school measures up. "Reviewers strive to get to know the school on its own ground, and in a context of respect and support" (Ancess, 1996:5).

Further, it is assumed that schools can make a difference by taking responsibility for building their own capacity to function more effectively. Review teams function as critical friends who raise questions about contradictions between their intents and the practices that are observed. "Working against the grain of most packaged professional development programs and prescriptions, a team's questions may leave a school community temporarily puzzled and frustrated, for they must unpack the questions in order to derive direction from them. When a school adopts a team's questions as a starting point for its inquiry, however, it can enter into a process of individual and collective reflection. The culture of inquiry that this can fuel can keep a school focused on its quest to achieve its goals" (Ancess, 1996:7).

According to Illinois accountability and assurance guidelines (Illinois State Board of Education, 1997–98):

> *Any school review process, whether internal or external, must assure that all stakeholders are able to contribute to the crafting of this process. It should affirm the critical importance of teaching and engage them in a discussion and review of teaching*

and learning. Schools should be afforded sufficient flexibility to represent their work in a manner they deem appropriate, both to their fellow professionals and to members of the wider community. . . . The Quality Review and Improvement Planning program will place great emphasis on supporting schools, and less on accumulating documentation; it will help to promote effective school inquiry and useful school improvement planning. It will be developed on a school by school basis, recognizing the different circumstances of schools, and linking school improvement to accountability. (2, 3)

While taking into account standardized test scores, both internal and external review teams place a great deal of emphasis on local standards and goals, on the grades that students earn, and on the actual work that they do. Thus, displays of student work in the halls and in classrooms, portfolios of student work, oral presentations, homework samples, daily classroom work, work derived from community service projects, and learnings from before and after school activities are also rigorously examined and taken into account in assessing a school. The Illinois quality review process "encourages schools to build on their previous work in this area, and provides flexibility in the continued development of assessment systems to ensure that they support a school's mission, curriculum and instruction. Review teams, therefore, review how a school assesses student progress, and how the school determines which procedures contribute to the overall assessment system" (Illinois State Board of Education, 1997–98:12).

An outline of an internal or external review includes attention to the following categories of information:

    I. Teaching and Learning
      Learning environment
      Instructional strategies
      Learning processes
      Student responses
    II. Student Learning, Progress, and Achievement
      Curriculum design and alignment
      Student work
      Assessment systems
    III. The Learning Community
      Mission and shared vision
      Leadership and administration
      Organizational structure
      Professional development and support for staff
      Community participation in the school-based learning community

A good quality review is based on both processes and substance, on both how things are done and what is accomplished, and on both school climate factors and student learning standards and achievements. Although focusing on results alone may be misguided, focusing on purposes alone may result in a weak review. This is why locally developed and rigorous standards for learning must be at the heart and soul of the quality review process.

If locals connected to a particular school are not comfortable with or able to develop learning standards alone, they should receive assistance from local school district or state experts. Locals should also be able to consult standards banks (lists of standards for the various disciplines that are retrievable on the Internet or in some other way). These standards banks could be made available by the state, by the various subject-matter specialty groups (e.g., National Council for Teachers of English), or by other groups (e.g., Council for Basic Education; Center on Learning, Assessment and School Structure; National Center on Education and the Economy). Some standards might be adopted for local use "as is," and others might be used to help frame the writing of local standards.

States have an important responsibility in this process. Their job is to develop metastandards and to use them to review local standards to be sure that they are legitimate. Thus, local standards will differ as one moves from school to school, but we would have some assurance that they will all be of good quality. Once schools have locally determined the standards they believe are important for each of the subject-matter areas taught, these standards should help guide the quality review process.

Who Should Be Responsible for What

Table 10.1 provides an overview of what might be one way to distribute responsibility among various stakeholders for setting standards and for assessing schools (see, for example, Chapter 6 in Sergiovanni, 2000). It proposes that there might be standards in five areas:

- Standardized standards for all schools in basic reading, writing, and math
- Focused and varied standards in key curriculum areas such as history, advanced math, English, art, music, and social sciences
- Focused and varied standards in social and emotional learning areas, including character development
- School standards in noncurriculum areas such as teacher development, use of resources, and sense of community
- Teacher standards in such areas as professionalism, collegiality, and professional growth

The state might assume responsibility for setting standardized standards in the *basic skills areas*. These areas would be assessed by standardized tests. For the *focused and varied standards in the key curriculum areas,* the state might assume 15 percent of the responsibility and the local school and its school district 85 percent of the responsibility. Perhaps something like 60 percent of the responsibility might be allocated to the individual school and 25 percent of the responsibility allocated to the district. For the area *focused and varied standards in social and emotional learning,* a

TABLE 10.1   Layered Standards, Shared Accountability

Standards in Five Areas:	Standardized standards in basic reading, math, & writing	Focused and varied standards in key curriculum areas such as history, advanced math, literature, art, social science, etc.	Focused and varied standards in social and emotional learning areas including character development	School standards in noncurriculum areas such as teacher development, use of resources, and sense of community	Teacher standards in such areas as professionalism, collegiality, professional growth, and quality of practice
Responsibility for Setting:	State 100%	State 15% Local 85%	State 40% Local 60%	State 40% Local 60%	State 60%* Local 40%
Primary Assessment Strategies:	Standardized tests	Tests, portfolios, performance exhibitions, internal review self-study, observation, interview	Portfolios, performance exhibitions, service requirement, internal review self-study, observation, interview	State indicator system, local self-study	State indicator system, local self-study
Responsibility for Assessment:	State with results considered by WSQR team	WSQR team, which includes state and local representatives, parents, teachers, students, local citizens	WSQR team	WSQR team	WSQR team
Product:	One report that provides an in-depth study of the school and a summary rating that takes into account all layers of standards and their assessments.				
Audience for the Report:	In order of importance: the local school, the school community, the school district, the state, the general public.				

Source: The Lifeworld of Leadership: Creating Culture, Community, and Personal Meaning in Our Schools (p. 120) by Thomas J. Sergiovanni, 2000, San Francisco: Jossey-Bass. Used with permission.

Note: WSQR = Whole School Quality Review

*If the state sets up an independent professional teaching board, then the distribution would be different with the board playing the major role.

40–60 split between state and local authorities might be agreed upon. With respect to *school standards in noncurriculum areas,* the state might assume 40 percent of the responsibility for setting standards and the local school and district 60 percent. With respect to *teachers' standards,* the state might take on 60 percent of the responsibility and the local school and school district 40 percent of the responsibility. If the state sets up an independent professional teaching board to oversee teaching standards, then the distribution would be different, with that board playing the major role. Such a board would presumably be heavily staffed by teachers and representatives of teacher organizations.

Though standardized tests would dominate in assessing standardized standards in basic reading, math, and writing, they would play a much less important role for focused and varied standards in key curriculum areas, a negligible role for focused and varied standards in social and emotional areas, and no role in assessing school standards and teacher standards. In these areas, the dominant assessment vehicle would be the whole school quality review process, involving both an internal self-study review and a visitation team that would engage in an intensive examination of each individual school. In the social and emotional learning areas, performance exhibitions, portfolios, and perhaps a service requirement would make sense. For school standards in noncurriculum areas, it might make sense for the state to develop some sort of an indicator system that the local school quality review team would have to consider along with local self-study data. A similar approach might work for teachers' standards, again assuming there is no independent teacher standards board in the state.

Who would be responsible for assessing? The state would be responsible for assessing standards in basic reading, math, and writing, and its findings would have to be considered by the whole school quality review team. The whole school quality review team would be the major player in all other assessments. This team would develop one report that provides an in-depth study of the school and a summary rating that takes into account all layers of standards and their assessment. In other words, if a state chooses to sort schools into categories such as exemplary, recognized, meets expectations, and needs improvement, *no one source of data would be used alone in reaching this summative evaluation.* In order of importance, the audience for the report would be the local school, the local school community, the school district, the state, and the general public.

We have no way of knowing if a system of whole school quality review will work in our context. It probably will not work if we wind up with the typical "inspection" system found in most other countries. The school quality review approach, however, has potential and should be experimented with. What are the obstacles to creating a school quality review system that incorporates layered standards and shared accountability? Certainly it is not a lack of talent. We already know how to assess with a high level of sophistication and we know that the concept of layered loyalties makes sense. It is, after all, a part of the everyday lives of most Americans who believe in their country, their churches, their lodges, their races, their ethnic backgrounds, their politics, their local communities, their families, and even their schools—all at the same time. Somehow all these layers of loyalties are held together by certain common characteristics that define Americans as Americans and Canadians as Canadians who share common traditions and values. Similarly, schools, like neighborhoods within a city, would be tied together by some common standards but would celebrate their diversity by being connected to different standards at the same time.

If talent is not an obstacle and disposition is not an obstacle, what is? I believe it is our blind commitment to the "one best way" ideology, our fear of diversity, and perhaps even our mistrust of grass-roots democracy.

Still, if we value democracy, we have no alternative but to adopt the layered approach to standards that ensures a viable lifeworld in each of our school communities. To do otherwise is to ignore what we know about creating effective schools—uniqueness and institutional character count. And if we adopt a comprehensive view of what a good school is, we simply must broaden our assessment strategies by adopting a version of the school quality review as our overarching framework.

Consider, for example, the recent report, *Promising Futures: A Call to Improve Learning for Maine's Secondary Students* (1998), issued by the Maine Commission on Secondary Education. This report identifies six core principles that successful secondary educational experiences require:

1. A safe, respectful and caring environment *that assures that every student can attend fully to her or his central mission: learning;*
2. *Adults to hold* high universal expectations of all students *and to provide a* variety of pathways *for students as they strive to meet these expectations;*
3. Frequent assessment of student learning *and review of these assessments among students, teachers, and parents so that all can* share responsibility for planning and carrying out *learning activities;*
4. *Teaching and procedures that* honor and build upon the unique contributions and needs of each learner *so that all students will make full use of their opportunities to learn;*
5. *Staff, parents, and especially* students to be engaged democratically in decisions about learning and the conduct of the school *so they learn civic responsibility and skills and so that respect and equity are assured among all members of the school community; and*
6. Internal coherence among school mission, goals, actions, and outcomes *so that the efforts of students, staff and community result in the fulfillment of mission and goals. (56)*

The Maine Commission on Secondary Education proposes that the best way to implement the core principles is by adopting 15 core practices for advancing teaching and supporting learning:

1. *Every student is respected and valued by adults and by fellow students.*
2. *Every teacher tailors learning experiences to the learner's needs, interests, and future goals.*

3. *Every teacher challenges learners both to master the fundamentals of the disciplines and to integrate skills and concepts across the disciplines to address relevant issues and problems.*
4. *Every student learns in collaborative groups of students with diverse learning styles, skills, ages, personal backgrounds and career goals.*
5. *Every student makes informed choices about education and participation in school life and takes responsibility for the consequences of those choices.*
6. *Every student employs a personal learning plan to target individual as well as common learning goals and to specify learning activities that will lead to the attainment of those goals.*
7. *Every teacher makes learning standards, activities, and assessment procedures known to students and parents and assures the coherence among them.*
8. *Every student who receives the secondary school diploma has demonstrated, through performance exhibitions, knowledge and skills at a level deemed by the school and by the state to be sufficient to begin adult life.*
9. *Students and teachers belong to teams that provide each student continuous personal and academic attention and a supportive environment for learning and growth.*
10. *Learning governs the allocation of time, space, facilities, and services.*
11. *Every teacher has sufficient time and resources to learn, to plan, and to confer with individual students, colleagues, and families.*
12. *Every staff member understands adolescent learning and developmental needs, possesses diverse instructional skills, and is a constructive model for youth.*
13. *Every school has a comprehensive professional development system in which every staff member has a professional development plan to guide improvement.*
14. *Staff, students, and parents are involved democratically in significant decisions affecting student learning.*
15. *Active leadership by principals and others inspires and mobilizes staff, students, and parents to work toward the fulfillment of the school's mission and, within it, their own learning and life goals. (Maine Commission on Secondary Education, 1998:57)*

And finally, the commission identifies six broad categories that provide the guiding principles for defining Maine's learning results that each student must exhibit before leaving school. The categories and principles are as follows:

Each Maine student must leave school as:

   I. *A Clear and Effective Communicator*
      • *uses oral, written, visual, artistic, and technological modes of expression;*
      • *reads, listens to and interprets messages from multiple sources; and*
      • *uses English and at least one other language*
  II. *A Self-Directed and Life-Long Learner*

- *creates career and education plans that reflect personal goals, interests and skills, and available resources;*
- *demonstrates the capacity to undertake independent study; and*
- *finds and uses information from libraries, electronic data bases, and other resources.*

III. *A Creative and Practical Problem Solver*
- *observes situations objectively to clearly and accurately define problems;*
- *frames questions and designs data collection and analysis strategies from all disciplines to answer those questions;*
- *identifies patterns, trends, and relationships that apply to solutions to problems; and*
- *generates a variety of solutions, builds a case for the best response, and critically evaluates the effectiveness of this response.*

IV. *A Responsible and Involved Citizen*
- *recognizes the power of personal participation to affect the community and demonstrates participation skills;*
- *understands the importance of accepting responsibility for personal decisions and actions;*
- *knows the means of achieving personal and community health and well-being; and*
- *recognizes and understands the diverse nature of society.*

V. *A Collaborative and Quality Worker*
- *knows the structure and functions of the labor market;*
- *assesses individual interests, aptitudes, skills, and values in relation to demands of the workplace; and*
- *demonstrates reliability, flexibility, and concern for quality.*

VI. *An Integrative and Informed Thinker*
- *applies knowledge and skills in and across English language arts, visual and performing arts, foreign languages, health and physical education, mathematics, science, social studies, and career preparation; and*
- *comprehends relationships among different modes of thought and methods associated with the traditional disciplines. (Maine Commission on Secondary Education, 1998:58)*

Having read the summaries of the Maine Commission on Secondary Education's work, how would you use its ideas to tackle the problem of assessing in your state? How would you provide the necessary information that each school needs to improve by gauging their progress in meeting the commission's standards and guidelines, and by embodying the commission's core practices and principles? Surely you would not rely on a standardized standards test formatted as multiple-choice questions in the basic skills areas of reading, writing, and mathematics. Even adding a portfolio of criterion-referenced tests that were linked to state standards in each of the subject-matter areas would add little in assessing the progress that each school in your state is making and in providing each school with the information they need to actually improve their performance. Moving to a school quality review framework that might include some testing as part of its repertoire but would include many other forms of assessment brings us much closer to what needs to be done. Borrowing a thought from Barth (1980), though the problems that schools face as they seek to improve may be the same, the solutions to these problems are likely to differ. A good assessment cannot be decontextualized but must be situated in a school's specific context and must include attention to that school's own goals, aspirations, needs, and dispositions.

References

Ancess, Jacqueline. 1996. *Outside/Inside, Inside/Outside Developing and Implementing the School Quality Review*. New York: National Center for Restructuring Education, Schools and Teaching.

Barth, Roland. 1980. *Run School Run*. Cambridge, MA: Harvard University Press.

Bryk, Anthony S., Valerie E. Lee, and Peter B. Holland. 1993. *Catholic Schools and the Common Good*. Cambridge, MA: Harvard University Press.

Clinchy, Evans. 1995, Spring. "Why Are We Restructuring?" *New Schools, New Communities* 11(3), 7–12.

Coleman, James S., and Thomas Hoffer. 1987. *Public and Private High Schools: The Impact of Communities*. New York: Basic Books.

Elias, Maurice J., et al. 1997. *Promoting Social and Emotional Learning Guidelines for Educators*. Alexandria, VA: Association for Supervision and Curriculum Development.

Gardner, Howard. 1983. *Dreams of Mind: The Theory of Multiple Intelligences*. New York: Basic Books.

Gardner, Howard. 1993. *The Multiple Intelligences: The Theory in Practice*. New York: Basic Books.

Goleman, Daniel. 1995. *Emotional Intelligence*. New York: Bantam.

Habermas, Jurgen. 1987. *The Theory of Communicative Action*. Vol. 2: *Lifeworld and System: A Critique of Functional Reason*. (T. McCarthy, trans.) Boston: Beacon Press.

Hill, Paul T., Gail E. Foster, and Tamar Gendler. 1990. *High Schools with Character*. Santa Monica, CA: RAND Corporation.

Hoff, David J. 1998, October 21. "At Long Last, California Board Adopts Standards for All Core Disciplines," *Education Week*, p. 12.

Illinois State Board of Education. 1997–98. *Accountability and Quality Assurance Guidelines: 1997–98, Draft II*. Springfield, IL: Center for Accountability and Quality Assurance.

Lightfoot, Sara Lawrence. 1983. *The Good High School: Portraits of Character and Culture*. New York: Basic Books.

Maine Commission on Secondary Education. 1998. *Promising Futures: A Call to Improve Learning for Maine's Secondary Students*. Augusta, ME: Department of Education.

McMullin, Lin. 1999, March 17. Letter to the editor. *Education Week*, p. 59.

Olson, Steve. 1998, Septemeber 30. "Science Friction," *Education Week*, pp. 25–29.

Sergiovanni, Thomas J. 2000. *The Lifeworld of Leadership: Creating Culture, Community, and Personal Meaning in Our Schools*. San Francisco: Jossey-Bass.

Sternberg, Robert J., and Richard K. Wagner. (Eds.). 1995. *Practical Intelligence*. New York: Cambridge University Press.

11

TEACHING, LEARNING, AND COMMUNITY

Just a few years ago, it seemed that the issue of defining effective teaching and understanding how students learn was settled. We had in hand a body of knowledge based on "effective teaching" research and on behaviorist learning principles that provided a crystal clear picture of how students learn and of what teachers needed to do to maximize this learning. Included in this picture were beliefs that learning was an individual matter involving the accumulation of bits and pieces of knowledge and skills. This learning could be facilitated by providing lots of direct teaching and guided practice, and could be motivated by providing the right rewards.

Things are different today. Whereas the effective teaching findings of the 1970s and early 1980s cannot be summarily dismissed, more recent research provides a different picture of how students learn and of what good teaching is. This research is based on constructivist cognitive psychology and on cultural views of human being and learning.

Comparing the Theories

In this chapter, the two views of teaching and learning are compared. If one believes that teaching is a deliberate act that is situationally responsive, then it is important that both views of teaching be understood and used. Direct instruction, for example, might make sense for some children in some contexts and for some purposes but not for other children in other contexts or for other purposes. The same is true for constructivist views of teaching and learning. It does makes a difference, however, which of the views is primary and which of the views is secondary; which view provides the overall framework for making decisions about curriculum, teaching, learning, and assessment and which view is a supplement; which view defines the overall pedagogical strategies a teacher or school uses and which view is a tactic that is used to serve a more narrow purpose or limited function.

Deciding which of the two views of teaching and learning should be the overall framework for curriculum building, supervision, staff development, and leadership practice is important because theories create the realities that we have to deal with. As theories change, so do the realities. In the image of teaching based on the early effective teaching research described on the previous page, the emphasis in curriculum building is on explicitness and on alignment of what will be learned with preset objectives, with approaches to teaching, and with assessment strategies. Supervision becomes a process of monitoring the various parts of this alignment and making the needed corrections. Staff development becomes training, and leadership becomes a process of planning, organizing, motivating, and evaluating the work of others. Within the constructivist cognitive view of teaching and learning, the emphasis is on emergent curriculum, collegial supervision, teacher development as inquiry and reflection, and leadership as community building. In both cases it is the theory of teaching and learning that determines what good practice is. If we want to change existing practice, we will first have to change what we believe is true about teaching and learning.

Exhibit 11.1 lists seven pairs of beliefs about teaching and learning. As you read the pairs, distribute 10 points to reflect the extent to which you think each is true. If, for example, you think belief *1a* and belief *1b* are equally true, give them each 5 points. If you think belief *1a* is absolutely true and *1b* is absolutely false, assign 10 points to *a* and none to *b,* and so forth.

By totaling the points you assigned to the *a* statements and to the *b* statements, you can get an idea of the extent to which you agree with each of the two theories of teaching and learning.

The choices we make about the beliefs we hold determine, for example, what is considered effective supervisory practice. The rating, inspecting, and inservicing practices that often account for what principals are expected to do are based on beliefs about teaching and learning implied by the *a* statements of each pair. This supervision takes the form of tightly linking teachers to detailed objectives, to curriculum content scripts, to teaching schedules, and to corresponding evaluation schemes that rely on checking to be sure that teachers are following the approved script. Effective teaching is expressed as research-validated generic behaviors. These behaviors often comprise lists that principals use in observing teachers.

The beliefs implied by the *b* statements are based on constructivist cognitive psychological principles that suggest different teaching and supervisory practices. Tyson (1990) describes some of these differences:

> *School structures and routines should be shaped more by students' needs than by the characteristics of the disciplines, and less by teachers' and administrators' need for control and convenience. Young children learn best when they become active workers rather than passive learners. They make more progress, and are much more interested in schoolwork, when they are permitted to work together in groups to solve complex tasks, allowed to engage in class discussions and taught to argue*

EXHIBIT 11.1   Beliefs about Teaching and Learning

1. (a) Learning is a process of accumulating isolated bits
   of information and skills.   (a) _____

   (b) Learning involves active construction of meaning
   and understanding.   (b) _____ = 10

2. (a) Students are empty vessels who receive and store
   information that is taught.   (a) _____

   (b) Students' prior understandings influence what
   they learn during instruction.   (b) _____ = 10

3. (a) Learning is defined as a change in student
   behavior.   (a) _____

   (b) Learning is defined as a change in a student's
   cognitive structure and world view.   (b) _____ = 10

4. (a) Teaching and learning involves interactions
   between teachers and students.   (a) _____

   (b) Teaching and learning involves active construction
   of meaning by students.   (b) _____ = 10

5. (a) Students are individual learners and motivation
   should be competitively based.   (a) _____

   (b) Learning in cooperation with others is important in
   motivating students and in enhancing outcomes.   (b) _____ = 10

6. (a) Teachers must work hard at delivering instruction
   to students to be successful.   (a) _____

   (b) Teachers must arrange for students to do the work
   of learning.   (b) _____ = 10

7. (a) Thinking and learning skills are generic across
   content areas and context.   (a) _____

   (b) Thinking and learning skills are content- and
   context-specific.   (b) _____ = 10
                                                                           _____
                                                                              70

Source: From *Supervision: A Redefinition,* 6th ed. (p. 107) by Thomas J. Sergiovanni and Robert J. Starratt, 1999, New York: McGraw-Hill. Reproduced with permission of The McGraw-Hill Companies.

convincingly for their approach in the midst of conflicting ideas and strategies. Even young children can do these things well with a little encouragement . . . many children, particularly those with little home support, learn best in a more familial school atmosphere. (22)

Believing that teaching is not the same as telling, Tyson (1990) concludes that

Generic pedagogy, which has spawned generic in-service training programs and generic teacher evaluation systems, overlooks the intimate and necessary connec-

tion between a discipline and teaching methods. Powerful, subject-specific and topic-specific pedagogy, most of it in mathematics and science, is becoming available. These new techniques make the battles over relative importance of content knowledge and pedagogical knowledge seem futile. Effective teaching requires both kinds of knowledge, developed to a high degree, and applied flexibly and artistically to particular topics and students. (24)

Much of the new research on teaching leads to the conclusion that script-following may have its place but that, overall, teaching is much more than script-following and supervision is much more than making sure that those scripts are followed (Brandt, 1993; Marzano, 1992; Resnick and Klopfer, 1989; Newmann and Associates, 1996). Several issues of *Educational Leadership* (April, 1992; April, 1993; November, 1994; March, 1997; November, 1998) provide readable and compelling summaries of this research.

Implications for Supervision

The *b* beliefs about teaching and learning provide a different image of how supervision should be thought about and practiced. According to Nolan and Francis (1992):

1. *Teachers will be viewed as active constructors of their own knowledge about teaching and learning;*
2. *Supervisors will be viewed as collaborators in creating knowledge about teaching and learning;*
3. *The emphasis in data collection during supervision will change from almost total reliance on paper and pencil observation instruments [designed] to capture the events of a single period of instruction to the use of a wide variety of data sources to capture a lesson as it unfolds over several periods of instruction;*
4. *There will be greater emphasis on context specific knowledge and skills in the supervisory process; and*
5. *Supervision will become more group oriented rather than individually oriented. (58)*

To this list we can add:

6. *The emphasis will be less on changing behaviors, per se, and more on changing theories, beliefs, and assumptions.*

This image suggests new roles and responsibilities for teachers. They will, for example, become more active as participants in knowledge and collaborators in creating new knowledge about teaching and learning. They must assume roles not only as cosupervisors with principals and other administrators, but also as cosupervisors with other teachers. They must join together with their principals to help the school become a learning and inquiring community. These themes will be further developed in Chapter 12. The following sections briefly review the research on effective teaching and then compare this research with the new insights that have emerged from constructivist cognitive psychology.

Research on "Effective Teaching"

Without question, the early research on effective teaching contributed to our understanding, provided a base upon which to build new insights into effective teaching, and still provides some useful ideas for certain teaching and learning situations. The findings are apt to sound familiar to experienced teachers and might even be considered applications of common sense. This research showed that certain teacher behaviors were related to student gains on both criterion- and norm-referenced tests. Examples of the behaviors most frequently cited by this research are:

> Provide classroom rules that allow pupils to take care of personal and procedural needs without having to check with the teacher.
>
> Communicate high expectations to students.
>
> Begin each class by reviewing homework and by reviewing material covered in the previous few classes.
>
> Make objectives of teaching clear to students.
>
> Teach directly the content or skills that will be measured on the tests.
>
> After teaching, assess student comprehension by asking questions and by providing practice.
>
> Provide opportunities for successful practice and monitor this practice by moving around the classroom.
>
> Be sure that students are directly engaged in academic tasks.
>
> Assign homework.
>
> Hold review sessions weekly and monthly.

How applicable are these teaching behaviors? Are they likely to be as effective in teaching complex subject matter that requires interpretation and teaching higher-order thinking skills as they are for teaching simple subject matter and basic skills? Are they equally effective for teaching music, physics, reading, arithmetic, or more advanced mathematics? Most effective teaching researchers would answer no. The research findings were never intended to be applicable to all situations. Many consultants, workshop providers, and policy makers, however, are often quick to answer yes. In their enthusiasm to find simple answers to complex questions, they tend to consider the findings as generic and thus applicable to all situations.

How teaching effectiveness is defined creates another problem. Definitions of effectiveness create realities. With different definitions we get different effective teaching practices. Some teacher evaluation instruments, for example, define effective teaching as the display of behavior associated with the research on direct instruction. Other instruments define effectiveness as the embodiment of constructivist teaching and learning principles. "Effectiveness," in each case, is a function of how effectiveness is defined originally.

Most of the studies that led to the effective teaching findings were concentrating on the teaching of basic skills in reading and arithmetic in the early grades of elementary schools. Whether these teaching behaviors are appropriate for higher-level learning in reading and mathematics or for learning in other areas such as history or music, is an open question. The indicators of teaching effectiveness are neither objective nor independent, but are directly linked to how researchers define effectiveness.

Process-Product Research

During the seventies and early eighties, teaching effectiveness researchers focused on linking teaching behaviors to outcomes such as achievement test scores. The teaching behaviors were known as *processes* and the outcomes as *products,* which gave rise to the name *process-product research.* The behaviors of teachers that correlated with high student outcomes were considered to be effective. This approach provided a limited definition of teacher productivity. A broader definition identifies the teacher as just one of several inputs into the process of producing student outcomes. Furthermore, it focuses on a teacher's contribution to learning rather than some arbitrary and absolute standard applied uniformly to all students. Productivity, in other words, is a relative, not an absolute, term. Thus, it is very possible for teacher *a* to be more productive than teacher *b,* even though at an absolute level, teacher *b*'s students score higher on tests than do teacher *a*'s (Schlock, Cowart, and Staebler, 1993).

The lessons learned from the process-product effective teaching research are important. This research tells us that some teachers elicit greater gains in student achievement on tests than others because of differences in how they teach; because they expect more from students, emphasize mastery, provide more opportunities to learn, and manage their classrooms well; and because they spend a great deal of time actively teaching their students (Brophy, 1992). Teachers who do these things are likely to be much more effective than teachers who don't. Nonetheless, because this research focused on basic aspects of teaching that differentiated least effective teachers from others, it does not highlight the critical, albeit more subtle, points of teaching that distinguish outstanding teachers.

Recent Research

What does the new research tell us? This research points out that learning requires knowledge, which comes in many forms. Some knowledge is limited and other knowledge is generative. Limited knowledge does not lead anywhere; it is simply accumulated, stored, and recalled. Generative knowledge, however, leads to more learning, new learning, more expansive learning, and the transfer of learning. Generative knowledge is used to create new knowledge. It is knowledge that can be used to understand new situations, to solve unfamiliar problems, to think and reason, and to continue to learn. Constructivist cognitive research reveals that before knowledge becomes generative in the minds of students, they must elaborate and question what they learn, be able to examine new information in relationship to other information, and build new structures of knowledge.

A further distinction is made between declarative knowledge and procedural knowledge. *Declarative knowledge* refers to subject-matter content, and *procedural knowledge* refers to processes such as how to think, and how we solve problems, and how we synthesize. Knowing what a virus is, how democracy works, what Federalist Paper No. 10 is about, what the Civil Rights Act includes, and who wrote *The Great Gatsby* are examples of declarative knowledge. Using coordinates to fix a position on a map, finding words in a dictionary, proofreading an essay, synthesizing existing information into new wholes, differentiating fact from fiction, and using a problem-solving strategy are examples of procedural knowledge.

Whether declarative knowledge turns out to be limited or generative depends on how content and thinking skills are taught. Are they taught separately or at the same time? A combination of the two is needed to create a curriculum that emphasizes thinking. Subject matter becomes the primary site for developing problem solving and reasoning. Resnick and Klopfer (1989) explain:

> *In this vision of the Thinking Curriculum, thinking suffuses the curriculum. It is everywhere. Thinking skills and subject-matter content are joined early in education and pervade instruction. There is no choice to be made between a content emphasis and a thinking-skills emphasis. No depth in either is possible without the other. (6)*

Teaching for Understanding

In the new research, the emphasis is on teaching subject matter for understanding and on generative use of knowledge. In order for knowledge to be understood and used, students must be involved in its active construction. This means not just telling and explaining, but providing students with opportunities to answer questions, to discuss and debate meanings and implications, and to engage in authentic problem solving in real contexts. According to Brophy (1992)*:

> *Early in the process, the teacher assumes most of the responsibility for structuring and managing learning activities and provides students with a great deal of information, explanation, modelling and cuing. As students develop expertise, however, they can begin regulating their own learning by asking questions and by working on increasingly complex applications with increasing degrees of autonomy. The teacher still provides task simplification, coaching, and other "scaffold-*

Source: From "Probing the Subtleties of Subject-Matter Teaching" by Jere Brophy, 1992, *Educational Leadership* 49(7), p. 6. Used by permission of the Association for Supervision and Curriculum Development. Copyright © 1992 by ASCD. All rights reserved.

ing" needed to assist students with challenges that they are not ready to handle on their own. Gradually, this assistance is reduced in response to gradual increases in student readiness to engage in self-regulated learning. (6)

Relying on the research of Anderson (1989) and Prawat (1989), as well as his own work, Brophy (1992)[*] identifies the following principles of good subject-matter teaching:

1. *The curriculum is designed to equip students with knowledge, skills, values, and dispositions useful both inside and outside of school.*
2. *Instructional goals underscore developing student expertise within an application context and with emphasis on conceptual understanding and self-regulated use of skills.*
3. *The curriculum balances breadth with depth by addressing limited content but developing this content sufficiently to foster understanding.*
4. *The content is organized around a limited set of powerful ideas (key understandings and principles).*
5. *The teacher's role is not just to present information but also to scaffold and respond to students' learning.*
6. *The students' role is not just to absorb or copy but to actively make sense and construct meaning.*
7. *Activities and assignments feature authentic tasks that call for problem solving or critical thinking, not just memory or reproduction.*
8. *Higher-order thinking skills are not taught as a separate skills curriculum. Instead, they are developed in the process of teaching subject-matter knowledge within application contexts that call for students to relate what they are learning to their lives outside of school by thinking critically or creatively about it or by using it to solve problems or make decisions.*
9. *The teacher creates a social environment in the classroom that could be described as a learning community where dialogue promotes understanding. (6)*

The Classroom as Learning Community

Two characteristics of Brophy's principles stand out. One is the importance of helping the classroom become a social community and the other is the power of learning through engagement in real work. Much of the earlier literature on effective teaching makes the assumption that teaching and learning is a rather solo affair and focuses primarily on the individual learner. Constructivist cognitive psychology points out the importance of social relationships and the need for classrooms to become learning communities and communities of inquiry. Much of the new research, for example, points to the value of cooperative living and learning within the classroom as a learning community.

In a learning community, knowledge exists as something that is both individually owned and community owned at the same time. The two feed off each other.

A particular student's own individual growth and accumulated knowledge contributes to the shared growth and accumulated knowledge that exists in a classroom as a whole. As this accumulated knowledge expands, so does individual knowledge. This view of shared knowledge is based on several assumptions.

> *First, learning is an active process of knowledge construction and sense-making by the student. Second, knowledge is a cultural artifact of human beings: we produce it, share it, and transform it as individuals and as groups. Third, knowledge is distributed among members of a group, and this distributed knowledge is greater than the knowledge possessed by any single member. (Leinhardt, 1992:23)*

Authentic Learning

Perhaps the most basic lessons that the constructivist cognitive research teaches are the importance of relating new learning to prior knowledge and the importance of immersing teaching in the world of real or "authentic" learning. Generative learning—learning that is understood and can be used to create new learning—doesn't just take place in a vacuum. It is always contextual. What is learned depends on one's prior knowledge; learning takes place best when bridges or scaffolds are developed that link the new with the old.

Sometimes prior knowledge interferes with learning or encourages one to learn the wrong thing. Students, for example, often bring misconceptions or naive theories and notions to their studies. Linking new ideas to prior knowledge that is wrong may result in the further accumulation of faulty learning. This problem highlights the importance of personalized learning, intimate settings for learning, and acknowledging the social nature of learning. Teachers have to get "up close" to understand where kids are coming from. This doesn't happen when the old tell-teach-practice-reteach practices are used.

The importance of authentic learning and the provision of "cognitive apprenticeships" to promote it cannot be underestimated. Students learn best by doing, and doing is best when it is lifelike—when it involves engagement with real or near real problem solving. Effective learning settings allow for learners to use shared knowledge to solve problems, allow students to practice their skills in real-life settings, and allow for the integration of abstract and practical learning activities. These are the conditions that increase the likelihood that teaching will be for understanding and that students will indeed be learning.

Standards for Authentic Learning

Newmann, Secada, and Wehlage (1995) define *authentic learning* as resulting in students being actively engaged with the materials of the curriculum. Authentic learning calls for student work to reflect the *construction of knowledge;* through *disciplined inquiry;* to produce discourse, products, and performances that have meaning to students *beyond being successful in school.* The authors propose four standards that need to be met to verify the presence of authentic learning:

1. *Higher order thinking (construction of knowledge): instruction involves students in manipulating information and ideas by synthesizing, generalizing, explaining, hypothesizing, or arriving at conclusions that produce new meaning and understandings for them. (29)*
2. *Deep knowledge (disciplined inquiry): instruction addresses central ideas of a topic or discipline with enough thoroughness to explore connections and relationships and to produce relatively complex understanding. (31)*
3. *Substantive conversation (disciplined inquiry): students engage in extended conversational exchanges with the teacher and/or their peers about subject matter in a way that builds an improved and shared understanding of ideas and topics. (35)*
4. *Connections to the world beyond the classroom (value beyond school): students make connections between substantive knowledge and either public problems or personal experiences. (40)*

But learning cannot be separated from teaching and neither learning nor teaching can be separated from the tasks, assignments, and other definers of the curriculum. Together, the three are referred to as *authentic pedagogy*. Newmann, Secada, and Wehlage (1995) propose a three-pronged strategy for assessing authentic pedagogy: assessing tasks that teachers give students to complete, assessing the dynamics of teaching and learning, and assessing the work students actually do. They then provide research-based standards and scoring criteria for assessing tasks, teaching and learning, and student work. The protocols for assessing tasks are provided in Appendix 11.1. Teacher-learning and student work protocols are available from the Wisconsin Center for Education Research (see, for example, Newmann, Secada, and Wehlage, 1995). Use the standards provided in Appendix 11.1 to examine the extent to which the tasks you assign to your students require the level of cognitive work described in each standard. Work together with two other teachers. As a group, how are you measuring up? How can the assessment protocols be used as a staff development vehicle in your school?

An Integrated View

Taking the new research on teaching and learning seriously means making some changes in the way we have thought about organizing the classroom, planning for teaching, and arranging the curriculum. The key will be changing from a coverage mentality to a mastery mentality. Gardner explains:

The greatest enemy of understanding is coverage. As long as you are determined to cover everything, you actually ensure that most kids are not going to understand. You've got to take enough time to get kids deeply involved in something so they can think about it in lots of different ways and apply it—not just at school but at home and on the street and so on. (Brandt, 1993:7)

Furthermore, we will have to rely far less on textbooks that provide the broad stroke and more on other materials that provide in-depth coverage of fewer topics. The curriculum will have to be revisited and serious inquiries made to identify essential and nonessential material, the fundamental structures of the disciplines that are generative by their very nature, and the aspects of the curriculum that comprise more limited or dead-end knowledge. Learning will have to emphasize solving problems. The curriculum will need to be more emergent as teachers and students, representing a community of learners, make decisions about what to do and when and how as they are involved in the process of thinking and learning.

Robert Marzano (1992:154–155) offers a "dimensions of learning" framework that is comprised of five sets of questions he believes teachers need to answer as they plan for teaching and learning. Exhibit 11.2 lists the dimensions and questions.

Answers to the questions in dimension 1 lay the groundwork for developing the kind of social relationships that provide students with shared meaning, shared funds of knowledge, and a shared basis for creating new knowledge. The remaining dimensions focus on teaching strategies and skills and decisions about knowledge.

Marzano (1992) recommends two broad strategies for teaching: presentation strategies and workshop strategies. Presentation strategies help students acquire and integrate new knowledge whether it be declarative or procedural, and thus help with the second dimension of learning. They also help extend and refine knowledge that helps with the third dimension of learning.

Presentation strategies incorporate many of the features of the original teaching effectiveness research. Examples are the importance of stimulating interest in the topic to be learned, relating the new information to existing information, providing clear goals and directions to students, modeling important activities, and providing closure. Yet, instead of viewing these functions in a linear stepwise fashion with one following the other, and instead of insisting that each of the functions be a part of every presentation type of teaching, the five are understood differently. Marzano points out that not all need to be part of every presentation nor do they need to be performed in any set order. The five functions might be depicted, then, not as a linear list, but as follows:

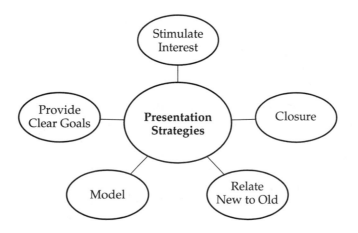

EXHIBIT 11.2   Dimensions of Learning

Dimension 1

1. What will be done to help students develop positive attitudes and perceptions about the learning climate?
   a. What will be done to help students feel accepted by the teacher and their peers?
   b. What will be done to help students perceive the classroom as a comfortable and orderly place?
2. What will be done to help students develop positive attitudes and perceptions about classroom tasks?
   a. What will be done to help students perceive classroom tasks as valuable?
   b. What will be done to help students believe they can perform classroom tasks?
   c. What will be done to help students understand and be clear about classroom tasks?

Dimension 2

Declarative Knowledge:
1. What are the general topics?
2. What are the specifics?
3. How will students experience the information?
4. How will students be aided in constructing meaning?
5. How will students be aided in organizing the information?

6. How will students be aided in storing the information?

Procedural Knowledge:
1. What skills and processes do students really need to master?
2. How will students be aided in constructing models?
3. How will students be aided in shaping the skill or process?
4. How will students be aided in internalizing the skill or process?

Dimension 3
1. What information will be extended and refined?
2. What activities will be used to help students extend and refine knowledge?

Dimension 4
1. What are the big issues?
2. How many issues will be considered?
3. Who will structure the tasks?
4. What types of products will students create?
5. To what extent will students work in cooperative groups?

Dimension 5
1. Which mental habits will be emphasized?
2. Which mental habits will be introduced?
3. How will the mental habits be reinforced?

Source: From A Different Kind of Classroom: Teaching with Dimensions of Learning by Robert J. Marzano. Alexandria, VA: Association for Supervision and Curriculum Development. Copyright © 1992 ASCD. Reprinted by permission. All rights reserved.

Students and teachers, for example, might begin a new unit with the end, with modeling what is to be learned, or with an activity that stimulates interest, and then move to one or another of the functions in any way that makes sense.

Marzano recommends workshop strategies for the questions included in dimension 4 of his learning framework. The metaphor of workshop suggests teaching is more student directed and activity oriented. A "workshop lesson" would generally begin with a mini-lesson designed to provide guidance and give assistance to students as they begin to work on projects. Mini-lessons provide students with essential information, resources, and so forth. The major block of teaching would be the *activity.* Here, students work individually, in pairs, or in small groups on projects. Finally, there would be a *sharing period* that allows students to discuss a variety of topics and issues. "The hallmark of a sharing period is that the students and teacher freely discuss their learning as students work on their projects" (Marzano, 1992:162).

Manager and Executive Roles of Teaching

One way to understand different theories of teaching is to examine various roles that teachers assume. What are the roles that teachers must assume, for example, when teaching for understanding and when their classrooms function as learning communities? How do these roles differ from those that are assumed when teachers function in accordance with the prescriptions of the earlier effective teaching research? Four roles are described in Table 11.1. They are manager, executive, mediator, and leader.

When teachers function as managers, they execute fairly specific teaching steps according to well-defined and structured protocols. When this role dominates, teaching begins to resemble a pipeline, with the role of the teacher to manage the flow of information through this line. Objectives are defined specifically for the student, students are motivated by extrinsic means, and both students and teachers are subordinate to a structured teaching system. Furthermore, two different teachers are likely to teach in the same way. The managerial role can be effective for teaching basic skills and simple subject-matter content, but it is inadequate for teaching higher-order thinking skills, teaching for understanding, and encouraging the mastery of generative knowledge.

TABLE 11.1   Roles of Teaching

Roles	Description	Characteristics	Strengths
Teacher as Manager	The teacher executes explicit teaching steps according to highly structured protocols associated with direct instruction. The teacher manages student behavior accordingly.	Teaching is conceived as a pipeline. The role of the teacher is to manage the flow of information through the line. Objectives are defined for the student. Motivation is typically extrinsic. Both teacher and students are subordinate to the structured teaching protocols. Reliability in teaching, therefore, is very high.	Very effective for teaching basic skills and effective for teaching simple subject-matter content.

Continued

TABLE 11.1 *Continued*

Roles	Description	Characteristics	Strengths
Teacher as Executive	The teacher uses research on effective teaching and psychological principles of learning to make proper teaching decisions in light of situations faced but within a set framework which provides decision-making rules. Within this framework, for example, the teacher makes important decisions about subject-matter content, grouping for and pacing of instruction, student assignments, and other instructional features. Decisions are typically made beforehand in the form of an executive plan for teaching. Effective teaching results when this plan is followed.	Teaching is conceived as executive decision making which requires that situations be diagnosed and that established teaching principles be applied correctly. Objectives are typically defined for the student. Motivation is typically extrinsic. Students are subordinate to the system (that is, they are viewed as objects of teaching rather than partners to the teaching). Teachers are active decision makers and are in control, provided that they follow the established teaching protocols.	Very effective for teaching simple subject-matter content and effective for teaching basic skills.
Teacher as Mediator	The teacher uses reciprocal and interactive teaching strategies which enable students to process new information and new learnings in light of their own personal meanings and experiences and prior learnings. Emphasis is on helping students make sense of learning encounters by constructing new understandings and by linking new to prior learnings.	Teaching is conceived as a mediating process within which students, with the help of teachers, interact with information and ideas in terms of personal meanings and previous learnings. Though at times teachers decide the actual learning outcomes of teaching, a balance is sought between teacher-determined and student-determined outcomes. The intent is to move away from students as absorbers of information to students as processors, synthesizers, creators, and users of information; from students being dependent upon the learning system provided to students using the learning system provided. Motivation is frequently intrinsic.	Very effective for teaching analysis, problem-solving, and higher-order skills; complex concepts, higher levels of comprehension, and having students extend what is learned for application to new situations.

TABLE 11.1 *Continued*

Roles	Description	Characteristics	Strengths
Teacher as Leader	The teacher models the importance of subject matter and learning intents by the manner and enthusiasm with which teaching is provided. Modeling dimensions include time (teaching reflects a great deal of effort), feeling (the teacher cares deeply about the content, learning outcomes, and students), and focus (teaching reflects a deep understanding of the subject taught; the whys as well as the whats, the structure of knowledge; and a focus on key issues and dimensions of importance).	Teaching is conceived as a sacred activity which reflects a reverence for the importance of knowledge and of learning as ends in themselves. Through modeling students find teaching and learning to be meaningful and significant and respond with higher levels of motivation and commitment.	Very effective for communicating the importance, meaning, and significance of subject matter and learning intents; for promoting learning attitudes and values in students.

Source: From *Supervision: A Redefinition*, 5th ed. (pp. 124–125) by Thomas J. Sergiovanni and Robert J. Starratt, 1993, New York: McGraw-Hill. Reproduced with permission of The McGraw-Hill Companies.

When assuming the role of executive, the teacher uses the research on teaching and principles of learning to make proper decisions in light of the situations, but within a fairly set framework for teaching. There is, for example, an executive plan for teaching, and effective teaching parallels this plan. The teacher makes important decisions about subject-matter content, grouping for and pacing of instruction, student assignments, and other teaching and learning considerations. Objectives are defined for the student by the teacher, and motivation is typically extrinsic. Students are not partners in the teaching, but objects of the teaching. Teachers are active decision makers who are very much in control providing that they follow the established teaching protocols and the approved executive plan. The executive role is workable for teaching straightforward kinds of subject-matter content and can be suitable as well for teaching basic skills. However, this role does not provide a powerful enough conception of what teaching is and how it works to encourage teaching for understanding, to build community, and to develop learning based on generative knowledge.

Mediator and Leader Roles of Teaching

The remaining two roles, mediator and leader, are more consistent with the principles of teaching and learning implied by the constructivist cognitive research. They are associated with higher-level learning and with the development in students of attitudes and commitments to learning as something that is worthwhile. Decision making is more collaborative as students assume increasing responsibility for making learning decisions and for doing the actual work of learning.

As mediator, the teacher uses reciprocal teaching strategies that enable students to process new information and new learning in light of their own personal meanings, experiences, and prior learnings. The idea is not to define what the nature or the value of a particular learning experience is, but to have the student search for this value. The emphasis is on helping students make sense of learning encounters by constructing new meanings, by linking new to prior learnings, and by helping students interact with information and ideas. At times, teachers decide the actual learning outcomes, but a balance is sought between teacher-determined and student-determined outcomes. The curriculum is emergent as decisions about what is worth learning are made as teaching and learning progresses. The purpose of this kind of teaching is to move students away from being absorbers of information to being processors, synthesizers, creators, and users of information; from being dependent on the learning system provided to using the learning system. Motivation is frequently intrinsic. The mediator role is very effective for teaching for understanding, for encouraging community building, and for helping students accumulate generative knowledge.

In many respects the role of teacher as leader is the most important of the four. Its purpose is to instill in students a love for, commitment to, and appreciation of learning that carries them not only through their school years, but throughout their lives. Here, the teacher models the importance of subject matter and learning intents by the manner and enthusiasm with which teaching is provided. When this role is successfully implemented, teaching and learning are conceived as sacred activities that reflect a reverence for knowledge as an end in itself.

On the surface it appears that teachers are active when assuming the managerial and executive roles, and passive when assuming mediator and leader roles; however, when we look deeper, we find that just the opposite is true. Mediator and leader roles require careful and skilled planning, diligent arrangement of the learning environment, close personal relationships with students, and intimate knowledge of the work that they do. Together, these requirements provide a more active and deeper involvement in teaching and learning than is the case when managerial and executive roles are assumed. These roles, by contrast, involve a lot of "show biz" that in reality requires only superficial involvement in students' learning and lives.

References

Anderson, L. 1989. "Implementing Instructional Programs to Promote Meaningful, Self-Regulated Learning," in J. Brophy (Ed.), *Advances in Research on Teaching, Vol. 1* (pp. 311–343). Greenwich, CT: JAI Press.

Brandt, Ron. 1993. "On Teaching for Understanding: A Conversation with Howard Gardner," *Educational Leadership* 50(7), 4–7.

Brophy, Jere. 1992. "Probing the Subtleties of Sub-ject-Matter Teaching," *Educational Leadership* 49(7), 4–8.

Educational Leadership 49(2). 1992, April.

Educational Leadership 50(7). 1993, April.

Educational Leadership 52(3). 1994, November.

Educational Leadership 54(6). 1997, March.

Educational Leadership 56(3). 1998, November.

Leinhardt, Gaea. 1992. "What Research on Learn-ing Tells Us about Teaching," *Educational Leadership* 49(7), 20–25.

Marzano, Robert J. 1992. *A Different Kind of Class-room: Teaching with Dimensions of Learning*. Alexandria, VA: Association for Supervision and Curriculum Development.

Newmann, Fred M., and Associates. 1996. *Authen-tic Achievement: Restructuring Schools for Intel-lectual Quality*. San Francisco: Jossey-Bass.

Newmann, Fred M., Walter G. Secada, and Gary G. Wehlage. 1995. *A Guide to Authentic Instruction and Assessment: Vision, Standards and Scoring*. Madison: Wisconsin Center for Education Research.

Nolan, James, and Pam Francis. 1992. "Changing Perspectives in Curriculum and Instruction," in Carl Glickman (Ed.), *Supervision in Transi-tion*, Yearbook of the Association for Supervi-sion and Curriculum Development (pp. 44–59). Alexandria, VA: Association for Supervi-sion and Curriculum Development.

Prawat, R. 1989. "Promoting Access to Knowledge, Strategy, and Disposition in Students: A Research Synthesis," *Review of Educational Research* 59, 1–41.

Resnick, Lauren B., and Leopold E. Klopfer. 1989. *Toward the Thinking Curriculum: Current Cog-nitive Research*, Yearbook of the Association for Supervision and Curriculum Develop-ment. Alexandria, VA: Association for Super-vision and Curriculum Development.

Schlock, Mark D., Bill Cowart, and Bonnie Stae-bler. 1993. "Teacher Productivity Revisited: Definition, Theory, Measurement, and Appli-cation," *Journal of Personnel Evaluation in Edu-cation* (7)2, 179–196.

Tyson, Harriet. 1990, March. "Reforming Science Education/Restructuring the Public Schools: Roles for the Scientific Community," pp. 22, 24. Prepared as a background paper for the New York Academy of Sciences and the Insti-tute for Educational Leadership Forum on Restructuring K–12 Education. New York: Academy of Sciences.

Appendix 11.1   Standards and Scoring Criteria for Assessment Tasks

Overview and General Rules

The main point here is to estimate, for a given task, the extent to which the teacher communicates to students expectations consistent with the standards. To what extent does successful completion of the task require the kind of cognitive work indicated by each standard?

The seven standards reflect three more general standards for authentic achievement as follows:

Construction of knowledge:	Organization of information
	Consideration of alternatives
Disciplined inquiry:	Disciplinary content
	Disciplinary process
	Elaborated written communication
Value beyond school:	Problem connected to the world beyond the classroom
	Audience beyond the school

A. If a task has different parts that imply different expectations (e.g., worksheet/ short answer questions and a question asking for explanation of some conclusions), the score should reflect the teacher's apparent dominant or overall expectations. Overall expectations are indicated by the proportion of time or effort spent on different parts of the task and by criteria for evaluation stated by the teacher.

B. Scores should take into account what students can reasonably be expected to do at the grade level.

Standard 1: Organization of Information

The task asks students to organize, synthesize, interpret, explain, or evaluate complex information in addressing a concept, problem, or issue.

Consider the extent to which the task asks the student to organize, interpret, evaluate, or synthesize complex information, rather than to retrieve or to reproduce isolated fragments of knowledge or to repeatedly apply previously learned algorithms and procedures. To score high, the task should call for interpretation of nuances of a topic that go deeper than surface exposure or familiarity.

Source: From *A Guide to Authentic Instruction and Assessment: Vision, Standards and Scoring* (pp. 80–85) by Fred M. Newmann, Walter G. Secada, and Gary G. Wehlage, 1995, Madison: Wisconsin Center for Education Research. Reprinted by permission.

Appendix 11.1   *Continued*

3 = high
2 = moderate
1 = low

When students are asked to gather information for reports that indicates some selectivity and organizing beyond mechanical copying, but are not asked for interpretation, evaluation, or synthesis, give a score of 2.

Standard 2: Consideration of Alternatives

The task asks students to consider alternative solutions, strategies, perspectives, or points of view as they address a concept, problem, or issue.

To what extent does success in the task require consideration of alternative solutions, strategies, perspectives and points of view? To score high, the task should clearly involve students in considering alternatives, either through explicit presentation of the alternatives or through an activity that cannot be successfully completed without examination of alternatives implicit in the work. It is not necessary that students' final conclusions include listing or weighing of alternatives, but this could be an impressive indicator that it was an expectation of the task.

3 = high
2 = moderate
1 = low

Standard 3: Disciplinary Content

The task asks students to show understanding and/or use of ideas, theories, or perspectives considered central to an academic or professional discipline.

To what extent does the task promote students' understanding of and thinking about ideas, theories or perspectives considered seminal or critical within an academic or professional discipline, or in interdisplinary fields recognized in authoritative scholarship? Examples in mathematics could include proportion, equality, central tendency, and geometric space. Examples in social studies could include democracy, social class, market economy, or theories of revolution. Reference to isolated factual claims, definitions, algorithms—though necessary to inquiry within a discipline—will not be considered indicators of significant disciplinary content unless the task requires students to apply powerful disciplinary ideas that organize and interpret the information.

3 = Success in the task clearly requires understanding of concepts, ideas, or theories central in a discipline.

2 = Success in the task seems to require understanding of concepts, ideas or theories central in a discipline, but the task does not make these very explicit.

Appendix 11.1   *Continued*

1 = Success in the task can be achieved with a very superficial (or even without any) understanding of concepts, ideas, or theories central to any specific discipline.

Standard 4: Disciplinary Process

The task asks students to use methods of inquiry, research, or communication characteristic of an academic or professional discipline.

To what extent does the task lead students to use methods of inquiry, research, communication, and discourse characteristic of an academic or professional discipline? Some powerful processes of inquiry may not be linked uniquely to any specific discipline (e.g., interpreting graphs), but they will be valued here if the task calls for their use in ways similar to important uses within the discipline.

3 = Success in the task requires the use of methods of inquiry or discourse important to the conduct of a discipline. Examples of methods of disciplinary inquiry would include looking for mathematical patterns or interpreting primary sources.

2 = Success in the task requires use of methods of inquiry or discourse not central to the conduct of a discipline.

1 = Success in the task can be achieved without use of any specific methods of inquiry or discourse.

Standard 5: Elaborated Written Communication

The task asks students to elaborate on their understanding, explanations, or conclusions through extended writing.

This standard is intended to measure the extent to which a task requires students to elaborate on their ideas and conclusions through extended writing in a discipline. Expectations for elaborated communication can vary between disciplines. We indicate criteria for mathematics and social studies.

4 = Analysis/Persuasion/Theory

Mathematics: The task requires the student to show his/her solution path and to justify that solution path, that is, to give a logical argument, explain his/her thinking, or to justify results.

Social studies: The task requires explanations of generalizations, classifications, and relationships relevant to a situation, problem, or theme. Examples include attempts to argue, convince, or persuade and to develop or test hypotheses.

3 = Report/Summary

Appendix 11.1   *Continued*

Mathematics: The task requires some organization of material. The student is asked to give clear evidence of his/her solution path but is not required to give any mathematical argument, to justify his/her solution path, or to explain his/her thinking.

Social studies: The task calls for an account of particular events or series of events ("This is what happened"), a generalized narrative, or a description of a recurrent pattern of events or steps in a procedure ("This is what happens"; "This is the way it is done").

2 = Short-answer exercises

Mathematics: The task requires little more than giving a result. Students may be asked to show some work, but this is not emphasized and does not request much detail.

Social studies: Only one or two brief sentences per question are expected.

1 = Multiple choice exercises; fill-in-the-blank exercises (answered with less than a sentence)

Standard 6: Problem Connected to the World Beyond the Classroom

The task asks students to address a concept, problem, or issue that is similar to one that they have encountered, or are likely to encounter, in life beyond the classroom.

To what extent does the task present students with a question, issue, or problem that they have actually encountered, or are likely to encounter, in their lives beyond school? In mathematics, estimating personal budgets would qualify as a real-world problem, but completing a geometric proof generally would not. In social studies, defending one's position on compulsory community service for students could qualify as a real-world problem, but describing the origins of World War II generally would not.

Certain kinds of school knowledge may be considered valuable as cultural capital or cultural literacy needed in social, civic, or vocational situations beyond the classroom (e.g., knowing how a bill becomes a law, or how to compute interest on an investment). However, task demands for culturally valued, "basic" knowledge will not be counted here unless the task requires applying such knowledge to a specific problem likely to be encountered beyond the classroom.

When students are allowed to choose topics of interest to them, this might also indicate likely application of knowledge beyond the instructional setting. But tasks that allow student choice do not necessarily connect to issues beyond the classroom. To score high on this standard, it must be clear that the question, issue, or problem which students confront resembles one that students have encountered, or are likely to encounter, in life beyond school.

Appendix 11.1   *Continued*

3 = The question, issue, or problem clearly resembles one that students have encountered, or are likely to encounter, in life beyond school. The resemblance is so clear that teacher explanation is not necessary for most students to grasp it.

2 = The question, issue, or problem bears some resemblance to real world experiences of the students, but the connections are not immediately apparent. The connections would be reasonably clear if explained by the teacher, but the task need not include such explanations to be rated 2.

1 = The problem has virtually no resemblance to questions, issues, or problems that students have encountered, or are likely to encounter, beyond school. Even if the teacher tried to show the connections, it would be difficult to make a personal argument.

Standard 7: Audience Beyond the School

The task asks students to communicate their knowledge, present a product or performance, or take some action to an audience beyond the teacher, classroom, and school building.

Authenticity increases when students complete the task with the intention of communicating their knowledge to an audience beyond the teacher and when they actually communicate with that audience. Such communication can include informing others, trying to persuade others, performing, and taking other actions beyond the classroom. This refers not to the process of working on the task, but to the nature of the student's final product.

4 = Final product is presented to an audience beyond the school.

3 = Final product is presented to an audience beyond the classroom, but within the school.

2 = Final product is presented to peers within the classroom.

1 = Final product is presented only to the teacher.

PART IV

THE DEVELOPMENT
OF HUMAN RESOURCES

12

TEACHER DEVELOPMENT AND SUPERVISION

A consensus is emerging that teacher learning is a key ingredient in any attempt to improve schools. David and Shields (1999), for example, found that the following are important contributors to improvement: (1) a strong and sustained district focus on teacher learning and quality instruction; (2) new conceptions of staff development that looked more like part of the everyday jobs of teachers; and (3) teacher learning strategies that emphasize learning new content and knowledge and new teaching approaches in one's own classroom by learning from colleagues, on-site staff developers, and one's own principal. David and Shields studied seven urban school districts involved in systemic standards-based reform. Reform was difficult to achieve, but where improvements were noted, the learning principles listed above were important.

In a study of 24 urban schools that were academically successful, Louis and Marks found that the most successful schools had teachers with a strong sense of community and a shared mission. Teachers had time to plan and talk together, to observe each other's teaching, and to reflect together on their practice. In other words, they had strong professional communities for support and these communities were linked to higher levels of student achievement (Viadero, 1999:27). After closely examining teachers' practice in three schools, Peterson, McCarthey, and Elmore (1996) suggest that teacher learning occurs mainly as a function of specific problems that teachers face in their classrooms; that changing one's practice is largely a problem of learning rather than of organization; that although school structures can provide opportunities for teacher learning, they do not cause the learning to occur; and that changes in school structure follow from good practice. Structures are important but do not lend themselves to forward mapping of changes in teaching practice. Instead, deciding on what is important in teaching and what kind of practice makes sense should come first, allowing the backward mapping to new structures. And this alternative involves learning. Teacher learning, it appears, is the springboard to school reform—not the other way around, as current policy now assumes.

How should principals help teachers learn more about themselves and their work? What should principals do to help teachers improve their teaching practice? Answers to these questions depend on the views that principals have about good teaching, how learning environments should be developed, what curriculum decisions make sense, how the schools should be organized for effective learning, and the extent to which schools are learning and inquiring communities not just for students but for teachers and other adults, as well. If a principal's view corresponds to the process-product effective teaching research discussed in Chapter 11, one answer would make most sense. If, however, a principal's view corresponds to the newer cognitive research on teaching, then a different set of decisions would make sense. There is a link between how principals want teachers to teach and how principals help them to teach in that way.

Let's review, for example, some of the principles of teaching and learning that are based on cognitive psychology:

> Learning is a process of making sense with the construction of personal meanings.
>
> Meanings are constructed by comparing existing understandings and developing connections among ideas, concepts, and blocks of information.
>
> Meanings are norm referenced and thus are constructed in social contexts and are influenced by the views of others.
>
> Motivation to learn is in part related to an individual's goals and aspirations, and in part influenced by an individual's connections to others and the resulting group norms that emerge.
>
> Learners differ in the time needed to learn the same thing and in the cognitive processes needed to learn.
>
> Learners differ in the kind of aptitudes and intelligences they bring to learning and are predisposed to learn when strengths are emphasized.
>
> Knowledge and skills are best learned in situations and under circumstances that resemble how they will actually be used.
>
> Learning is facilitated by emphasizing the mastery of generative knowledge, which helps learners to acquire new knowledge on their own.

In this image of teaching and learning, learners are not consumers of knowledge but constructors, and the personal meanings they bring to learning are critical determinates of what will be learned and how well it will be learned. Helping teachers to learn to teach or to improve their teaching along these lines requires a shift in our understanding of teacher development. This view of teaching cannot be mastered by emphasizing consumption, memorization, and replication. Training alone just won't do. Instead, principals will need to *emphasize* professional development and renewal improvement strategies. Training, professional development, and renewal strategies are described and contrasted in Table 12.1.

TABLE 12.1   Models of Teacher Development

	Training	Professional	Renewal
Assumptions	Knowledge stands above the teacher.	The teacher stands above knowledge.	Knowledge is in the teacher.
	Knowledge is therefore instrumental. It tells the teacher what to do.	Knowledge is therefore conceptual. It informs the teacher's decisions.	Knowledge is therefore personal. It connects teachers to themselves and others.
	Teaching is a job and teachers are technicians.	Teaching is a profession and teachers are experts.	Teaching is a calling and teachers are servants.
	Mastery of skills is important.	Development of expertise is important.	Development of personal and professional self is important.
Roles	Teacher is consumer of knowledge.	Teacher is constructor of knowledge.	Teacher is internalizer of knowledge.
	Principal is expert.	Principal is colleague.	Principal is friend.
Practices	Emphasize technical competence.	Emphasize clinical competence.	Emphasize personal and critical competencies.
	Build individual teacher's skills.	Build professional community.	Build caring community.
	Through training and practice.	Through problem solving and inquiry.	Through reflection and reevaluation.
	By planning and delivering training.	By emphasizing inquiry, problem solving, and action research.	By encouraging reflection, conversation, and discourse.

The term *emphasize* is key. All three strategies have important roles to play, but not all three strategies are equal. If we value teaching for understanding, the development of thinking, and the mastery of generative knowledge, then we will need to give less attention to training models and more attention to professional development and renewal models.

Training Models

Training models of teacher development have important roles to play. They resemble traditional inservice programs that are well known to teachers and principals and need little elaboration. They are best suited for when a problem can be defined as a deficit in knowledge of some kind—for example, when teachers don't know about something or need to improve their skills in some area. Outside or inside experts do the training. Training is linked to clear objectives and relies on conventional well-executed instruction. Teachers, for example, might be introduced to various ways in which interest centers can be set up, methods for evaluating student portfolios, new techniques for using simulation for teaching world history, tips on how to monitor student progress, or some basic teaching skills that help keep students "on task." Teachers generally assume passive roles. Techniques most often used are oral presentations, illustrated presentations, demonstrations, and observations of good practice. Effective training programs provide opportunities for teachers to practice what it is that they learn. They receive coaching as they actually begin to use what they learned in their classrooms.

Professional Development Models

Although training has its place, most observers believe that it should no longer be the primary model for teacher development. Implementing lists of do's and don'ts, standard skill repertoires, and other scripts is not the way to help teachers to teach for understanding, to develop student thinking, and to promote generative knowledge. Instead, teachers need to learn how to think on their feet, inventing their practice as they go.

The relationship between teachers and the knowledge base for teaching is understood differently in professional development than in training. Professional development assumes that teachers are superordinate to the research on teaching. Unlike technicians who are trained to apply research findings, professionals view research as knowledge that informs the decisions that they make. Professionals create their practice in use.

Professional development approaches emphasize providing teachers with a rich environment loaded with teaching materials, media, books, and devices. With encouragement and support, teachers interact with this environment and with each other through exploration and discovery. Thelan (1971) suggests that the most useful teacher development programs are characterized by "intensity of personal involvement, immediate consequences for classroom practice, stimulation and ego support by meaningful associates in the situation, and initiating by teacher rather than outside" (72–73). Judith Warren Little (1993), a thoughtful commentator on teacher development, proposes six principles that she believes should guide the design of professional development experiences for teachers:

1. *Professional development offers meaningful intellectual, social and emotional engagement with ideas, with materials, and with colleagues both in and out of teaching.*
2. *Professional development takes explicit account of the context of teaching and the experience of teachers. Focused study groups, teacher collaboratives, long-term partnerships, and similar models of professional development afford teachers a means of locating new ideas in relation to their individual and institutional histories, practices, and circumstances.*
3. *Professional development offers support for informed dissent. In the pursuit of good schools, consensus may prove to be an over-stated virtue. . . . Dissent places a premium on the evaluation of alternatives and the close scrutiny of underlying assumptions.*

4. *Professional development places classroom practice in the larger context of school practice and the educational careers of children. It is grounded in a big-picture perspective on the purposes and practices of schooling, providing teachers with a means of seeing and acting upon the connections among students' experience, teachers' classroom practice, and school-wide structures and cultures.*

5. *Professional development prepares teachers (as well as students and their parents) to employ the techniques and perspectives of inquiry. . . . It acknowledges that the existing knowledge is relatively slim and that our strength may derive less from teachers' willingness to consume research knowledge than from their capacity to generate knowledge and to assess the knowledge claimed by others.*

6. *The governance of professional development ensures bureaucratic restraint and a balance between the interests of individuals and the interests of institutions. (138–139)*

Little offers the principles as alternatives to training models that when used excessively provide teachers with shallow and fragmented content and subject them to passive roles as they participate in scripted workshops. The principles are anecdotes to the "one-size-fits-all" problem that training too often presents. Furthermore, she argues that the principles challenge the view that teaching is a narrowly defined technical activity. Little believes that today's emphasis on teacher inservice is dominated by "a district-subsidized marketplace of formal programs over which teachers exert little influence or in which they play few leadership roles" (139). In professional development models, the teacher's capacities, needs, and interests are paramount. They are actively involved in contributing data and information, solving problems, analyzing, and so forth. Principals are involved as colleagues. Together, principals and teachers work to develop a common purpose themed to the improvement of teaching and learning. Together, principals and teachers work to build a learning and inquiring community.

Renewal Models

Both training and professional development models share the purpose of helping teachers improve their practice. Bolin and Falk (1987) point out that although improvement may be a legitimate goal, it is not powerful enough to tap the potential for teachers to grow personally and professionally. Bolin (1987), for example, writes:

What would happen if we set aside the question of how to improve the teacher and looked instead at what we can do to encourage the teacher? . . . Asking how to encourage the teacher places the work of improvement in the hands of the teacher. It presupposes that the teacher desires to grow, to be self-defining, and to engage in teaching as a vital part of life, rather than as unrelated employment. This leads to looking at teaching as a commitment or calling, a vocation . . . that is not adequately contained in the term profession *as it has come to be used. (11)*

Bolin believes that when the emphasis shifts from improving teachers to encouraging them, then both training and professional development give way to renewal. In her view, renewal is not driven so much by professional problems as by a teacher's commitment to teaching as a vocation. Renewal implies doing over again, revising, making new, restoring, reestablishing, and revaluing as teachers individually and collectively reflect on not only their practice but themselves and the practice of teaching that they share in the school.

In training, the emphasis is on building each individual's teaching skills by planning and delivering instruction. In development, the emphasis is on building professional community by helping teachers become inquirers, problem solvers, and researchers of their own practice. In renewal, the emphasis is on building a caring community by encouraging teachers to reflect and to engage in conversation and discourse.

Teacher Development and Types of Teacher Competence

Zimpher and Howey (1987) describe four major types of teaching competence that can help sort out when each of the approaches—training, development, and renewal—might make the most sense. The four types of competence depicted and discussed in Table 12.2 are technical, clinical, personal, and critical. Teaching as an expression of technical competence is probably the most popular of the four. It remains the area that receives the most attention in teacher education programs and in school district and state-mandated teacher evaluation instruments. An example of an emphasis on technical competence is focusing on lists of teaching behaviors as found in the earlier process-product teaching effectiveness research. Technical competence is important to successful teaching and learning, but once technical competence is ensured, primary attention should be given to developing the clinical, personal, and critical competencies of teachers.

When addressing clinical competence, the emphasis is on helping teachers become better problem solvers who are able to frame problems and issues and come to grips with solutions. The purpose of teacher development in this case is to enhance inquiry, encourage reflection, build problem-solving skills, and help teachers make more informed decisions about their practice.

When the emphasis is on personal competence, the intent is to help teachers understand and interpret their own teaching in a manner that provides them meaning and significance. Personal competence is enhanced as teachers increase their awareness and understand more fully their teaching practice.

Critical competence is concerned with issues of value and with the hidden meanings underlying teaching practice. Critical competence is developed as teachers are able to differentiate between effective and good practice, take ethical stands, and be concerned with worth and purpose.

Although training can help enhance the teacher's technical competence, it seems not to be powerful enough to enhance the other three types. Clinical competence seems best addressed by professional development models. Professional

TABLE 12.2　**Zimpher and Howey: Framework for Examining Four Types of Teaching Competence**

	Technical Competence	Clinical Competence	Personal Competence	Critical Competence
Conception of the Teacher	Determines in advance what is to be learned, how it is to be learned, and criteria by which success is to be measured	Instructional problem solver; clinician frames and solves practical problems; takes reflective action; inquirer	Understanding of self, self-actualized person who uses self as effective and humane instrument	Rational, morally autonomous, socially conscious change agent
Focus of Supervision	Mastery of methods of instruction: specific skills (how to ask good questions); how to apply teaching strategies; how to select and organize curriculum content; how to structure the classroom for learning what techniques to use to maintain control	Reflective decision making and action to solve practical problems (what should be done about disruptive behavior) as well as reconsideration of intents and practices to take action to solve practical problems	Increase self-awareness, identity formation, and interpretive capacities, e.g., self confrontation; values clarification; interpersonal involvement; small-group processes; develop personal style in teaching role	Reflective decision making and action to form more rational and just schools, critique of stereotypes/ideology, hidden curriculum, authoritarian/permissive relationships, equality of access, responsibilities, and forms of repressive social control
Conception of the Supervisor	Technical expert/master provides for skill development and efficient/effective use of resources in classroom; translator of research theory into technical rules for application in classrooms	Fosters inquiry regarding the relationship of theory and practice; fosters reflection about the relationship of intents and practice and reconsideration/modification of intent/practice in light of evaluation of their conscience	Expert in interpersonal competence and theories of human development; nondirective participant; warm and supportive learning environment, responsiveness to teacher-defined needs and concerns, wisdom in guiding free exploration of teaching episodes, diagnosing theories-in-use	Collaborator in self-reflective communities of practitioner-theorists committed to examining critically their own/institutional practices and improving them in interests of nationality and social justice; provides challenges and support as do other participants in dialogue
Type of Theoretical Knowledge	Technical guidelines from explanatory theory; analytic craft knowledge about what constitutes "good" practice	Synthesis of normative, interpretive, and explanatory knowledge to form intellectually and morally defensible practical judgments about what to do in a particular situation	Analytic and interpretive theory to understand and make explicit reasons underlying symbolic interaction essentially those which occur in the class	Critical theory of education; unite philosophical analysis and criticism and causal and interpretive science

Continued

TABLE 12.2 *Continued*

	Technical Competence	Clinical Competence	Personal Competence	Critical Competence
Mode of Inquiry	Applied science, functional and task analysis, linear problem solving to determine how to accomplish given ends	Practical action research to articulate concerns, plan action, monitor action, and reflect on processes and consequences to improve our teaching practices; rationale-building	Phenomenological, ethnographic, hermeneutic analysis and interpretation; analyze elements of teaching episodes	Collaborative action and reflection to transform the organization and practice of education; group inquiry regarding conditions of communicative interaction and social control
Level of Reflectivity	Specific techniques needed to reach stated objectives involve instrumental reasoning; means-end (if, then) relative to efficiency/effectiveness	Practical reasoning and judgment relative to what should be done (best course of action under the circumstances)	Interpretation of intended meaning of verbal and nonverbal symbols and acts; introspection relative to self-awareness/identity	Critical self-reflection/reflexivity and social critique to uncover contradictions/inadequacies and different conceptions of educational practice as values with society

Source: From "Adapting Supervisory Practices to Different Orientations of Teaching" by Nancy L. Zimpher and Kenneth R. Howey, 1987, *Journal of Curriculum and Supervision* 2(2), pages 104–105. Reprinted with permission of the Association for Supervision and Curriculum Development. Copyright © 1987 by ASCD. All rights reserved.

Note: The authors wish to acknowledge the major contribution of Sharon Strom in the development of this framework.

development can also help build personal competence, with renewal models being most appropriate for enhancing personal and critical competence.

The Nature of Professional Expertise

Many principals, policy makers, and others who influence how schools are run and the way teaching and learning is perceived and practiced have different views of the nature of professional expertise in teaching. Kennedy (1987) has identified several dimensions of professional expertise, including the accumulation and use of certain technical skills; the development and application of conceptual knowledge, general principles, and theories; and the ability to engage in deliberative action.

Principals who view professional expertise as primarily the accumulation of technical skills promote teacher development strategies that emphasize mastering the specific tasks that teachers must perform and the skills they must demonstrate to engage in these tasks successfully. These tasks and skills might include learning how to plan lessons, organize workstations, redirect student behavior, use small groups, conduct Socratic seminars, and discipline students. Skills are valuable to professional practice but skills alone provide only a narrow and decontextualized view of teaching. Avoiding this problem requires that skills be accompanied by the other two dimensions of professional expertise. When this happens, teachers are able to decide which skills to use and when to use these skills. They also understand why they are using these skills. When professional expertise is defined only as the accumulation and use of skills, then teaching winds up being much less of a profession than most would like, and managing teaching and learning by direct supervision, standardizing the work, and standardizing outcomes become the primary strategies for monitoring the work of teachers. Teacher discretion would not be a high priority in this image of professional expertise.

Principals who view professional expertise in teaching as the application of general principles that provide teachers with the body of knowledge that enables them to treat specific cases and situations they face as examples of categories about something which is known take a different stance. They believe that this body of knowledge enables teachers to solve problems, find solutions, and make decisions about what to do and when to do it, even in ambiguous situations (Kennedy, 1987).

Principals who view professional expertise as deliberative action take still another stance. They emphasize teachers learning how to think like teachers who model high levels of intellectual artisanship. Deliberative action recognizes that teaching practice is situated in a context that involves different resources, students, needs, time constraints, and curriculum frameworks. Indeed, deliberate teachers bring to this context different purposes and the interaction between purposes and contexts shapes what they do. Teachers analyze different situations and monitor how situations change as practice unfolds. They craft strategies that combine action with thinking. One idea leads to another until a pattern begins to emerge (Mintzberg, 1987:68). Once a pattern emerges, teachers are able to use both knowledge of general principles and their experiences to make good decisions. Since this analysis occurs within the context of one's unique teaching practice, it resembles the generation of knowledge in use (Schön, 1983). Professionals generate knowledge in use as they engage in the particulars of practice, spontaneously forming intuitions and discovering new paths that they were not able to anticipate beforehand.

Wilson and Peterson (1997) point out that teachers are intellectuals who think about students and subject matter and construct bridges between the two. In their words:

> *Good teachers must think hard about what they want their students to learn, contemplating myriad questions. A teacher must consider questions like: What is interesting about this subject for my students? What ideas and concepts are particularly difficult? Why? What are the different means I can use to help students grapple with these ideas? What do my students already know that might help? What do they believe that might get in the way? What time of the day is it? the year? What resources do I have access to? How do students construct their understandings? What teaching moves can I make to help that process of meaning construction? (8–9)*

Futhermore, Wilson and Peterson point out that teachers are listeners and inquirers who research their practice by investigating students' thinking and searching for ways to teach for understanding.

The three dimensions of professional expertise are not mutually exclusive. When appropriately applied to teaching, they are nested (Sergiovanni, 2000). The acquisition of skills is embedded in and flows from the development and use of general principles. General principles, in turn, are embedded in and flow from deliberative action. Deliberative action, with its concept of teacher as intellectual, encompasses the other two dimensions, providing a challenging, complex, yet realistic view of teaching and learning. Such a view contrasts sharply with a skills-only approach or even a skills and general principles approach. Professional expertise in teaching, in other words, requires that teachers do more than master and apply a set of generalizations and regularities expressed as lists of skills that are context free and thus thought to apply to all students, on all occasions, everywhere (Sergiovanni, 2000). If professional expertise is, indeed, more appropriately understood as deliberative action, then teacher development needs to emphasize more the clinical, personal, and critical competencies that Zimpher and Howey propose and the professional and renewal models of teacher development discussed in Table 12.1.

The definition of *high-quality professional development* offered by the National Foundation for the Improvement of Education (Renyi, 1996) provides a practical framework for how schools might respond to clinical, personal, and critical teaching competencies. At the heart of their definition is the connection between teacher learning and student performance and the importance of sustained, in-depth, in-school teacher learning directly connected to improvements in levels of student academic achievement, civility, and other purposes. According to the foundation, high-quality professional development has the goal of improving student learning and behavior; helps teachers to be effectively responsible to diversity in learning and culture; provides time for inquiry, reflection, and mentoring as an ordinary part of the teachers' workdays; is rigorous, sustained, and directed to long-term changes in practice; is directed to teachers' intellectual development; fosters understanding of subject matter, pedagogy, and student needs; is designed by teachers, directed by teachers, and incorporates principles of adult learning; uses new technology; is school and classroom based; and is linked to a clear vision for students (6–7).

Reflecting on Supervision

Teacher development and supervision go hand in hand. Principals have a responsibility to help teachers improve their practice and to hold them accountable for meeting their commitments to teaching and learning. These responsibilities are usually referred to as *supervision*. Done well, supervision enhances teacher development.

A first step in building a practical and meaningful supervisory program is willingness by the principal and by teachers to face up to, struggle with, and accept a more complex view of supervision and evaluation. Required next is dealing with the negative stereotypes of supervision emerging from its history of hierarchy, dominance, and control.

From the start it should be clear that no one-best-way strategy, model, or set of procedures for supervision makes sense. Instead, a differentiated system of supervision more in tune with growth levels, personality characteristics, needs and interests, and professional commitments of teachers is needed.

Supervision and Evaluation

When the focus of supervision is on teaching and learning, evaluation is an unavoidable aspect of the process. The literature is filled with reports and scenarios highlighting the disdain with which teachers regard evaluation (see, for example, Blumberg, 1980). One reason for such attitudes is that evaluation has been too narrowly defined in both purpose and method. Evaluation is, and will remain, a part of supervision, and this reality cannot be ignored. Attempts to mask evaluation aspects of supervision by avoiding use of the term, by denying that evaluation occurs, or by declaring that evaluation is reserved only for the annual administrative review of one's teaching performance will not be helpful. Such claims are viewed suspiciously by teachers and for good reason—evaluation cannot be avoided. We are constantly evaluating everything that we experience, and our experiences with teachers and their teaching is no different.

Evaluation can be less of a problem if we expand its meaning within supervision. Evaluation, for example, is often defined narrowly as a process for calculating the extent to which teachers measure up to *preexisting standards*. Standards might be a program goal or teaching intent, or perhaps a list of "desirable" teaching competencies or performance criteria. Broader conceptions of evaluation include describing what is going on in a particular classroom, discovering learning outcomes actually achieved, and assessing their worth. In broader conceptions, the focus of evaluation is less on measuring and more on describing and illuminating teaching and learning events, as well as on identifying the array of meanings that these events have for different people. Evaluation broadly conceived involves *judgment* more than measurement. Judgments of teaching and learning are less fixed, more personal, and embedded in a particular context or situation (Dewey, 1958). Of interest in judgmental evaluation are *particular* teachers and students; *specific* teaching situations and events, and the *actual* teaching and learning issues, understandings, and meanings emerging from teaching. Although measuring against preexisting standards has its place in the process of supervision and evaluation, the present onerous view of evaluation will be greatly lessened if principals emphasize judgmental aspects.

Using the word *evaluation* in its ordinary, rather than technical, sense will also help dissipate its negative effects among teachers. Commonplace in our ordinary lives, evaluation is an inescapable aspect of most of what we do. Whether we are buying a pair of shoes, selecting a recipe for a dinner party, rearranging the living room furniture or enjoying a movie, baseball game, or art show, evaluation is part of the process. In its ordinary sense, evaluation means to discern, understand, and appreciate, on the one hand, and to value, judge, and decide on the other. These very same natural and ordinary processes are at play in evaluating teaching. As in ordinary life, these processes serve to heighten our understanding and appreciation of teaching and to inform our intuition as we make decisions about teaching. Heightened sensitivity and informed intuition are the trademarks of accomplished practice in all the major professions. It is by increasing and informing their sensitivities and intuitions that attorneys, architects, and physicians make better practice decisions and improve their performance. Professional practice in teaching, supervision, and the principalship improve similarly.

Supervision and evaluation of teaching should look for answers to the following questions:

What is actually going on in this classroom?

What is the teacher and what are students actually doing?

What are the actual learning outcomes?

What ought to be going on in this classroom, given our overall goals, educational platform, knowledge of how children learn, and understandings of the structure of the subject matter to be taught?

What do these events and activities of teaching and learning mean to teachers, students, and others?

What are the personal meanings that students accumulate regardless of teacher intents?

How do teacher and principal interpretations of teaching reality differ?

What actions should be taken to bring about even greater understanding of teaching and learning and better congruence between our actions and beliefs?

These questions provide a broader and more complex conception of the supervisory process than that implied just in rating teachers or in measuring outcomes for comparison with stated intents. Indeed, for supervision to work the way it should, teachers must share responsibility for its success. This means teachers have to assume roles as supervisors—working with each other to improve their teaching and even to help maintain quality control. Unless teachers accept this responsibility, supervision will remain what it too often is today—principals going into classes with checklists and making quick evaluations that have doubtful validity and little or no meaning to most teachers.

Purposes

The multifaceted nature of teacher supervision and evaluation can be illustrated by providing a framework for describing and bringing together key dimensions of the process. Included in this framework are general purposes of supervision and evaluation, specific perspectives that stem from these purposes, key competency areas that serve as benchmarks for evaluation, and critical knowledge areas that help define and describe teaching competence. This framework is designed to help principals analyze supervisory problems and plan supervisory strategies.

What is supervision for? Who is to be served? Why evaluate? How one answers such questions determines how one approaches the tasks of supervision and evaluation and influences the relationships emerging among teachers and between teachers and the principal. Supervision and evaluation have many purposes. These range from ensuring that minimum standards are being met and that teachers are being faithful to the school's overall purposes and educational platform, to helping teachers grow and develop as persons and professionals. Purposes can be grouped into three major categories:

1. *Quality Control.* The principal is responsible for monitoring teaching and learning in her or his school and does so by visiting classrooms, touring the school, talking with people, and visiting with students.
2. *Professional Development.* The principal is responsible for helping teachers to grow and to develop in their understanding of teaching and classroom life, in improving basic teaching skills, and in expanding their knowledge and use of teaching repertoires.
3. *Teacher Motivation.* The principal is responsible for building and nurturing motivation and commitment to teaching, to the school's overall purposes, and to the school's defining educational platform.

One hallmark of a good supervisory system is that it reflects these multiple purposes. No supervisory system based on a single purpose can succeed over time. A system that focuses only on quality control invites difficulties with teachers and lacks needed expansive qualities. By the same token, a supervisory system concerned *solely* with providing support and help to teachers (and thus, by omission, neglects teaching deficiencies and instances where overriding purposes and defining platforms are ignored) is not sufficiently comprehensive. Quality control and teacher improvement are therefore basic purposes that should drive any system of supervision and evaluation. A third purpose, often neglected but important in the long run, is that of teacher motivation. Overwhelming evidence exists suggesting that "knowledge of results" is an important ingredient in increasing a person's motivation to work and in building commitment and loyalty to one's job (Hackman and Oldham, 1976; Hackman et al., 1975).

Different Purposes, Different Standards

Different teacher-evaluation purposes require different teacher-evaluation standards and criteria. When the purpose is quality control to ensure that teachers measure up, standards, criteria, expectations, and procedures take one form. When the purpose is professional improvement to help increase teachers' understanding and enhance teaching practice, standards, criteria, expectations, and procedures take on a different form. In evaluation for quality control, the process is formal and documented; criteria are explicit and standards are uniform for all teachers; criteria are legally defensible as being central to basic teaching competence; the emphasis is on teachers meeting requirements of minimum acceptability; and responsibility for evaluation is in the hands of administrators and other designated officials. When the purpose of teacher evaluation is professional improvement, the process is informal; criteria are tailored to the needs and capabilities of individual teachers; criteria are considered to be appropriate and useful to teachers before they are included in the evaluation; the emphasis is on helping teachers reach agreed-upon professional development goals; and teachers assume major responsibility for the process by engaging in self-evaluation and collegial evaluation and by obtaining evaluation information from students.

The outcome of evaluation for quality control is the protection of students and the public from incompetent teaching. Unquestionably, this is an important outcome and a highly significant responsibility for principals and other supervisors. The outcome of evaluation for professional improvement is quite different. Rather than ensuring minimum acceptability in teaching, professional improvement guarantees quality teaching and schooling for the students and the public.

The *80/20 quality rule* spells out quite clearly what the balance of emphasis should be as schools engage in teacher evaluation. *When more than 20 percent of the principal's time and money is expended in evaluation for quality control or when less than 80 percent of the principal's time and money is spent in professional improvement, quality schooling suffers.* The 80/20 quality rule provides a framework for those responsible for evaluation of teachers to evaluate whether their efforts are indeed directed toward quality schooling. In making this assessment, one should give less attention to the rhetoric that one hears (i.e., to what those responsible for teacher evaluation say their purposes are) and more to the standards and procedures that they use. The standards and procedures associated with each of the two purposes of evaluation are outlined in Exhibit 12.1. If the standards at the left side of the exhibit are emphasized, quality control is the purpose of the evaluation regardless of what is claimed.

Teaching Competency Areas

The typical evaluation program puts the emphasis on the wrong thing. It relies almost exclusively on classroom observations of teaching behaviors and recording the presence or absence of these behaviors on instruments and forms. This results in placing the emphasis on whether the teacher can do the job as required while being observed. Even if it were possible to identify the correct list of teaching behaviors, the approach is still narrow. A good evaluation is not only concerned with "can do," but with other teaching competency areas, as well.

What are the major competency areas for which teachers should be accountable? Teachers should *know how* to do their jobs and to keep this knowledge current. The areas of knowledge for professional teaching include purposes, students, subject matter to be taught, and teaching techniques. However, knowing and understanding are not enough; teachers should be able to put this knowledge to work—to demonstrate that they *can do* the job of teaching. Demonstrating knowledge, however, is a fairly low-level competency. Most teachers are competent enough and adept enough to come up with the right teaching performance when they are required to do so. More important is whether they *will do* the job well consistently and on a sustained basis. Finally, all professionals are expected to engage in a lifelong commitment to self-improvement. Self-improvement is the *will-grow* compe-

---

EXHIBIT 12.1 Purposes and Standards for Evaluation

Purposes

Quality control (ensuring that teachers meet acceptable levels of performance)

Professional improvement (increasing understanding of teaching and enhancing practice)

Standards

The process is formal and documented.

The process is informal.

Criteria are explicit, standard, and uniform for all teachers.

Criteria are tailored to needs and capabilities of individual teachers.

Criteria are legally defensible as being central to basic teaching competence.

Criteria are considered appropriate and useful to teachers.

Emphasis is on meeting minimum requirements of acceptability.

Evaluation by administrators and other designated officials counts the most.

Emphasis is on helping teachers reach agreed-upon professional development goals.

Self-evaluation, collegial evaluation, and evaluation information for students count the most.

Outcome

Protects students and the public from incompetent teaching.

Guarantees quality teaching and schooling for students and the public.

The 80/20 Quality Rule: When more than 20 percent of supervisory time and money is expended in evaluation for quality control *or* less than 80 percent of supervisory time and money is expended in professional improvement, quality schooling suffers.

Source: From *Supervision: A Redefinition,* 6th ed. (p. 231) by Thomas J. Sergiovanni and Robert J. Starratt, 1999, New York: McGraw-Hill. Reproduced with permission of The McGraw-Hill Companies.

tency area. Self-employed professionals, such as physicians and attorneys, are forced by competition and by more visible performance outputs to give major attention to the will-grow dimension. Teachers are "organizational" professionals whose "products" are difficult to measure and who have not felt as much external pressure for continued professional development. Increasingly, however, school districts are making the will-grow dimension a significant part of their supervision and evaluation program. As teachers strive for further professionalism, they too recognize the importance of this dimension.

Thus, a comprehensive system of supervision and evaluation is concerned with all four professional development competency areas: knowledge about teaching, ability to demonstrate this knowledge by actual teaching under observation, willingness to sustain this ability continuously, and demonstration of a commitment to continuous professional growth. Although each of the competency areas represents a discrete category that suggests different evaluation strategies, the four remain largely interdependent in practice. When observing classrooms, principals naturally are interested in the knowledge base exhibited by teachers. Most observations, in turn, lead to issues and ideas that form the basis for informing continuing growth plans and more formal staff development programs.

Substantive Aspects of Professional Development

When one speaks of knowledge about teaching, demonstrating this knowledge, and improving one's teaching, what substance areas are of concern? Rubin (1975) has identified four critical areas in good teaching that he believes can be improved through supervision:

- The teacher's sense of purpose
- The teacher's perception of students
- The teacher's knowledge of subject matter
- The teacher's mastery of technique

Sense of purpose and perception of students represent values, beliefs, assumptions, and action theories that teachers hold about the nature of knowledge, how students learn, appropriate relationships between students and teachers, and other factors. Composing the teacher's educational platform, they thus become the basis for decisions made about classroom organization and teaching. For example, a teacher who views teaching as primarily the dissemination of information will likely rely heavily on direct instruction as a teaching methodology and on formally structured classroom arrangements as a method of organizing for teaching. A teacher who views children as being basically trustworthy and interested in learning is likely to share responsibility for decisions about learning, and so forth. A principal who was interested in reducing the amount of teacher talk in a given classroom or in increasing the amount of student responsibility in another would have to contend with the critical considerations of purposes and perceptions as key components of the teachers' educational platforms.

The third factor in good teaching is the teacher's knowledge of subject matter to be taught. Rubin (1975) notes:

There is considerable difference between the kind of teaching that goes on when teachers have an intimate acquaintance with the content of the lesson and when the acquaintance is only peripheral. When teachers are genuinely knowledgeable, when they know their subject well enough to discriminate between the seminal ideas and the secondary matter, when they go beyond what is in the textbook, the quality of pedagogy becomes extraordinarily impressive. For it is only when a teacher has a consummate grasp of, say, arithmetic, physics, or history, that their meaning can be turned outward and brought to bear upon the learner's personal experience. Relevancy lies less in the inherent nature of a subject than in its relationship to the child's frame of reference. In the hands of a skilled teacher, poetry can be taught with success and profit to ghetto children. (47)

Although content versus process arguments continue in teaching, both aspects are necessary. The less a teacher knows about a particular subject, the more trivial her or his teaching is likely to be. Content is important. Still, one can have a great appreciation of a particular field of study and not be able to disclose its wonder and excitement effectively. Shulman (1989) believes that teaching what one knows to someone else represents a distinct level of knowledge different from each of the other five levels of Bloom's taxonomy. The substance of this level is the ability to create a bridge between what a teacher knows and the students' experiences. To Shulman, content and pedagogy are inseparable. Mastery of technique, knowing how this technique relates to the subject matter one wants to teach (Stodolsky, 1988), classroom organization and management, and other pedagogical skills make up the fourth critical dimension of effective teaching. A comprehensive system of supervision and evaluation is concerned with all four substance areas: the teacher's conception of purpose, sensitivities to students, intimacy with subject matter, and basic repertoires of teaching techniques.

Figure 12.1 combines professional development competency areas and teaching substance areas to provide an "angle" for appreciating the complexity involved in supervision and evaluation, for analyzing existing supervisory programs, and for planning future strategies. Professional competency areas represent the range that should be included in a comprehensive supervision and evaluation system. Substance areas represent the content concerns to be included.

In summary, supervision and evaluation are concerned with the extent to which teachers demonstrate they know how, can do, will do, and will grow in such teaching knowledge areas as purpose, students, subject matter, and teaching techniques. The following questions provide examples of evaluation concerns raised in Figure 12.1. Within each substance area, *know how, can do, will do,* and *will grow* questions are provided:

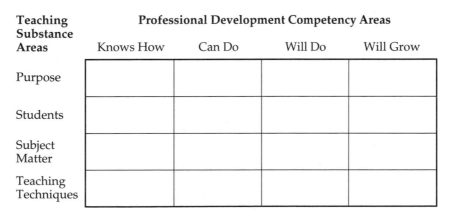

FIGURE 12.1   Competency and Substance Areas in Supervision and Evaluation

1. *Sense of Purpose.* To what extent does a teacher know and understand how behavior modification classroom management techniques work, what the philosophical base of this approach is, what the advantages and disadvantages are, and under which circumstances this approach would be more or less effective? Can and will the teacher demonstrate this approach to classroom management when circumstances call for it? Does the teacher know when to avoid this approach? Is there evidence that the teacher is growing in knowledge and skill in using this and other classroom management techniques? Does the teacher, for example, understand and use developmental approaches and morally based approaches to student discipline?

2. *Knowledge of Students.* Is the teacher sensitive to, and does the teacher know about, problems of peer identity among students and pressures for conformity that students face at certain ages and grade levels? Does the teacher understand how peer pressure can affect student motivation, classroom attention, voluntary participation in class, and other activities? Does the teacher exhibit knowledge about how to cope with peer pressure? Can and will the teacher demonstrate this knowledge by effective planning and teaching? Does the teacher show a commitment to increasing competence and skill in this area?

3. *Knowledge of Subject Matter.* Does the teacher have a firm grasp of the subject matter in the area she or he is teaching? Is there evidence, for example, that the teacher has an adequate cognitive map of the subject, appreciates the structure of knowledge inherent in the disciplinary base of the subject, and understands the major concepts undergirding this structure? Does the teacher demonstrate this mastery in her or his teaching? Is there evidence that concept attainment and other higher-level cognitive concerns are continuously emphasized? In what ways does the teacher keep up with expanding knowledge in her or his field?

4. *Mastery of Technique.* Is the teacher knowledgeable about an array of teaching methods and strategies? Does the teacher show sensitivity to the conditions under which each is more or less effective? Can the teacher demonstrate a variety of techniques in teaching? Does this ability to demonstrate variety occur continuously? Is there evidence that the teacher expands her or his repertoire of teaching over time? Is there evidence that the teacher is becoming more effective in matching teaching strategies to circumstances? What is the link between the subject being taught and how it is taught? Do methods change when content changes? How successful is the teaching in building bridges between the teacher's knowledge and student experiences?

When one takes into account different evaluation purposes and perspectives and different teaching competence and substance areas, it becomes clear that limiting one's supervision and evaluation strategy to only classroom observation, rating scales, paper and pencil tests, target setting, clinical supervision, portfolio development, or any other *single* strategy does not account for the complexities involved in providing a comprehensive, meaningful, and useful system of evaluation. In summary, principals are responsible for the school's supervisory program. At the very minimum, this responsibility includes ensuring that a helpful, useful, and comprehensive system of supervision is operating. Teachers should report that they find the system helpful and satisfying. The following are questions that can reasonably be asked in evaluating a school's supervisory program:

- Are teachers involved in shaping, implementing, and evaluating the supervisory program?
- Are multiple purposes provided for? Does the program, for example, address issues of quality control, professional development, and teacher motivation and commitment? Are formative, summative, and diagnostic perspectives all included in the program?
- Is the program sufficiently comprehensive to include *know how, can do, will do,* and *will grow* as basic teaching performance expectations?
- Does the program focus on improving knowledge and skill in such basic teaching essentials as purpose, student needs and characteristics, subject matter, and teaching techniques?

These questions highlight the importance of including teacher development programs as part of the school's overall design for supervision. The major emphasis in supervision should be on teacher growth and development. Both supervision and teacher development should be planned and provided as *interdependent* parts of a school's overall commitment to striving for quality.

Linking Teacher Development to School Effectiveness

This chapter began by acknowledging the link between teacher learning and school improvement and it is on this theme that the chapter ends. It is now widely accepted that for schools to be effectively responsive to new demands to teach all students at a high level, teacher development must become a top priority. Writing in *The Education of Teachers: Ninety-Eighth Yearbook of the National Society for the Study of Education* (1999), Darling-Hammond points out:

> *A growing body of research finds that teacher expertise is one of the more important school factors influencing student achievement, followed by the smaller but generally positive influences of small schools and small class sizes. That is, teachers who know much about teaching and learning and who work in environments that allow them to know students well are critical elements of successful learning. Studies of student achievement in Texas [Ferguson, 1991], Alabama [Ferguson and Ladd, 1996], and New York [Armour-Thomas et al., 1989], for example, have concluded that teachers' qualifications (based on measures of knowledge, education, and experience) account for a larger share of the variance in students' achievement than any other single factor. (228)*

Little (1997) sums up the importance of teacher development to school success as follows:

> *Schools that exhibit a high level of success with students, sometimes against con-*
> *siderable odds, supply consistent portraits of work environments conducive to*
> *teacher learning. In these portraits, teacher learning arises out of close involvement*
> *with students and their work; shared responsibility for student progress; sensibly*
> *organized time; access to the expertise of colleagues inside and outside the school;*
> *focused and timely feedback on individual performance and on aspects of classroom*
> *or school practice; and then overall ethos in which teacher learning is valued and*
> *professional community cultivated. (Chapter 12:1)*

Little found that schools are likely to be successful to the extent that they emphasize teachers' individual and collective responsibility for student learning; organize teachers' work in ways that provide enhanced opportunities for teacher learning; use staff development resources to increase the school's ability to obtain feedback on its own performance and use this feedback in making better decisions; and redirect its staff development and other assessment efforts in a manner which is consistent with teacher learning.

Helping Teachers Achieve Goals

The key to developing a supervisory approach that supports student learning is a very simple but deceptive axiom. Teachers have professional goals that are important to them. Given the opportunity, they will work very hard at achieving these goals. In many respects, supervision is little more than a system of help for teachers as they achieve goals that they consider important. Principals are needed to provide help as this process unfolds.

House (1971) proposed a "path-goal" theory of leadership that summarizes much of our discussion and provides a handle on key aspects of effective helping. He believes that leaders are responsible for "increasing the number and kinds of personal payoffs to the subordinates for the work-goal attainment and making paths to these payoffs easiest to travel by clarifying the paths, reducing roadblocks and pitfalls, and increasing the opportunities for personal satisfaction en route" (323).

Translated to teacher supervision, principals assume responsibility for "clarifying and clearing the path" toward goals that teachers consider important. Clarifying the path requires that goals be set and reasonably defined and understood. Ambiguous and unstructured situations and unclear expectations can be a source of frustration and dissatisfaction for teachers. Thus, it becomes important to provide the necessary task emphasis to help clarify goals. Clearing the path requires that principals provide the necessary assistance, education, support, and reinforcement to help achieve goals. Key to a path-goal approach is understanding that the richer sources of satisfaction for teachers come not from an emphasis on human relationships and social interaction separate from the accomplishment of work but from having accomplished worthwhile and challenging tasks within a pleasant atmosphere.

Providing the right system of differentiated supervision is one way in which principals can create the necessary paths that enable teachers to accomplish goals they consider to be important. Appendix 12.2 provides a description of how one principal began the process of changing supervision and evaluation in her school. Beginning with the assumption that a principal and her teachers need to "bend" the existing system of evaluation in order to create one that encourages learning from one another, she invited her teachers to consider alternatives. Not surprisingly, they responded enthusiastically. Her story is a fitting place to end our discussion of teacher development and supervision. Neither teacher development nor supervision are things that we can do for teachers, but are things that they must do for themselves. The test of leadership is to be able to extend to teachers an invitation to accept responsibility for themselves, and to have them accept it.

References

Armour-Thomas, Eleanor, et al. 1989. *An Outline Study of Elementary and Middle Schools in New York City: Final Report.* New York: New York City Board of Education.

Blumberg, Art. 1980. *Supervisors and Teachers: A Private Cold War* (2nd ed.). Berkeley, CA: McCutchan.

Bolin, Frances S. 1987. "Reassessment and Renewal in Teaching," in F. S. Bolin and J. McConnel Falk (Eds.), *Teacher Renewal: Professional Issues, Personal Choices.* New York: Teachers College Press.

Bolin, Frances S., and Judith McConnell Falk (Eds.). 1987. *Teacher Renewal: Professional Issues, Personal Choices.* New York: Teachers College Press.

Darling-Hammond, Linda. 1999. "Educating Teachers for the Next Century: Rethinking Practice and Policy," in Gary A. Griffin (Ed.), *The Education of Teachers: Ninety-Eighth Yearbook of the National Society for the Study of Education* (pp. 221–256). Chicago: University of Chicago Press.

David, Jane L., and Patrick M. Shields. 1999, April 14. "Standards Are Not Magic," *Education Week*, pp. 40, 42.

Dewey, John. 1958. *Art as Experience.* New York: Putnam.

Ferguson, R. F. 1991, Summer. "Paying for Public Education: New Evidence on How and Why Money Matters," *Harvard Journal on Legislation* 28(2), 465–498.

Ferguson, R. F., and H. F. Ladd. 1996. "How and Why Money Matters: An Analysis of Alabama Schools," in Helen Ladd (Ed.), *Holding Schools Accountable* (pp. 265–298). Washington, DC: Brookings Institution.

Hackman, J. R., and Greg Oldham. 1976. "Motivation through the Design of Work: Test of a Theory," *Organizational Behavior and Human Performance* 16(2), 250–279.

Hackman, J. R., G. Oldham, R. Johnson, and K. Purdy. 1975. "A New Strategy for Job Enrichment," *California Management Review* 17(4).

House, Robert J. 1971. "A Path Goal Theory of Leader Effectiveness," *Administrative Science Quarterly* 16(3), 321–338.

Kennedy, Mary M. 1987. *Inexact Sciences: Professional Education and the Development of Expertise.* East Lansing, MI: The National Center for Research on Teacher Education.

Little, Judith Warren. 1993. "Teachers' Professional Development in a Climate of Educational Reform," *Educational Evaluation and Policy Analysis* 15(2), 129–151.

Little, Judith Warren. 1997, March. "Excellence in Professional Development and Professional Community," Working Paper, Benchmarks for Schools. Washington, DC: Office of Educational Research and Improvement, U.S. Department of Education.

Mintzberg, Henry. 1987, July–August. "Crafting Strategy," *Harvard Business Review* 65(4), 66–75.

Peterson, Penelope L., Sarah J. McCarthey, and Richard F. Elmore. 1996. "Learning from School Restructuring," *American Educational Research Journal* 33(1), 119–153.

Renyi, Judith. 1996. *Teachers Take Charge of Their Learning: Transforming Professional Development for Student Success,* Executive Summary. Washington, DC: The National Foundation for the Improvement of Education.

Rubin, Louis. 1975. "The Case for Staff Development," in Thomas J. Sergiovanni (Ed.), *Professional Supervision for Professional Teachers* (pp. 33–49). Washington, DC: Association for Supervision and Curriculum Development.

Schön, Donald. 1983. *The Reflective Practitioner: How Professionals Think in Action.* New York: Basic Books.

Sergiovanni, Thomas J. 2000. *The Lifeworld of Leadership: Creating Culture, Community and Personal Meaning in Our Schools.* San Francisco: Jossey-Bass.

Shulman, Lee. 1988, January 28. "Teaching the Disciplines Liberally." The Third Annual Meeting of The Holmes Group, Atlanta.

Stodolsky, Susan S. 1988. *The Subject Matters.* Chicago: University of Chicago Press.

Thelan, Herbert. 1971. "A Cultural Approach to In-Service Education," in Louis Rubin (Ed.), *Improving In-Service Education* (pp. 72–73). Boston: Allyn and Bacon.

Viadero, Debra. 1999, February 10. "A Key to High Achievement," *Education Week,* p. 27.

Wilson, Susan M., and Penelope L. Peterson. 1997. "Theories of Learning and Teaching: What Do They Mean for Educators?" Working Paper, Benchmarks for Schools. Washington, DC: Office of Educational Research and Improvement, U.S. Department of Education.

Zimpher, Nancy L., and Kenneth R. Howey. 1987. "Adapting Supervisory Practice to Different Orientations of Teaching," *Journal of Curriculum and Supervision* 2(2), 101–127.

Appendix 12.1   Clinical Supervision, Peer Inquiry, and Teacher Learning

It is difficult to justify any approach to supervision unless its primary emphasis is on teacher learning. When teacher learning is not the prime beneficiary of supervision, the costs of supervision in time and effort are poor investments in enhancing the opportunities for student learning and in increasing the success rates of student learning. This is why changes are needed in typical approaches to supervision that are top down, unduly scripted by evaluation instruments, and view teachers as objects of—rather than participants in—supervision.

The rationale for a differentiated approach to supervision is simple: Teachers are different. They have different needs and temperaments, and these needs should be recognized. When they are, teachers are likely to respond more positively to supervision than when a one-best-way approach is used. To change the system, the roles of principals and teachers also have to change. Teachers will have to assume the responsibility for developing approaches to supervision that are responsive to the issues they face in their practice. They will also have to play key roles in deciding which options for supervision make most sense to them. Most importantly, they will have to accept responsibility for making the options work. They will, in other words, have to become supervisors, too—not supervisors in the old factory sense of monitoring, inspecting, and evaluating, but in the sense of colleagues working together to help each other understand their own teaching and to improve their practices.

In any professional field, supervision that is responsive to the needs of practice must be responsive as well to the learning requirements of professional practitioners. A good place to start is with what is known about how adults, particularly professionals, learn. They learn best when they have opportunities to become self-reliant, depending less on their institution and its programs and less on formal supervision. They learn best when what is being learned emerges from the problems they face in their everyday practice and when learning is situated in a real context. They learn best when they function as members of a community of practice who are connected together by reciprocal commitments and obligations to each other and to shared goals. They learn best when they have an opportunity to discover for themselves and to experiment with ideas and practices in their own contexts. They learn best when they have the time and encouragement to reflect on their practice and that of their colleagues.

In such a design, principals would not be excluded. They have important roles to play. They need to give leadership to the supervisory program, marshall resources to make sure the program works, help provide the administrative structures and other arrangements that will enable teachers to work effectively together, and participate as supervisors—engaging in dialogue and helping in the improvement of teaching wherever they can.

Appendix 12.1   Continued

Clinical Supervision as an Option

In the late 1950s, Robert Goldhammer (1969), Morris Cogan (1973), and their colleagues at Harvard University began to develop the clinical supervision concept as they sought more effective ways to supervise graduate students enrolled in the Master of Arts in Teaching program. Since then, this idea has been further developed to accommodate not only preservice supervision of teachers but also inservice supervision of beginning teachers and of seasoned professional teachers. Cogan (1973) defines *clinical supervision* as follows:

> *The rationale and practice is designed to improve the teacher's classroom performance. It takes its principal data from the events of the classroom. The analysis of these data and the relationships between teacher and supervisor form the basis of the program, procedures, and strategies designed to improve the students' learning by improving the teacher's classroom behavior. (54)*

Clinical supervision is considered by many experts (Garman, 1982; Goldhammer, Anderson, and Krajewski, 1993) to be a very effective strategy for bringing about improvements in teaching. It requires a more intense relationship between supervisor and teacher than typically is found in supervisory strategies. The perspective for clinical supervision is basically formative. Its focus is on building teacher motivation and commitment on the one hand, and on providing for "online" staff development for teachers on the other. Because teachers assume active roles in the process, they often find this a satisfying approach. Furthermore, clinical supervision need not be hierarchical; that is, it lends itself to peer and collegial relations among teachers. Teachers, for example, can organize themselves into teams of three or so to help each other research their practice using the clinical supervision framework.

The purposes of clinical supervision are to help teachers to understand their practice better and to examine existing patterns of teaching in ways that make sense to them. Evaluation is therefore responsive to the needs and desires of the teacher. It is the teacher who decides the course of a clinical supervisory cycle, the issues to be discussed, and for what purpose. Obviously, principals and teacher colleagues who serve as clinical supervisors will bring to this interaction a considerable amount of influence; however, ideally, this influence should stem from their being in a position to provide the help and clarification needed by teachers. The supervisor's job is to help the teacher select goals to be improved and teaching issues to be illuminated, and to understand better her or his practice. This emphasis on understanding provides the avenue by which more technical assistance can be given to the teacher; thus, clinical supervision involves, as well, the systematic analysis of classroom events. Clinical supervision, then, is a framework for helping teachers research their practice. The role of supervision can be assumed by a teacher, principal, or other colleague.

Appendix 12.1   *Continued*

The Cycle of Clinical Supervision

Most authorities (e.g., Goldhammer, 1969) suggest that a sequence of clinical supervision contain five general steps or stages, as follows:

1. Preobservation conference
2. Observation of teaching and collection of other material that might be helpful
3. Analysis and strategy
4. Postobservation conference
5. Postconference analysis

Preobservation Conference.   No stage is more important than the preobservation conference. It is here that the framework for observations is developed and an agreement is reached between the person who is "supervising" and the person who is teaching. After a brief warm-up period, the supervisor needs to become familiar with the class and with the teacher's way of thinking about teaching. How does the teacher view this class? What are the qualities and characteristics of this class? What frames of reference regarding purposes, models of teaching, classroom management, and so forth does the teacher bring to teaching? Getting into the teacher's "corner" and understanding the class from her or his perspective should help the supervisor understand what the teacher has in mind for the particular teaching sequence that will be observed. How the particular lesson in question fits into the teacher's broader framework of purposes and view of teaching is also essential to provide the supervisor with a perspective beyond the particular lesson at hand.

The supervisor is now ready to engage the teacher in a mental or conceptual *rehearsal* of the lesson. The teacher provides an overview of her or his intents, outcomes not formally anticipated but likely or possible, and problems likely to be encountered. An overview of how teaching will unfold, what the teacher and students will be doing, and anticipated responses from students should also be provided. The supervisor might wish to raise questions for clarification and, depending on the relationship existing between supervisor and teacher, to make suggestions for improving the lesson before it unfolds.

Typically, this conceptual rehearsal by the teacher identifies an array of teaching issues of interest. Clinical supervision is *selective* in the sense that an intense and detailed study is made of only a handful of issues at a time. Thus, supervisor and teacher must decide what aspects of teaching will be considered, with the teacher assuming major responsibility for setting the supervisory agenda. What would the teacher like to know about this class and the teaching that will take place? On what aspects of teaching would she or he like feedback? Teachers inexperienced with clinical supervision may have initial difficulty in suggesting agenda items, but careful prodding and guiding by the supervisor usually help to elicit meaningful issues that become the basis for a particular cycle of supervision. This phase of the conference concludes with the teacher and supervisor reaching a fairly explicit agreement or "contract" about the reasons for supervision, along with the teaching

Appendix 12.1   *Continued*

and learning agendas to be studied. The contract might contain, as well, some indication of the information to be collected, how this information will be collected, what the supervisor will be doing, and what the supervisor should not do. Clinical supervision advocates feel that the teacher should have as complete as possible a picture of events to occur as the process of supervision unfolds.

Observation of Teaching.   The second stage in a clinical supervision cycle—and basic to it—is the actual and systematic observation of teaching. Attention is given to the teacher *in action* and to the classroom story unfolding as a result of this action. Clinical supervision purists would argue that "canned" or standardized devices, or scales for ratings of general teaching characteristics, may well be useful but in themselves are not sufficient; and when used, they should stem from, and be related to, the actual observation of teaching and learning at issue. It is what the teacher actually says and does, how students react, and what actually occurs during a specific teaching episode under study that remains the center of evaluation to advocates of clinical supervision. Student interviews, collections of classroom artifacts, development of evaluation portfolios, bulletin board and classroom arrangements, photo essays, inventories of lessons accomplished by children or books read, and other evaluative data collection strategies should supplement and illuminate this actual teaching.

The teacher will know what to expect because of the preobservation conference. He or she should understand that the supervisor wishes to make an unobtrusive entrance and to remain as unobtrusive as possible. During the observation, the clinical supervisor may take copious notes attempting to record all classroom events. Notes should be descriptive—that is, free from inferences; for example, the supervisor would avoid writing "during the questioning of students on the use of microscopes by criminologists, the students were bored" in favor of something such as "John and Mary both did not hear the question when it was asked" and "two students were looking out the window; a third was playing with materials in his desk during the microscope questioning time." Sometimes the information collected is focused on a particular issue, such as cognitive level of questions, attention spans of children, time on task, or cooperative relationships among students. Then, instead of attempting to record everything that takes place during the lesson, the supervisor might record and rate each question asked on the Bloom Taxonomy of Educational Objectives or collect similar, more detailed information. Many clinical supervision purists insist on a written transcript or the collection of firsthand data by the supervisor, and many supervisors using clinical methods have been successful by using television and videotaping equipment or by using audiotaping equipment to record actual teaching. At the conclusion of the observation, the supervisor leaves the classroom as unobtrusively as possible.

Analysis and Strategy.   The third step in the cycle of clinical supervision is the analysis of teaching and the building of a supervisory strategy. The analysis stage

Appendix 12.1 *Continued*

requires that the supervisor convert the raw data or information collected from the observation into a manageable, meaningful, and sensible form. Clinical supervision advocates recommend that the analysis yield significant teaching patterns and that critical incidents be identified for use in the supervisory conference. Of paramount importance is the contract initially struck with the teacher. What was the purpose of the observation? How did the information collected illuminate this purpose? Can the supervisor arrange this information in a fashion that communicates clearly to the teacher the feedback she or he seeks but at the same time does not prejudge the teaching? This process identifies teaching patterns: recurring teacher verbal and nonverbal behaviors discovered in the course of teaching. Critical incidents are those occurrences that have a particularly noticeable positive or negative effect on the teaching and learning.

Having organized the information, the supervisor now gives attention to building a strategy for working with the teacher. The supervisor takes into account the nature of the contract originally struck, the evaluation issues uncovered during the observation and analysis, the quality of interpersonal relationships existing between teacher and supervisor, the authority base from which she or he is operating, and the competency or experience level of the teacher in deciding on this strategy.

Postobservation Conference.   The fourth stage in the cycle of clinical supervision is the supervisory conference. The supervisor uses the specific information gathered to help the teacher analyze the lesson. Typically, this postobservation conference focuses on a handful of issues previously agreed on by the teacher and supervisor. It is appropriate as well for the supervisor to introduce new issues as circumstances warrant, but these issues should be few and cautiously introduced. The emphasis remains on providing information to the teacher for fulfilling the contract that was the basis for the observation cycle. Furthermore, the emphasis is not on providing evaluative information but on providing *descriptive* information. The process of making sense of this information is a joint one shared by teacher and supervisor.

Let's assume that the most important issue identified and agreed to in the pre-conference is "level of cognitive questioning" used by the teacher and cognitive level of assignments given to the students. The teacher uses objectives that span all six levels of the Bloom Taxonomy of Educational Objectives but wishes to emphasize the higher-level objectives of analysis and synthesis. Perhaps this teacher is not confident that actual teaching emphasizes these levels; or perhaps the supervisor, suspecting that teaching is not matching teacher intents, suggests that the level of cognitive questionings be examined. In either event, teacher and supervisor agree to use an inventory that enables the sorting of questions asked into the Bloom categories: remembering, understanding, solving, analyzing, creating, and judging. During the observation of teaching, each question asked by the teacher is classified into an appropriate level. A transcript of actual questions asked could be prepared.

Appendix 12.1   *Continued*

During the analysis and strategy stage of the supervisory cycle, the supervisor tallies questions and computes percentages.

The supervisor then decides on a strategy whereby the teacher is asked to restate her or his purposes for the lesson as well as for the unit of which the lesson is a part. The cognitive level of questioning information is then presented and compared with the teacher's intents. The supervisor is careful to avoid drawing conclusions or to elaborate on possible discrepancies, considering these conclusions to be the responsibility of the teacher. The teacher and supervisor might decide that it would be helpful to collect homework assignments given for other lessons in this particular teaching unit as well as to examine questions on tests that have been used. These assignments and test questions could also be categorized into the cognitive level of questioning format. Throughout the process, the supervisor's role is not to condemn, cajole, or admonish, but to provide information useful to the teacher and in a supportive atmosphere. Some suggestions for providing helpful feedback to teachers are provided in Exhibit A.

Postconference Analysis.   The fifth and final stage in a cycle of clinical supervision is the postconference analysis. The postconference phase is a natural springboard to staff development for both teacher and supervisor. The supervisor evaluates what happened in the supervisory conference and throughout the supervisory cycle for purposes of improving her or his own efforts. Was the integrity of the teacher protected? Did the teacher participate in the process as a cosupervisor? Was feedback given in response to the teacher's needs and desires? Was the emphasis more on teaching and the improvement of teaching than on teacher and evaluating the teacher? What can the supervisor do to improve her or his skills in clinical supervision? A typical outcome of the first four phases of clinical supervision is agreement on the kinds of issues to be pursued next as further cycles are undertaken. The postconference analysis is, therefore, both the end of one cycle and the beginning of another.

Is Clinical Supervision for Everyone?

Clinical supervision, as just outlined, is demanding in the time it requires from both supervisor and teachers. Principals who have difficulty finding the time to use this approach with all teachers might reserve it for working with two or three teachers at a time. If it is desirable for more teachers to be involved, then using collegial or peer clinical supervision may be the answer. Here, teachers take turns assuming the role of clinical supervisor as they help each other. Collegial clinical supervision, however, often results in teachers being burdened with additional time demands. Furthermore, participation requires much more training in conferencing, information collecting, interpreting, and other supervisory techniques than is typically necessary for other forms of supervision. If teachers are to be clinical supervisors, they

Appendix 12.1 *Continued*

EXHIBIT A Some Suggestions for Providing Helpful Feedback to Teachers

1. *When giving feedback to teachers, be descriptive rather than judgmental.* Clinical supervision is designed to help teachers improve ongoing teaching and should not be used as a device for summative evaluation designed to determine the value of a person or program. For example, instead of saying to a biology teacher, "You are spending too much time in lecture and not enough time with students engaged in field work and laboratory," try "Your time log shows that you spent 85 percent of class time these past two weeks in lecture. Let's look at your objectives and plans for this unit and see if this is what you intended."

2. *When giving feedback to teachers, be specific rather than general.* General statements tend to be misunderstood more than specific statements. Instead of saying to a teacher, "You interrupt students and tend not to listen to what they are saying," try, "When you asked John a question, you interrupted his response and seemed uninterested in what he had to say." A cassette transcript of the question, response attempt, and interruptions would be helpful.

3. *When giving feedback to teachers, concentrate on things that can be changed.* A teacher may have little control over a nervous twitch or voice quality, but much can be done about arranging seats, grouping students, improving balance between knowledge level and other objectives, and disciplining students.

4. *When giving feedback to teachers, consider your own motives.* Often, feedback is given to impress teachers with one's knowledge or for some other reason that builds the supervisor's status. Feedback is intended for only one purpose—to help the teacher know and understand her or his actual behavior as a teacher and consequences of this behavior on teaching and learning.

5. *Give the teacher feedback at a time as close to the actual behavior as possible.* Details of events are likely to be forgotten easily. Furthermore, fairly prompt attention is likely to upgrade and personalize the importance of clinical supervision.

6. *When giving feedback to teachers, rely as much as possible on information whose accuracy can be reasonably documented.* Photographs of bulletin boards, audio- and videotapes of teachers and students at work, a portfolio of classroom tests, a record of books borrowed from the class library, the number of students who return to shop during free periods or after school, and a tally of questions asked by the teacher sorted into the hierarchy of educational objectives are examples of documented feedback. It will not always be possible or desirable to provide this type of highly descriptive feedback, but it is important, nevertheless, as a technique, for clinical supervision cannot be overemphasized.

---

will need to receive the proper training; this, too, can present problems because training takes time and is expensive.

A further issue is that *formal clinical supervision may be too much supervision for some teachers.* Although all teachers would profit from clinical supervision from time to time, it does not appear that this strategy should be used all the time for all teachers. Going through this process every second, third, or fourth year may be less

Appendix 12.1   *Continued*

burdensome and tiresome for some. Unfortunately, this supervisory process can become too routinized and ritualized if overused. Finally, teacher needs and dispositions as well as work and learning styles vary. Formal clinical supervision may be suitable for some teachers but not for others when these concerns are taken into consideration.

Collegial Supervision

An alternative to structured and formal approaches to clinical supervision is to rely on teachers working with teachers as colleagues who research each other's practice more informally. Sometimes specific steps and protocols are followed, but the teachers decide together which will be used and how they will be used. Sometimes the structure for supervision emerges from conversations about the issues being investigated and from other concerns unique to the teachers' context. For example, in some schools, teachers might be organized into teams of three. In forming such teams, teachers would have an opportunity to indicate with whom they might like to work. Often, one member of the team is selected by the principal, but there are no rigid rules for selecting teams. Once formed, the teams may choose to work together in a number of ways, ranging from formal clinical supervision to less intensive and more informal processes. They may, for example, simply agree to observe each other's classes, providing help according to the desires of the teacher being observed. The teachers then might confer, giving one another informal feedback and otherwise discussing issues of teaching that they consider to be important. An approach relying on specific teaching steps and elements of lesson design might be used on another occasion. In this case, the emphasis on teaching might be narrowly focused on specific issues identified by the teacher. On still another occasion, the emphasis might be quite unfocused in order to provide a general feel or rendition of teaching. All that is needed is for team members to meet beforehand to decide "the rules and issues" for the observation and for any subsequent conversations or conferences.

It is a good idea for collegial supervision to extend beyond classroom observation. It should provide a setting in which teachers can informally discuss problems they are facing, share ideas, help one another in preparing lessons, exchange tips, and provide other support to one another. Some suggestions for principals seeking to implement collegial supervision are provided in Exhibit B.

Appendix 12.1 *Continued*

EXHIBIT B Guidelines for Implementing Collegial Supervision

1. Teachers should have a voice in deciding with whom they work.
2. Principals should retain final responsibility for putting together collegial supervisory teams.
3. The structure for collegial supervision should be formal enough for the teams to keep records of how and in what ways time has been used and to provide a general *nonevaluative* description of collegial supervisory activities. This record should be submitted annually to the principal.
4. The principal should provide the necessary resources and administrative support enabling collegial supervisory teams to function during the normal range of the school day. The principal might, for example, volunteer to cover classes as needed, to arrange for substitutes as needed, to provide for innovative schedule adjustments enabling team members to work together readily.
5. If information generated within the team about teaching and learning might be considered even mildly evaluative, it should stay with the team and not be shared with the principal.
6. Under no circumstances should the principal seek evaluation data from one teacher about another.
7. Each teacher should be expected to keep a professional growth log that demonstrates that she or he is reflecting on practice and growing professionally as a result of collegial supervisory activities.
8. The principal should meet with the collegial supervisory team at least once a year for purposes of general assessment and for sharing of impressions and information about the collegial supervisory process.
9. The principal should meet individually at least once a year with each collegial supervisory team member to discuss her or his professional growth log and to provide any encouragement and assistance that may be required.
10. Generally, new teams should be formed every second or third year.

References

Cogan, Morris. 1973. *Clinical Supervision.* Boston: Houghton Mifflin.

Garman, Noreen. 1982. "The Clinical Approach to Supervision," in Thomas J. Sergiovanni (Ed.), *Supervision of Teaching* (pp. 35–52). Alexandria, VA: Association for Supervision and Curriculum Development.

Goldhammer, Robert. 1969. *Clinical Supervision: Special Methods for the Supervision of Teachers.* New York: Holt, Rinehart and Winston.

Goldhammer, Robert, Robert H. Anderson, and Robert A. Krajewski. 1993. *Clinical Supervision: Special Methods for the Supervision of Teaching* (3rd ed.). New York: Holt, Rinehart and Winston.

Appendix 12.2   Rethinking Teacher Evaluation

No More "Super"vision
Joanne Rooney, Principal
Pleasant Hill School

Our teacher evaluation system wasn't working.... After examining our evaluation system, I realized that it was based on several assumptions:

1. The power to change teacher behavior is inherent in my role as principal.
2. Teachers are all, in some way, "broken" and need "fixing." My job is to repair and improve (somewhat like bringing in a car for a brake job).
3. Clinical supervision is the model for our evaluation system. This, done well, requires multiple observations and a *coaching* relationship—not an evaluative one.
4. Because a small minority of teachers could be considered "incompetent," the system of remediation is used for all.
5. The ranking of teachers as *Excellent, Satisfactory,* and *Unsatisfactory* in some way relates to improved instruction.

Personally, I subscribed to none of these beliefs.

A change was needed; yet, because the evaluation system had been negotiated between the teachers' union and district officials, it was imperative that any modifications of the given procedure stay within the negotiated parameters. Our challenge was to bend, without breaking, the existing teacher evaluation system.

Were teachers ready to try something different? I decided to ask them.

Early in the school year, I met with teachers who were to be evaluated that year. We addressed some basic questions: Did the "yellow tablet" system improve their teaching? Could the many hours expended in our current evaluation system be used more creatively? Was it possible to devise a new and worthwhile system within given parameters?

The teachers were amazingly candid. Their response was unanimous. They, too, felt we could "massage" the process, use our time more advantageously, and learn more about instruction.

A Giant Step Forward
The ball was in their court. The improvement of instruction belonged to them, as, in fact, it always had. By acknowledging this premise, we allowed the power of action to pass to the professional staff. We left that meeting committed to a new sys-

Appendix 12.2   *Continued*

tem in which the letter of the law had been preserved, and that which had value was salvaged. We all agreed on the following:

- This initial planning meeting would be called the "pre" conference. Previous policy did not specify that this initial conference had to be done on an individual basis. This decision itself saved time.
- All of my visits were designated as "formal." As there was no definition of "formal" in the Teacher Evaluation Handbook, we defined it to mean any and all visits. I promised to be in classrooms more often, not less.
- In lieu of my formal observation, teachers agreed to visit one another. In some cases, teachers paired up; others decided to work with two others. The speech pathologist and music teacher decided to visit their counterparts in other schools—something they had never had the opportunity to do.
- I volunteered to substitute for the teachers when they were observing. (All thought this was an excellent use of my time!) Being back in the classroom would also give me a fresh insight into their teaching.
- The "visiting" teachers would meet. I would be present, thus fulfilling the requirement for a "post" conference. I would facilitate the conversation between the two teachers, asking thoughtful questions and staying away from any evaluative remarks.
- We would repeat the procedure during the second semester, when teachers could observe the same person or choose another.
- The final conference would be maintained. We felt strongly that principal and teacher needed to talk—one on one—at some point.
- Any teacher who preferred the "old" system was free to stay with it. None did.
- We would evaluate this plan at the end of the year, asking if any changes needed to be made or if we wanted to go back to the old system.

The year went well. Teachers gained many insights into one another's teaching and became thoroughly immersed in discussing instruction. And we took a giant step toward working together.

A Learning Experience
We are in year two of our new procedure, and, as with any change of this sort, we are learning more than we expected.

- Barriers between teachers and classrooms are breaking down. In some instances, teachers had taught next to each other for years, yet this was their first chance to actually see one another in action. Many want to return and see more.
- Peer coaching, long accepted as an effective way for teachers to improve instruction, is becoming the norm.

Appendix 12.2   *Continued*

- Individual differences in teachers are respected. Some, a bit uncertain about teaching in front of someone else, chose their friends as partners. Others reviewed the lesson as though they now had the yellow tablet, making suggestions for improvement. Teachers are more tolerant of one another, and of me, as we sometimes stumble through this learning process.
- The spirited exchange of the post-conference often continues long after the formal time is over. Each visit and conference is very different, but all agree that we are learning. Many plan to visit again—to observe, learn, and discuss.
- When we subsequently planned an inclusion program for special education students, teachers devised a coteaching model. Not only have classroom doors been unbolted, but teachers' minds have opened more widely, too.

That our system of teacher evaluation is currently in place does not limit contact with teachers. Concerns can be expressed—and are—if they are productive for kids and do not demean those who struggle each day to do their very best for kids. However, I have found that support and encouragement have much more effect than criticism—however thinly veiled under the guise of supervision.

What happens to the teacher who needs help? Who is incompetent? Who truly has much to improve in teaching? The matter should be pursued diligently, but we principals work with few teachers who are so incompetent that they could be terminated. Nevertheless, our evaluation systems are technically based on the process through which incompetent teachers can be dismissed.

What has changed in our system—more than anything else—is the concept of the principal. I am no longer the one responsible for a teacher's behavior. Teachers are now responsible for their own professional growth—both individually and as a group.

Principals are overwhelmed with the job of leading schools. To think that we also have some kind of "super"vision is simply ludicrous. Teachers are, and should be, the instructional leaders in our schools. We must rely on the collective expertise of the staff to bring our schools into the 21st century.

13

MOTIVATION, COMMITMENT, AND THE TEACHER'S WORKPLACE

Much is known about how to arrange job dimensions and work conditions within schools so that teachers are more personally satisfied and are inspired to work harder and smarter on behalf of teaching and learning. When teaching is intellectually satisfying, professionally rewarding, and just plain more fun for teachers, they are likely to keep improving their effectiveness as the years go by. Students are more successful learners as a result. That is why few topics are more important. When high motivation and strong commitment are absent, teachers are likely to be connected to their jobs on a "fair day's work for a fair day's pay" basis (Sergiovanni, 1968). Instead of giving their best, teachers emphasize meeting basic work requirements in exchange for material and other extrinsic benefits. If teachers become dissatisfied, their performance is likely to fall below even this fair day's work level (Brayfield and Crockett, 1955; Vroom, 1964). If they experience loss of meaning and significance with what they are doing, they are likely to become detached, even alienated, from their jobs (Argyris, 1957). Commitment erodes and performance decreases.

Despite what is known about how to improve teacher motivation and commitment and the links between such improvement and effective schooling, this knowledge base does not inform policy development and administrative practice very much. State and local policy makers, for example, frequently mandate changes in school organizational patterns, curriculum, and teacher evaluation in ways that contradict the motivation research. Although well intended, these policy initiatives can actually inhibit—even lower—teacher motivation and commitment, with predictable effects on effective schooling.

Problems and Contradictions in Policy and Practice

Two examples of policies and practice that contradict what motivation research tells us are examined in this section: mandating and implementing highly structured, prescriptive, and standardized curriculum and teaching formats that result in increasing bureaucracy in the classroom; and school organizational patterns that encourage isolation, privatism, and lack of social interaction among teachers.

Bureaucracy in the Classroom

Exhibit 13.1 contains the "Quality of Work Life in Teaching," scale that is adapted from a more general one developed by Marshall Sashkin and Joseph J. Lengermann (Pfeiffer and Goodstein, 1984). The scale is designed to assess perceptions of job conditions in one's work setting. If you are a teacher, please respond to the ques-

---

EXHIBIT 13.1   Quality of Work Life in Teaching

Directions: The following questions ask you to describe the objective characteristics of your job, as well as the activities of your co-workers and supervisor. Try not to use these questions to show how much you like or dislike your job; just be as factually correct as possible—imagine what an outside observer would say in response to these questions. Circle the appropriate letter.

(A)ll of the time, (M)ost of the time, (P)art of the time, (N)ever

1. Teachers in my school are allowed to make some decisions, but most of the decisions about their work have to be referred to their supervisor or are shaped by rules, curriculum requirements, or testing requirements.	A	M	P	N
2. Teachers in my job normally move on to better jobs as a direct result of the opportunities my job offers.	A	M	P	N
3. Teachers in my school are required to produce or cover a specific amount of work each day or each week.	A	M	P	N
4. Teachers in my school perform tasks that are repetitive in nature.	A	M	P	N
5. My work requires me to coordinate regularly with other teachers.	A	M	P	N
6. Teachers in my school have a great deal of control over their work activities.	A	M	P	N
7. Teachers in my job have the opportunity to learn new skills in the course of their work.	A	M	P	N
8. Teachers in my school must work according to a fixed schedule; it is not possible to let the work go for a time and then catch up on it later.	A	M	P	N
9. Teachers in my job are required to follow certain procedures in doing their work that they wouldn't choose if it were up to them.	A	M	P	N
10. Teachers in my position work alone, on their teaching, with little or no contact with other teachers.	A	M	P	N
11. When they encounter problems in their teaching, teachers in my school must refer these problems to their supervisor; they cannot take action on their own.	A	M	P	N

Continued

EXHIBIT 13.1 *Continued*

12.	My work requires me to learn new methods in order to keep up with changes and new developments.	A	M	P	N
13.	Teachers in my position must work very rapidly.	A	M	P	N
14.	My work involves completing a "whole" task.	A	M	P	N
15.	Teachers in my position are able to help out one another as they teach.	A	M	P	N
16.	My principal acts on some of the suggestions of teachers in my school.	A	M	P	N
17.	Teachers in my position are encouraged to try out methods of their own when teaching.	A	M	P	N
18.	Teachers in my position have considerable control over the pace or scheduling of work.	A	M	P	N
19.	Jobs at my level fail to bring out the best abilities of teachers because they are designed too simply.	A	M	P	N
20.	Teachers in my position must interact with other teachers as they teach.	A	M	P	N
21.	Teachers at my level can make their own decisions without checking with anyone else or without consulting approved teaching and curriculum requirements.	A	M	P	N
22.	Teachers at my level have the opportunity to learn about the teaching that is occurring at other grade levels and in other departments.	A	M	P	N
23.	My work must be completed on a set schedule.	A	M	P	N
24.	Teachers in my position perform the same series of tasks all day.	A	M	P	N
25.	My work requires a great deal of contact with other teachers.	A	M	P	N

Source: Adapted from "Quality of Work Life Conditions" by Marshall Sashkin and Joseph J. Lengermann, 1984, *The 1984 Annual,* pages 140–141, San Francisco: Pfeiffer/Jossey-Bass. Copyright © 1984 Pfeiffer/Jossey-Bass Inc., Publishers. Used with permission.

tions following the directions provided. If you are a principal, respond in the way you think the teachers in your school would respond.

Response patterns indicate the extent to which one perceives her or his job to be growth-oriented on a number of dimensions considered important by job-enrichment theorists and researchers. Later in this chapter, the instrument will be scored, and response patterns will be examined as the concept of job enrichment is discussed.

The instrument can also be used to assess the extent to which one's job is bureaucratized. Responses to items 1, 3, 4, 6, 8, 11, and 24 hint at the extent to which the teaching job you describe is bureaucratic. Item 6 is scored in reverse. The more prevalent the job characteristics described in the items, the more bureaucratic that job is likely to be.

It is generally assumed that teaching is a profession, although perhaps a fledgling one. Professionals and bureaucrats operate quite differently at work. The work of bureaucrats is programmed for them by their work system. The work of professionals emerges from an interaction between available professional knowledge and individual client needs. Webster, for example, describes a bureaucrat as "a government official following a narrow, rigid, formal routine." In contrast, professionals are assumed to command a body of knowledge enabling them to make informed judgments in response to unique situations and individual client needs. Essential to professionalism is sufficient discretion for professionals to use informed judgment as they practice.

Beginning in the seventies, there has been a trend toward greater centralization in deciding what will be taught in schools: when, with what materials, to whom, and for how long. During that time, approximately two-thirds of the states enacted policies that sought to standardize and regulate teacher behavior (Darling-Hammond, 1984). States were even more active during the 1980s. There are many legitimate and desirable reasons for the state to be involved in matters of education, and many alternatives are open to states as they set standards, provide guidelines, promote equity, and ensure accountability. However, the problem lies in how far the state should go and the consequences of going too far. Providing leadership to local districts is an important responsibility. Legislating learning to the point of installing a system of bureaucratic teaching is quite another matter (Wise, 1979).

Some standards advocates argue that the standards-based reforms introduced in the nineties promoted professionalism by giving teachers and schools discretion over means. Schools and their teachers, so the argument goes, are free to make decisions they think are necessary providing state standards are reached. These standards are measured by tests the state provides. But in reality, as pointed out in Chapter 10, the ends invariably drive the means. Thus, the tests soon become the curriculum. That curriculum is soon linked (*aligned with* is the jargon) to specific models of teaching, scheduling formats, and other scripts that must be followed. The rhetoric of empowerment and the reality of standardized outcomes and assessments are like oil and water.

When curriculum and teaching decisions are programmed in a way that diminishes the influence of students and teacher in making teaching and learning decisions, then impersonal, standard, and formal learning goals dominate; teaching and learning become "teacher proof" and "student proof"; instructional leadership is discouraged as the teacher spends more time managing the learning process by monitoring, inspecting, regulating, and measuring; and commitment to teaching and learning by both teacher and students is lessened. For students, the consequences can be more emphasis on learnings and meanings defined by the school, which functions as an agent of the state (Coombs, 1959; MacDonald, 1964) and less emphasis on intrinsic motivation for learning, on responding to students' needs and interests, on students setting standards for themselves, and on other locally defined learnings and meanings. Student learning is enhanced when teaching is characterized by a balanced emphasis on personally and school-defined meanings and learning outcomes and on students being intrinsically motivated to learn. These characteristics are not encouraged by bureaucratic teaching.

In sum, recent years have seen schools racing toward adopting uniform standards mandated by states as part of a high-stakes, standards-based approach to school improvement (see, for example, Tucker and Codding, 1998). The approach is high stakes because standards are measured by state-mandated tests. School scores are published in the newspaper. Schools that do well on the tests are rewarded. Most states provide for low-scoring students to receive special assistance but if test scores do not improve, negative sanctions quickly follow. Often, there are exit tests that students must pass as a requirement for graduation or as a requirement to pass on to the next grade.

As pointed out in Chapter 10, setting high standards and assessing progress makes sense when most of the standards are decided at the local level by teachers, parents, students, and others. Uniform standards mandated from afar or imported en masse from afar, by contrast, too often erode local discretion, place a school's organizational character at risk, and compromise the school's ability to be responsive to local aspirations and needs. Over time, this erosion hampers efforts to provide effective teaching and learning.

Testing expert George F. Madaus (1999) points out, *"If important decisions are presumed to be related to test results, then teachers will teach to the test"* (80). Teachers are inclined to disregard the subjects that are not tested and, with the subjects that are being taught, to neglect the topics that are not tested, resulting in a narrowing, even skewing, of the curriculum. Madaus states further, *"In every setting where a high-stakes test operates, a tradition of past exams develops, which eventually de facto defines the curriculum"* (83). Making the test the curriculum may seem like a rational and reasonable response that teachers and schools face. But, as Madaus points out, when a teacher's professional worth is determined by test scores, she or he will corrupt the concepts and skills assessed by reducing them to strategies in which students are drilled. Still another principle offered by Madaus is, *"Teachers pay particular attention to the form of questions on a high-stakes test (for example, short answer, essay, multiple-choice) and adjust their instruction accordingly"* (85). As Meier points out (in Madaus, 1999:86), teaching reading (and other subjects) comes to resemble closely the practice of taking reading tests. Curriculum materials are added or discarded based on what is tested rather than on what is valued. And finally, Madaus asserts, *"A high-stakes test transfers control over the curriculum to the agency which sets or controls the exam"* (87). These are hardly empowering conditions that encourage teachers to behave as self-managing professionals. Nor, as we discuss next, do these conditions build efficacy in teaching and encourage teachers to behave as "origins."

The research on motivation to work suggest that Madaus's observations are troublesome (see, for example, Deci, 1995 and Kohn, 1993). In a recent study of the motivational impact of school-based performance awards, Kelley (1999) observes:

> *When incentive systems work as they are intended, employees will shift behaviors toward what is being rewarded and away from everything else.* . . . *Thus, the design of the incentive system and the assessment instrument is critical because outcomes that are not measured, or not readily measurable, will be deemphasized in the curriculum.* . . . *Some teachers indicated that the focus of the assessment on higher-order skills was leading to decreased attention to basic skills. Other teachers indicated that the need to cover a large amount of material was forcing them to main-*

tain a strict schedule. For example, one teacher indicated that when a student asked an interesting but tangential question, in the past she would have pursued it in order to encourage and stimulate students' love of learning. With the high-stakes assessment in place, she felt the need to deflect these questions and maintain a focus on the skills and topics to be assessed. (320)

Teachers as "Origins" and "Pawns"

What are the consequences of legislated learning and bureaucratic teaching on motivation and commitment of teachers? Is there a link between teacher motivation and commitment and school effectiveness? In successful schools, teachers are more committed, harder workers, more loyal to the school, and more satisfied with their jobs. The research on motivation to work (Hackman and Oldham, 1980; Herzberg, 1966; Peters and Waterman, 1982) suggests that these highly motivating conditions are present when teachers:

- Find their work lives to be *meaningful,* purposeful, sensible, and significant, and when they view the work itself as being worthwhile and important
- Have reasonable *control over their work activities* and affairs and are able to exert reasonable influence over work events and circumstances
- Experience *personal responsibility* for the work and are personally accountable for outcomes

Meaningfulness, control, and personal responsibility are attributes of teachers functioning as "Origins" rather than as "Pawns." According to De Charms (1968), "An Origin is a person who perceives his behavior as determined by his own choosing: a Pawn is a person who perceives his behavior as determined by external forces beyond his control." He continues:

An Origin has a strong feeling of personal causation, a feeling that the locus for causation of effects in his environment lies within himself. . . . A Pawn has a feeling that causal forces beyond his control, or personal forces residing within others, or in the physical environment determine his behavior. This constitutes a strong feeling of powerlessness or ineffectiveness. (274)

Personal causation is an important dimension of motivation. People strive to influence the events and situations of their environment, to be Origins of their own behavior.

Legislated learning and bureaucratic teaching threaten personal causation by creating work conditions more associated with Pawn feelings and behavior. In referring to Pawn feelings and behavior among teachers, the economist and Nobel laureate Theodore Schultz (1982) states:

Most of these attitudes of school teachers should have been anticipated in view of the way schools are organized and administered. The curriculum is not for them to decide; nor is the content of the course to be taught and the plans to be followed.

. . . In assessing the performance of teachers, it is a dictum of economics that incentives matter. School teachers are responding to the much circumscribed opportunities open to them. They are not robots but human agents who perceive, interpret, and act in accordance with the worthwhile options available. (43)

There is a paradox at play here. On the one hand, clear mandates, mission statements, lists of standards, goals and purposes, and high achievement expectations for teachers provide them with a needed sense of direction and clear signal of what is important and significant. This realization was an important leadership theme of earlier chapters, which discussed the concepts of purposing and symbolic and cultural aspects of leadership. On the other hand, if such mandates are described and prescribed in such detail that teachers come to feel and behave like Pawns rather than Origins, problems in motivation arise. Mandates that provide direction, define meaning, and promote significance in one's work are motivating and contribute to building commitment. Mandates that reduce the decision-making prerogatives of teachers and make teaching "teacher-proof" discourage motivation and contribute to detachment, even alienation, rather than to commitment. Widely accepted motivational theories that policy makers rely on in developing mandates are also paradoxical. States and other authorities with the power to mandate rely on goal-setting theories of motivation that suggest goals that take the form of specific, measurable, and achievable outcomes motivate teachers to higher levels of performance (Locke, 1968; Rowan, 1996). But expectancy theory (Vroom, 1964), which is a cousin of goal-setting theory, suggests that teachers are motivated when goals are understood, when teachers believe they have the means and resources to achieve the goals, and when achieving the goals will result in outcomes that they personally value. Taken together, these two powerful cousins provide still another tightrope for principals to walk. Goals make sense, but they will backfire if they are so pervasive and so detailed that they script what teachers do.

Principals are responsible for monitoring the delicate balance between goals. The balance may be thought of as settings on a compass, providing a sense of direction and the goals may be seen as roadmaps that script the journey. It helps if principals seek to ensure that mandates are sensibly interpreted and articulated into administrative, supervisory, and teaching practices that promote Origin feelings and behaviors among teachers. They must ask whether interpretation and implementing decisions will promote professionalism or bureaucracy in teaching. Responsive to unique situations, professionals take their cues from the problems they face and the students they serve. They draw on the wealth of knowledge and technology available to them as they create professional knowledge in use in response to student needs. Bureaucrats, by contrast, are not driven by student problems but by the technology itself. They are appliers of rules, regulators of formats, direction followers, and managerial implementers. They strive for a one-best-way to treat all cases, and, pursuing standard outcomes, they apply formal procedures in standardized ways. It is in this sense that legislated learning and bureaucratic teaching encourage Pawn feelings and behaviors among teachers and students, contributing to less effective teaching and learning.

In bureaucratic schools even the best of intentions are often displaced by other intentions. This displacement occurs without people being aware of what is going on. Rules, procedures, and processes, for example, that are originally devised to help the school run better, to help teachers teach better, and to help students learn better become ends in themselves.

Teachers are particularly vulnerable to goal displacement. Faced with a fast-paced and tight schedule, a prescribed curriculum, a list of student behavior rules and consequences that must be implemented, a universal grading policy, and other "rules" to follow, these frameworks become ends in themselves, displacing such ends as caring for students and doing one's best to teach them well. Soon, teachers become transformed from skilled and caring teachers to expert deliverers of instruction to detached clients.

Bimber (1993) believes that the transformation from caring to bureaucratic teacher is a natural response to how schools are organized and operated. He differentiates between "functional" rationality and "substantial" rationality to show how this transformation happens.

> When workers strive to carry out procedures and adhere closely to rules, they are exercising functional *rationality: They use their judgment and skills to adhere to the rules to perform a well-defined function. This is rational because it is the behavior for which they are best rewarded. On the other hand, when workers use their judgment and skills to devise solutions to client problems on their own, when they judge for themselves what would be best in a given situation, they are exercising substantial *rationality: Rather than follow rules they make substantial decisions about their work. . . . Functional and substantial rationality do not arise because of personality traits or individual's temperaments, but from the system of rewards and sanctions that structures the work environment. (29)*

If Bimber's analysis is correct, then it appears that much of what we do in schools first victimizes our teachers and then victimizes our students.

Isolation in Teaching

Teaching can be aptly described as a lonely profession. Typically, teachers work alone; as a result, no one else in the school knows what they are doing or how well they are doing it (Bidwell, 1975; Lortie, 1975; Waller, 1932). Related to isolation in teaching are tendencies to encourage the value of privatism and the consequences of this value on social interaction. Privatism forces teachers to look inward, discourages sharing, and encourages competition; furthermore, it promotes feelings of inadequacy and insecurity. Lack of social interaction deprives teachers of opportunities to help and seek help from others, to give feedback, and to get feedback from others—both essential ingredients in most motivation to work models. These conditions not only contradict what is known about sound management practices but they also impede professional growth and effective teaching. Despite the debilitating effects of isolation in teaching, schools persist in organizational structures and supervisory and evaluation practices that encourage these conditions. Let's examine further the effects of isolation, privatism, and lack of social interaction in teaching.

Rosenholtz (1984) identifies isolation as one of the major impediments to school improvement. Her recent review of the research on this topic leads to the following conclusions:

> *In isolated settings, teachers come to believe that they alone are responsible for running their classrooms and that to seek advice or assistance from their colleagues constitutes an open admission of incompetence.*
>
> *Teacher isolation is perhaps the greatest impediment to learning to teach, or to improving one's existing skills, because most learning by necessity occurs through trial and error. One alarming consequence of trial and error learning is that teachers' limits for potential growth depend heavily on their own personal ability to detect problems and to discern possible solutions.*
>
> *Another consequence is that teachers in isolated settings have few role models of good teaching to emulate. As a matter of fact, it is more typical of teachers in isolated settings to use role models that they recall from their own student days than to seek models of teaching excellence among their contemporaries.*
>
> *. . . in interpreting and formulating solutions to classroom problems, teachers realize little benefit from the advice, experience, or expertise of colleagues with whom they work. That is, any pre-existing practical knowledge is seldom passed along to new recruits, who must then, of their own accord, sink or swim.*
>
> *For teachers restricted to trial-and-error learning then, there is a limit to their capacity to grow in the absence of others' professional knowledge. . . . Teachers teach their prime after about four or five years and thereafter, perhaps because of little teaching input, their effectiveness with students actually begins to decline. (4–6)*

Lieberman and Miller (1984) point out that being private means not sharing experiences about teaching, classes, students, and learning. By being private, teachers forfeit the opportunity to share their successes with colleagues but gain the security of not having to disclose shortcomings. Having worked in isolation and not having accurate knowledge of the teaching of others, teachers tend to assume that they are not measuring up to colleagues.

Isolation and privatism contribute to fewer social interaction opportunities among teachers. The three conditions combine to force teachers to look inward for sources of feedback and rewards. Indeed, teachers rely almost exclusively on interactions with students as sources of satisfaction in teaching (Lortie, 1975; Waller, 1932). The question, though, is whether the satisfaction derived from student social interaction is enough to provide the kind of motivation and commitment needed for effective schooling. How does social interaction with adults fit into the picture?

Social interaction is a key ingredient in the supervisory process. Contrary to myth, teachers report increases in satisfaction as supervision increases moderately (Dornbush and Scott, 1975). Moderate increases in supervision seem also to be related to increases in teaching effectiveness. From his research, Natriello (1984) concludes: "Teachers who report more frequent evaluation activities also report being markedly more effective in teaching tasks" (592). Social interaction, as a form of feedback about one's teaching, is a contributor to these findings. Social interaction is also the medium by which recognition is given and received. Furthermore, social interaction seems to be a key factor in evoking the achievement, power-influence, and affiliation motives of persons at work and is an integral part of most motivation-to-work and job-enrichment models emerging from the research (Hackman and Oldham, 1980).

Many experts believe that social interaction among teachers, and between teachers and supervisors, is essential for promoting and institutionalizing change in schools and is related as well to successful staff-development efforts. With respect to institutionalizing changes, Clark, Lotto, and Astuto (1984) point out that the focus of staff development must reach beyond the development of new teaching skills to the development of new concepts and behaviors within a supportive school climate. Their review of the research on effective school improvement efforts leads them to conclude that interaction among teachers, and between teachers and administrators, provides the needed opportunities for technical and psychological support that enhances effective implementation. "Teachers report that they learn best from other teachers. Teacher-teacher interactions provide for technical and psychological support as well as personal reinforcement" (Clark, Lotto, and Astuto, 1984:58). Although more than social interaction opportunities may be necessary for school improvement efforts to be successful, success will not be likely without social interaction. Informal professional development efforts are also linked to social interaction among teachers. When provided with opportunity and encouragement, teachers learn a great deal from one another and trust one another as sources of new ideas and as sharers of problems they face (Glatthorn, 1984; Keenan, 1974).

Appendix 13.1, "Studying the Climate of Your School," provides a brief overview of the concept of school climate and how this climate can be assessed. The appendix relies on the work of Rensis Likert, a pioneer in the organizational climate literature.

Legislated learning and bureaucratic teaching, isolation in the workplace, the tradition of privatism, and lack of social interaction are urgent problems that principals and their faculties must address as they work to improve the quality of work life in schools, encourage professional development, increase teacher motivation and commitment, and build professional community in our schools. Community, McLaughlin and Talbert (Bradley, 1993:7) conclude, is not only good for teachers but it is also good for students. Their research reveals that teachers who belong to learning communities have more positive views of students and are more successful in changing their practice for the better.

Using Motivation Theory and Research to Inform Practice

In Chapter 6, it was pointed out that leadership practice might usefully be understood through use of the metaphor "developmental stages." Four stages were discussed: leadership by bartering, building, bonding, and binding. Virtually all the available research on motivation addresses the first two stages, leadership by bartering and building. Leadership by bartering makes the assumption that the interests of leaders and those being led are different, and therefore a bargain needs to be struck whereby the leader gives to the led something they want in return for their compliance with the leader's wishes. For the most part, the trading that takes place in leadership by bartering focuses on extrinsic factors. Tradeoffs occur in leadership by building as well, although they tend to address higher-order need factors and intrinsic motives of the led.

These ideas are captured by the theorizing of the psychologist Abraham Maslow (1943) and by the research of Frederick Herzberg (1966). These experts make the assumption that people have many needs and that the needs stem from at least two human desires—avoidance of pain, hardship, and difficulty; and the desire for growth and development in an effort to realize one's potential (e.g., Herzberg, 1966:56). Perhaps most well known is the need classification scheme proposed by Maslow (1943). He proposed that human needs could be classified into five broad categories: physiological, security-safety, social-belonging, esteem, and self-actualization. Key to Maslow's theory is that the need categories are arranged in a hierarchy of prepotency, with individual behavior motivated to satisfy the need most important at the time. Furthermore, according to theory, the strength of this need depends on its position in the hierarchy and the extent to which lower-order needs are met or satiated. The press from esteem needs, for example, will not be very great for individuals whose security needs are not met. Maslow's ideas form much of the basis for the material and psychological bartering that takes place between leader and led as each seeks an accommodation of their needs. The leader needs to get work done in a certain way. The led need to get certain needs met. One is traded for the other.

Maslow's ideas are helpful, but have limitations. When applied in the management literature, an assumption is often made that some of the needs in his theory are more valued than others. Esteem, autonomy, and self-actualization, for example, are considered to be better than belonging. Indeed, belonging needs are sometimes considered to be a nuisance that must be met to get a person motivated at a higher level. The higher the level, the more motivated a person will be and the more productive that person will be. This is spurious thinking, especially when applied to young people. To most students, belonging is the most important need.

Another problem is that Maslow's needs are typically viewed as being universally applicable, however, needs are culturally determined. Belonging may be less valued in one culture and more valued in another. The same thing is true of achievement and the other needs in Maslow's formulation.

The work of Frederick Herzberg (1966) and his colleagues (Herzberg, Mausner, and Snyderman, 1959) provides a more sophisticated set of ideas for engaging in this kind of bartering. Herzberg's approach, often referred to as *two-factor theory*, is based on the premise that job characteristics contributing to work motivation are different from those contributing to work dissatisfaction. He called the first set of factors *motivators* and the second *hygienic*. According to the theory, if hygienic factors are not attended to by principals, poor work hygiene will occur, with corresponding feelings of teacher job dissatisfaction and poor performance. However, tending to these factors and eliminating job dissatisfaction will not result in increased teacher commitment or job performance. The motivation factors that contributed to increased teacher performance when present seemed not to result in job dissatisfaction or work performance that was below par when absent. According to the theory, if principals do not attend to the motivation factors, teachers will not be motivated to work, but they will not be dissatisfied either. They will perform up to a certain level considered satisfactory, but will make little or no effort to exceed this level (Sergiovanni, 1966).

The factors identified by Herzberg and his associates as being related to work hygiene included interpersonal relationships with students, teachers, and supervisors; quality of supervision; policy and administration; working conditions; and personal life. The factors related to work motivation were achievement, recognition, the work itself, responsibility, and advancement.

The two-factor theory suggests that job satisfaction and motivation to work are related to two decision possibilities for teachers: participation and performance (Sergiovanni, 1968). The decision to participate in one's job is associated with the fair day's work concept. When participating, one takes a job and does all that is necessary to meet minimum commitments; in return, one receives "fair pay" in the form of salary, benefits, social acceptance, courteous and thoughtful treatment, and reasonable supervision. Because these dimensions are *expected* as part of fair pay, they tend not to motivate a person to go beyond. The decision to perform, however, results in exceeding the fair day's work for a fair day's pay contract. This decision is voluntary because all that school districts can require from teachers is fair work. Rewards associated with the fair day's work are for the most part extrinsic, focusing on the conditions of work. Rewards associated with the performance investment tend to be more intrinsic (e.g., recognition, achievement, feelings of competence, exciting and challenging work, interesting and meaningful work).

Principals need to be concerned with both extrinsic and intrinsic rewards. Schools cannot function adequately unless the participation investment is made and continued by teachers. However, schools cannot excel unless the majority of teachers make the performance investment as well. The two-factor theory can provide principals with a cognitive map for ensuring that administrative, organizational, curricular, and teaching practices provide for both levels of work investment by teachers. Yet, a map is different than a recipe, not everything will work for everyone. Much trial and error will be necessary as principals practice leadership by bartering.

The Potential of Work Itself as a Motivator

A major problem with leadership by bartering is that it relies heavily on making deals. At the heart of the deals are bureaucratic and psychological authority as the means to obtain compliance. Bureaucratic authority promises sanctions and punishments if compliance is not forthcoming. Psychological authority gives rewards in exchange for compliance. Both forms of authority are limited in two ways. First, they lead to calculated involvement. A person's compliance is contingent on either the avoidance of penalties or the obtaining of rewards. When neither is forthcoming, continued compliance is often risky and sometimes nonexistent.

Both rewards and penalties are based on the economic concept of utility function. Human beings are driven by a desire to maximize their self-interests, thus, they continually calculate the costs and benefits of all their options, choosing the course of action that either makes them a winner or keeps them from losing. In Chapter 3, it was pointed out that the concept of utility function is now being successfully challenged by a new economics that does not dismiss the importance of self-interest but gives equal weight to emotions and values—to expressive and moral authority as motivators (Etzioni, 1988). Leadership by bartering is based on the principle that "what gets rewarded gets done." Leadership by building, by contrast, is based on the principle "what *is* rewarding gets done." Here, the emphasis is on intrinsic returns and expressive reasons for involvement in one's work. To these, Etzioni would add the principle "what is right and good gets done." He has in mind the addition of moral authority as a means to understand why people choose to do something and to do it well.

Flow Theory

Csikszentmihalyi (1990) proposes *flow theory* as a way to understand the potential of work itself as a source of motivation. He studied highly accomplished and motivated experts (e.g., rock climbers, composers, surgeons, authors) in a number of different fields. Although the work of these experts differed, each experienced a certain flow that Csikszentmihalyi attributes to intrinsic motivation. Flow is characterized by opportunity for action; the merging of action and awareness; focused attention characterized by concentration, narrowing of consciousness, and being absorbed in what one is doing; the loss of self-consciousness as one works; the clarity of goals and norms; direct and immediate feedback; and feelings of competence and of being in control of what one does. He concludes that the satisfaction derived from this total absorption in one's work provides a powerful source of motivation.

Csikszentmihalyi is convinced that experiencing flow can be a very common experience under the right conditions. One must first be faced by a *challenge* that is not too great for the *skills* needed to meet it, but great enough for a person to meet the challenge with enjoyment on the one hand and to grow in competence, confidence, and/or skill on the other. Should one's skills be greater than the challenge, then boredom is likely to result. One can speculate, for example, that when teachers are bored with their work, their available skills may not be used fully enough. Some experts maintain that this is the likely consequence of teachers who are subjected to curriculum and supervisory mandates that specify unduly what it is they must do and how. Such specification can lead to work simplification and the subsequent "de-skilling" of teachers (McNeil, 1987).

Sometimes teachers are faced with levels of challenge that far exceed their skills, with the result being feelings of anxiety. When neither level of challenge nor level of skill is very high, the response is likely to be one of apathy, another version of the de-skilling hypothesis. It might be useful at this point to inventory one's own personal experience with teachers and with students. Compare occasions when they responded to work with apathy, boredom, anxiety, or total absorption (flow). What are the mixes of challenge and skills levels that seemed to contribute to these states?

The message of flow theory for principals is that maintaining the right balance between level of skill and level of challenge makes good motivational sense. When challenge is up, principals need to provide the necessary support on the skill dimension to avoid frustration and fear of failure. In areas where teacher skill levels are high, challenging opportunities will need to be provided. Successful matching of challenge and skill, according to the theory, is likely to result in flow—total absorption in one's work.

Job-Enrichment Theory

Another window through which one might view the potential of the work itself to motivate is provided by the research of Hackman and Oldham (1980). These scholars have developed a theory of job enrichment—the Job Characteristics model—that has been successfully applied in practice. Key to the model is the presence of three psychological states found to be critical in determining a person's work motivation and job satisfaction:

- Experience meaningfulness, *which is defined as the extent to which an individual perceives her or his work as being worthwhile or important by some system of self-accepted values*
- Experience responsibility, *which is defined by the extent to which a person believes that she or he is personally accountable for the outcomes of efforts*
- Knowledge of results, *which is defined as the extent to which a person is able to determine, on a fairly regular basis, whether or not performance is satisfactory and efforts lead to outcomes (Hackman et al., 1975:57)*

According to the Job Characteristics model, when these psychological states are experienced, one feels good and performs better—internal work motivation occurs. Internal work motivation means how much an individual experiences positive feelings from effective performance. Hackman and Oldham have found that the content of one's job is an important critical determiner of internal work motivation. Furthermore, when certain characteristics of one's job are improved or enhanced, internal work motivation can be increased. They found, for example, that experiencing meaningfulness is enhanced by jobs characterized by skill variety, task identity, and task significance. Autonomy was the job characteristic related to experiencing responsibility, and feedback was related to knowledge of results.

The Job Characteristics model suggests that in teaching, jobs that require (1) different activities in carrying out the work and the use of a variety of teacher talents and skills (skill variety); (2) teachers to engage in tasks identified as whole and comprising identifiable pieces of work (task identity); (3) teachers to have substantial and significant impact on the lives or work of other people (task significance); (4) substantial freedom, independence, and direction be provided to teachers in scheduling work and in deciding classroom organizational and instructional procedures (autonomy); and (5) teachers be provided with direct, clear information about the effects of their performance (feedback) are likely to evoke the psychological states of meaningfulness, responsibility, and knowledge of results. Hackman and Oldham's research reveals that these conditions result in high work motivation, high-quality performance, high job satisfaction, and low absenteeism among teachers.

Figure 13.1 illustrates the Job Characteristics model. In addition to job dimensions, psychological states, and personal and work outcomes, an "implementing concepts" panel is included. Implementing concepts are suggestions the researchers offer to principals interested in building more of the job dimensions into the work of the school. The principle of combining tasks, for example, suggests that as much as possible, fractionalized aspects of teaching should be put together into larger, more holistic modules. Comprehensive curriculum strategies, interdiscipli-

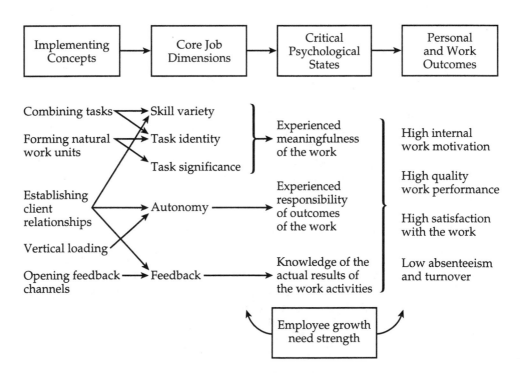

FIGURE 13.1   Job Enrichment Concepts and Practices

Source: From "A New Strategy for Job Enrichment" by J. R. Hackman, G. Oldham, R. Johnson, and K. Purdy. © 1975 by the Regents of the University of California. Reprinted from *California Management Review*, Vol. XVII, no. 4, p. 62 by permission of the Regents.

nary teaching approaches, and team-group teaching modes all contribute to the combining of teaching and curriculum tasks. Combining teaching tasks increases not only skill variety for teachers, but their identification with the work as well.

Although establishing close relationships with students ("clients") is a natural part of teaching and learning, some patterns of school organization and teaching encourage impersonal relationships between teachers and students. Forming "natural work units" points to the importance of thinking in community terms. The intent of such units would be to increase one's sense of ownership and continuing responsibility for identifiable aspects of the work by more closely connecting people to each other and by connecting them more closely to their work. The self-contained elementary school classroom comes closer to this concept than does the departmentalized and quick-moving secondary school teaching schedule. But even in the elementary setting, the building of teaching teams that plan and work together and whose members share a common responsibility for students is often lacking. "Vertical loading" suggests strategies that bring together actual teaching and planning to teach. Providing teachers with more control over schedules, work methods, evaluation, and even the training and supervision of less experienced teachers might be examples of vertical loading.

"Opening feedback channels" is another way of saying that the more principals are able to let teachers know how well they are doing, the more highly motivated they will be. Indeed, motivation and satisfaction are neglected benefits of teacher-evaluation supervisory programs designed to provide teachers with helpful feedback. Examples of helpful programs would be those that include clinical supervision, peer supervision, target settings, and similar formats. Principals should strive to create ways in which feedback to teachers occurs naturally from their day-to-day activities and from working closely with colleagues.

The Job Characteristics model suggests that virtually every decision principals make about schooling, classroom organization, curriculum development and implementation, selection of materials, and teaching itself has implications for building motivation and commitment of teachers. Principals need to assess the consequences of a particular decision on promoting job-enrichment opportunities for teachers.

Friendship opportunities and opportunities to work with others are two other dimensions identified in the Job Characteristics model (Sashkin and Morris, 1984). "Friendship opportunities" refers to the extent to which the work setting provides for the development of close contacts among teachers and the development of friendly patterns of interaction. "Working with others" refers to the extent to which the accomplishment of tasks requires that teachers interact with other teachers in order to complete the work successfully. These dimensions seem related to the extent to which workers are involved in their jobs, experience satisfaction, and report improvements in work quality (Sashkin and Morris, 1984).

In summary, the Job Characteristics model provides principals with a conceptual framework allowing them to make informed decisions about the nature and structure of the work of teaching to help teachers feel that their job is meaningful, to enable them to learn the actual outcomes of their efforts, to provide them with feelings of control and responsibility for results, and to help them become part of a social unit. These conditions are related to high intrinsic work motivation, increases in quality performance, high job satisfaction, and lower absence and turnover rates.

Appendix 13.2 contains a key that allows you to score your responses to the Quality of Work Life in Teaching form. Please score by following the directions provided. Note that five subscores are provided, each corresponding to an important dimension of most job-enrichment models. With the exception of work speed and routine, the higher the score, the more enriched is the job, the greater are the possibilities for increased motivation and commitment, and the more likely that connections between and among people will embody community.

Women as a Special Case

Much of the available motivation literature is subject to male bias; thus, the accompanying prescriptions for practice may not apply to women. The problem, according to Shakeshaft (1987), is *androcentrism,* defined as "the practice of viewing the world and shaping reality from a male perspective [and] the elevation of the masculine to the level of the universal and the ideal and honoring of men and the male principle above women and female" (94). Maslow's theory, the two-factor theory, and the job enrichment theory, for example, give heavy emphasis to competition, the setting of task goals, individual achievement, the building of self-competence and self-esteem, individual autonomy, and self-actualization. Women, by contrast, give emphasis to such themes as cooperation, intimacy, affiliation, the construction of interpersonal networks, and community building. In using teamwork as an example, Shakeshaft (1987) points out that men tend to view the concept in terms of goals, roles, and responsibilities. A team must first define what needs to be done and then allocate responsibilities to roles making clear not only what is expected, but how one person's niche fits that of others who comprise the team. The metaphor for team, in this context, is sport in the form of baseball, basketball, or football. For women, teamwork is not the parallel play of men, but the meshing of individual identities to create a new configuration and the bonding together of people in a common cause.

Key in applying the concepts from traditional motivation theory is redefining concept indicators. Achievement, for example, can mean the accumulation of a series of individual successes on the one hand or the successful constructing of a learning community on the other. Application of the motivation theory and research should therefore be idiosyncratic. If you want to know what motivates people start by asking them.

Motivation, Efficacy, and Student Performance

When motivation is down and discretion is low, a teacher's sense of self-esteem becomes blurred, resulting in the erosion of professional confidence. Ultimately, efficacy is affected. As suggested earlier in our discussion of Origin and Pawn feelings and their effects, teacher efficacy is directly related to how teachers behave in the classroom, to students' behavior in the classroom, and to the quality of student achievement they obtain.

"All students can learn" has become a slogan that is repeated by administrators trying to urge teachers to work harder or to change their practice. Most teachers will swear allegiance to this slogan publicly but privately many do not believe it. In their research, Ashton and Webb (1986) found, for example, that teachers with a low sense of efficacy had come to believe that many students cannot learn and will not learn and that there is not much they can do about it. Teachers with a high sense of efficacy, by contrast, believe that all students are capable of learning and that teachers can do a great deal to increase student achievement.*

Ashton and Webb note that there is a second dimension to teachers' sense of efficacy. Not only does it refer to one's belief that students can learn if taught, but to a particular teacher's belief that she or he has the ability to do the right kind of teaching that will result in student performance. With this two-part definition of efficacy in hand, Ashton and Webb found that teachers with a high sense of efficacy exhibited teacher behaviors that were characterized by warmth. They were more accepting of student responses, more accepting of student initiatives, and more attentive to student needs. Students responded by being more enthusiastic and by initiating more interactions with the teachers. Further, student achievement was higher in both tests of high school mathematics and tests of language basic skills.

Enhancing Efficacy

The good news is that teachers' sense of efficacy can change. Teachers can come to feel more efficacious or less efficacious depending on a variety of factors. Further, higher levels of motivation and commitment and higher levels of efficacy seem to be related to each other. What are the factors that contribute to these higher levels? How do these factors interact with each other? Ashton and Webb (1986) found that school climates that are supportive, teaching and learning environments that are characterized by collegial values and shared decision making, and a school culture that provides a sense of purpose and a shared covenant as a basis for accountability are important. Together, these factors contribute to cooperative relationships and higher levels of interaction; higher levels of personal responsibility for outcomes; and higher standards and expectations as well as a sense that the work of teaching is meaningful and significant. These relationships, summarized from Ashton and Webb's research, are provided here:

1. a. A *school climate* where teachers support each other, and principals support teachers, encourages cooperative relationships and high levels of social interaction among teachers.

*This discussion follows closely the discussion of efficacy and student achievement in Chapter 7, "Teachers, Keys to School Improvement" in Sergiovanni (2000).

     b. *Collegial values* where shared decision making is present and shared inquiry prevails encourages feelings of high personal causation among teachers and high responsibility for work outcomes.

     c. A *school culture* where sense of purpose, shared values and ideas, and a system of accountability based on these ideas is found encourages high standards and expectations, high pride and self-esteem, and the feeling that one's work is meaningful and significant.

2. a. *Cooperative relationships* and *high levels of social interaction* among teachers encourage a high sense of efficacy, motivation, and commitment by teachers.

     b. Feelings of *high personal causation* and *high responsibility for work outcomes* encourage a high sense of efficacy, motivation, and commitment by teachers.

     c. Having *high standards and expectations, high levels of pride and self-esteem,* and *expanding personal meaning and significance* at work encourage a high sense of efficacy, motivation, and commitment by teachers.

3. A high sense of teacher *efficacy, motivation,* and *commitment:*

     a. Leads to teacher behaviors that are *warm and accepting of student responses,* accepting of *student initiatives,* and attentive to the *needs of students.*

     b. Leads to student behaviors characterized by *student enthusiasm for learning* and *student initiation of interaction with teachers.*

     c. Leads to *higher student achievement* as measured by high school mathematics and language basic skills test scores.

In sum, efficacy is important. Individual efficacy is an important part of the professional and cultural world of teachers, and collective efficacy is an important part of the professional and cultural world of schools. Both suffer when bureaucratic policies, management systems, and mandated one-size-fits-all standards and assessments are placed at the center and thus determine the cultural worlds of teachers and other locals.

The Power of Beliefs

In this and other chapters, adding moral authority as a basis for leadership to bureaucratic and psychological authority was recommended. Doing so depends on schools being able to develop a set of shared values and beliefs that spells out who they are, what they want to accomplish, and how. These centers of ideas, once accepted, function as covenants that provide the basis for bonding people together as members of a learning community that knows why it exists. Further, covenants detail what the community owes its members and what its members in turn owe the community. This theme was at the heart of earlier discussions of leadership and school culture and will be returned to in the final chapter, "Administering as a Moral Craft."

    Interpreted properly, the theory and research in the area of teacher motivation and commitment can be helpful in understanding why covenants that lead to building professional communities of practice for teachers are important and how they enable more effective teaching and learning. Often, our policy mandates, administrative directives, and complacency in insisting on "business as usual" present conditions and practices at odds with this knowledge base. School practices, for example, too often encourage bureaucratic teaching, promote isolationism among teachers, encourage privatism, and discourage social interaction. These conditions are typically associated with decreases in teacher motivation and commitment. Effective teaching and learning and other school improvement efforts are enhanced as teachers work harder and smarter and as their commitment to the school and its success is increased. This gap between present practice and what we know represents a test of leadership for principals.

Even more challenging is the attempt to broaden present conceptions of the nature of human potential. Without dismissing the importance of self-interest, principals and faculties must give far more attention to expressive and moral reasons for determining courses of action. As expressive and moral authority gain acceptance as legitimate ways of working with teachers, professional learning communities emerge. Attention will need to be given, as well, to applying these same ideas to students.

References

Argyris, Chris. 1957. *Personality and Organization.* New York: Harper & Row.

Ashton, Patricia T., and Rodman B. Webb. 1986. *Making a Difference: Teachers' Sense of Efficacy and Student Achievement.* New York: Longman.

Bidwell, Charles E. 1975. "The School as a Formal Organization," in James O. March (Ed.), *Handbook of Organizations* (pp. 972–1022). Chicago: Rand McNally.

Bimber, Bruce. 1993. *School Decentralization: Lessons from the Study of Bureaucracy.* Institute on Education and Training, Santa Monica, CA: The Rand Corporation.

Bradley, Ann. 1993, March 31. "By Asking Teachers about 'Context' of Work, Center Moves to Cutting Edge of Research," *Education Week,* p. 7.

Brayfield, A. H., and W. H. Crockett. 1955. "Employee Attitudes and Employee Performance," *Psychological Bulletin* 52(1), 415–422.

Clark, David L., Linda S. Lotto, and Terry A. Astuto. 1984. "Effective Schools and School Improvement: A Comparative Analysis of Two Lines of Inquiry," *Educational Administration Quarterly* 20(3), 41–68.

Coombs, Arthur W. 1959. "Personality Theory and Its Implication for Curriculum Development," in Alexander Frazier (Ed.), *Learning More about Learning.* Washington, DC: Association for Supervision and Curriculum Development.

Csikszentmihalyi, Mihaly. 1990. *Flow: The Psychology of Optimal Experience.* New York: Harper & Row.

Darling-Hammond, Linda. 1984. *Beyond the Commission Reports: The Coming Crisis in Teaching.* Santa Monica, CA: The Rand Corporation.

De Charms, Richard. 1968. *Personal Causation.* New York: Academic Press.

Deci, Edward L. 1995. *Why We Do What We Do.* New York: G. B. Putnam's Sons.

Dornbush, S. M., and W. R. Scott. 1975. *Evaluation and the Exercise of Authority.* San Francisco: Jossey-Bass.

Etzioni, Amitai. 1988. *The Moral Dimension: Toward a New Economics.* New York: The Free Press.

Glatthorn, Allan A. 1984. *Differentiated Supervision.* Alexandria, VA: Association for Supervision and Curriculum Development.

Hackman, J. R., and G. R. Oldham. 1980. *Work Redesign.* Reading, MA: Addison-Wesley.

Hackman, J. R., G. Oldham, R. Johnson, and K. Purdy. 1975. "A New Strategy for Job Enrichment," *California Management Review* 17(4).

Herzberg, F. 1966. *Work and the Nature of Man.* New York: World Publishing.

Herzberg, F., B. Mausner, and B. Snyderman. 1959. *The Motivation to Work.* New York: Wiley.

Keenan, Charles. 1974. *Channels for Change: A Survey of Teachers in Chicago Elementary Schools.* Doctoral dissertation. Urbana: Department of Educational Administration, University of Illinois.

Kelley, Carolyn. 1999. "The Motivational Impact of School-Based Performance Awards," *Journal of Personnel Evaluation in Education* 12(4), 309–326.

Kohn, Alfie. 1993, September–October. "Why Incentive Plans Cannot Work," *Harvard Business Review.*

Lieberman, Ann, and Lynne Miller. 1984. *Teachers, Their World, and Their Work.* Alexandria, VA: Association for Supervision and Curriculum Development.

Locke, E. A. 1968. "Toward a Theory of Task Motivation and Incentives," *Organizational Behavior and Union Performance* 3, 157–189.

Lortie, Dan. 1975. *School Teacher.* Chicago: The University of Chicago Press.

MacDonald, James. 1964. "An Image of Man: The Learner Himself," in Ronald R. Doll (Ed.), *Individualizing Instruction.* Washington, DC: Association for Supervision and Curriculum Development.

Madaus, George F. 1999. "The Influence of Testing on the Curriculum" in Margaret J. Early and Kenneth J. Rehage (Eds.), *Issues in Curriculum: A Selection of Chapters from NSSE Yearbooks.* Ninety-Eighth Yearbook of the National Society for the Study of Education. Part II. Chicago: University of Chicago Press. (Note: This chapter originally appeared in the 1988 Yearbook.)

Maslow, A. H. 1943. "A Theory of Human Motivation," *Psychological Review* 50(2), 370–396.

McNeil, Linda M. 1987. "Exit Voice and Community: Magnet Teachers Responses to Standardization," *Educational Policy* 1(1).

Natriello, Gary. 1984. "Teachers' Perceptions of the Frequency of Evaluation and Assessments of Their Effort and Effectiveness," *American Educational Research Journal* 21(3), 579–595.

Peters, Thomas J., and Robert H. Waterman, Jr. 1982. *In Search of Excellence.* New York: Harper & Row.

Pfeiffer, J. William, and Leonard D. Goodstein. 1984. *The 1984 Annual: Developing Human Resources.* San Diego, CA: University Associates.

Rosenholtz, Susan J. 1984. "Political Myths about Educational Reform: Lessons from Research on Teaching." Paper prepared for the Education Commission of the States, Denver, CO.

Rowan, Brian. 1996. "Standards as Incentives for Instructional Reform" in Susan H. Fuhrman and Jennifer A. O'Day (Eds.), *Rewards and Reform: Creating Educational Incentives that Work.* San Francisco: Jossey-Bass.

Sashkin, Marshall, and William C. Morris. 1984. *Organizational Behavior Concepts and Experiences.* Reston, VA: The Reston Co.

Schultz, Theodore W. 1982. "Human Capital Approaches in Organizing and Paying for Education," in Walter McMahan and Terry G. Geste (Eds.), *Financing Education: Overcoming Inefficiency and Inequity* (pp. 36–51). Urbana: University of Illinois Press.

Sergiovanni, Thomas J. 1966. "Factors Which Affect Satisfaction and Dissatisfaction of Teachers," *Journal of Educational Administration* 5(1), 66–82.

Sergiovanni, Thomas J. 1968. "New Evidence on Teacher Morale: A Proposal for Staff Differentiation," *The North Central Association Quarterly* 62(3), 259–266.

Sergiovanni, Thomas J. 2000. *The Lifeworld of Leadership: Creating Culture, Community, and Personal Meaning in Our Schools.* San Francisco: Jossey-Bass.

Shakeshaft, Charol (1987). *Women in Educational Administration.* Beverly Hills, CA: Sage Publications.

Tucker, Marc S., and Judy B. Codding. 1998. *Standards for Our Schools: How to Set Them, Measure*

Them, and Reach Them. San Francisco: Jossey-Bass.

Vroom, V. H. 1964. *Work and Motivation.* New York: Wiley.

Waller, Willard. 1932. *Sociology of Teaching.* New York: Wiley.

Wise, Arthur E. 1979. *Legislated Learning: The Bureaucratization of the American Classroom.* Berkeley: University of California Press.

Appendix 13.1   Studying the Climate of Your School

The pioneering work of Rensis Likert and his colleagues at the Institute for Social Research, University of Michigan, from the late 1950s through the 1960s, placed the concept climate in the mainstream of management thought. This research introduced into practice the idea that principals and other school administrators needed to focus not only on "end results" indicators of effectiveness of their policies, actions, and decisions, but on the "mediating" indicators as well (Likert, 1961, 1967).

Mediating Variables

According to Likert's theory, school policies, standard operating procedures, and accompanying administrative actions and decisions do not influence school effectiveness and other end results variables directly. Instead, they influence how teachers, students, and others perceive and feel, the attitudes and values they share, the trust and support binding them together, and the degree to which they are motivated to work and are committed to school goals and purposes. It is these mediating indicators that in turn influence school effectiveness.

Initiating —> mediating —> school effectiveness variables

Likert reached these conclusions by studying the characteristics of more and less effective work groups and organizations. He found that differences in the mediating variables of these group and organization types followed consistent patterns. He was able to identify four distinct patterns of management: Systems 1, 2, 3, and 4. System 1 resembles a rigid bureaucracy and is characterized by little mutual confidence and trust among supervisors and workers, direct supervision, high control, centralized decision making, detailed rules and regulations and work operating procedures, top-down communications, and routine work regulation by inspection. System 4 reflects a commitment to the development and use of human resources and is characterized by trust, supportive relationships, goal clarity and commitment, autonomy with responsibility, group decision making, authority more closely linked with ability, team work, social interaction, and controls linked to agreed-upon goals and purposes. Systems 2 and 3 are at intermediate positions on this continuum. Although they represent a distinct improvement over the rigid bureaucratic management of System 1, they do not recognize human potential as fully as does System 4.

The basic features of Likert's theory are illustrated in Figure A, "How Management Systems 1 and 4 Influence Mediating and School Effectiveness Variables." The principal's assumptions and resulting behavior with regard to leadership, control, organization, goals and purposes, and the motivation of teachers and students provide a specific pattern of management that can be described on a continuum from System 1 to 4. This management system elicits a predictable response from teachers at work that influences their motivation and performance. Teacher attitudes and behavior, it follows, have predictable consequences on school effectiveness. The effects of management systems 2 and 3 on mediating and school effectiveness variables would fall somewhere between the indicators provided in Figure A.

Appendix 13.1   *Continued*

Evaluating the Climate of Your School

Likert (1967) developed the Profile of Organizational Characteristics (POC) as a tool for measuring and charting system characteristics of the organizations he studied. The POC provides an indication not only of which management system characterizes a particular organization, but of that organization's climate as well.

The POC was adopted for school use in the form of The Profile of a School. An abbreviated version of the profile appears in Figure B. Figure C provides a score sheet for the profile. Use the instrument and the score sheet to evaluate your school or another school you know very well. Try to imagine how most of the teachers who work in this school would respond if they had the chance. Following the directions, plot your scores on the score sheet and draw a profile depicting your perceptions of that school's climate.

There are limitations in evaluating school "secondhand"; nonetheless, comparing your responses with those of others who know this school should reveal some similarities. Chances are your profile line reveals that this school can be characterized as System 2 or 3. Consistencies are likely in your ratings as you move from item to item, although your profile line probably has certain peaks toward System 4 and dips toward System 1. Peaks represent unusually strong qualities of the school's climate. Dips, by contrast, suggest areas where improvements are needed. Analyzing peaks and dips on the profile line allows principals and teachers to diagnose their school climate.

Dips can also be used as benchmarks for evaluating school climate improvement efforts. Imagine a school with relatively low climate scores on dimensions describing the extent to which students trust teachers and feel free to consult with them on academic and nonacademic matters. Principals and teachers might agree on a plan to improve this situation. Perhaps they decide to initiate voluntary open forum sessions for students and teachers on a weekly basis. They might agree as well to conduct weekly "that was the week that was" sessions in homerooms, in which students are free to summarize their academic week, pointing out highs and lows. More informally, teachers might resolve to be more sensitive to this issue as they interact with students. After several months, a second reading of the school climate might be taken; new responses could be compared with benchmark responses to detect improvements.

One implicit benefit of the POS and other climate instruments is that they provide handy structures for encouraging conversation and dialogue about events and conditions that ordinarily are difficult to discuss. It is much easier, for example, for teachers and principals to discuss items and item responses and their meanings than to engage in more unstructured conversations about school conditions and school improvements.

Take a moment to reflect on the climate of the school that you just evaluated. Using the POS, in its entirety, or a shortened version comprised of items that you select, evaluate the climate by first indicating how you would like it to be. What discrepancies do you note between your ideal and real responses? Assume that your

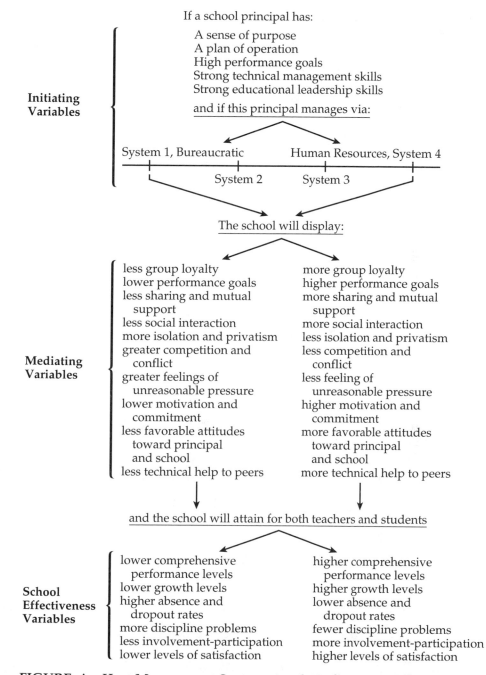

FIGURE A   How Management Systems 1 and 4 Influence Mediating and School Effectiveness Variables

Sources: Summarized from *New Patterns of Management* by Rensis Likert, 1961, New York: McGraw-Hill and *The Human Organization: Its Management and Value* by Rensis Likert, 1967, New York: McGraw-Hill.

Organizational Variable	System 1		System 2		System 3		System 4	
A. Leadership Processes used:	**RARELY**		**SOMETIMES**		**OFTEN**		**VERY OFTEN**	
1. How often is your behavior seen by students as friendly and supportive?	①	②	③	④	⑤	⑥	⑦	⑧
How often does the principal seek and use your ideas about:								
2. academic matters	①	②	③	④	⑤	⑥	⑦	⑧
3. non-academic school matters	①	②	③	④	⑤	⑥	⑦	⑧
4. How often do you see the principal's behavior as friendly and supportive?	①	②	③	④	⑤	⑥	⑦	⑧
	VERY LITTLE		**SOME**		**QUITE A BIT**		**A VERY GREAT DEAL**	
5. How much confidence and trust does the principal have in you?	①	②	③	④	⑤	⑥	⑦	⑧
6. How much confidence and trust do you have in the principal?	①	②	③	④	⑤	⑥	⑦	⑧
	NOT FREE		**SOMEWHAT FREE**		**QUITE FREE**		**VERY FREE**	
7. How free do you feel to talk to the principal about school matters?	①	②	③	④	⑤	⑥	⑦	⑧
	VERY LITTLE		**SOME**		**QUITE A BIT**		**A VERY GREAT DEAL**	
8. How much confidence and trust do you have in students?	①	②	③	④	⑤	⑥	⑦	⑧
9. How much confidence and trust do students have in you?	①	②	③	④	⑤	⑥	⑦	⑧
	NOT FREE		**SOMEWHAT FREE**		**QUITE FREE**		**VERY FREE**	
10. How free do students' feel to talk to you about school matters?	①	②	③	④	⑤	⑥	⑦	⑧
How often are students' ideas sought and used by the principal about:	**RARELY**		**SOMETIMES**		**OFTEN**		**VERY OFTEN**	
11. academic matters	①	②	③	④	⑤	⑥	⑦	⑧
12. non-academic school matters	①	②	③	④	⑤	⑥	⑦	⑧
13. How often does the principal use small group meetings to solve school problems?	①	②	③	④	⑤	⑥	⑦	⑧
B. Character of Motivational Forces:	**DISLIKE**		**SOMETIMES DISLIKE IT, SOMETIMES LIKE IT**		**USUALLY LIKE IT**		**LIKE IT VERY MUCH**	
14. What is the general attitude of students toward your school?	①	②	③	④	⑤	⑥	⑦	⑧
How often do you try to be friendly and supportive to:	**RARELY**		**SOMETIMES**		**OFTEN**		**VERY OFTEN**	
15. the principal	①	②	③	④	⑤	⑥	⑦	⑧
16. other teachers	①	②	③	④	⑤	⑥	⑦	⑧
	USUALLY A WASTE OF TIME		**SOMETIMES A WASTE OF TIME**		**OFTEN WORTH-WHILE**		**ALMOST ALWAYS WORTH-WHILE**	
17. In your job is it worthwhile or a waste of time to do your best?	①	②	③	④	⑤	⑥	⑦	⑧
	NOT SATISFYING		**SOMEWHAT SATISFYING**		**QUITE SATISFYING**		**VERY SATISFYING**	
18. How satisfying is your work at your school?	①	②	③	④	⑤	⑥	⑦	⑧
To what extent do the following feel responsible for seeing that educational excellence is achieved in your school:	**VERY LITTLE**		**SOME**		**CONSIDER-ABLE**		**VERY GREAT**	
19. principal	①	②	③	④	⑤	⑥	⑦	⑧
20. department heads	①	②	③	④	⑤	⑥	⑦	⑧
21. teachers	①	②	③	④	⑤	⑥	⑦	⑧
22. To what extent do students help each other when they want to get something done?	①	②	③	④	⑤	⑥	⑦	⑧
23. To what extent do students look forward to coming to school?	①	②	③	④	⑤	⑥	⑦	⑧
24. To what extent do students feel excited about learning?	①	②	③	④	⑤	⑥	⑦	⑧
25. To what extent do you look forward to your teaching day?	①	②	③	④	⑤	⑥	⑦	⑧
26. To what extent are you encouraged to be innovative in developing more effective and efficient educational practices?	①	②	③	④	⑤	⑥	⑦	⑧

FIGURE B Profile of a School: Teacher Form

Items and scoring formats are from The Profile of a School, Form 3, Teacher Form. Items have been regrouped and renumbered, and system designations have been added. The original questionnaire contains additional items that enable evaluation of high school departments, grade levels, or teaching teams. Used by permission of Rensis Likert Associates, Inc., Ann Arbor, Michigan 48104. Copyright © 1977 by Jane Gibson Likert and Rensis Likert. Distributed by Rensis Likert Associates, Inc. All rights reserved. No further reproduction in any form authorized without written permission of Rensis Likert Associates, Inc., Ann Arbor, Michigan 48104.

Organizational Variable	System 1	System 2	System 3	System 4
C. Character of Communication Process:	VERY LITTLE	SOME	QUITE A BIT	A VERY GREAT DEAL
27. How much do students feel that you are trying to help them with their problems?	① ②	③ ④	⑤ ⑥	⑦ ⑧
28. How much accurate information concerning school affairs is given to you by students?	① ②	③ ④	⑤ ⑥	⑦ ⑧
D. Character of Interaction-influence:				
How much influence do the following *have* on what goes on in your school?	VERY LITTLE	SOME	QUITE A BIT	A VERY GREAT DEAL
29. principal	① ②	③ ④	⑤ ⑥	⑦ ⑧
30. teachers	① ②	③ ④	⑤ ⑥	⑦ ⑧
31. central staff of your school system	① ②	③ ④	⑤ ⑥	⑦ ⑧
32. students	① ②	③ ④	⑤ ⑥	⑦ ⑧
How much influence do you think the following *should have* on what goes on in your school?				
33. principal	① ②	③ ④	⑤ ⑥	⑦ ⑧
34. teachers	① ②	③ ④	⑤ ⑥	⑦ ⑧
35. central staff of your school system	① ②	③ ④	⑤ ⑥	⑦ ⑧
36. students	① ②	③ ④	⑤ ⑥	⑦ ⑧
37. How much influence do you think students *have* on what goes on in your school?	① ②	③ ④	⑤ ⑥	⑦ ⑧
38. How much influence do you think students *should have* on what goes on in your school?	① ②	③ ④	⑤ ⑥	⑦ ⑧
	USUALLY IGNORED	APPEALED BUT NOT RESOLVED	RESOLVED BY PRINCIPAL	RESOLVED BY ALL THOSE AFFECTED
39. In your school, how are conflicts between departments usually resolved?	① ②	③ ④	⑤ ⑥	⑦ ⑧
	VERY LITTLE	SOME	QUITE A BIT	A VERY GREAT DEAL
40. How much do teachers in your school encourage each other to do their best?	① ②	③ ④	⑤ ⑥	⑦ ⑧
	EVERY ONE FOR SELF	LITTLE COOPERATIVE TEAMWORK	A MODERATE AMOUNT OF COOPERATIVE TEAMWORK	A VERY GREAT AMOUNT OF COOPERATIVE TEAMWORK
41. In your school, is it "every one for self" or do principals, teachers, and students work as a team?	① ②	③ ④	⑤ ⑥	⑦ ⑧
	VERY LITTLE	SOME	QUITE A BIT	A VERY GREAT DEAL
42. How much do different departments plan together and coordinate their efforts?	① ②	③ ④	⑤ ⑥	⑦ ⑧
E. Character of Decision-Making Processes:	RARELY	SOMETIMES	OFTEN	VERY OFTEN
43. How often do you seek and use students' ideas about academic matters, such as their work, course content, teaching plans and methods?	① ②	③ ④	⑤ ⑥	⑦ ⑧
44. How often do you seek and use students' ideas about non-academic matters, such as student activities, rules of conduct, and discipline?	① ②	③ ④	⑤ ⑥	⑦ ⑧
	VIEWED WITH GREAT SUSPICION	SOME VIEWED WITH SUSPICION, SOME WITH TRUST	USUALLY VIEWED WITH TRUST	ALMOST ALWAYS VIEWED WITH TRUST
How do students view communication from:				
45. you	① ②	③ ④	⑤ ⑥	⑦ ⑧
46. the principal	① ②	③ ④	⑤ ⑥	⑦ ⑧
	NOT WELL	SOMEWHAT WELL	QUITE WELL	VERY WELL
47. How well do you know the problems faced by students in their school work?	① ②	③ ④	⑤ ⑥	⑦ ⑧
	VERY LITTLE	SOME	CONSIDER-ABLE	VERY GREAT
48. To what extent is the communication between you and your students open and candid?	① ②	③ ④	⑤ ⑥	⑦ ⑧
49. To what extent does the principal give you useful information and ideas?	① ②	③ ④	⑤ ⑥	⑦ ⑧
	FROM THE TOP DOWN	MOSTLY DOWN	DOWN AND UP	DOWN, UP AND LATERALLY
50. What is the direction of the flow of information about academic and non-academic school matters?	① ②	③ ④	⑤ ⑥	⑦ ⑧

FIGURE B *Continued*

Organizational Variable	System 1	System 2	System 3	System 4
		SOME VIEWED WITH SUSPICION, SOME WITH TRUST		
	VIEWED WITH GREAT SUSPICION		USUALLY VIEWED WITH TRUST	ALMOST ALWAYS VIEWED WITH TRUST
51. How do you view communications from the principal?	① ②	③ ④	⑤ ⑥	⑦ ⑧
	USUALLY INACCURATE	OFTEN INACCURATE	FAIRLY ACCURATE	ALMOST ALWAYS ACCURATE
52. How accurate is upward communication to the principal?	① ②	③ ④	⑤ ⑥	⑦ ⑧
	NOT WELL	SOMEWHAT WELL	QUITE WELL	VERY WELL
53. How well does the principal know the problems faced by the teachers?	① ②	③ ④	⑤ ⑥	⑦ ⑧
To what extent is communication open and candid:	VERY LITTLE	SOME	CONSIDER-ABLE	A VERY GREAT DEAL
54. between principal and teachers	① ②	③ ④	⑤ ⑥	⑦ ⑧
55. among teachers	① ②	③ ④	⑤ ⑥	⑦ ⑧
	VERY LITTLE	SOME	QUITE A BIT	A VERY GREAT DEAL
56. How much help do you get from the central staff of your school system?	① ②	③ ④	⑤ ⑥	⑦ ⑧
	VERY LITTLE	SOME	QUITE A BIT	A VERY GREAT DEAL
57. How much are students involved in major decisions affecting them?	① ②	③ ④	⑤ ⑥	⑦ ⑧
	AT MUCH TOO HIGH LEVELS	AT SOMEWHAT TOO HIGH LEVELS	AT QUITE SATISFAC-TORY LEVELS	AT THE BEST LEVELS
58. Are decisions made at the best levels for effective performance?	① ②	③ ④	⑤ ⑥	⑦ ⑧
	VERY LITTLE	SOME	CONSIDER-ABLE	VERY GREAT
59. To what extent are you involved in major decisions related to your work?	① ②	③ ④	⑤ ⑥	⑦ ⑧
60. To what extent are decision makers aware of problems, particularly at lower levels?	① ②	③ ④	⑤ ⑥	⑦ ⑧
F. Character of Goal Setting:				
61. To what extent does the principal make sure that planning and setting priorities are done well?	① ②	③ ④	⑤ ⑥	⑦ ⑧
G. Character of Control Processes:	HIGHLY AUTHORI-TARIAN	SOMEWHAT AUTHORI-TARIAN	CONSUL-TATIVE	PARTICI-PATIVE GROUP
What is the administrative style of:				
62. the principal	① ②	③ ④	⑤ ⑥	⑦ ⑧
63. the superintendent of schools	① ②	③ ④	⑤ ⑥	⑦ ⑧
How competent is the principal:	NOT COMPETENT	SOMEWHAT COMPETENT	QUITE COMPETENT	VERY COMPETENT
64. as an administrator	① ②	③ ④	⑤ ⑥	⑦ ⑧
65. as an educator	① ②	③ ④	⑤ ⑥	⑦ ⑧
H. Performance Goals:	VERY LITTLE	SOME	CONSIDER-ABLE	VERY GREAT
66. To what extent does the principal try to provide you with the materials, equipment and space you need to do your job well?	① ②	③ ④	⑤ ⑥	⑦ ⑧
	VERY LITTLE	SOME	QUITE A BIT	A VERY GREAT DEAL
67. How much do you feel that the principal is interested in your success as a teacher?	① ②	③ ④	⑤ ⑥	⑦ ⑧
68. How much interest do students feel you have in their success as students?	① ②	③ ④	⑤ ⑥	⑦ ⑧
69. How much does the principal try to help you with your problems?	① ②	③ ④	⑤ ⑥	⑦ ⑧
70. To what extent do students accept high performance goals in your school?	① ②	③ ④	⑤ ⑥	⑦ ⑧
	INADEQUATE	SOMEWHAT INADEQUATE	QUITE ADEQUATE	VERY ADEQUATE
71. How adequate are the supplies and equipment the school has?	① ②	③ ④	⑤ ⑥	⑦ ⑧
	LOW	ABOUT AVERAGE	QUITE HIGH	VERY HIGH
72. How high are the principal's goals for educational performance?	① ②	③ ④	⑤ ⑥	⑦ ⑧

FIGURE B *Continued*

FIGURE C Profile of a School Scoring Sheet

Item	System 1		System 2		System 3		System 4	
1	1	2	3	4	5	6	7	8
2	1	2	3	4	5	6	7	8
3	1	2	3	4	5	6	7	8
4	1	2	3	4	5	6	7	8
5	1	2	3	4	5	6	7	8
6	1	2	3	4	5	6	7	8
7	1	2	3	4	5	6	7	8
8	1	2	3	4	5	6	7	8
9	1	2	3	4	5	6	7	8
10	1	2	3	4	5	6	7	8
11	1	2	3	4	5	6	7	8
12	1	2	3	4	5	6	7	8
13	1	2	3	4	5	6	7	8
14	1	2	3	4	5	6	7	8
15	1	2	3	4	5	6	7	8
16	1	2	3	4	5	6	7	8
17	1	2	3	4	5	6	7	8
18	1	2	3	4	5	6	7	8
19	1	2	3	4	5	6	7	8
20	1	2	3	4	5	6	7	8
21	1	2	3	4	5	6	7	8
22	1	2	3	4	5	6	7	8
23	1	2	3	4	5	6	7	8
24	1	2	3	4	5	6	7	8
25	1	2	3	4	5	6	7	8
26	1	2	3	4	5	6	7	8
27	1	2	3	4	5	6	7	8
28	1	2	3	4	5	6	7	8
29	1	2	3	4	5	6	7	8
30	1	2	3	4	5	6	7	8
31	1	2	3	4	5	6	7	8
32	1	2	3	4	5	6	7	8
33	1	2	3	4	5	6	7	8
34	1	2	3	4	5	6	7	8
35	1	2	3	4	5	6	7	8
36	1	2	3	4	5	6	7	8
37	1	2	3	4	5	6	7	8
38	1	2	3	4	5	6	7	8
39	1	2	3	4	5	6	7	8
40	1	2	3	4	5	6	7	8
41	1	2	3	4	5	6	7	8
42	1	2	3	4	5	6	7	8
43	1	2	3	4	5	6	7	8
44	1	2	3	4	5	6	7	8
45	1	2	3	4	5	6	7	8
46	1	2	3	4	5	6	7	8
47	1	2	3	4	5	6	7	8
48	1	2	3	4	5	6	7	8
49	1	2	3	4	5	6	7	8
50	1	2	3	4	5	6	7	8

Continued

FIGURE C *Continued*

Item	System 1		System 2		System 3		System 4	
51	1	2	3	4	5	6	7	8
52	1	2	3	4	5	6	7	8
53	1	2	3	4	5	6	7	8
54	1	2	3	4	5	6	7	8
55	1	2	3	4	5	6	7	8
56	1	2	3	4	5	6	7	8
57	1	2	3	4	5	6	7	8
58	1	2	3	4	5	6	7	8
59	1	2	3	4	5	6	7	8
60	1	2	3	4	5	6	7	8
61	1	2	3	4	5	6	7	8
62	1	2	3	4	5	6	7	8
63	1	2	3	4	5	6	7	8
64	1	2	3	4	5	6	7	8
65	1	2	3	4	5	6	7	8
66	1	2	3	4	5	6	7	8
67	1	2	3	4	5	6	7	8
68	1	2	3	4	5	6	7	8
69	1	2	3	4	5	6	7	8
70	1	2	3	4	5	6	7	8
71	1	2	3	4	5	6	7	8
72	1	2	3	4	5	6	7	8

responses represent average responses for the entire faculty. Based on the scoring profile that you prepare, what improvements need to be made in the climate of this school?

An important strength of the POS is that climate is not conceived as the product of only the principal's behavior or of any other single source. As one reads the items, it becomes clear that climates are based on a mix of attitudes, beliefs, and behaviors of everyone who lives and works in the school. They are manifestations of the school's culture. This being the case, school improvement efforts require that teachers and principals work together. Striving toward a System 4 climate, for example, requires a shared commitment. As you review the climate profile of the school you evaluated, what ideas come to mind as to how you as principal (and the faculty whose responses are represented by your responses) can plan to work together to improve the school?

References

Likert, Rensis. 1961. *New Patterns of Management.* New York: McGraw-Hill.

Likert, Rensis. 1967. *The Human Organization: Its Management and Value.* New York: McGraw-Hill.

Appendix 13.2   Quality of Work Life in Teaching Scoring Form

Instructions: Transfer your answers to the questions on the QWLinT instrument (Exhibit 13.1) to the scoring grid below, circling the number below the letter of the answer you selected. When you have transferred all answers and circled the appropriate numbers, add up all the numbers circled in each of the columns and enter the total in the empty box at the bottom of the column. Each of these totals refers to one of the scales of the QWLinT. Note that high scores for autonomy, personal growth, work complexity, and task-related interaction indicate a strong presence of these characteristics and suggest high job-enrichment opportunities in one's job. High scores for work speed and routine indicate a weak presence of this characteristic and low job enrichment.

Q.1	Q.2	Q.3	Q.4	Q.5
A M P N 1 2 3 4	A M P N 4 3 2 1	A M P N 1 2 3 4	A M P N 1 2 3 4	A M P N 4 3 2 1
Q.6	**Q.7**	**Q.8**	**Q.9**	**Q.10**
A M P N 4 3 2 1	A M P N 4 3 2 1	A M P N 1 2 3 4	A M P N 1 2 3 4	A M P N 1 2 3 4
Q.11	**Q.12**	**Q.13**	**Q.14**	**Q.15**
A M P N 1 2 3 4	A M P N 4 3 2 1	A M P N 1 2 3 4	A M P N 4 3 2 1	A M P N 4 3 2 1
Q.16	**Q.17**	**Q.18**	**Q.19**	**Q.20**
A M P N 4 3 2 1	A M P N 4 3 2 1	A M P N 4 3 2 1	A M P N 1 2 3 4	A M P N 4 3 2 1
Q.21	**Q.22**	**Q.23**	**Q.24**	**Q.25**
A M P N 4 3 2 1	A M P N 4 3 2 1	A M P N 1 2 3 4	A M P N 1 2 3 4	A M P N 4 3 2 1
Autonomy	Personal Growth Opportunity	Work* Speed and Routine	Work Complexity	Task-Related Interaction

Scale Score Interpretation:
5 to 9, low job enrichment
10 to 15, moderate job enrichment
16 to 20, high job enrichment

---

*High scores for work speed and routine indicate low job enrichment.

14

THE CHANGE PROCESS

Schools in the United States and Canada are busy changing: New standards have been mandated, curriculum is being developed that is aligned with these standards, assessments follow to complete the instructional delivery package, and everywhere teachers are being trained in how to teach to the test, to align things to get students ready, to adapt mandates to local situations, to beef up their subject-matter knowledge so they can competently teach to higher standards, and to learn new pedagogies. Despite this frenzy of change activity, one wonders what is really going on. Are teachers changing their practice for the better? Are students better off? Will the changes of the nineties sustain themselves over time? Do the things that have changed the most really matter the most?

Some schools, provinces, and states, for example, can point to sharp increases in student test scores as a result of changes introduced to help students meet "world-class standards." But are the gains achieved indicators that students are learning to use their minds well? Are they able to problem solve, particularly when confronted with new information? Are they more self-sufficient learners able to tackle new tasks? We don't know the answers to these questions. Though many changes have been introduced, though schools appear to be doing things differently, and though higher test scores indicate some improvements in learning—at least in what is being tested—real changes come hard. Adopting changes is not the same as implementing changes and implementing changes may not produce the intended results.

More than Adoption, More than Implementation

Much of the literature on change in schools assumes that adoption is the same as implementation. The two, however, are different (Gaynor, 1975). Schools frequently adopt innovations that are not implemented or, if implemented, innovations are shaped to the way things were to the point that the "change is hardly noticeable." The open-space concept, popular during the late 1960s and early 1970s, is an example. "Implementation" of open space was characterized by carving schools into traditional classrooms through the use of bookcases, room dividers, lockers, and other partitions. Goodlad and Klein (1970) make a similar observation with respect to the adoption of team teaching and the ungraded classroom concept. Frequently, implementation was characterized by "turn" teaching and the creation of grades within grades. From your own experiences you probably know of a junior high school that has adopted, but not really implemented, the middle school concept. In a similar vein, today's standards movement is intended to ensure a broad yet deep education for students. Yet, the standards, curriculum, and assessment changes seem to be narrowing the curriculum and limiting what is learned.

Sometimes changes have unanticipated consequences that, when forced on the system, make things worse than they were. Site-based management, for example, has been widely adopted, but instead of becoming a means to help us get somewhere, it often is an end in itself. Not only can site-based management become a non-event in the teaching and learning life of the school but it can also create problems. Lichtenstein, McLaughlin, and Knudsen (1992) explain:

> We observed and read about instances in which site-based authority resulted in little of consequence in the classroom. Rather than feeling empowered to exercise greater authority in their teaching, many teachers found their time bound up with committees wrestling with decisions about what color to make the curtain on the auditorium stage, or whether to spend $500.00 on a slide projector or bookcases. In some cases, we discovered that "restructuring" mandates provided weak school administrators an excuse to delegate significant responsibilities to teachers who then floundered because of insufficient orientation, resources, support, and expertise. Further, we saw instances where efforts to expand teacher's authority without also attending to their capacity resulted in the ironic outcome of diminished performance of school, classroom, or system. (39)

Too often, changes are introduced that contradict each other. As a result, they raise havoc and cause confusion. Espousing Deming's (1993) philosophy and touting "Total Quality Management" (TQM) or using TQM to create "The Quality School" are good examples. Deming rarely uses the word *quality* in his writing and lectures, and does not recommend its use. Furthermore, the notion of totally managing something is alien to him. To Deming, the secret is not to manage for control (the word *management*, for example, is derived from the Latin word *manus* and its Italian cousin *maneggio*, which means the training or handling of a horse), but to honor variation. He takes exception to the use of the word *customer* in educational settings. Unlike most appliers of TQM to practice, Deming believes that one cannot view his 14 principles as a buffet of ideas from which one picks and chooses only the ideas that are liked. Deming's ideas comprise a whole and must be applied as a whole. That means the slogan *TQM* has to be dropped because slogans are out. It means that grading and testing students as well as evaluating teachers, honor rolls, and other student rankings cannot be used because they violate two of his principles (eliminating work standards on the one hand and extrinsic rewards on the other).

At times, Deming's ideas are packaged together with other movements, such as Outcomes-Based Education (OBE) or today's standards movement. But like oil and water, Deming's philosophy and theses approaches cannot be readily mixed. In OBE, process is not important; one must focus on outcomes and let process take care of itself. People are free to do whatever they want as long as the job gets done. The only requirement is to "design down" what you do from the outcomes. To Deming, outcomes are part of the problem; his answer is to focus on process. It is the activity of teaching and learning, the curriculum, the classroom climate, and the numerous social contracts that are struck between teachers and students, among teachers, and among students that count the most. Tend to these and the outcomes will take care of themselves. No wonder change comes so hard—new ideas are accompanied by mixed signals. Too often, new ideas come in prepackaged forms and are marketed as if they were a new breakfast food.

Even successful implementation of a change in schooling is not enough. School improvement requires that such implementation be sustained over time; this, in turn, requires that the change be institutionalized. Institutionalization means that the change is "built in" to the life of the school (Miles, 1983). As Huberman and Crandall (1982) point out: "New practices that get built into the training, regulatory, staffing, and budgetary cycles survive, others don't. Innovations are highly perishable goods" (cited in Miles, 1983:14). Institutionalization is a process of making a change routine; it becomes part of the ordinary life of the school. Changes requiring new dollars, for example, become institutionalized when these new dollars become regularly budgeted dollars. Changes requiring new structural arrangements become institutionalized when regular school policies are revised to reflect these arrangements. Changes requiring new patterns of behavior become institutionalized when the regular reward system (salary, promotions, psychological rewards) is adjusted to reflect these patterns. Institutionalization cannot be taken for granted. Thus, school improvement requires that adoption, implementation, *and* institutionalization become the principal's goals.

The "One-Best-Way" Problem

For every successful school improvement effort, one hears horror stories about unsuccessful efforts. One reason for failure, beyond lack of management and leadership effort by the principal, is a limited view of what the process of change involves. Unsuccessful school improvement efforts tend to put "all their eggs in one basket" by using a one-best-way to approach the problem.

Some experts advocate engineering the social and political context within which the school exists in an effort to provide the necessary support and momentum for change (see, for example, Baldridge, 1971; Gaynor, 1975). Other experts emphasize the development of favorable school climates that provide the necessary interpersonal support for change. In recent years, scholars from this group have focused on the concept of school culture and have emphasized the importance of developing values and norms that include the proposed changes (Likert, 1967; Sergiovanni and Corbally, 1984). Still other experts concentrate almost exclusively on the individual and her or his needs, dispositions, stages of concern for the proposed change, and the driving and restraining forces that pull and tug, causing resistance to the change (Bennis, Benne, and Chin, 1969; Reddin, 1970). Finally, some experts give primary attention to engineering the work context as a means to program and structure teacher behavior to ensure that the school improvement effort is implemented properly (Hunter, 1984). All these concerns are important, but none alone is an adequate model for school improvement.

A Systems View of Change

When one brings together each of these concerns, a systems view begins to emerge—one that provides a dynamic, integrative, and powerful view of change. Within this view, the unit of change is not limited to the individual teacher, the school, the work flow of teaching and schooling, or the broader political and administrative context. Instead, the four are viewed as interacting units of change, all requiring attention. When attended to properly, these units of change are the roads to successful school improvement.

The systems view is depicted in Figure 14.1. Note that the direct road to changes relating to teaching and learning is through structuring the work flow of schooling. However, teaching is human-intensive, which means that regardless of how hard one might try to introduce change, teachers cannot be ignored. They count, whether one wants them to or not. They make the day-to-day and minute-to-minute decisions influencing what happens to students. For changes in the work flow of teaching to count, they must be directly linked to changes in teaching behavior, and this inevitably means changes in the attitudes and beliefs of individual teachers and the faculty as a whole. Teaching and learning change as teachers change.

Teachers typically work alone. This isolation has telling negative consequences on teaching effectiveness and school improvement (Lieberman and Miller, 1984; Rosenholtz, 1989). Still, teachers are members of social groups that make up the larger school faculty. Social groups create norms, customs, and traditions that define ways of living. *School culture* is the term often used to refer to the sense of order and being that emerges. School culture defines what is of worth for teachers, specifies acceptable limits of behavior and beliefs, and is a powerful factor in promoting or resisting school improvement efforts (Saranson, 1971).

Schools do not exist in isolation; thus, another dimension of importance in the school improvement process is the broader administrative, social, and political environment. School climates, for example, are influenced by actions and attitudes of the teachers' union, the school board, and central office school district administrators (Kirst, 1984). Influences from this political system trickle down from the school level to the individual teacher and finally to the work flow. All four levels—individual, school, work flow, and political context—are interacting units of change needing attention as principals promote school improvement. Deep, continuous, meaningful, and effective change cannot be just top down or just bottom up. In the following sections, each of the four units of change is examined more closely.

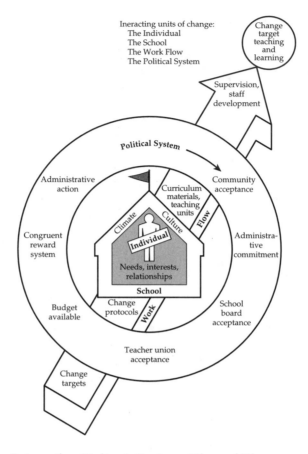

FIGURE 14.1   Interacting Units: A Systems View of Change

The Individual as the Unit of Change

When considering the individual teacher as the unit of change, needs, values, beliefs, and levels of readiness are important. Change is often frightening. So much is at stake as present circumstances, norms, and ways of operation are threatened. Before most teachers are able to examine the worth of a proposed new idea for improving teaching and learning, they are apt to view this idea selfishly. The first reaction is likely to be: How will this proposed change affect me? For example, the prospect of family grouping, team teaching, or a new pattern of organization (e.g., school within the school or middle school) raises such questions in teachers' minds as: How will my relationship with other teachers change? How will my view of myself change? How will my authority over students and my influence in the school change? How will the amount of work I do change? How will my relationship with parents and administrators change? Will I be more or less successful as a teacher? Who will be the team leader or master teacher? What will other teachers think of me as a person? What will other teachers think of me as a teacher?

These questions reflect concerns that are normal and that deserve answering. Unless these human concerns are adequately resolved, continued emphasis on educational and other job-related aspects of the change will likely increase anxiety and promote skepticism. Principals react similarly when faced with the prospects of change, as do professors and superintendents. Healthy individuals are naturally concerned with how changes will affect them, their work, and their relationships with others; all these concerns require attention.

For some time, researchers have been interested in the concerns of teachers and how these concerns focus their attention on a limited range of issues relating to change (Fuller, 1969; Hall and Loucks, 1978; Hord et al., 1987). This work has led to the development of the "concern-based adoption model," which describes the changing feelings of people as they learn about a proposed change, prepare to use it, use it, and modify it as a result. The model proposes seven stages of concern as follows (Hall and Loucks, 1978):

1. Awareness   I am not concerned about it.
2. Informational   I would like to know more about it.
3. Personal   How will using it affect me?
4. Management   I seem to be spending all my time getting material ready.
5. Consequence   How is my use affecting my students?
6. Collaboration   I am concerned about relating what I am doing with what other teachers are doing.
7. Refocusing   I have some ideas about something that would work even better.

The developers of the model do not maintain that every teacher marches through all the stages beginning with awareness and ending with refocusing or that the stages are mutually exclusive with only one being tended to at a time. The stages do, however, represent the general kind of development that takes place as changes are adopted and used on a continuous basis. They are therefore developmental *in nature* rather than being strictly developmental.

The progression of concerns seems to follow this pattern. In the early stages of a change effort, teachers are likely to have self-concerns that center on learning more about the proposed change and how the change will affect them personally. Once these concerns are taken care of, they tend next to focus on the management problems they are likely to face as they begin to implement the change. Next, their attention shifts to the impact the change is likely to have on their students and, as this change is remediated, to issues of collaboration with other teachers in an effort to implement the change and to improve its effects. Finally, because teachers are different and their situations are varied, adaptions are made in the change in an effort to improve its fit.

Principals and others who are interested in promoting change can use the concern-based model as a general framework for evaluating where various individuals are with respect to change concerns and for matching their own strategies to these levels. It makes little sense, for example, to spend an inordinate amount of time worrying about management concerns or consequences that a particular change is likely to have for students when teachers are still pretty much focused on such personal concerns as whether they will indeed be able to successfully adopt the change, how it will affect their relationships with other teachers, and so forth.

Resistance to change occurs when one's basic work needs are threatened. Although individual differences among teachers exist in the relative importance of specific work needs, four fairly universal needs can be identified (Mealiea, 1978):

1. *The Need for Clear Expectations.* Most of us require fairly specific information about our jobs to function effectively. We need to know what is expected of us, how we fit into the total scheme of things, what our responsibilities are, how we will be evaluated, and what our relationships with others will be. Without such information, our performance is likely to decline and our job satisfaction will be lessened (Katz and Kahn, 1978). Change upsets this "equilibrium" of role definition and expectations.

2. *The Need for Future Certainty.* Closely related to knowing how we fit into the job system is being able to predict the future. We need to have some reliability and certainty built into our work lives to provide us with security and allow us to plan ahead (Coffer and Appley, 1964). Change introduces ambiguity and uncertainty, which threaten our need for a relatively stable, balanced, and predictable work environment.

3. *The Need for Social Interaction.* Most of us value and need opportunities to interact with others. This interaction helps us to define and build our own self-concepts and to reduce anxiety and fear we experience in the work environment. We seek support and acceptance from others at work. Change is often perceived as threatening to these important social interaction patterns, and the prospects of establishing new patterns can present us with security problems. Collaborative cultures and communities of practice have been persistent themes in this book and both are powerful means to promote the support and direction teachers need for learning. Learning, in return, is a prerequisite for changing.

4. *The Need for Control over Our Work Environment and Work Events.* Most of us want and seek a reasonable degree of control over our work environment (Argyris, 1957). We do not wish to be at the mercy of this system. As suggested in the last chapter, we want to be Origins and not Pawns (De Charms, 1968) when it comes to making decisions that affect our work lives.

When control is threatened or reduced, the net effect for teachers is not only less job satisfaction but also a loss of meaning in work that can result in job indifference and even alienation. Change efforts that do not involve teachers and changes that threaten to lessen their control over teaching, learning, and other aspects of schooling can have serious consequences for school effectiveness.

Teachers vary in the intensity with which the four universal needs are held. The greater the intensity, the more likely change threats will be felt. Still, for all teachers, change will likely create some disturbance in their present situation. Principals can help get teachers back onto a more comfortable and stable course by providing as much relevant information as possible about the change and how it affects the work of teaching. Teachers need to know what will be expected of them as the change is put into operation. This theme will be discussed further, when the work flow as the unit of change is considered. Allowing—indeed, welcoming—teacher participation in planning the proposed change will help provide for these needs and will very likely result in ideas about how to improve the proposal. Keeping the proposed change simple and implementing aspects of the change gradually will increase teachers' confidence in themselves as successful implementers.

Mealiea (1978) suggests that changes be accompanied by a nonevaluation period during which the teacher's performance cannot have a negative effect on income, career ladder promotion, or other school benefits. During this period, the emphasis would be solely on providing feedback to teachers to help them learn more about the change and to increase proficiency in implementing the change. Directing change efforts first to teachers who might be considered as role models and who optimally would become early adopters of the change can be helpful to successful school improvement. If teachers who are widely respected by others are moving ahead with the change, a certain confidence and calm are likely to occur and resistance is likely to be lessened.

The School as the Unit of Change

Concentrating on individual teachers as units of change is important, but many experts maintain that too much emphasis has been given to this level. The well-known social psychologists Daniel Katz and Robert Kahn (1978) state: "Attempts to change organizations by changing individuals have a long history of theoretical inadequacy and practical failure. Both stem from a disregard of the systematic properties of organizations and from the confusion of individual changes with modifications in organizational variables" (658).

Katz and Kahn believe that individuals and individual behavior remain important in change considerations but take on different qualities and meanings when viewed within the context of the group. Consider, for example, recent interactions you had with your supervisor one to one and in a group context. In many respects, you were two different persons. Many individuals, for example, feel more an equal with supervisors when interacting within a group context rather than interacting on a one-to-one basis.

The school as a community needs to be considered as an important unit of change. Schools have cultures and these cultures are governed by the webs of meaning and the customs, rituals, and other patterns of life that teachers create. A culture is manifested in norm systems that determine what it is that people think, believe, and do.

The distinguished sociologist Willard Waller (1932) pointed out the following many years ago:

> *Schools have a culture that is definitely their own. There are, in the school, complex rituals of personal relationships, a set of folk ways, mores, and irrational sanctions, a moral code based on them. There are games, which are sublimated wars, teams,*

and an elaborate set of ceremonies concerning them.There are traditions, and traditionalists waging their world-old battle against innovators. (103)

Lieberman and Miller (1984) identified four themes within the school culture—rhythms, rules, interactions, and feelings—that are played out in the daily lives of teachers. The elementary school teaching day, for example, has morning activities, lunch hour, afternoon activities, recess, and so forth. Bells ring in the high school to signal the passing of classes. The school day is divided into periods or hours, with collections of hours comprising courses. Within each class period, a universal routine is followed. Attendance is taken, new material is introduced, and then homework is assigned for the next day. This routine is repeated five times a day, five days a week, four weeks a month for nine months. Soon, teachers become such a part of this daily rhythm that a proposed change in any part of it upsets the whole, and this is often too much to take. In many respects, teachers become victims of the rhythm of the day, the week, the month, and the school year. Although they may want to escape the rhythm, they simply are not able to.

Lieberman and Miller point out that teaching has its rules, both codified and informal. Codified rules are stated up front and informal ones are held tacitly. Teachers, for example, must keep their distance from students to maintain a certain objectivity that enables them to deliver expert services fairly and equitably. Prime among the rules is for teachers to be practical and to be private.

Practical knowledge in schools is defined in terms of its opposites. Being practical is the opposite of being theoretical; being practical is the opposite of being idealistic. . . . New teachers in search of practical knowledge, then, must reject the university professors who train them as well as their own tendencies to seek ideal solutions to difficult problems. Practical knowledge is lodged in the experiences and practices of teachers at work in their classrooms. (Lieberman and Miller, 1984:7)

Ideas are practical when they have immediate application, when they are offered by practical people, and when they address such practical problems as discipline, attendance, order, and achievement.

The norm of privatism runs deep within the school culture. Lieberman and Miller point out that new teachers learn their place in the school quickly and learn to keep their practice to themselves. "What does private mean? It means not sharing experiences about teaching, about classes, about students, about perceptions" (Lieberman and Miller, 1984:8).

The norms of practicality and privatism limit the depth and scope of interactions that teachers have. There is little opportunity for teachers to visit among themselves. All that is left are the interactions that they have with their students, and from these they must derive any rewards that they experience. The accumulated effects of the rhythms, rules, and interactions that characterize the daily lives of teachers takes its toll on feelings. There is conflict, frustration, satisfaction, joy, self-doubt, vulnerability, and uncertainty.

In accounting for the changes we need in the teaching workforce for schools to pursue more vigorously school improvement goals, Lieberman and Miller (1999:24) propose the development of *new social realities of teaching* as follows:

From	*To*
Individualism	Professional community
Teaching at the center	Learning at the center
Technical work	Inquiry into practice
Controlled work	Accountability
Managed work	Leadership
Classroom concerns	Whole-school concerns and beyond
A weak knowledge base	A broad knowledge base

These transformations, Lieberman and Miller argue, are occurring as school staffs reorganize their world and their work. Key is the shift from principal leadership based on bureaucratic authority and personal authority to a leadership based on ideas, values, common commitments, and common quests that is shared by everyone.

Deal (1987) points out that there is a basic contradiction between culture and change. Culture, he argues, is something people invent in order to find meaning. Its purpose is to provide stability, certainty, and predictability. Meaning is derived through symbols that create a sense of control. Change challenges all of this; it threatens to eat away at the very essence of what culture is supposed to do for people. In a sense, change requires the creation of a new culture, and that is difficult to accomplish. Deal points out that in order to create a new culture we have to struggle with the loss of the old. This involves re-creating the history of the school and articulating new shared values and conceptions, while at the same time celebrating the old in ceremonies that enable them to be let go. Little will be accomplished in dealing with culture without addressing the school itself as the unit of change.

The Work Flow as the Unit of Change

Change experts who focus their efforts almost entirely on the individual and school as units of change are often successful in promoting adoption of a school improvement idea but not in implementing it. Adoption goals create the necessary readiness and enthusiasm for change and result from a bit of salespersonship on the one hand and psychological reassurance on the other. Too often, however, enthusiasm wanes, teachers experience frustration with implementation attempts, and the proposed change is modified to resemble the familiar "business as usual" or abandoned entirely. Focusing almost exclusively on the individual or the school or the two in combination results in "up-front" commitment (Crandall, 1983:7), but this commitment may not be expanded or sustained as teachers begin to put the change into practice. Up-front commitment, of course, is important because it gets us into the water. Now we need help learning how to swim differently, and this requires that we focus on the work flow as the unit of change.

Work flow focus *builds commitment during and after teachers are actually engaged in new practices* (Crandall, 1983). Sure, change is facilitated when teachers believe in what they are doing, but belief in the value of a change increases, as well, when it is successfully implemented. This interaction is missed if we take an either-or stance on this issue. That is why both top down and bottom up change, gracefully interwoven and sensitively implemented, is a principal's best bet.

No secrets are involved in focusing on the work flow. The process is simple and direct. It involves making known specifically what is to be accomplished; defining carefully how this will be accomplished; giving specific attention to what teachers will actually be doing that is different; providing the necessary teaching apparatus, equipment, and curriculum materials; and providing the necessary ongoing training, assistance, supervision, and evaluation for ensuring that teachers' attempts to implement the change will be successful. Sometimes changes have unanticipated consequences that when forced on the system make things worse than they were.

The dimensions of the work flow requiring attention from principals can be summarized as follows:

1. *The Change Goal.* This is what the school wants to accomplish.
2. *The Change Targets.* These are practical and operational definitions, descriptions, and examples of the goal.
3. *The Change Protocols.* These are practical and operational definitions, descriptions, and examples of arrangements and behaviors that need to be provided or articulated to reach targets.
4. *The Curriculum and Teaching Requirements.* These are the curriculum and teaching materials and units that teachers will need for them to work differently and successfully.
5. *The Supervisory and Staff Development Support.* This is the help teachers will need before they begin the process of change and while the process of change continues.

As suggested in the last chapter, expectancy theory of motivation can help us understand the importance of the dimensions of the work flow. According to expectancy theory, before motivation to change occurs, teachers need answers to the following questions:

1. Do I know what it is that needs to be accomplished?
2. Are the benefits of accomplishment important to me and desired by me?
3. Do I have a clear idea of exactly what it is that I need to do to accomplish this?
4. Should I attempt accomplishment; will I be successful?

A "no" answer to any of these questions means that teachers will not be motivated to participate in the school improvement effort. "Yes" answers that result in motivation depend on the attention principals give to the work flow as the unit of change. Particularly key is the supervisory support available to teachers to ensure successful implementation.

The Political System as the Unit of Change

Adoption and implementation are not the same as institutionalization of a change. Institutionalization occurs when the change is no longer viewed as an innovation; instead, it is considered part of the regular pattern of operation within the school and school district. Institutionalization requires changes in school district policies, rules, and procedures; actual budget allocations; school structural and administrative arrangements; and the official reward system that is made available to teachers. In school settings very few change attempts ever reach the institutional level; this explains, in part, why changes tend not to stick.

Principals are the main characters in bringing about adoption and implementation goals. They play key roles in planning and providing leadership for changes addressed to individuals, the school, and the work flow as units of change. Yet, when it comes to institutionalizing changes, they do not have much power. The reality is that principals will need the help of the superintendent and central office staff and, at the very least, the acquiescence of the school board and teachers' union. There is no way around this reality. The best of ideas and the most enthusiastic of responses to these ideas at the school level are not enough to make an adopted and implemented school improvement attempt a permanent fixture of the school.

It is common practice among the best school districts in the country for the superintendent and the central office staff to meet regularly with school principals. These meetings are typically held monthly, but often more frequently. They can last for a full day and often well into the evening. The purpose of the meetings is to exchange information and ideas about what is occurring in each of the schools. Principals are given an opportunity to update the superintendent and other administrators, including peers, on the last month's happenings in each school and to share plans for the next month. Superintendents and principals do not view these sessions as evaluation and review but as communication and assistance. Good ideas from schools become better ones as other principals and central office staff consider them. More importantly, these sessions allow the superintendent to "buy in" to local school improvement initiatives, and this buying in is the first step to ensure that the necessary support for institutionalization will be forthcoming.

Michael Fullan (1991) points out that adoption of a change does not occur without an advocate, and one of the most powerful advocates is the superintendent of schools with her or his staff in combination with the school board. This conclusion is supported by many other studies (e.g., Berman and McLaughlin, 1977, 1979).

Leadership for School Improvement

The systems view of change depicted in Figure 14.1 emphasizes interactions among individual teachers, the school, the work flow of teaching and learning, and the broader political context as units of change. This view represents a strategy map for planning school improvement efforts and for increasing the possibility that such efforts not only will be adopted but also implemented and institutionalized. Yet, the question remains: What should the principal do to help things along as each of the units of change is addressed? What are the *specific* principal behaviors associated with successful school improvement efforts?

Change Facilitator Styles

Let's begin our inquiry into this topic by describing the behavior of a principal whose school is, or has recently been, involved in a change effort. It is hard to separate all the aspects of a principal's change facilitator style from her or his general style or orientation; thus, you will want to focus on both the general style and the change style as we begin our analysis. What kind of leadership does the principal bring to the school? What does the leader stand for and how effective is she or he in communicating these standards to teachers? What kind of interpersonal leader is the principal? How does the principal work to facilitate change that will result in school improvement? Before continuing further, turn to the Change Facilitator Styles Inventory (CFSI), which appears as Appendix 14.1; following the directions, describe the principal you have been thinking about.

The CFSI is based on an extensive research program investigating links between principal behaviors and successful school improvements (Hall et al., 1983). This research was conducted at the Research and Development Center for Teacher Education at the University of Texas at Austin. The investigators were able to group principal leadership behaviors into three general change facilitator styles: Responder, Manager, and Initiator. These three styles correspond to the *R, M,* and *I* response categories on the CFSI and are described in the following extract (Hall and Rutherford, 1983):

> Responders *place heavy emphasis on allowing teachers and others the opportunity to take the lead. They believe their primary role is to maintain a smooth-running school by focusing on traditional administrative tasks, keeping teachers content, and treating students well. Teachers are viewed as strong professionals who are able to carry out their instructional role with little guidance. Responders emphasize the personal side of their relationships with teachers and others. Before they make decisions they often give everyone an opportunity to have input so as to weigh their feelings or to allow others to make the decision. A related characteristic is the tendency toward making decisions in terms of immediate circumstances rather than in terms of longer-range instructional or school goals. This seems to be due in part to their desire to please others and in part to their limited vision of how their school and staff should change in the future.*
>
> Managers *represent a broader range of behaviors. They demonstrate both responsive behaviors in answer to situations or people and they also initiate actions in support of the change effort. The variations in their behavior seem to be linked to their rapport with teachers and central office staff as well as how well they understand and buy into a particular change effort. Managers work without fanfare to provide basic support to facilitate teachers' use of the innovation. They keep teachers informed about decisions and are sensitive to teacher needs. They will defend their teachers from what are perceived as excessive demands. When they learn that the central office wants something to happen in their school, they then become very*

involved with their teachers in making it happen. Yet, they do not typically initiate attempts to move beyond the basics of what is imposed.

Initiators *have clear, decisive long-range policies and goals that transcend but include implementation of the current innovation. They tend to have very strong beliefs about what good schools and teaching should be like and work intensely to attain this vision. Decisions are made in relation to their goals for the school and in terms of what they believe to be best for students, which is based on current knowledge of classroom practice. Initiators have strong expectations for students, teachers, and themselves. They convey and monitor these expectations through frequent contacts with teachers and clear explication of how the school is to operate and how teachers are to teach. When they feel it is in the best interest of their school, particularly the students, Initiators will seek changes in district programs or policies or they will reinterpret them to suit the needs of the school. Initiators will be adamant but not unkind, they solicit input from staff and then decisions are made in terms of the goal of the school even if some are ruffled by their directness and high expectations. (84)*

Which of these general change facilitator styles best corresponds with your response patterns on the CFSI? Can you estimate which of these styles were most and least associated with successful school improvement efforts? Hall and Rutherford (1983) found that Initiator principals were more likely to be successful than were Manager and Responder principals. Responders were least likely to be successful. As you review the principal behavior descriptions on the CFSI associated with each of these styles, note that Initiators have a clear sense of what needs to be accomplished and take more active roles in planning, prodding, encouraging, advising, participating, checking, stimulating, monitoring, and evaluating change efforts. Furthermore, they assume more direct roles in obtaining and providing the necessary material and psychological support for successful change efforts. Initiators are able to empower the change process by both enabling and empowering teachers to be active in their change roles. To this end, they are neither laissez-faire supporters nor micromanagers of the change process.

Levels of Leadership Behavior

As a result of their research on principals at work, Leithwood and Montgomery (1986) identified four levels of leadership behavior, each with a different focus and style and each with different consequences for principal effectiveness. They found that the "higher" the level of principal behavior, the more effective the school. Effectiveness was defined as gains in student achievement in the "basics" and increases in student self-direction and problem solving.

Each of the levels represents increasingly complex and effective principalship behaviors. Principals functioning at level one, the *Administrator*, believe that it is the teacher's job to teach and the principal's job to run the school. Principals functioning at level two, the *Humanitarian*, believe that the basis of a sound education is a good interpersonal climate. Principals functioning at level three, the *Program Man-*

ager, believe that their job is to provide the best possible programs for students. Principals functioning at level four, the *Systematic Problem Solver*, are committed to doing whatever is necessary by way of invention and delivery in order to give students the best possible chance to learn. Program Managers and Systematic Problem Solvers both bring to their practice a focus on students, but Program Managers are largely committed to proper implementation of officially sanctioned goals and programs. They are more dependent on established guidelines, resources, and procedures than are Systematic Problem Solvers.

> *Systematic Problem Solvers are "bottom liners" virtually all of the time; the bottom line is the goals held for students by their school. Their focus is largely unconstrained by established practice and their client orientation leads them to the invention and delivery of whatever legitimate services are likely to realize the goals held by their school for students. (Leithwood and Montgomery, 1986:83)*

Important to Leithwood and Montgomery's formulation is the concept of level. What administrators do at level one is not necessarily ineffective, only less effective than the other three levels if this behavior pattern is dominant. Humanitarians at level two carry with them some of the Administrator's style but focus primarily on more complex behaviors that emphasize human relationships. Although more effective than Administrators, Humanitarians are not as effective as Program Managers. Program Managers bring aspects of the Administrator and Humanitarian style to their practice but focus primarily on more complex matters of educational program development and implementation. Finally, the strategic Problem Solvers focus primarily on students' success. This entrepreneurial stance is supported, nonetheless, by competent administrative, human relations, and program management skills.

Leithwood and Montgomery's research suggests that as principals come to view their jobs in more complex ways they become more effective operating at higher levels of practice. They recognize, of course, the important management demands in their job and the need to provide an environment that supports and enhances human relationships. Yet, neither management nor human relations processes are viewed as ends in themselves. They believe that process always serves substance. The substance of the school is defined by its educational programs and levels of commitment to teaching and learning. Yet, neither process nor substance can be viewed as something static, they are, instead, pursued in a context characterized by an array of demands, constraints, and choices. Realizing that expanding choices results in better schooling, principals at level four work for this expansion by taking a problem-solving, even entrepreneurial, approach to their leadership practice.

Some Ethical Questions

Principals often feel uncomfortable when they are asked to assume fairly direct roles in bringing about change. Change is, after all, a form of "social engineering";

and, as one becomes more skilled at bringing about change, ethical issues are naturally raised. Are we talking about leadership or are we really talking about manipulation? No easy answer exists to this question, but one thing is certain—principals have an obligation to provide leadership to the school, and this involves following a course of action leading to school improvement. The change agent role is therefore unavoidable.

Benne (1949) proposes a set of guidelines for principals to ensure that their change behavior is ethical. He believes that the engineering of change and the providing of pressure on groups and organizations to change must be collaborative. Collaboration suggests that principals and teachers form a change partnership, with each being aware of the intentions of others. Change intents are honest and straightforward. Teachers, for example, do not have to endure being "buttered up" today for the announced change of tomorrow.

First, the engineering of change should be educational to those involved in the process. "Educational" suggests that principals will try to help teachers become more familiar with the process of problem solving and changing so that they are less dependent on her or him. Giving a teacher a solution is not as educational as helping the teacher muddle through a problem. Second, the engineering of change should be experimental. "Experimental" implies that changes will not be implemented for keeps but will be adopted tentatively until they have proven their worth or until a better solution comes along.

Finally, engineering of change should be task-oriented; that is, controlled by the requirements of the problem and its effective solution rather than oriented to the maintenance or extension of prestige or power of the principal and others who are encouraging changes. Task orientation refers to one's primary motive for change. The principal should have job-related objectives in mind first—objectives that are concerned with improving teaching and learning for students. If such school improvement efforts are successful, the principal and others responsible for the change enjoy personal success and a certain amount of fame as well. These are the rewards for hard work, but they are not the reasons for bringing about the change in the first place. Principals who emphasize change to get attention from their supervisors or to improve their standing or influence in the school district may well be violating this ethical principle.

The Change Facilitating Team

This is a book for principals; therefore, it is natural to emphasize the principal's role and its significance in school improvement efforts. Yet, the principal cannot do it alone. In highlighting this issue, Hord, Hall, and Stiegelbauer (1983:1) point out: "This rhetoric, abundant in literature, quite obviously hangs like a heavy mantle on the principal. However, what is becoming equally certain and abundantly clear is that the principal does not bear the weight of leadership responsibility alone." Their research reveals that often one or two other key people in the school emerge as key change facilitators. As a result of their research on school improvement and analysis of the change literature, Loucks-Horsley and Hergert (1985:ix) conclude: "The principal is not *the* key to school improvement. Although the principal is important so are many other people." Teachers and supervisors have important roles to play, as do superintendents and specialists at the central office.

The research suggests that it may be more useful to view the principal as the leader of the change facilitating team (Hall, 1988), with as many as four change facilitators serving on the team. The principal, for example, might be viewed as the primary change facilitator. Very often, a second change facilitator (assistant principal, department chairperson, resource teacher, or teacher on a special assignment) was identified by the researcher. Frequently, a third level of change facilitator existed. Typically, facilitators at this level were teachers whose roles were less formalized but whose help was substantial and sought by their peers (Hord et al., 1987). This group of facilitators served the process of change primarily by modeling the use of the new practices, disseminating information to other teachers, cheerleading, and providing support. The principals who were most effective in implementing change were team-oriented, working closely with these other levels of change facilitators. Often, structures were built that allowed them to work together as a change facilitator team.

> In some schools, they may meet each week to review data about the school improvement process, generate ideas, and plan who will do what during the ensuing week. When they meet again, they debrief to ascertain what went well and what needs more attention. In other schools we observe a more hierarchical organization of facilitators: the first CF (the principal) appeared to interact only with the second CF, who in turn related to the third CF. All communications flowed through this "chain of command." Whether the team of CFs has a "flat" or horizontal collegial structure or a more hierarchical one, however, the important aspects to remember are what they need to do as group. (Hord et al., 1987:85)

These researchers identified even a fourth category, the *external facilitator*. Frequently, this role was filled by someone from the central office who served as a facilitative link between the office resources and the school.

The Meaning of Educational Change

One theme emerges from this discussion of the process of change. Although principals are important and their visions key in focusing attention on change and in successfully implementing the process of change, what counts in the end is bringing together the ideas and commitments of a variety of people who have a stake in the success of the school. As this process unfolds, principals can often find themselves on thin ice. They need to be clear about what it is that they want but cannot be so clear that they are providing people with road maps. They need to allow people to have an important say in shaping the direction of the school and deciding on the changes needed to get there, but they cannot be so detached that these individual aspirations remain more rhetorical than real. Michael Fullan (1991), after reviewing Lighthall's (1973) work, points out that there is strong support for the assertion that

> *leadership commitment to a particular version of a change is negatively related to ability to implement it. . . . Educational change is a process of coming to grips with the multiple realities of people who are the main participants in implementing change. The leader who presupposes what the change should be and acts in ways which preclude others' realities is bound to fail. (95)*

Key, of course, are the visions of teachers. If change is not responsive to the world of teaching as teachers experience it, it is likely to be viewed as irrelevant if not frivolous (Lortie, 1975). Fullan (1991) believes that the assumptions that principals and others make about change are key because they represent powerful, although frequently unconscious, sources of one's actions. His analysis of the process of change leads him to identify certain do's and don'ts assumptions as being basic to the successful implementation of educational change:

1. *Do not assume that your vision of what the change should be is the one that should or could be implemented. On the contrary, assume that one of the main purposes of the process of implementation is to exchange your reality of what should be through interaction with implementers and others concerned. Stated another way, assume that successful implementation consists of some transformation or continual development of initial ideas. (Particularly good discussions of the need for this assumption and the folly of ignoring it are contained in Lighthall, 1973; Morris, 1975, Ch. XVIII; Schön, 1971, Ch. 5; Louis & Miles, 1990).*
2. *Assume that any significant innovation, if it is to result in change, requires individual implementers to work out their own meaning. Significant change involves a certain amount of ambiguity, ambivalence, and uncertainty for the individual about the meaning of the change. Thus, effective implementation is a process of clarification. It is also important not to spend too much time in the early stages on needs assessment, program development, and problem definition activities—school staff have limited time. Clarification is likely to come in large part through practice (see Cohen, 1987; Loucks-Horsley & Hergert, 1985).*
3. *Assume that conflict and disagreement are not only inevitable but fundamental to successful change. Since any group of people possess multiple realities, any collective change attempt will necessarily involve conflict. Assumptions 2 and 3 combine to suggest that all successful efforts of significance, no matter how well planned, will experience an implementation dip in the early stages. Smooth implementation is often a sign that not much is really changing (Huberman & Miles, 1984).*
4. *Assume that people need pressure to change (even in directions that they desire), but it will be effective only under conditions that allow them to react,*

to form their own position, to interact with other implementers, to obtain technical assistance, etc. Unless people are going to be replaced with others who have different desired characteristics, relearning is at the heart of change.

5. Assume that effective change takes time. It is a process of "development in use." Unrealistic or undefined time lines fail to recognize that implementation occurs developmentally. Significant change in the form of implementing specific innovations can be expected to take a minimum of two or three years; bringing about institutional reforms can take five or more years. Persistence is a critical attribute of successful change.

6. Do not assume that the reason for lack of implementation is outright rejection of the values embodied in the change, or hard-core resistance to all change. Assume that there are a number of possible reasons: value rejection, inadequate resources to support implementation, insufficient time elapsed.

7. Do not expect all or even most people or groups to change. The complexity of change is such that it is impossible to bring about widespread reform in any large social system. Progress occurs when we take steps (e.g., by following the assumptions listed here) that increase the number of people affected. Our reach should exceed our grasp, but not by such a margin that we fall flat on our face. Instead of being discouraged by all that remains to be done, be encouraged by what has been accomplished by way of improvement resulting from your actions.

8. Assume that you will need a plan that is based on the above assumptions and that addresses the factors known to affect implementation.... Evolutionary planning and problem-coping models based on knowledge of the change process are essential (Louis & Miles, 1990).

9. Assume that no amount of knowledge will ever make it totally clear what action should be taken. Action decisions are a combination of valid knowledge, political considerations, on-the-spot decisions, and intuition. Better knowledge of the change process will improve the mix of resources on which we draw, but it will never and should never represent the sole basis for decision.

10. Assume that changing the culture of institutions is the real agenda, not implementing single innovations. Put another way, when implementing particular innovations, we should always pay attention to whether the institution is developing or not. *

In his classic book *Change Forces*, Fullan (1993) summarizes eight basic lessons that should be taken to heart as principals and faculties ponder the complexities of the change process:

- *You Can't Mandate What Matters*
  (The more complex the change, the less you can force it)

- *Change Is a Journey, Not a Blueprint*
  (Change is non-linear, loaded with uncertainty and excitement, and sometimes perverse)
- *Problems Are Our Friends*
  (Problems are inevitable and you can't learn without them)
- *Vision and Strategic Planning Come Later*
  (Premature visions and planning blind)
- *Individualism and Collectivism Must Have Equal Power*
  (There are no one-sided solutions to isolation and groupthink)
- *Neither Centralization nor Decentralization Works*
  (Both top-down and bottom-up strategies are necessary)
- *Connection with the Wider Environment Is Critical for Success*
  (The best organizations learn externally as well as internally)
- *Every Person Is a Change Agent*
  (Change is too important to leave to the experts, personal mind set and mastery is the ultimate protection) (21–22)

School improvement may not be easy, but it is well within reach of most schools. Successful efforts depend on the principals taking a comprehensive view of the problem. This view acknowledges the importance of leadership density and emphasizes implementation and institutionalization of change as well as adoption. Furthermore, successful change efforts are directed to the four levels of the school's interacting system: individual, school, work flow, and administrative-political context.

References

Argyris, Chris. 1957. *Personality and Organizations.* New York: Harper & Row.

Baldridge, Victor A. 1971. "The Analysis of Organizational Change: A Human Relations Strategy versus a Political Systems Strategy." Stanford, CA: R & D Memo #75, Stanford Center for R & D in Teaching, Stanford University.

Benne, Kenneth D. 1949. "Democratic Ethics and Social Engineering," *Progressive Education* 27(4).

Bennis, Warren, Kenneth D. Benne, and Robert Chin. 1969. *The Planning of Change* (2nd ed.). New York: Holt, Rinehart and Winston.

Berman, Paul, and Milbrey Wallin McLaughlin. 1977. *Federal Programs Supporting Educational Change. Vol. VII: Factors Affecting Implementation and Continuation.* Santa Monica, CA: Rand Corporation.

Berman, Paul, and Milbrey Wallin McLaughlin. 1979. *An Explanatory Study of School District Adaptations.* Santa Monica, CA: Rand Corporation.

Coffer, C. N., and M. H. Appley. 1964. *Motivation: Theory and Research.* New York: Wiley.

Cohen, M. 1987. "Designing State Assessment Systems," *Phi Delta Kappan* 70(8), 583–588.

Crandall, David P. 1983. "The Teacher's Role in School Improvement," *Educational Leadership* 41(3), 6–9.

Deal, Terence E. 1987. "The Culture of Schools," in Linda T. Sheive and Marian B. Schoenheit (Eds.), *Leadership Examining the Illusive,* 1987 Yearbook of the Association for Supervision and Curriculum Development. Alexandria, VA: Association for Supervision and Curriculum Development.

De Charms, Richard. 1968. *Personal Causation: The Internal Affective Determinants of Behavior.* New York: Academic Press.

Deming, W. Edwards. 1993. *The New Economics for Industry, Government, and Education.* Cambridge, MA: M.I.T. Press.

Fullan, Michael. 1991. *The New Meaning of Change* (2nd ed.). New York: Teachers College Press.

Fullan, Michael. 1993. *Change Forces.* London: Falmer Press.

Fuller, Frances F. 1969. "Concerns of Teachers: A Developmental Conceptualization," *American Educational Research Association Journal* 6(2).

Gaynor, Alan K. 1975, March 27–30. "The Study of Change in Educational Organizations: A Review of the Literature." Paper presented at the University Council for Educational Administration, Ohio State University Career Development Seminar, Columbus.

Goodlad, John I., and Frances M. Klein. 1970. *Behind the Classroom Door.* Worthington, OH: Charles A. Jones.

Hall, Gene E. 1988. "The Principal as Leader of the Change Facilitating Team," *Journal of Research and Development in Education* 22(1).

Hall, Gene E., Shirley M. Hord, Leslie L. Huling, William L. Rutherford, and Suzanne M. Stiegelbauer. 1983, April. "Leadership Variables Associated with Successful School Improvement." Papers presented at the Annual Meeting of the American Educational Research Association, Montreal, Canada.

Hall, Gene E., and Susan F. Loucks. 1978. "Teacher Concerns as a Basis for Facilitating Staff Development," *Teachers College Record* 80(1).

Hall, Gene E., and William L. Rutherford. 1983, April. "Three Change Facilitator Styles: How Principals Affect Improvement Efforts." Paper presented at the Annual Meeting of the American Educational Research Association, Montreal, Canada.

Hord, Shirley M., Gene E. Hall, and Suzanne Stiegelbauer. 1983, April. "Principals Don't Do It Alone: The Role of the Consigliere." Paper presented at the Annual Meeting of the American Educational Research Association, Montreal, Canada.

Hord, Shirley M., William L. Rutherford, Leslie Huling-Austin, and Gene E. Hall. 1987. *Taking Charge of Change.* Alexandria, VA: Association for Supervision and Curriculum Development.

Huberman, A. M., and D. P. Crandall. 1982. *People, Policies and Practices: Examining the Chain of School Improvement. Vol. IX: Implications for Action.* Andover, MA: The Network.

Huberman, M., and M. Miles. 1984. *Innovation up Close.* New York: Plenum.

Hunter, Madeline. 1984. "Knowing, Teaching and Supervising," in Philip L. Hosford (Ed.), *Using What We Know about Teaching.* Alexandria, VA: Yearbook of the Association for Supervision and Curriculum Development.

Katz, Daniel, and Robert L. Kahn. 1978. *The Social Psychology of Organization* (2nd ed.). New York: Wiley.

Kirst, Michael W. 1984. *Who Controls Our Schools?* New York: Freeman.

Leithwood, Kenneth A., and Deborah J. Montgomery. 1986. *Improving Principal Effectiveness: The Principal Profile.* Toronto: Ontario Institute for Studies in Education Press.

Lichtenstein, Gary, Milbrey W. McLaughlin, and Jennifer Knudsen. 1992. "Teacher Empowerment and Professional Knowledge" in Ann Lieberman (Ed.), *The Changing Context of Teaching,* Ninety-First Yearbook of the National Society for the Study of Education, Part I. Chicago: The University of Chicago Press.

Lieberman, Ann, and Lynne Miller. 1984. *Teachers, Their World and Their Work: Implications for School Improvement.* Alexandria, VA: Association for Supervision and Curriculum Development.

Lieberman, Ann, and Lynne Miller. 1999. *Teachers—Transforming Their World and Their Work.* New York: Teachers College Press.

Lighthall, F. 1973, February. "Multiple Realities and Organizational Nonsolutions: An Essay on Anatomy of Educational Innovation," *School Review.*

Likert, Rensis. 1967. *The Human Organization: Its Management and Value.* New York: McGraw-Hill.

Lortie, Dan. 1975. *Schoolteacher: A Sociological Study.* Chicago: The University of Chicago Press.

Loucks-Horsley, Susan, and Leslie F. Hergert. 1985. *An Action Guide to School Improvement.* Arlington, VA: Association for Supervision and Curriculum Development and The Network.

Louis, K., and M. B. Miles. 1990. *Improving the Urban High School: What Works and Why.* New York: Teachers College Press.

Marris, P. 1975. *Loss and Change.* New York: Anchor Press/Doubleday.

Mealiea, Laird W. 1978. "Learned Behavior: The Key to Understanding and Preventing Employee Resistance to Change," *Group and Organizational Studies* 3(2), 211–223.

Miles, Matthew B. 1983. "Unraveling the Mystery of Institutionalization," *Educational Leadership* 41(3), 14–19.

Reddin, W. J. 1970. *Managerial Effectiveness.* New York: McGraw-Hill.

Rosenholtz, Susan J. 1989. *Teachers Workplace: A Social-Organizational Analysis.* New York: Longman.

Saranson, Seymour B. 1971. *The Culture of the School and the Problem of Change.* Boston: Allyn and Bacon.

Schön, D. 1971. *Beyond the Stable State.* New York: Norton.

Sergiovanni, T. J., and John E. Corbally (Eds.). 1984. *Leadership and Organizational Culture.* Urbana-Champaign: University of Illinois Press.

Waller, Willard. 1932. *The Sociology of Teaching.* New York: Wiley.

Appendix 14.1   Change Facilitator Styles Inventory

This inventory contains descriptions of principal behavior grouped by style. The items are drawn from actual research comparing more and less effective principals involved in school improvement. The inventory provides an opportunity for you to describe a principal you know (or perhaps yourself) and to compare your responses with the change facilitator styles of these principals.

Each item comprises three different descriptors of principal behavior. Using a total of 10 points, distribute points among the three to indicate the extent to which each describes your principal's behavior. Record your responses on the score sheet provided.

Score Sheet

Principal Behaviors		R	M	I	Totals
A. Vision	1. 2. 3.	____ ____ ____	____ ____ ____	____ ____ ____	10 10 10
B. Structuring the school as a workplace	4. 5. 6. 7. 8.	____ ____ ____ ____ ____	____ ____ ____ ____ ____	____ ____ ____ ____ ____	10 10 10 10 10
C. Structuring involvement with change	9. 10. 11. 12. 13. 14.	____ ____ ____ ____ ____ ____	____ ____ ____ ____ ____ ____	____ ____ ____ ____ ____ ____	10 10 10 10 10 10
D. Sharing of responsibility	15. 16. 17.	____ ____ ____	____ ____ ____	____ ____ ____	10 10 10
E. Decision making	18. 19. 20.	____ ____ ____	____ ____ ____	____ ____ ____	10 10 10
F. Guiding and supporting	21. 22. 23. 24. 25. 26.	____ ____ ____ ____ ____ ____	____ ____ ____ ____ ____ ____	____ ____ ____ ____ ____ ____	10 10 10 10 10 10

Appendix 14.1 *Continued*

Principal Behaviors		R	M	I	Totals
G. Structuring his/her professional role	27.	____	____	____	10
	28.	____	____	____	10
	29.	____	____	____	10
	30.	____	____	____	10
	31.	____	____	____	10
	32.	____	____	____	10
	33.	____	____	____	10
	34.	____	____	____	10
	35.	____	____	____	10
	36.	____	____	____	10
	37.	____	____	____	10
Totals					370

Score	Style Emphasis
0–39	Very Low
40–136	Low
137–233	Medium
234–330	High
331–370	Very High

Change Facilitator Styles Inventory (CFSI)

Principal Behaviors	R	M	I
A. Vision	1. Accepts district goals as school goals	Accepts district goals but makes adjustments at school level to accommodate particular needs of the school	Respects district goals but insists on goals for school that give priority to this school's student need
	2. Future goals/direction of school are determined in response to district level goals/priorities	Anticipates the instructional and management needs of school and plans for them	Takes initiative in identifying future goals and priorities for school and in preparing to meet them

Continued

Appendix 14.1 *Continued*

Principal Behaviors	R	M	I
	3. Responds to teachers', students' and parents' interest in the goals of the school and the district	Collaborates with others in reviewing and identifying school goals	Establishes framework of expectations for the school and involves others in setting goals within that framework
B. Structuring the school as a work place	4. Maintains low profile relative to day-by-day operation of school	Very actively involved in day-by-day management	Directs the ongoing operation of the school with emphasis on instruction through personal actions and clear designation of responsibility
	5. Grants teachers autonomy and independence, provides guidelines for students	Provides guidelines and expectations for teachers and students	Sets standards and expects high performance levels for teachers, students, and self
	6. Ensures that district and school policies are followed and strives to see that disruptions in the school day are minimal	Works with teachers, students, and parents to maintain effective operation of the school	First priority is the instructional program; personnel and collaborative efforts are directed at supporting that priority
	7. Responds to requests and needs as they arise in an effort to keep all persons involved with the school comfortable and satisfied	Expects all involved with the school to contribute to effective instruction and management in the school	Insists that all persons involved with the school give priority to teaching and learning
	8. Allows school norms to evolve over time	Helps establish and clarify norms for the school	Establishes, clarifies, and models norms for the school
C. Structuring involvement with change	9. Relies on information provided by other change facilitators, usually from outside the school, for knowledge of the innovation	Uses information from a variety of sources to gain knowledge of the innovation	Seeks out information from teachers, district personnel, and others to gain an understanding of the innovation and the changes required

Appendix 14.1 *Continued*

Principal Behaviors	R	M	I
	10. Supports district expectations for change	Meets district expectations for change	Accommodates district expectations for change and pushes adjustments and additions that will benefit his/her school
	11. Sanctions the change process and strives to resolve conflicts when they arise	Involved regularly in the change process, sometimes with a focus on management and at other times with a focus on the impact of the change	Directs the change process in ways that lead to effective use by all teachers
	12. Expectations for teachers, relative to change, are given in general terms	Tells teachers that they are expected to use the innovation	Gives teachers specific expectations and steps regarding application of the change
	13. Monitors the change effort principally effort through brief, spontaneous conversations and unsolicited reports	Monitors the change effort through planned conversations with individuals and groups from informal observations of instruction	Monitors the change effort through classroom observation, review of lesson plans, reports that reveal specific teacher instruction involvement, and specific attention to the work of individual teachers
	14. May discuss with the teacher information gained through monitoring	Discusses information gained through monitoring with teacher in relation to teacher's expected behavior	Gives direct feedback to teacher concerning information gained through monitoring, which includes a comparison with expected behaviors and a plan for next steps, possibly including improvements
D. Sharing of Responsibility	15. Allows others to assume the responsibility for the change effort	Tends to do most of the intervening on the change effort but will share some responsibility	Will delegate to carefully chosen others some of the responsibility for the change effort

Continued

Appendix 14.1 *Continued*

Principal Behaviors	R	M	I
	16. Others who assume responsibility are more likely to be outside the school, e.g., district facilitators	Others who assume responsibility may come from within or from outside the school	Others who assume responsibility are likely to be from within the school
	17. Others who assume responsibility have considerable autonomy and independence in which responsibilities they assume and how they carry them out	Coordinates responsibilities and stays informed about how others are handling these responsibilities	First establishes which responsibilities will be delegated and how they are to be accomplished, then works with others and closely monitors the carrying out of tasks
E. Decision making	18. Makes decisions required for ongoing operation of the school as deadlines for those decisions approach	Actively involved in routine decision making relative to instructional and administrative affairs	Handles routine decisions through established procedures and assigned responsibilities, thereby requiring minimal time
	19. Makes decisions influenced by the immediate circumstances of the situation and formal policies	Makes decisions based on the norms and expectations that guide the school and the management needs of the school	Makes decisions based on the standard of high expectations and what is best for the school as a whole, particularly learning outcomes and the longer-term goals
	20. Willingly allows others to participate in decision making or to make decisions independently	Allows others to participate in decision making but maintains control of the process through personal involvement	Allows others to participate in decision making and delegates decision making to others within carefully established parameters of established goals and expectations

Appendix 14.1 *Continued*

Principal Behaviors	R	M	I
F. Guiding and supporting	21. Believes teachers are professionals and leaves them alone to do their work unless they request assistance or support	Believes teachers are a part of the total faculty and establishes guidelines for all teachers to be involved with the change effort	Believes teachers are responsible for developing the best possible instruction, so expectation for their involvement with innovation is clearly established
	22. Responds quickly to requests for assistance and support in a way that is satisfying to the requester	Monitors the progress of the change effort and attempts to anticipate needed assistance and resources	Anticipates the need for assistance and resources and provides support as needed as well as sometimes in advance of potential blockages
	23. Checks with teachers to see how things are going and to maintain awareness of any major problems	Maintains close contact with teachers involved the change effort in an attempt to identify things that might be done to assist teachers with the change	Collects and uses information from a variety of sources to be aware of how the change effort is progressing and to plan interventions that will increase the probability of a successful, quality implementation
	24. Relies on whatever training is available with the innovation in order to aid in the development of teacher's knowledge and skill relative to the innovation	In addition to the regularly provided assistance, seeks out and uses sources within and outside the school to develop teacher knowledge and skills	Provides increased knowledge or skill needed by the teachers through possible utilization of personnel and resources within the building
	25. Provides general support for teachers as persons and as professionals	Provides support to individuals and to subgroups for specific purposes related to the change as well as to provide for their personal welfare	Provides direct programmatic support through interventions targeted to individuals and to the staff as a whole

Continued

Appendix 14.1   *Continued*

Principal Behaviors	R	M	I
	26. Tries to minimize the demands of the change effort on teachers	Moderates demands of the change effort to protect teachers perceived overload	Keeps ever-present demands on teachers for effective implementation
G. Structuring her/ his professional role	27. Sees role as administrator	Sees role as avoiding or minimizing problems so instruction may occur	Sees role as one of ensuring the school has a strong instructional program with teachers teaching students so they are able to learn
	28. Believes others will generate the initiative for any school improvement that is needed	Engages others in regular review of school situation to avoid any reduction in school effectiveness	Identifies areas in need of improvement and initiates action for change
	29. Relies primarily on others for introduction of new ideas into the school	Is alert to new ideas and introduces them to faculty or allows others in school to do so	Sorts through new ideas presented from within and from outside the school and implements those deemed to have high promise for school improvement
	30. Is concerned with how others view him	Is concerned with how others view the school	Is concerned with how others view the impact of the school on students
	31. Accepts the rules of the district	Lives by the rules of the district but goes beyond minimum expectations	Respects the rules of the district but determines behavior by what is required for maximum school effectiveness
	32. Opinions and concerns of others determine what will be accomplished and how	Is consistent in setting and accomplishing tasks and does much of it herself/himself	Tasks determined and accomplished are consistent with school priorities but responsibility can be delegated to others

Appendix 14.1 *Continued*

Principal Behaviors	R	M	I
	33. Maintains a general sense of "where the school is" and of how teachers are feeling about things	Is well informed about what is happening in the school and who is doing what	Maintains specific knowledge of all that is going on in the school through direct contact with the classroom, with individual teachers, and with students
	34. Responds to others in a manner intended to please them	Responds to others in a way that will be supportive of the operation of the school	Responds to others with concern but places student priorities above all else
	35. Develops minimal knowledge of what use of the innovation entails	Becomes knowledgeable about general use of the innovation and what is needed to support its use	Develops sufficient knowledge about use to be able to make specific teaching suggestions and to troubleshoot any problems that may emerge
	36. Indefinitely delays having staff do tasks if perceiving that staff are overloaded	Contends that staff are already very busy and paces requests and task loads accordingly	Will knowingly sacrifice short-term feelings of staff if doing a task now is necessary for the longer-term goals of the school
	37. Ideas are offered by each staff member, but one or two have dominant influence	Some ideas are offered by staff and some by the principal; then consensus is gradually developed	Seeks teachers' ideas as well as their reactions to her/his ideas; then priorities are set

Note: The items on this inventory were identified as a result of an extensive research program investigating the relationship between principal behavior and successful school improvement. This program was conducted at the Research and Development Center for Teacher Education, University of Texas, Austin. The items are from Gene E. Hall and William L. Rutherford (1983), "Three Change Facilitator Styles: How Principals Affect Improvement Efforts," paper presented at the Annual Meeting of the American Educational Research Association, Montreal, April. Available from the RDCTE, Austin, TX, document number 3155. See also "Leadership Variables Associated with Successful School Improvement" (Austin, TX: RDCTE, 1983).

PART V

THE MORAL DIMENSION

15

ADMINISTERING AS
A MORAL CRAFT

In this book, a number of conceptions of the principal have been discussed: Strategic problem solver, cultural leader, barterer, and initiator are examples. It's fair to ask whether these are the roles and images of leadership that one should follow in order to be an effective principal. The answer is yes—well, no—actually maybe. Similarly, what about the motivational concepts and ideas presented in Chapter 13, the new principles of management and leadership presented in Chapter 3, the characteristics of successful schools, the forces of leadership, strategies for bringing about change, and the dimensions of school culture discussed in other chapters? Will these ideas, if routinely applied, help one to be an effective principal? The answer is the same: yes—well, no—actually maybe. Unfortunately, there is no guarantee that the concepts presented in this book will fit all readers or the contexts and problems they face in the same way. Leadership is a personal thing. It comprises three important dimensions—one's heart, head, and hand.

The Heart, Head, and Hand of Leadership

The *heart* of leadership has to do with what a person believes, values, dreams about, and is committed to—that person's *personal vision,* to use a popular term. To be sure, sharing personal conceptions of what is a good school will reveal many common qualities, but what often makes them personal statements is that they will differ, as well. The *head* of leadership has to do with the theories of practice each of us has developed over time and our ability to reflect on the situations we face in light of these theories. This process of reflection combined with our personal vision becomes the basis for our strategies and actions. Finally, the *hand* of leadership has to do with the actions we take, the decisions we make, the leadership and management behaviors we use as our strategies become institutionalized in the form of school programs, policies, and procedures. As with heart and head, how we choose to manage and lead are personal reflections not only of our vision and practical theories but also of our personalities and our responses to the unique situations we face. In this idiosyncratic world, one-best-way approaches and cookie-cutter strategies do not work very well. Instead, diversity will likely be the norm as principals practice. Each principal must find her or his way, develop her or his approach if the heart, head, and hand of leadership are to come together in the form of successful principalship practice.

Does that mean that the concepts presented in this book are not true? If they are not truths to be emulated and imitated, what are they? They comprise a different kind of truth. They represent a concept boutique on one hand and a metaphor repository on another. The idea is to visit the boutique, trying on one idea after another, seeking a fit here or there, and to visit the repository, seeking to create new understandings of situations one faces and new alternatives to one's practice. As boutique and repository, the role of knowledge about schooling changes from being something that principals apply uniformly to being something useful that informs the decisions they make as they practice. This is the nature of reflective practice.

The Moral Imperative

Although many may prefer the work of administration to be some sort of an applied science that is directly connected to a firm knowledge base of theory and research, the reality we face is that it is much more craftlike. The message from this reality is equally clear. Successful practice requires the development of craft know-how. Craft know-how according to Blumberg (1989:47) includes the following:

- Being able to develop and refine "a nose for things."
- Having a sense of what constitutes an acceptable result in any particular problematic situation.
- Understanding the nature of the "materials" with which one is working. This includes oneself as a "material" that needs to be understood, as well as others. It also includes understanding the way other parts of the environment may affect the materials and the acceptableness of the solution at a particular point in time.
- Knowing administrative techniques and having the skill to employ them in the most efficacious way possible.
- Knowing what to do and when to do it. This involves not only pragmatic decisions—what behavior or procedure is called for at a particular time—but also implies issues of right and wrong. Much as Tom's (1984) description of teaching is that of a "moral" craft, so too is the practice of administration one in which there are moral dimensions to every action taken, with the possible exception of those that are simply mundane. This is not to suggest that administrators are aware of these moral dimensions at all times; it is simply to suggest that they are present.

- Having a sense of "process"—that is, being able to diagnose and interpret the meaning of what is occurring as people interact in any problematic situation.

Yet, administering schools, as Blumberg suggests, is no ordinary craft. Bringing together head, heart, and hand in practice; the unique nature of the school's mission; and the typically loosely structured, nonlinear, and messy context of schooling combine to make administering a *moral* craft, a fate shared with teaching (Tom, 1984) and supervision (Sergiovanni and Starratt, 1988). The reasons for this moral imperative are as follows:

1. The job of the principal is to transform the school from being an ordinary organization concerned with technical functions in pursuit of objective outcomes into an *institution*. Organizations are little more than technical instruments for achieving objectives. As instruments, they celebrate the value of effectiveness and efficiency by being more concerned with "doing things right" than with "doing right things." Institutions, however, are effective and efficient and more. They are responsive, adaptive enterprises that exist not only to get a particular job done but as entities in and of themselves. As Selznick (1957) points out, organizations become institutions when they transcend the technical requirements needed for the task at hand. In his words, "Institutionalization is a *process*. It is something that happens to an organization over time, reflecting the organization's own distinctive history, the people who have been in it, the groups it embodies and the vested interests they have created, and the way it has adapted to its environment" (Selznick, 1957:16). He continues:

> *Organizations become institutions as they are* infused with value, *that is, prized not as tools alone but as sources of direct personal gratification and vehicles of group integrity. This infusion produces a distinct identity for the organization. Where institutionalization is well advanced, distinctive outlooks, habits, and other commitments are unified, coloring all aspects of organizational life and lending it a* social integration *that goes well beyond formal coordination and command.* (Selznick, 1957:40)

Selznick's conception of institution is similar to the more familiar conception of school as *learning community*. To become either, the school must move beyond concerns for goals and roles to the task of building purposes into its structure and embodying these purposes in everything that it does with the effect of transforming school members from neutral participants to committed followers. The embodiment of purpose and the development of followership are inescapably moral.

2. The job of the school is to provide students with knowledge and skills and to build *character* and instill *virtue*. As Cuban (1988) points out, both technical and moral images are present in teaching and administering. "The technical image contains values that prize accumulated knowledge, efficiency, orderliness, productivity, and social usefulness; the moral image, while not disregarding such values, prizes values directed at molding character, shaping attitudes, and producing a virtuous, thoughtful person" (xvii). Technical and moral images of administration cannot be separated in practice. Every technical decision has moral implications. Emphasizing orderliness, for example, might serve as a lesson in diligence for students and might be a reminder to teachers that professional goals cannot be pursued to the extent that bureaucratic values are compromised.

3. Whether concern is for virtue or efficiency, some *standard* has to be adopted. What is efficient in this circumstance? How will virtue be determined? Determining criteria for effective teaching, deciding on what is a good discipline policy, or coming to grips with promotion criteria standards, for example, all require value judgments. Answers to questions of how and what cannot be resolved objectively as if they were factual assertions, but must be treated as normative assertions. Normative assertions are true only because we decide that they are. "We must decide what ought to be the case. We cannot *discover* what ought to be the case by investigating what is the case" (Taylor, 1961:248). Normative assertions are moral statements.

4. Despite commitments to empowerment and shared decision making, relationships between principals and others are inherently unequal. Although often downplayed, and whether they want it or not, principals typically have more *power* than teachers, students, parents, and others. This power is in part derived legally from their hierarchical position, but for the most part it is obtained de facto by virtue of the greater access to information and people that their position affords them. Principals are not chained to a tight schedule. They do a lot of walking around. They are the ones who get the phone calls, who are out in the streets, who visit the central office, who have access to the files, and so forth. As a result, principals function more frequently in the roles of figurehead and liaison with outside agencies. They have greater access to information than do other people in the school. This allows principals to decide what information will be shared with others, what information will be withheld, and frequently what information will be forgotten. Often, teachers and others in the school rely on the principal to serve as the "coordinating mechanism" that links together what they are doing with what others are doing. In teaching, where much of the work is invisible, the coordinating function is a powerful one. Furthermore, much of the information that principals accumulate is confidential. When teachers have problems, they frequently confide in the principal. Information is a source of power, and the accumulation of power has moral consequences.

Whenever there is an unequal distribution of power between two people, the relationship becomes a moral one. Whether intended or not, leadership involves an offer to control. The follower accepts this offer on the assumption that control will not be exploited. In this sense, leadership is not a right but a responsibility. Morally speaking, its purpose is not to enhance the leader's position or make it easier for the leader to get what she or he wants but to benefit the school. The test of moral leadership under these conditions is whether the competence, well-being, and independence of the follower are enhanced as a result of accepting control and whether the school benefits. Tom (1980) makes a similar argument in pointing out that "the teacher-student relationship is inherently moral because of its inequality" (317).

5. The context for administration is surprisingly loose, chaotic, and ambiguous. Thus, despite demands and constraints that circumscribe the principal's world, in actuality, *discretion* is built into the job, and this discretion has moral implication.

For example, frequently how things look is different from how things work. In their research on the reality of managing schools, Morris and colleagues (1984) discovered numerous instances in which principals and schools were able to develop implicit policies and pursue courses of action that only remotely resembled officially sanctioned policies and actions. They noted that not only maintaining student enrollment levels but increasing them was often viewed as a managerial necessity by principals. However, principals were not motivated for official "educational" or "societal" reasons, but to protect or enhance the resource allocation base of their schools. Staffing patterns and budget allocations were often linked to a principal's standing among peers and were related as well to morale and productivity levels among teachers. Furthermore, principals of larger schools had more clout with the central office. Simply put, more staff and bigger budgets were viewed as being better. Schools losing resources, however, "usually suffer a decline in purposefulness, security, and confidence that goes beyond the loss of operating funds" (128).

As a result, principals tended to view monitoring, protecting, and increasing school enrollments and attendance as one of their key, albeit implicit, tasks. This led them to engage in courses of action that were at variance with the officially sanctioned definition of their tasks and roles. There was, for example, a concerted effort to change existing programs and revise the existing curriculum so they were more attractive to students and thus better able to hold their enrollment. One of the principals reported, "We may have to cut physics, for instance, and add environmental science. It's in. . . . I've got to get my faculty to see that they have to reshape the traditional curriculum of the school. Their jobs are at stake" (Morris et al., 1984:128–129). Another principal in their study worked to change his school's kindergarten program so that it was more structured and "rigorous," not for educational reasons or philosophical commitments but so that the school would be better able to compete with the neighborhood Catholic school.

Despite clear guidelines governing attendance procedures (e.g., fixed attendance boundaries and age requirements), principals became flexible by bending the rules for student admissions and taking liberties with reporting enrollment information to the central office. In the words of one principal, "In general, I'm not picky about where the students in the school live," noting further that if a child subsequently became a behavioral problem or was suspected of being a behavioral problem she always checked the home address (Morris et al., 1984:30). Some principals were inclined to look the other way even when they knew that students came from other school districts if they thought the students were "extremely bright." Some principals used leniency in enforcing attendance boundaries as the lever to extract better behavior and more achievement from students. Principals stressed that they were doing the parents and students a favor and expected good behavior in return. Not all students were treated equally. While bright students were encouraged to attend, "troublemakers" were not. In the words of one principal, "Let him go, that guy's been nothing but trouble for us" (Morris et al., 1984:131).

Although discretion can provide principals with a license for abuse, it is also a necessary prerequisite for leadership. "From choice comes autonomy. Autonomy is the necessary condition for leadership to arise. Without choice, there is no autonomy. Without autonomy, there is no leadership" (Cuban, 1988:xxii). Discretion, therefore, is necessary if principals are to function effectively. Yet, how principals handle discretion raises moral issues and has moral consequences for the school.

Normative Rationality

Key to understanding the moral dimension in leadership is understanding the difference between *normative rationality* (rationality based on what we believe and what we consider to be good) and *technical rationality* (rationality based on what is effective and efficient). Happily, the two are not mutually exclusive. Principals want what is good and what is effective for their schools, but when the two are in conflict, the moral choice is to prize the former over the latter. Starratt makes the point poignantly as follows: "'Organizational effectiveness' employs technical rationality, functional rationality, linear logic. Efficiency is the highest value, not loyalty, harmony, honor, beauty, truth. One can run an efficient extermination camp or an efficient monastery. The principles of efficiency are basically the same in either context" (Sergiovanni and Starratt, 1988:218).

Normative rationality provides the basis for moral leadership. Instead of just relying on bureaucratic authority to force a person to do something or a psychological authority to manipulate a person into doing something, the leader—principal or teacher, as the case may be—provides reasons for selecting one alternative over another. The reasons are open to discussion and evaluation by everyone. To pass the test of normative rationality, the reasons must embody the purposes and values that the group shares—the sacred covenant that bonds everyone in the school together as members of a learning community.

One might properly ask: What is the place of scientific authority in the form of expertness established by educational research in getting a person to do something? Isn't it enough that research says we ought to do this or that? Scientifically speaking, teaching, management, and leadership are underdeveloped fields. As a result, research findings are often so general as to comprise common understandings widely known to the general public (e.g., a positive school climate provides a better setting for learning than a negative one; students who spend more time learning learn more; relating school content to personal experiences helps students understand better; teachers are more likely to accept a decision they help shape and make) or so idiosyncratic (e.g., discovering that making Billy a blackboard monitor has helped his behavior in class; or noting that teacher Barbara does not respond well to one-on-one supervision but seems to get a lot out of collegial supervision) that they are difficult to apply beyond the setting from which they come.

Nonetheless, research and reflecting on personal experience can often provide us with patterns of characteristics to which many students or teachers are likely to respond in the same way. These insights can help, and this form of knowledge is often invaluable to principals. But this knowledge cannot represent a source of authority for action that replaces moral authority. As Smith and Blase (1987) explain,

> *A leader in moral terms is one who fully realizes the . . . serious limitations on our ability to make accurate predictions and master the instructional process. Moreover, such a leader must encourage others to fully realize these limitations. Based on this awareness, a moral leader refuses to allow discussions of major pedagogical issues to be dominated by what the research supposedly demonstrates. . . . To do so would be to perpetuate the fiction that we have the kind of knowledge that we do not in fact possess. Rather, disagreements over how and what to teach must be played out in terms of reasoned discourse. The generalizations of educational inquiry can of course be part of these reasons, but they are not epistemologically privileged— they must share the stage with personal experience, a recounting of the experience of others, with philosophical and sociological considerations, and so on. (39)*

The key is the phrase "epistemologically privileged." It is not that research findings are unimportant but that they are *no more important than other sources of authority.* One "so on" that might be added to Smith and Blase's list is conceptions of what is valued by the school that define it as a unique learning community.

Normative rationality influences the practice of leadership in schools in two ways. Principals bring to their job normative baggage in the form of biases and prejudices, ways of thinking, personality quirks, notions of what works and what doesn't, and other factors that function as personal theories of practice governing what they are likely to do and not do, and school cultures are defined by a similar set of biases that represent the center of shared values and commitments that define the school as an institution. Both are sources of norms that function as standards and guidelines for what goes on in the school. As a school's culture is strengthened and its center of values becomes more public and pervasive, normative rationality becomes more legitimate. Everyone knows what the school stands for and why and can articulate these purposes and use them as guidelines for action. This in-building of purpose "involves transforming [persons] in groups from neutral, technical units into participants who have a peculiar stamp, sensitivity, and commitment" (Selznick, 1957:150).

The Four Competencies

In his book *Why Leaders Can't Lead* (1989), Bennis suggests that leadership rests on four basic competencies: management of attention, management of meaning, management of trust, and management of self (19). The *management of attention* focuses the principalship on values, ideas, goals, and purposes that bring people together and that provide a rationale, a source of authority, for what goes on in the school. Principals have important roles to play in setting this idea agenda, but just as important is seeing to it that an idea structure emerges from the visions of others.

The *management of meaning* focuses the principalship on connecting teachers, parents, and students to the school in such a way that they find their lives useful, sensible, and valued. Even the seemingly mundane routines of school are valued and are connected to the larger purposes and meaning that define who people are, why they are in school, why the school needs them, and why their participation is worthwhile. Attention and meaning helps people connect to each other and to the school.

The *management of trust* ensures that the principal's role in the school and the leadership she or he expresses are viewed as credible, legitimate, and honest. Bennis (1989) uses the term *constancy* to communicate that whether or not parents, teachers, or students like what the principal does or says, they always know where that principal is coming from and what she or he stands for. The *management of self* is the ability of principals to know who they are, what they believe, and why they do the things that they do. When a principal's behavior can be defended by that principal in a way that others at least understand and respect, self-knowledge has been achieved. These four competencies are expressed, in part, as the principal struggles to develop a shared followership and to build up the character of her or his school. School character, as will be described later in this chapter, is an essential ingredient in school effectiveness.

Followership Is the Goal

The importance of purposing to leadership changes how it is understood and practiced. With purposing in place in a school, one cannot become a leader without first becoming a follower. The concept of followership was discussed in Chapters 5, 6, and 7. It was pointed out that what it means to be a follower and what it means to be a subordinate are very different. Subordinates respond to bureaucratic authority and sometimes to personal authority. Followers, by contrast, respond to ideas. You can't be a follower unless you have something to follow. Furthermore, as Zaleznik (1989) suggests, subordinates may cooperate with the management system but are rarely committed to it. By contrast, one of the hallmarks of being a follower is commitment. As Kelly (1988) points out, followers "are committed to the organization and to a purpose, principle, or person outside themselves. . . . [And as a result, they] build their competence and focus their efforts for maximum impact" (144). Followers, by definition, are never constrained by minimums but are carried by their commitment to performance that typically exceeds expectations. Subordinates, by contrast, do what they are supposed to; they tend not to do more.

When subordinateness is transcended by followership, a different kind of hierarchy emerges in the school. Principals, teachers, students, parents, and others find themselves equally "subordinate" to a set of ideas and shared conceptions to which they are committed. As a result, teachers respond and comply not because of the principal's directives but out of a sense of obligation and commitment to these shared values. That's what it means to be a follower.

The principal's job is to provide the kind of purposing to the school that helps followership to emerge. She or he then provides the conditions and support that allow people to function in ways that are consistent with agreed-upon values. At the same time, the principal has a special responsibility to continually highlight the values, to protect them, and to see that they are enforced. The true test of leadership under these conditions is the principal's ability to get others in the school to share in the responsibility for guarding these values. This litany of roles was discussed in the text as leadership by purposing, empowerment and enablement, outrage, and finally kindling outrage in others.

One of the persistent problems of administration is obtaining compliance, which is at the heart of the principal's role. Invariably, compliance occurs in response to some sort of authority, but not all sources of authority are equally powerful or palatable. In this book, four sources of authority have been described: bureaucratic, personal, professional, and moral. All four have a role to play if schools are to function effectively, however, the four compete with each other. When principals use bureaucratic authority, they rely on rules, mandates, and regulations in efforts to direct thought and action. When principals use personal authority, they rely on their own interpersonal style, cleverness, guile, political know-how, and other forms of managerial and psychological skill in order to direct thought and action. When principals rely on professional authority, they appeal to expertness, expecting everyone to be subordinate to a form of technical rationality that is presumably validated by craft notions of what constitutes best educational practice or scientific findings from educational research. When principals rely on moral authority, they bring to the forefront a form of normative rationality as discussed above that places everyone subordinate to a set of ideas, ideals, and shared values and asks them to respond morally by doing their duty, meeting their obligations, and accepting their responsibilities. All are important, but the art of administration is balancing the four competing sources of authority in such a way that moral and professional authority flourish without neglecting bureaucratic and personal authority.

The Challenge of Leadership

In the principalship, the challenge of leadership is to make peace with two competing imperatives: the managerial and the moral. The two imperatives are unavoidable and the neglect of either creates problems. Schools must be run effectively and efficiently if they are to survive. Policies must be in place. Budgets must be set. Teachers must be assigned. Classes must be scheduled. Reports must be completed. Standardized tests must be given. Supplies must be purchased. The school must be kept clean. Students must be protected from violence. Classrooms must be orderly. These are essential tasks that guarantee the survival of the school as an organization. Yet, for the school to transform itself into an institution, a learning community must emerge. Institutionalization is the moral imperative that principals face.

Discussing the moral imperative in administration; proposing such leadership values as purposing, empowerment, outrage, and kindling outrage in others; and arguing for the kind of balance among bureaucratic, psychological, professional, and moral sources of authority in schools that noticeably tilts toward professional and moral challenge the "professional manager" conception of the principalship by placing concerns for substance firmly over concerns for process.

On the upside, the development of school administration as a form of management technology brought with it much needed attention to the development of better management know-how and of organizational skills badly needed to deal with an educational system that continues to grow in technical, legal, and bureaucratic complexity. On the downside, professionalism has too often resulted in principals thinking of themselves less as statespersons, educators, and philosophers, and more as organizational experts who have become absorbed in what Abraham Zaleznik (1989) refers to as the *managerial mystique*. "As it evolved in practice, the mystique required managers to dedicate themselves to process, structures, roles, and indirect forms of communication and to ignore ideas, people, emotions, and direct talk. It deflected attention from the realities [of education] while it reassured and rewarded those who believed in the mystique" (2). The managerial mystique holds so strongly to the belief that "the right methods" will produce good results that the methods themselves too often become surrogates for results, and to the belief that management and bureaucratic controls will overcome human shortcomings and enhance human productivity that controls become ends in themselves. School improvement plans, for example, become substitutes for school improvements; scores on teacher appraisal forms become substitutes for good teaching; accumulating credits earned in courses and required inservice workshops become substitutes for changes in school practice; discipline plans become substitutes for student control; leadership styles become substitutes for purpose and substance; congeniality becomes a substitute for collegiality; cooperation becomes a substitute for commitment; and compliance becomes a substitute for results.

Zaleznik (1989) maintains that the managerial mystique is the antithesis of leadership. The epitome of the managerial mystique is the belief that anyone who can manage one kind of enterprise can also manage any other kind. It is the generic management techniques and generic interpersonal skills that count rather than issues of purpose and substance. Without purpose and substance, Zaleznik argues, there can be no leadership. "Leadership is based on a compact that binds those who lead and those who follow into the same moral, intellectual and emotional commitment" (15).

Building the Character of Your School

One of the major themes of this book is the importance of the school's culture. For better or for worse, culture influences much of what is thought, said, and done in a school. Character is a concept similar to culture but much less neutral. A school's character is known by how the school is viewed by members and outsiders in ethical and moral terms. Building and enhancing the school's character is the key to establishing its credibility among students, teachers, parents, and administrators and externally in the broader community. Wilkins (1989) notes that the components of an organization's character are its common understandings of *purpose* and identity that provide a sense of "who we are"; faith of members in the fairness of the leadership and in the ability of the organization to meet its commitments and to get the job done; and the distinctive cultural attributes that define the tacit customs, networks of individuals, and accepted ways of working together and of working with others outside of the organization. How reliable are the actions of the school? How firm is the school in its convictions? How just is its disposition? Wilkins points out that purpose, faith, and cultural attributes "add up to the collective organizational competence" (1989:27). To him, faith is a particularly important component of an organization's character, and loss of faith in either the organization or its leadership results in loss of character. Building faith restores character. Enhancing faith increases character. Without faith and character the organization and its members are not able to move beyond the ordinary to extraordinary performance. With faith such a transformation is possible. No matter how relentlessly principals pursue their managerial imperative, reliability in action, firmness in conviction, and just disposition are the consequences of the moral imperative. Without tending to the moral imperative there can be no organizational character, and without character a school can be neither good nor effective (Sergiovanni, 2000).

A Commitment to Democratic Values

The inescapable moral nature of administrative work and in particular seeking to establish moral authority embodied in the form of purposing and shared values and expressed as "cultural leadership" raises important questions of manipulation and control. Cultural leadership can provide principals with levers to manipulate others that are more powerful than the levers associated with bureaucratic and psychological authority. Lakomski (1985) raises the question squarely:

> To put the objection more strongly, it may be argued that if all cultural analysis does is to help those in power, such as principals and teachers, to oppress some students more effectively by learning about their views, opinions, and "student cultures," then this method is just another and more sophisticated way to prevent students (and other oppressed groups) from democratic participation in educational affairs. (15)

Her comments apply as well to teachers and others. Furthermore, cultural leadership can become a powerful weapon for masking the many problems of diversity, justice, and equality that confront schools. There is nothing inherently democratic about cultural leadership, and, indeed, depending on its substance this kind of leadership can compromise democratic values. Consensus building and commitment to shared values can often be little more than devices for maintaining an unsatisfactory status quo and for discouraging dissent. Finally, not all covenants are equal. The values that define the "center" of different school communities are not interchangeable.

Cultural leadership can be understood and practiced as a technology available to achieve any goal and to embody any vision or as a means to celebrate a particular set of basic values that emerge from the American democratic tradition. It makes a difference, for example, whether the basic values that define a school community revolve around themes of efficiency, effectiveness, and excellence or whether these are considered to be mere means values in service to such ends values as justice, diversity, equality, and goodness. In the spirit of the latter point of view, Clark and Meloy (1984) propose the Declaration of Independence as a metaphor for managing schools to replace bureaucracy. This metaphor guarantees to all persons that school management decisions will support such values as equality, life, liberty, and the pursuit of happiness based on the consent of the governed.

Discussion of democracy in schools typically wins nods from readers. However, as Quantz, Cambron-McCabe, and Dantley (1991) point out, democracy is not always understood as both process and substance:

> There is often a confusion of democracy with pure process—the belief that as long as there is some form of participatory decision-making that democracy has been achieved. We argue, however, that democracy implies both a process and a goal, that the two, while often contradictory, cannot be separated. We believe that democratic processes cannot justify undemocratic ends. For example, we cannot justify racial and gender inequity on the basis that the majority voted for it. While this dual-reference test for democracy is not simple or clean, while it often requires us to choose between two incompatible choices, both in the name of democracy, we can conceive of no other way to approach it. In other words, even though an appeal to democratic authority cannot provide a clear and unequivocal blueprint for action in every particular instance, it can provide a general and viable direction for intelligent and moral decision-making by school administrators.

One of the challenges of moral leadership in schools is to engage oneself and others in the process of decision making without thought to self-interest. Can we discuss and decide our grading policies, discipline procedures, student grouping practices, supervisory strategies, and so forth without regard to whether we will be winners or losers? Sending children routinely to the principal's office for discipline, for example, or favoring homogeneous grouping of students may be in the interest of teachers but not students. Requiring all teachers to teach the same way may make it easier for the principal to hold teachers accountable, but not for teachers who want to teach in ways that make sense to them. Discouraging parental involvement in school governance makes for fewer headaches for school people but disenfranchises the parents. What is just under these circumstances? John Rawls (1971) has suggested that decisions such as these should be made by people choosing in a hypothetical position of fairness under what he called "a veil of ignorance." The idea is to pretend that we don't know anything about ourselves—our sex, our race, our position in the school, our talents, and so forth. We don't know, in other words, whether we are black or white, principal or teacher, student or custodian, parent or teacher aide. Our identities are only revealed when the veil of ignorance is lifted. Rawls maintains that in this way we are likely to fashion our principles and make decisions regardless of who we turn out to be. With bias diminished, chances are that the principles would be fairer and the decisions more just.

A Personal Note

How committed are you to becoming a successful school principal? Generally speaking, commitment to your present job provides a good idea of one's overall commitment to work. For an indication of your present job commitment, respond on the Job Commitment Scale Exhibit 15.1. This scale contains 16 items about how people feel about their jobs. Indicate the extent to which you agree or disagree with each item. As you count your score, reverse-score items 6, 8, and 16. Your score will

---

EXHIBIT 15.1   Job Commitment Index

Responses: 4—Strongly Agree, 3—Agree, 2—Disagree, 1—Strongly Disagree

	1	2	3	4
1. Most of the important things that happen to me involve my work.	—	—	—	—
2. I spend a great deal of time on matters related to my job, both during and after hours.	—	—	—	—
3. I feel badly if I don't perform well on my job.	—	—	—	—
4. I think about my job even when I'm not working.	—	—	—	—
5. I would probably keep working even if I didn't have to.	—	—	—	—
6. I have a perspective on my job that does not let it interfere with other aspects of my life.	—	—	—	—
7. Performing well on my job is extremely important to me.	—	—	—	—
8. Most things in my life are more important to me than my job.	—	—	—	—
9. I avoid taking on extra duties and responsibilities in my work.	—	—	—	—
10. I enjoy my work more than anything else I do.	—	—	—	—
11. I stay overtime to finish a job even if I don't have to.	—	—	—	—
12. Sometimes I lie awake thinking about the next day's work.	—	—	—	—
13. I am able to use abilities I value in doing my job.	—	—	—	—
14. I feel depressed when my job does not go well.	—	—	—	—
15. I feel good when I perform my job well.	—	—	—	—
16. I would not work at my job if I didn't have to.	—	—	—	—

The Job Commitment Index is generally adapted from the Occupational Commitment Scale developed by Becky Heath Ladewig and Priscilla N. White, The Department of Human Development and Family Life, University of Alabama, University, AL.

range from a low of 16 to a high of 64, with 64 representing the highest level of commitment. Keep in mind that there is always the chance that a person's commitment to work may be high, but that her or his present job presents such unusual difficulties that low commitment and a low score result.

Anyone aspiring to the principalship had better have a strong commitment to work. This assertion should perhaps be modified as follows: Anyone who is aspiring to be a *successful* principal had better have a strong commitment to work. Success has its price. Consider, for example, the following statement:

> *A passion for excellence means thinking big and starting small: excellence happens when high purpose and intense pragmatism meet. This is almost but not quite, the whole truth. We believe a passion for excellence also carries a price, and we state it simply: the adventure of excellence is not for the faint of heart.*
>
> *Adventure? You bet. It's not just a job. It's a personal commitment. Whether we're looking at a billion dollar corporation or a three-person accounting department, we see that excellence is achieved by people who muster up the nerve (and the passion) to step out—in spite of doubt, or fear, or job description (to maintain face-to-face contact with other people, namely customers and colleagues). They won't retreat behind office doors, committees, memos or layers of staff, knowing this is the fair bargain they make for extraordinary results. They may step out for love, because of a burning desire to be the best, to make a difference, or perhaps, as a colleague recently explained, "because the thought of being average scares the hell out of me." (Peters and Austin, 1985:414)*

In his studies of high-performing leaders, Vaill (1984) found that "(1) Leaders of high-performing systems put in extraordinary amounts of *time;* (2) Leaders of high-performing systems have very strong *feelings* about the attachment of the system's purposes; and (3) Leaders of high-performing systems *focus* on key issues and variables" (94). Vaill notes that "there are of course many nuances, subtleties, and local specialists connected with the leadership of many high-performing systems, but over and over again, Time, Feeling, and Focus appear no matter what else appears" (94). The three go hand in hand. Vaill states, for example, that administrators who put in large amounts of time without feeling or focus are exhibiting "workaholism." Time and feeling without focus, however, often lead to dissipated energy and disappointment. Finally, time and focus without feeling seem to lack the necessary passion and excitement for providing symbolic and cultural leadership. Successful leaders—principals among them—are not afraid of hard work. By putting in large amounts of time, they demonstrate that they are not afraid of hard work; however, they don't dissipate this time by taking on everything. Instead, they concentrate their efforts on those characteristics and values that are clearly more important to the success of their organization than are others. Furthermore, unlike cold, calculated, objective, and uninvolved managers, they bring to their enterprises a certain passion that affects others deeply.

As a result of his extensive studies of the principalship and school leadership, Greenfield (1985) concludes that principals need to be more passionate about their work, clearer about what they seek to accomplish, and more aggressive in searching for understandings that lead to improved schooling. Greenfield speaks of passion as "believing in the worth of what one seeks to accomplish and exhibiting in one's daily action a commitment to the realization of those goals and purposes" (17). He maintains that clarity about goals and outcomes should be accompanied by a commitment to flexibility regarding processes, procedures, and other means to attain ends.

Finally, anyone who is aspiring to be a good principal needs to have some sense of what she or he values, something to be committed to, a compass to help navigate the way—a personal vision. Barth (1990) points out:

> *Observers in schools have concluded that the lives of teachers, principals, and students are characterized by brevity, fragmentation, and variety. During an average day, for instance, a teacher or principal engages in several hundred interactions. So do many parents. A personal vision provides a framework with which to respond and to make use of the many prescriptions and conceptions of others. But more important, these ideas centered around schools as communities of learners and leaders have provided me with a road map which has enabled me to respond to the hundreds of daily situations in schools . . . in a less random and more thoughtful way. Without a vision, I think our behavior becomes reflexive, inconsistent, and shortsighted as we seek the action that will most quickly put out the fire so we can get on with putting out the next one. In five years, if we're lucky, our school might be fire free—but it won't have changed much. Anxiety will remain high, humor low, and leadership muddled. Or as one teacher put it in a powerful piece of writing, "Without a clear sense of purpose we get lost, and our activities in school become but empty vessels of our discontent." Seafaring folk put it differently: "For the sailor without a destination, there is no favorable wind." (211)*

One of the great secrets of leadership is that before one can command the respect and followership of others, she or he must demonstrate devotion to the organization's purposes and commitment to those in the organization who work day by day on the ordinary tasks that are necessary for those purposes to be realized. As Greenleaf (1977) points out, people "will freely respond only to individuals who are chosen as leaders because they are proven and trusted as servants" (10). This perspective has come to be known as *servant leadership* (Greenleaf, 1977), with its basic tenets found in the biblical verse: "Ye know that the rulers of the Gentiles lorded over them, and that their great ones exercised authority over them. Not so shall it be among you: but whosoever would become great among you shall be your minister and whosoever would be first among you shall be your servant" (Matthew 20:25).

Servant leadership describes well what it means to be a principal. Principals are responsible for "ministering" to the needs of the schools they serve. The needs are defined by the shared values and purposes of the school's covenant. They minister by furnishing help and being of service to parents, teachers, and students. They minister by providing leadership in a way that encourages others to be leaders in their own right. They minister by highlighting and protecting the values of the school. The principal as minister is one who is devoted to a cause, mission, or set of ideas and accepts the duty and obligation to serve this cause. Ultimately, her or his success is known by the quality of the followership that emerges. Quality of followership is a barometer that indicates the extent to which moral authority has replaced bureaucratic and psychological authority. When moral authority drives leadership practice, the principal is at the same time a leader of leaders, follower of ideas, minister of values, and servant to the followership.

References

Barth, Roland S. 1990. *Improving Schools from Within.* San Francisco: Jossey-Bass.

Bennis, Warren. 1989. *Why Leaders Can't Lead: The Unconscious Conspiracy Continues.* San Francisco: Jossey-Bass.

Blumberg, Arthur. 1989. *School Administration as a Craft.* Boston: Allyn and Bacon.

Clark, David L., and Judith M. Meloy. 1984. "Renouncing Bureaucracy: A Democratic Structure for Leadership in Schools," in T. J. Sergiovanni and J. H. Moore (Eds.), *Schooling for Tomorrow: Directing Reforms to Issues that Count.* Boston: Allyn and Bacon.

Cuban, Larry. 1988. *The Managerial Imperative and the Practice of Leadership in Schools.* Albany: State University of New York Press.

Greenfield, William D. 1985, June 29. "Instructional Leadership: Muddles, Puzzles, and Promises." Athens: The Doyne M. Smith Lecture, University of Georgia.

Greenleaf, Robert K. 1977. *Teacher as Servant.* New York: Paulist Press.

Kelly, Robert E. 1988, November–December. "In Praise of Followers," *Harvard Business Review.*

Lakomski, Gabriele. 1985. "The Cultural Perspective in Educational Administration," in R. J. S. Macpherson and Helen M. Sungaila (Eds.), *Ways and Means of Research in Educational Administration.* Armidale, New South Wales: University of New England.

Morris, Van Cleave, Robert L. Crowson, Cynthia Porter-Gehrie, and Emanual Hurwitz, Jr. 1984. *Principals in Action.* Columbus, OH: Merrill.

Peters, Tom, and Nancy Austin. 1985. *A Passion for Excellence.* New York: Random House.

Quantz, Richard A., Nelda Cambron-McCabe, and Michael Dantley. 1991. "Preparing School Administrators for Democratic Authority: A Critical Approach to Graduate Education," *The Urban Review,* 23(1), 3–19.

Rawls, John. 1971. *A Theory of Justice.* Cambridge, MA: Harvard University Press.

Selznick, Philip. 1957. *Leadership in Administration: A Sociological Interpretation.* New York: Harper & Row. California Paperback Edition 1984. Berkeley: University of California Press.

Sergiovanni, Thomas J. 2000. *The Lifeworld of Leadership: Creating Culture, Community and Personal Meaning in Our Schools.* San Francisco: Jossey-Bass.

Sergiovanni, Thomas J., and Robert J. Starratt. 1988. *Supervision: Human Perspectives.* New York: McGraw-Hill.

Smith, John K., and Joseph Blase. 1987. *Educational Leadership as a Moral Concept.* Washington, DC: American Educational Research Association.

Taylor, Paul W. 1961. *Normative Discourse.* Englewood Cliffs, NJ: Prentice-Hall.

Tom, Alan. 1980. "Teaching as a Moral Craft: A Metaphor for Teaching and Teacher Education," *Curriculum Inquiry* 10(3).

Tom, Alan. 1984. *Teaching as a Moral Craft.* New York: Longman.

Vaill, Peter B. 1984. "The Purposing of High-Performing Systems," in Thomas J. Sergiovanni and John E. Corbally (Eds.), *Leadership and Organizational Culture.* Urbana-Champaign: University of Illinois Press.

Wilkins, Alan L. 1989. *Developing Corporate Character.* San Francisco: Jossey-Bass.

Zaleznik, Abraham. 1989. *The Managerial Mystique: Restoring Leadership in Business.* New York: Harper & Row.

INDEX